AMERICAN PRESIDENTS, DEPORTATIONS, AND HUMAN RIGHTS VIOLATIONS

Of the many issues polarizing societies today, immigration is one of the most contentious. In the United States, as in Europe, immigration was a defining issue in recent national elections. Immigration not only involves government policies, but also the human rights of millions of people. *American Presidents, Deportations, and Human Rights Violations* studies how immigration policies in the United States developed during the Obama administration and are now being expanded in the early period of the Trump presidency. Documenting the harsh treatment of immigrants over the past twenty years, Bill Ong Hing shows how mass detention and deportation of immigrants, from Clinton's two terms and the Bush administration, have escalated even higher. This book questions what price the United States is willing to pay for such harsh immigration policies in terms of its national values, and the impact on the lives of the millions of immigrants who deserve the full protection of universal human rights obligations.

Bill Ong Hing is Professor of Law and Migration Studies at the University of San Francisco and the founder of the Immigrant Legal Resource Center. He is the author of multiple books including, *Ethical Borders: NAFTA, Globalization, and Mexican Migration* (2010) and *Deporting Our Souls: Values, Morality, and Immigration Policy* (2006). He is also the lead author of *Immigration Law and Social Justice* (2018). He was co-counsel in the precedent-setting Supreme Court asylum case, *INS* v. *Cardoza-Fonseca* (1987), and represented the State Bar of California in *In re Sergio Garcia* (2014) before the California Supreme Court helping to grant a law license to an undocumented law graduate.

American Presidents, Deportations, and Human Rights Violations

FROM CARTER TO TRUMP

BILL ONG HING

University of San Francisco

CAMBRIDGE
UNIVERSITY PRESS

University Printing House, Cambridge CB2 8BS, United Kingdom

One Liberty Plaza, 20th Floor, New York, NY 10006, USA

477 Williamstown Road, Port Melbourne, VIC 3207, Australia

314–321, 3rd Floor, Plot 3, Splendor Forum, Jasola District Centre, New Delhi – 110025, India

79 Anson Road, #06-04/06, Singapore 079906

Cambridge University Press is part of the University of Cambridge.

It furthers the University's mission by disseminating knowledge in the pursuit of education, learning, and research at the highest international levels of excellence.

www.cambridge.org
Information on this title: www.cambridge.org/9781108472289
DOI: 10.1017/9781108559690

© Bill O. Hing 2019

First published 2019

Printed in the United States of America by Sheridan Books, Inc.

A catalogue record for this publication is available from the British Library.

ISBN 978-1-108-47228-9 Hardback
ISBN 978-1-108-45921-1 Paperback

I dedicate this book to the women and children – past and present – held at the ICE family detention centers in Artesia, New Mexico, Dilley, Texas, and Karnes City, Texas. You fled unimaginable violence, surviving a treacherous journey to our nation's border seeking humanitarian compassion. You were greeted with hostility and treated as criminals. Your detention is heartless and shameful. The anxiety and sad expressions on the faces of detained toddlers – many the same age as my two-year-old granddaughter Maddie – broke my heart at Dilley. The migrant children deserve the same kind of happy experiences she has had.

Contents

Tables

Acknowledgments

A number of students and friends provided excellent research assistance for this project: Ryan Blackney, Leandra Gamboa, Ned Juri-Martinez, Brooke Longuevan, Carla Lopez-Perez, Anna Manuel, Dyvianne Martinez, Denise Oki, Kaitlin Talley, Katy Tang, Carolyn Widman, and particularly law research librarian John Shafer. Special thanks to my colleagues at the University of San Francisco Immigration and Deportation Defense Clinic for their unwavering dedication and inspirational work on behalf of children, women, and men from the Northern Triangle and Mexico: Vanessa Saldivar, Alex Mensing, Monica Valencia, Martin Steinman, Roxana Quintero, Gabriela Mendez, and especially Jacqueline Brown Scott.

Introduction

Deportation Champion

President Barack Obama was dubbed "deporter-in-chief" by immigrant rights advocates for good reason.[1] During his eight years in office, his administration formally removed more than three million noncitizens, compared to two million during George W. Bush's tenure and about 900,000 under the Clinton administration.[2] On the other hand, the Clinton and Bush administrations apprehended and returned millions more without formal proceedings at the US–Mexico border than during the Obama administration. But the reason is likely because far fewer Mexican migrants were attempting to enter without inspection during Obama's eight years in office.[3] So the Obama administration focused more on formal removals instead of border returns, with formal removals under Obama far outpacing those of the Bush and Clinton administrations even as returns were far lower. At the time he left office, Obama was definitely the reigning Deportation Champion.

Enter Donald Trump. Given the immigration enforcement exploits of President Trump and his administration, Obama's clutch on the title of "deporter-in-chief" is in serious jeopardy. In spite of early court actions constraining Trump's travel ban and Congress's hesitance to fund the construction of a border wall or a deportation army, Trump's enforcement henchmen have initiated a frightening deportation campaign with resources that were already in place. Interior enforcement is up, and his threat to local law enforcement officials to take away federal funds if they refuse to cooperate is working. Between his tweeting and the unleashing of mean-spirited Immigration and Customs Enforcement (ICE) agents, noncitizens in the country

---

[1] Amanda Sakuma, *Obama Leaves Behind a Mixed Legacy on Immigration*, NBC News, April 17, 2015.

[2] Muzaffar Chishti, Sarah Pierce, and Jessica Bolter, *The Obama Record on Deportations: Deporter in Chief or Not?*, Migration Policy, January 26, 2017.

[3] That trend, which began under the Bush administration, is due to improved economic conditions in Mexico, reduced post recession job demand in the United States, ramped-up enforcement, and the increased use of different enforcement tactics at the border. Ibid.

are scared. Trump is easily on his way to yanking the deportation champ moniker away from Obama.

Time and again, the enforcement of US immigration laws over the past four decades should make us wonder about the cost we are willing to pay to enforce the nation's immigration laws. We should wonder not simply in terms of the billions of dollars spent on enforcement, but also in terms of the cost to our basic humanity. In the name of border integrity and an enforcement regime based on ill-informed claims of economic competition, hundreds of migrants die each year attempting to cross our southern border due to the expanded militarization of the border that began with Operation Gatekeeper. Hardworking immigrants were victimized by Bush-era ICE raids, and thousands more lost their jobs each year because of the Obama administration's silent raids on employers. The Obama administration also took a page from the Bush era, instituting raids at workplaces frequented by Latinos in New Orleans and other parts of the country. The result was family separation – usually involving US citizen children. The destruction of families also resulted from the expansion of the so-called "Secure Communities" program under the Obama administration's watch. The deportation of refugees and longtime lawful permanent residents convicted of aggravated felonies has become the unquestioned, politically accepted routine – in spite of an acknowledgment in criminal justice communities that engaging in rehabilitation efforts would be wiser. Obama's Department of Homeland Security (DHS) also made credible fear standards for refugees fleeing to our borders more rigorous, then more inhumanely called for expeditious removal of the thousands of unaccompanied children (UACs) arriving at our border who are fleeing violence.

To achieve its formal removal numbers, the Obama enforcement priorities and policies represented a significant departure from those of the Bush and Clinton administrations. The Obama-era policies focused on two key groups: The deportation of criminals and recent unauthorized border crossers. So, for example, in 2016, Obama's last year in office, 85 percent of all removals were of noncitizens who had recently crossed the US border unlawfully, were apprehended, and then were formally ordered removed. Of the remainder, who were removed from the US interior, more than 90 percent had been convicted of what the DHS regarded as serious crimes.[4]

A central focus of this book is on an important segment of Obama's removal priority at the border that helped him earn the deporter-in-chief title – the apprehension, detention, and removal prioritization of women and children fleeing violence in Central America. In my view, those efforts were reprehensible and cast a dark shadow on Obama's legacy, even though he took some remarkably courageous steps on behalf of immigrants as well. On the positive side, most notably, he responded to Congress's failure to pass comprehensive immigration reform by taking executive

[4]   Ibid.

action on behalf of DREAMers – young, undocumented immigrants who grew up here – through the Deferred Action for Childhood Arrivals (DACA) program. Those who qualified were granted permission to stay and work without the threat of deportation. Some 800,000 DREAMers benefited from the DACA program. However, on the negative side, Obama's policy on women and children fleeing Central America has visited great and unnecessary hardship and trauma on migrants victimized by violence.

As background, I also review other aspects of Obama's enforcement efforts and major tools used by earlier presidents, including Jimmy Carter, Ronald Reagan, Bill Clinton, and George W. Bush. Those presidents established the immigration enforcement policies that my clients have faced since I started practicing immigration law and deportation defense in the 1970s. That backdrop is important for contextualizing ICE enforcement under Obama as well as under Trump. Although the main focus of this project is on President Obama's soiled legacy, the back end of the book hones in on the new Trump ICE age. As you will see, however, Obama and Trump were provided templets for deportation by other presidents of recent vintage. Carter ordered all Iranian students to report to immigration authorities and turned away Haitian boat people as "economic" migrants rather than admit them as political refugees. Reagan rejected asylum claims by El Salvadorans and Guatemalans fleeing the devastations of civil war, as well as providing even less due process for Haitians seeking asylum. He also criminally prosecuted and jailed sanctuary workers trying to help Central Americans. Bush became infamous for inspiring anti-Muslim, anti-Arab hate that evolved into his own Muslim bans, while his ICE engaged in some of the most harrowing gun-wielding raids ever experienced in the history of immigration enforcement. And Clinton left us with the legacy of Operation Gatekeeper – a death trap along the southern border that results in an average of one avoidable death each day because it funnels migrants to the deadliest border crossing trails.

I.1. MARIA AND MAYNOR

"Why are we here?" the young boy asked me. "Because you and your mother need to talk with the judge about staying in the United States," I responded. I did not tell him what else I was thinking: that we were there because the Obama administration was determined to quickly deport migrants like Maynor and his mother Maria back to one of the most violent regions in the world. That the Obama administration was trying to make an example of Maynor and Maria and send a message to tens of thousands of Central American migrants, in spite of the fact that they had never broken the law and were on solid footing seeking asylum. They were two of dozens of clients that my law school immigration clinic was assisting within months of opening our doors.

After more than an hour, the precocious nine-year-old looked at me and asked me once more, "Why do we have to wait so long?" I told him again, "You and your mother are near the end of the long list of people that have been ordered to speak with the judge this morning. It won't be much longer." About fifteen minutes later, federal Immigration Judge Dana Marks called out, "Maria Garrido and Maynor Garrido, cases A– 094 500 and 501." Five minutes later after a brief discussion, Judge Marks set their final removal and asylum hearing for November 5, 2015, 10 am. This time Maria asked, "Will she grant us asylum?" I responded, "Time will tell. She is a fair judge."

Maria and Maynor were part of the "rocket docket" process that was set up for the surge in Unaccompanied Alien Children (UACs) and family units (mostly mothers and children) who had fled the Northern Triangle of Central America (Honduras, Guatemala, and El Salvador). The influx caught the nation's attention in the summer of 2014. The law school clinic was simply one of many pro bono attorneys and legal services programs in the San Francisco Bay Area that had stepped up to assist the migrants subjected to the rocket dockets. The migrants who made it to the San Francisco Bay Area were relatively lucky; others who were still in detention centers or who were sent to areas of the country with few legal services programs often were left to fend for themselves in the Byzantine world of immigration law and procedure.

The number of migrants fleeing Central America in 2014 was impressive. Over 60,000 UACs arrived that year, while a similar number of women with children traveling as "family units" crossed into the United States as well. The numbers dipped somewhat in 2015, only to swell once again in 2016 and 2017.

As the influx of 2014 hit the news headlines across the country, immigrants and immigrant rights advocates realized that we were in trouble when a Ku Klux Klan "knight" called for shooting UACs arriving at the border, and the Obama administration expedited removal proceedings of UACs and other families arriving at the border. As the Loyal White Knights of the Klan advocated a "shoot-to-kill" border policy, another North Carolina Klan leader made clear why he thought the policy should apply to UACs: "If we pop a couple of 'em off and leave the corpses laying on the border, maybe they'll see we're serious about stopping immigrants."[5] Seemingly in tandem, although the White House initially labeled the influx of UACs a "humanitarian crisis," the DHS and Department of Justice responded by sending a "surge" of immigration judges and government attorneys to the border to start deportation hearings immediately. Immigration courts around the country were ordered to prioritize UAC-related cases for those children or family units who were no longer in custody. That's how Maria and Maynor landed on the San Francisco rocket docket and came to be represented by the law school's immigration clinic.

In addition to expediting deportation proceedings against both groups, the Obama administration decided to rely on a policy of detention in large part to send a message to Central Americans that they were not welcome. Ignoring the fact that

---

[5] Leslie Savan, *The KKK Wants a 'Shoot to Kill' Policy to Include Migrant Children*, The Nation, July 30, 2014.

the migrants were fleeing violence that could give rise to valid asylum claims, family detention facilities in Karnes, TX were expanded, while a makeshift prison-like operation was opened in Artesia, NM. Both were located far away from immigration attorneys who might be willing to help the migrants assert their rights.

More than a year later, in October 2015, after the Artesia facility was forced to close due to challenges to its poor human rights conditions and a replacement facility was opened in Dilley, TX, several of my law students traveled to Texas to help the detainees. They returned after a week, sickened by the conditions – physically and emotionally – in disbelief that this was happening in the United States. One student, Kaitlin Tally debriefed:

> The detainees are fleeing truly unimaginable threats of violence in their home countries. Gang-rapes of young women who refuse to become involved in a gang, brutal violence from domestic partners or husbands that refuse to let them file for divorce or leave the relationship, threats from gang members to kill women, kidnap their children, or kill the families of those who do not comply with the gang's recruitment or other demands are just a few of the fears often expressed...
>
> [M]any suffer further violence en route to the United States. Upon arriving to the United States, they were not welcomed with the promise of freedom and basic right to life, but were immediately vilified, interrogated, placed into cold jail cells notoriously known as *hieleras* ("freezers"), and then incarcerated into family "residential" centers only to suffer again from sexual abuse, lack of basic healthcare, and no mental healthcare in spite of their PTSD...
>
> [M]others reported that their children started crying through the entire night, a 12-year-old would start wetting the bed again, or that their children simply refused to eat. They report waiting hours in the detention center's medical clinic for medical treatment for their child's fever, headache, stomach ache or other complaints, only being told to put ice cubes under their armpits, to drink honey and water, that the child had allergies, or if they were lucky given a Tylenol to help with the pain.

Maria and Maynor were held in the despicable *hieleras* for a couple days, but fortunately they averted detention at Artesia because Maria was able to reach her husband in San Francisco. ICE officials at the border allowed her to join him on the condition that she wear an ankle monitor.

I.2. UAC ENFORCEMENT PRIORITIZATION

The sharp increase in Central American migration generated tremendous media coverage and speculation by elected officials and others about the reasons for the surge. Many of the explanations were misguided. Some Obama critics claimed the influx resulted from promises of immigration reform or administrative reforms in enforcement that sent encouraging signals to Central Americans; the migrants were said to be hoping to enjoy a "de facto amnesty" if they got across the United States–Mexico border. Others thought the children were being drawn by rumors about special protections for migrant children by the Obama administration, and pointed to the DACA program announced in 2012.

In reality, the migration has been mostly forced with little due to pull factors. The migration of youth arose out of longstanding, complex problems in their home countries – that is, the growing influence of youth gangs and drug cartels, plus targeting of youth by gangs and police. Women are fleeing because of gender-based violence, rising poverty, and continuing unemployment as well as the gang and drug violence. Violence clearly has been the main reason that the women and children are fleeing their countries, not because of some nebulous lure of promised amnesty in the United States.

The prevalence of violence is apparent in what is termed the Northern Triangle of Honduras, El Salvador, and Guatemala. Honduras, from where the largest numbers of unaccompanied minors have fled, has become one of the most dangerous countries in the world. In 2017, Honduras was ranked first with the highest homicide rate in the world.[6] El Salvador and Guatemala were ranked fourth and fifth respectively. In 2015, El Salvador had been bestowed with the tragic title of murder capital of the world.[7] Besides that, gender-based violence is at epidemic levels in Guatemala and the country ranks third in femicide worldwide. According to the United Nations, two women are killed there every day.[8]

Children in the region are at a greater risk of gang violence. Collaboration between drug cartels and gangs has led to a significant increase in violence, with children and teens being the primary targets. For example, more than nine hundred Honduran children were murdered in the first three months of 2012. In El Salvador, gangs have increasingly targeted children at their schools, resulting in El Salvador having one of the lowest school attendance rates in Latin America.

Human and drug trafficking also are rampant. The influence of cartels in Mexico and at the border connects the current migratory experience with human and drug trafficking. The United Nations High Commissioner for Refugees (UNHCR) reported that organized criminal groups coerce children into prostitution or to work as hit men, lookouts, and drug mules. Drug traffickers may target minors in their home country and force them to traffic drugs across the border and once they are in the United States. Because these youth often travel alone and are escaping death in their home countries, they are often faced with no choice but to carry drugs or work for drug cartels in order to cross the border.

Gang and drug trafficking in Central America are increasingly recruiting girls to smuggle and sell drugs in their home countries, using gang rape as a means of

---

[6] H. Petr, 25 *Countries With the Highest Murder Rates in the World*, June 8, 2017, available at: http://list25.com/25-countries-with-the-highest-murder-rates-in-the-world/

[7] *It's Official San Salvador is the Murder Capital of the World* – LA Times, March 2, 2016.

[8] Julie Guinan, *Nearly 20 Years After Peace Pact, Guatemala's Women Relive Violence*, CNN, April 7, 2015.

forcing them into compliance. Many gangs are targeting younger girls, some as young as nine-year-old, for rape and sexual assault. Gangs also use the threat of rape as a tactic to gain money through extortion and kidnapping.

I.3. DETENTION OF UNACCOMPANIED MIGRANT CHILDREN

The Office of Refugee Resettlement (ORR), a branch of the Department of Health and Human Services, is the federal agency responsible for the care and custody of unaccompanied migrant children. Under the William Wilberforce Trafficking Victims Protection Reauthorization Act of 2008, unaccompanied, non-Mexican, migrant children must be transferred to ORR custody within 72 hours of their arrest. For several years, ORR has operated temporary shelters throughout the United States to house children while ORR caseworkers sought to reunify them with family members or family friends in the United States. In response to the dramatic increase in numbers of children apprehended by Customs and Border Patrol, ORR opened three large facilities housed on military bases: Joint Base San Antonio – Lackland in San Antonio, TX; Fort Sill Army Base in Oklahoma; and Port Hueneme Naval Base in Ventura, CA. Advocates raised significant concerns about the conditions in which children were held at these facilities and the difficulty in gaining access by attorneys and legal workers due to security procedures at these military facilities.

More than 200,000 migrant kids traveling without their parents have been detained at the United States–Mexico border over the past five years. Most are part of the wave of Central American children fleeing violence, as criminal gangs in El Salvador and neighboring countries have come to wield terrifying power with impunity, and weak governments struggle to respond. That violence is a legacy of the civil wars of the 1980s, subsequent migrations to the United States, and the deportation of gang members back to their home countries in the 1990s.

When adults are picked up at the border, they are dealt with by the DHS. But unaccompanied children are turned over to ORR. As the number of migrant kids has multiplied, ORR's job has grown. In 2011, the agency took custody of 7,000 children. In 2014 it was 57,000.

The vast majority of these children spend about a month in a licensed ORR-funded shelter, and then they are placed with a relative or a sponsor while they await their day in immigration court. A small fraction – roughly 500–700 in any given year – are placed in jail-like settings: locked group homes or juvenile detention facilities. Those children are held for two to three months, on average, but some are detained much longer.[9]

---

[9] Tyche Hendricks, *Hundreds of Migrant Teens Are Being Held Indefinitely in Locked Detention*, KQED News, April 11, 2016.

I.4. DETENTION OF FAMILIES

In a 2014 change in policy, Obama's ICE began detaining families apprehended at the border, rather than releasing them from custody to appear for removal proceedings at a later date. ICE opened a family detention center in Artesia, NM, in July 2014 and opened another family detention center in Karnes City, TX, in August. Due process violations became the norm in how cases were being handled at these facilities. For example, concerns were raised about how credible fear asylum screening interviews were being conducted. These interviews determine whether the adult family member will be given the opportunity to have her or his asylum claim heard before an immigration judge. Other problem areas included hearings being conducted remotely via video teleconferencing and, of course, lack of access to counsel.

A friend, Helen Lawrence, was one of the first pro bono attorneys who traveled to assist detainees in Artesia. She emailed me her observations:

On average our days in Artesia ran from 5:30 am to 1:30 am, logging in around 4 hours of sleep a day. We entered the facility in the cool dawn hours and left at dusk. In between those hours, when we would step out of the attorney trailer or the court trailer to move between trailers, the bright sun and the bland backdrop of the white trailers that comprise the detention center and the neutral Southwest landscape were blinding. After leaving the detention center, we went to the church to meet together to troubleshoot cases, receive updates, and dole out the next day's cases and workload. After the group meeting, we would begin preparing our cases for the next day.

Our team filled a variety of roles. At the detention center, some of us would meet with women and kids in the attorney trailer to prepare their cases. The list of these consultations was on average around 60. Others would be in court representing the women in their bond and asylum hearings in two court dockets that averaged around 15 cases a court. Still others would stay behind at the community church to prepare innumerable filings.

The women we saw were mostly from El Salvador, Guatemala and Honduras. They were all fleeing either gang or domestic violence or both. They shared stories of kidnapping, rape, abuse, extortion and threats. The weight that these women carry is profound. Most of the women came to the attorney trailer for consultations with their children. They often have to recount these horrific stories of rape, domestic violence, abuse, and other threats within earshot of their children. We would do our best to remove the children during these moments, but even separating mom from child(ren) was cruel in itself. As a distraction, ICE would put on a children's video and tear out pages of coloring books and give the children crayons that they have to return when they leave the legal trailer.

Most of the children had coughs, some had sores on their faces, one kid had a growth on his face. There have been chicken pox outbreaks here, leading to quarantines. Many of the children who are old enough to be weaned from bottles have regressed to bottles. Some moms reported their children were sleeping for distressingly long hours. I read medical records of a 5-year-old reporting to the clinic here that expressed that his level of pain was between 7 to 8 on a scale of 10.

We heard that some of the little boys have started to pretend they are ICE agents, mimicking them at count (when the guards count the detainees to confirm that everyone is still there).

Another disturbing observation from our team is how quiet the kids are in Artesia. All day we are surrounded by them either in our consultation area in the detention center or in court. They all seem so sedated and low energy. I spent two days working with one mother and her 16-month-old. The child's face was always tear-stained and yet he never made a peep or fussed.[10]

After great uproar over the deplorable conditions at Artesia, ICE closed the facilities, but opened new barracks in Dilley, TX. Meanwhile, the Karnes facility was expanded. To no one's surprise, the conditions at Dilley and Karnes were no improvement over Artesia.

A major part of the problem with Dilley and Karnes is that both sites are operated by private prison companies. Yes, ICE has contracted with GEO Group and CCA (Corrections Corporation of America , recently renamed: CoreCivic) to detain families – mostly women and children – who are anything but criminals. These are the same private prison companies who have been under scrutiny for their lobbying expenditures and relationships with government officials. For instance, the discovery that two of Arizona Governor Jan Brewer's top advisors were former CCA lobbyists raised concerns that these affiliations influenced the creation of SB1070, Arizona's infamous "show me your papers" law, which would have generated significant business for CCA with the state.

Worse still, these are the same companies whose operations are so bad, that complaints against them are difficult to keep track of:

- A 2010 Associated Press report revealed that CCA's Idaho Correctional Center (ICC) had more assaults than all other Idaho prisons combined. Dubbed the "Gladiator School," video footage showed a prisoner being severely beaten by another inmate, pleading for help as CCA guards looked on. CCA lost its $30 million contract for the prison with the state, and the FBI launched an investigation into the company in 2014.
- In 2013, the Texas Observer called the state's CCA-run Dawson State Jail for nonviolent offenders in Dallas "the worst state jail in Texas." Seven inmates have died in Dawson since 2004, generally due to medical neglect and malpractice. One prisoner gave birth to a premature baby at twenty-six weeks after CCA guards refused her cries for medical attention. The baby was delivered in a prison toilet with no medical assistance and died four days later.

[10] Email from Helen Lawrence, Esq., October 22, 2014.

- CCA's Don T. Hutto facility, a "family residential facility" for immigrant detainees and their children, was found to be violating nearly every standard for minors in ICE custody. Families were crammed into small cells with no privacy, children were dressed in prison scrubs, and conditions were appalling. After an ACLU lawsuit, the facility is no longer used for family detention. Yet in 2011, two federal sexual abuse investigations and a class action lawsuit were filed on behalf of immigrant women who alleged they were sexually assaulted by guards in the facility. One CCA guard was sentenced to ten months in federal prison.
- In 2011, an Oklahoma jury ordered GEO Group to pay $6.5 million to the family of Ronald Sites, an inmate who was strangled to death by his cellmate in 2005.
- Also in 2011, the Florida Department of Children and Families said GEO Group's neglect contributed to the death of a South Florida State Hospital patient. The man was being escorted by GEO Group employees to an appointment at Jackson Memorial Hospital when he hurled himself from the eighth story of a parking garage.
- In 2009, a Texas appeals court upheld a $42.5 million verdict after a prisoner at a GEO Group facility was beaten to death four days before he was to be released.
- In 2007, Texas canceled an $8 million contract with GEO and closed the Coke County Juvenile Justice Center. Inspectors found feces on floors and walls, padlocked emergency exits and the overuse of pepper spray on young inmates.
- A former employee of GEO Group revealed that at the Adelanto, CA, Immigration Detention Center, Muslim men were put into solitary confinement simply for quietly saying their daily prayers. A government report found that GEO Group's medical mismanagement at Adelanto directly led to the death of at least one detainee, Fernando Dominguez, in March 2012. Another Adelanto detainee was denied treatment for his severe hip infection because "it was too expensive." The infection ultimately developed into a life-threatening condition that required six-week hospitalization at an outside hospital.

Immigration detention is big business for private companies. CCA, the largest private prison corporation, reported $1.65 billion in revenue in 2014; 44 percent was from federal contracts: 20 percent US Marshals, 12 percent Bureau of Prisons, and 12 percent from ICE. Despite GEO Group's embattled reputation, ICE announced plans to expand the available bed space at Adelanto by 640 beds, and for the first time may house women and lesbian, gay, bisexual, transgender, queer (LGBTQ) individuals at the facility. According to their annual report, GEO Group expects to generate $21 million in additional annualized revenue from this expansion. Both companies have significantly augmented their profits since the implementation of an immigration bed quota that was inserted into federal law in 2007. CCA's net profits went from $133,373,000 in 2007 to $195,022,000 in 2014. GEO experienced an even more dramatic profit increase from $41,845,000 in 2007 to $143,840,000 in 2014, a 244 percent increase.[11]

In spite of the problems and criticism, CCA and GEO Group were selected to run the family detention centers housing women and children fleeing violence from Central America. The CCA-operated South Texas Family Residential Center in Dilley opened in December 2014 to hold 480 women and children. But capacity was increased to 2,400 by May 2015 – making Dilley the largest immigrant detention center in the country. The GEO-run Karnes County Residential Center opened in June 2014 and now holds around 1,200 women and children.

It did not take long for horrendous conditions at both facilities to develop and get exposed. In one scandal, detainees rioted over poor medical care, as well as things like overflowing sewage and overcrowding. The facilities have been plagued with allegations of sexual and physical abuse, maggots in inmates' food, and inmates' wash loads mixed with mops and cleaning equipment. By the summer of 2015, a federal judge called the detention centers and temporary holding cells along the border "deplorable" and has said they "failed to meet even the minimal standard" for "safe and sanitary" conditions. The judge ordered that children not be held for more than 72 hours unless they are a significant flight risk or a danger to themselves and others. However, ICE continues to drag its feet. Two more of my students who volunteered at the Dilley facility in the summer of 2016, returned with these sobering observations:

From Zulma Munoz:

I did a lot of everything... I did my own CFI preps, I attended bond hearings, I helped prepare bond motions, I attended CFI interviews as a consultant, I spoke to family members of women who had "split family" and/or "medical issues" to ensure them that we had found the missing father and/or child, I helped input a ton of information into Law Lab, I interpreted and translated declarations, and the list goes on.

Currently I am in touch with two families. I exchanged contact information with those families. One is a split family (separated from husband at the *hielera*) who is currently in medical isolation because both children have been diagnosed with chickenpox. It is virtually impossible for Blanca to communicate with her family because she and her two children are isolated in a tiny room. I have taken the initiative to communicate with her USC sister who lives in Colorado. When I prepped Blanca for her interview, I did so over the phone since she is not allowed outside of the room. I told her that I'd find her husband. She imagined he'd be dead. I found her husband at the East Hidalgo Detention Center using the ICE detainee detector. With the help of the Dilley offsite team (who tracked his A#) and

[11] Bethany Carson and Eleana Diaz, *Payoff: How Congress Ensures Private Prison Profit with an Immigrant Detention Quota*, April 2015. Grassroots Leadership, http://grassrootsleadership.org/reports/payoff-how-congress-ensures-private-prison-profit-immigrant-detention-quota

with my persistence in pressuring the team to help find this father, we were able to locate him ASAP. Blanca and her sister and the kids are feeling much better. I've been texting and calling Blanca's sister, Reina.

The other family I exchanged numbers with is a mother with two children who escaped the *maras* [gangs]. She reminded me of my mother in so many ways. I saw myself in her children and I thought about her other children that were left behind... She did an amazing job at her interview. I can't wait to hear from her. I also have her parents' information.

Leaving Dilley was very difficult for me. Is anyone ever ready to really leave? I wasn't. I didn't want to go... Packing up my nice clothes and oatmeal bars and fruity-smelling lotions, made my heart feel even more heavy.

From Gabriela Garcia:

Being in that place was horrible, the women had to check in with a guard all of their moves and eat at certain times only and couldn't eat dinner after 6 pm. As I talked to them I asked if they missed having another dinner like they did back in their countries and most would say yes, but they were content with at least having food. One of the things that made me feel extremely sad was seeing children who were about 10 asking if they could work instead of their mothers once they were released; seeing them act as adults I couldn't stop thinking their childhood had been stolen by the person who had also harmed their mom and that drew tears in my eyes. At the end of the trip Zulma and I thought a second week there would have been great, we didn't want to leave until we saw the women we helped get out of there, but unfortunately we had to continue with our other commitments and be ready for school so once we graduate we can do more for the immigrant community. I hope by then these centers are closed. I'm still trying to recover from seeing all the suffering the women went through, and trying to stop dreaming about being in the detention center.

I.5. THE USE OF "ROCKET DOCKETS"

Another significant development was the implementation of expedited removal proceedings, so-called "rocket dockets," for UACs and families who have been released from custody. Maria and Maynor were subjected to this process. Relatives or close family friends can sponsor children in order to have them released from custody. Their deportation cases are then transferred to the immigration court near the relative or family friend.

Rocket dockets were rolled out in immigration courts across the country. Children and families were provided as few as three days' notice of their court hearing date, severely limiting their ability to find counsel. Continuances (periods of time in between hearings) were granted for very short periods of time – in some instances as little as a week – to find an attorney.

These expedited hearings for children and families gained some national attention. On July 22, 2014, Dana Leigh Marks, President of the National Association of Immigration Judges, sent a letter to Senator Harry Reid, US Senate Majority Leader, and Senator Mitch McConnell, US Senate Minority Leader, expressing serious concerns about immigration judges' caseloads and the use of expedited procedures in children's cases. Coordinated efforts by service providers to respond to the rocket dockets in many parts of the country have helped, but the stress and pressure on these providers has been immense. Some jurisdictions, including the State of California and San Francisco County, tried to help by appropriating funds for community legal services providers to hire additional staff.

1.6. OPERATION BORDER GUARDIAN

In spite of critique of its detention policies and being chastised by immigrants and immigrant rights groups for rushing to place migrants from Central America in removal proceedings, the Obama administration doubled down. As many American families celebrated and welcomed the 2016 New Year, for some UACs and families from Central America, the New Year was the beginning of a nightmare. News leaked in early December that ICE raids would be conducted at the beginning of the year in order to send a message to migrants trying to cross the border. The *Washington Post* reported that the "ICE operation would target only adults and children who have already been ordered removed from the United States by an immigration judge." The *Los Angeles Times* quoted an ICE official who explained that "ICE is working to secure the US–Mexico border," and that the deportations were "part of a plan to convince migrants that entering the country illegally is 'fruitless.'"

As the roundups – dubbed Operation Border Guardians – unfolded, DHS Secretary Jeh Johnson issued a press release on "Southwest Border Security" on January 4, 2016, stating: "[t]his past weekend, ICE engaged in concerted, nationwide enforcement operations to take into custody and return at a greater rate adults who entered this country illegally with children. This should come as no surprise. I have said publicly for months that individuals who constitute enforcement priorities, including families and unaccompanied children, will be removed... I know there are many who loudly condemn our enforcement efforts as far too harsh, while there will be others who say these actions don't go far enough. I also recognize the reality of the pain that deportations do in fact cause. But, we must enforce the law consistent with our priorities. At all times, we endeavor to do this consistent with American values, and basic principles of decency, fairness, and humanity."

Operation Border Guardian essentially was a sweep for Central American migrants who failed to appear at their hearings. Many were instantly deported, but the Board of Immigration Appeals intervened in one case: nineteen-year-old Yefri Hernandez of El Salvador was granted a new hearing so that he could apply for asylum. At the time that he arrived in the United States a couple years earlier fleeing a gang that was targeting him and his family, he could not find legal help initially. When he did, his attorney did not know how to apply for asylum and did not inform Yefri about his deportation hearing date. ICE arrested Yefri on the morning of January 27, 2016, when he was waiting at the school bus stop. Even after ICE realized that Yefri had missed his hearing date through no fault of his own, officials opposed Yefri's motion to open and continued to detain him until the BIA decision.

Alexander Soriano-Cortez, a nineteen-year-old from Honduras, also was granted a motion to reopen by the immigration court. An immigration judge had ordered Alexander deported when he failed to show up for his hearing. The immigration judge later realized that Alexander's absence was caused by lack of notice of the court hearing date. Yet, Alexander also continued to be held in ICE detention after being swept up in a predawn ICE raid, when agents entered his home without consent, and roused him from his sleep.

Kimberly Pineda Chavez, another Operation Border Guardian victim, was also initially represented by incompetent counsel. She entered the United States as a minor to escape violence and threats in her native Honduras. Kimberly was on her way to school when the car she was riding in was stopped by ICE agents. She was arrested and detained for more than ten weeks. After an hour-long hearing in which the ICE attorney aggressively argued against bond, an immigration judge granted release on a $1,500 bond. Kimberly fled Honduras in 2014 at age seventeen to escape gangsters who threatened to make her and her younger sister their "sexual property." Immigration authorities apprehended the sisters at the southwest border in September of that year, and Kimberly was ordered deported because her attorney did not know the process for asylum.

The insanity of the arrest policy was obvious. By April, the *New York Times* argued that the Border Guardian roundup "taints all who touch it, from the ICE director, Sarah Saldaña, to Homeland Security Secretary Jeh Johnson, to President Obama himself."

> While legal advocates have been scrambling, ICE has been running amok, raiding homes and public spaces in search of deportable youths. In North Carolina and Georgia, where organized advocacy is sparse, the dragnet has been unusually aggressive. Agents seized students at home and on their way to school. Appalled teachers, students and community leaders have been signing petitions and marching, pleading for justice and putting a human face on the victims of coldblooded policies...
>
> Students are being locked up while they appeal deportation orders, though they pose no threat of violence or flight. Ms. Saldaña has rebuffed pleas for mercy, saying the administration – which has flown more than 28,000 people back to Central America since October – needs "to send a message" that the borders are closed to illegal immigration. But pleading for refuge is not illegal. More than 100 members of Congress have denounced the raids. Both Bernie Sanders and Hillary Clinton have pledged not to deport children if they win the presidency.[12]

---

[12] Editorial Board, *The Dark Side of Immigration Discretion*, New York Times, April 16, 2016.

I.7. FACES OF THE CHILDREN

In spite of the criticism, family detention, rocket dockets, and enforcement like Operation Border Guardian flourished on Obama's watch. On August 3, 2016, Secretary Johnson announced that deportations of Guatemalans, Hondurans, and El Salvadorans would continue at the rate of fifteen to eighteen flights per week. While acknowledging that those countries have among the highest homicide rates in the world, he insisted that the United States had to continue sending the message that "our borders are not open borders."[13]

The implementation of these policies was hard for me to believe. One need only spend a little time with the migrants – especially the children – to understand that prioritizing their removal is wrong-headed. Maria and Maynor should not be subjected to a further nightmare after fleeing one in El Salvador. Nor should another of our child clients, Marlon, who told us about his harrowing journey to the United States:

> I lived in El Salvador with my mother, Sandra Patricia Majano Henriquez, and my younger brother, Oscar Steven Ortiz Majano. My father left El Salvador to come to the United States when I was about 5 years old. My father would call to our house in El Salvador from the United States regularly and I spoke with him occasionally. He was very concerned about the gang situation in our home town, and he warned me to avoid any gang activity. He was very concerned about my safety. Santa Tecla, my home town, was often the scene of intense gang rivalry between the two major street gangs in the area, the "MS-13" and the "M-18." My uncle had been killed in his own home, just a few doors from our house, by a stray bullet shot by gang members looking for someone nearby. When the MS-13 gang would come into town to harass the last of the M-18 members around, they would try to force my friends and me to be look-outs for them to warn them when police were on the way. If we refused, they would threaten us with violence. I was beaten with a baseball bat by one of the gang members when they accused me of "tagging" a wall because they were afraid it would draw police attention to the area. My mother was in constant fear for my safety and future because of the gang situation. She told me to stay away from the gangs, but there was nothing that she could do to protect me or keep me safe. If she went to the police to complain about the threats, recruitment activity or assaults, the police would do nothing to help. Her complaints only make her and the family a target of gang retaliation. In fact, it was some of the anti-gang police unit members, the "anti-pandillas," who also beat me with their batons, several times. Sometimes, when my friends and I would be on our way home from playing soccer under the lights at night, we would be rounded up, forced to get on our knees and beaten on the back or shoulders by these men in dark uniforms with ski masks, who accused us of being gang members. My mother was very concerned with what was happening. She was concerned with my safety and was very worried

[13] Franco Ordonez, *Despite Danger, U.S. to Continue Deportations to Central America*, McClatchy Washington Bureau, August 3, 2016.

that she could not keep me away from the gangs. The police were not helpful and
in fact I was beaten by them as well. Eventually, fearing for my safety and her inability to protect me, she counseled me to flee El Salvador. My uncle told me what
to do to get ready and we left together to travel through Mexico to the United States
Border. We traveled by bus to the Guatemalan border, crossed a river by raft and
then walked all day, hiding from the Mexican immigration authorities by hiding in
trees. We had to sometimes wait for trains for days, standing up so we wouldn't fall
asleep. We rode on the top of the trains, switching trains several times as we headed
north through Mexico. For a while a guide travelled with us who knew all the train
schedules. Sometimes there was hard rain and tree branches almost knocked us off
the tops of the trains. It was very frightening. I also heard a lot of scary stories about
a lot of people being injured or killed by falling off of trains. When we finally got
to Reynosa I had to travel without my uncle, with a guide and some other people,
to cross the Mexico–US border. We crossed a river together, walked about three
hours and hid for a while, but then when we walked out again toward a fence and
a bridge we were discovered and detained by the US border patrol. I was taken to a
detention center in Texas and kept about 7–8 days. Then I was transferred to New
York where I stayed about three weeks.[14]

And consider this typical reflection that one of my students, Brooke Longuevan,
offered after she labored to put together the story of another of our child clients:

One of my clients was a boy from Honduras who fled to the United States after
gang members killed multiple family members and threatened to do the same to
him. Three of his immediate family members were killed over a span of 2 years.
At the time my client was 11 years old and his mother sought to shield him from
details of his family member's deaths, she also moved the family around frequently
in hopes of avoiding the gang. Because of his youth and his mother's protection he
could not remember specifically when his family members were killed or where the
murders occurred. These murders were obviously central to his asylum claim and it
became imperative that we find this information somehow. Luckily his mother also
is living in the United States and was able to provide some general dates but was
herself unsure of many details. It was obvious that both my client and his mother
were suffering from PTSD. The mother was most affected by events that occurred
in Honduras and the murders of her family members. Because of my client's age
and mental health we decided to leave specific questions about the murders for the
mother. However, this also was problematic as she was perhaps more emotionally
harmed by the murders than her son because she was old enough to recognize their
magnitude. The effect of PTSD on memory also was an issue in discerning when
my client entered the United States and how he traveled here. During interviews
it was obvious that his PTSD had blurred his memory of his journey. I asked him
how long he thinks it took him to get from Honduras to the border, I realized that
he probably didn't have exact dates, but he could not even give a rough estimate.

14 Declaration of [Name Kept Confidential], July 20, 2015 (on file with author).

I asked, "Do you think it was days? Or weeks?" and he couldn't remember. The only thing he remembers from his journey was taking the train through Mexico to the border. I asked him why he thought he remembered that and not the other parts of his journey and he replied that it was because he had to stay awake the whole time, if you fell asleep you could fall off [from] the top of the train. He said that he had seen kids that fell asleep fall off the train and die.

On the eve if of his final state of the union address, President Obama faced embarrassing criticism from more than 140 fellow Democrats accusing the administration of wrongfully deporting women and children from Central America who had come here seeking refuge from violence. To mollify those critics, administration officials announced a new program that would seek United Nations help to screen migrants fleeing violence from the region to set up processing centers in several Latin American countries in the hopes of stemming a flood of families crossing our southern border illegally.[15] The truth is, movement on those efforts was negligible and the migrant flow continues at a high level.

Sadly, Obama's Department of Justice and DHS strongly defended their misguided deportation efforts in court. For example, they emphatically resisted challenges to the conditions at the detention centers. They also battled against the right to appointed counsel in cases involving children facing deportation on their own. Unbelievably, the Department of Justice offered this incredible testimony in defense of its refusal to appoint counsel to unrepresented children: Jack H. Weil, a long-time immigration judge who is responsible for training other judges, testified for the government that toddlers can learn immigration law well enough to represent themselves in court, "I've taught immigration law literally to 3-year-olds and 4-year-olds," Weil said. "It takes a lot of time. It takes a lot of patience. They get it. It's not the most efficient, but it can be done."[16]

I.8. THIS PROJECT

I was moved to develop this project because the story needs to be told about what in my view is a tragic mistake in so-called immigration enforcement – a mistake that began at the hands of Obama. While much of the migrant rights community's attention understandably has been focused nationally on the escalation of immigration enforcement under Trump and internationally on serious refugee crises like those involving Syrians and the Rohingya, our own humanitarian crisis in this hemisphere has been grossly mishandled starting long before President Trump took office. As a decent, caring people, Americans need to stand up, take note of the violations of

---

[15] Julia Preston, David M. Herszenhorn, and Michael D. Shear, *U.N. to Help U.S. Screen Central American Migrants*, New York Times, January 12, 2016.

[16] Jerry Markon, *Can a 3-Year Old Represent Herself in Immigration Court? This Judge Thinks So*, Washington Post, March 5, 2016.

human rights visited upon Central Americans reaching our borders, and embrace the migrants fleeing violence – at least until the dust has settled. Of course, Trump himself has exacerbated the situation by making it even harder for refugees to get across the border to apply for asylum – and that's just one of dozens of harsh policies that he is pursuing in the name of immigration enforcement.

While the project began as an effort to shed light on the dark side of Obama's immigration legacy, the evolution to a more comparative work given Trump's no-holds-barred harsh immigration enforcement strategies was necessary. His full court attack on immigrants – from Mexicans, to Muslims and those who would be regarded as "low priority" by Obama – has been constant. There is no denying that immigrants and their advocates are constantly on call under Trump.

In Chapter 1, I set the stage by providing a review of several immigration enforcement tools that have been implemented beginning with the Clinton administration. They include Operation Gatekeeper, Bush ICE raids, Obama's silent raids, the Secure Communities program, the removal of lawful permanent residents without meaningful due process, and separating mixed families – those comprised of citizen and undocumented members.

The next section of the book is its heart, comprised of several chapters on Obama's response to the flight of unaccompanied child and women and children to the United States that surged in 2014.

Chapter 2 focuses principally on the Obama administration's response to the flood of unaccompanied minors. This includes prioritizing their deportation, detaining them in facilities operated by the ORR around the country, creating "rocket dockets" in various parts of the country, the difficulty in getting representation for the children in deportation proceedings, the actual deportation of thousands of the unaccompanied children, and the fact that many of the children have been murdered upon their return to Central America. I also include a discussion on the difference in treatment between Mexican children and children from the Northern Triangle of Central America.

Chapter 3 is on the treatment of women and children by the Obama administration – their detention in "family" detention centers first in New Mexico, then in three facilities operated in Texas and Pennsylvania. These facilities are operated by ICE, subcontracted to private prison companies, under atrocious conditions. The treatment of these family units that came during the surge stands in contrast with how family units were treated much better prior to the surge. The conditions in these facilities – lack of health care, sanitation, access to counsel, abuse, mental health issues – are covered. I also describe a federal lawsuit over the conditions.

In Chapter 4, I describe what is going on in Honduras, Guatemala, and El Salvador. The conditions that have forced children as well as mothers with their children to flee are clear. The levels of gang violence, murders, drug cartels, and domestic violence in Honduras, Guatemala, and El Salvador, are among the highest in the world. Cartels there and in Mexico are violent and control many parts of the country. Domestic violence also is a key factor.

Chapter 5 is a discussion on the challenges of obtaining relief and fighting against deportation on behalf of children and family units. I explain why asylum laws do not fit well in some of these circumstances. There are also practical challenges to a different form of relief – Special Immigrant Juvenile Status – because of variations in law and procedure from state to state. The legal representation challenge, while critical, is only the tip of the iceberg in terms of the needs of the client group. Mental health, educational assistance, and social service needs for the migrants are tremendous. Because legal representation is so important to obtaining relief, I discuss due process issues and legal challenges on behalf of children.

The next section of the book is devoted to the new Trump enforcement era. Chapter 6 reviews his proposals and actual ICE strategies today compared to what has occurred in the past. In this chapter, I highlight enforcement efforts that were put in place by other presidents, especially President Jimmy Carter and President Ronald Reagan. I also discuss the real fear that Trump has instilled in immigrant communities, and why that fear is well-founded.

Chapter 7 is an analysis of how the United States has failed to use a humanistic approach to situations that involve real lives. I am disappointed over the failure to address the human rights crisis in human rights terms. I discuss what I believe the United States should be doing – most notably using an available legal provision, "Temporary Protected Status," to benefit these groups. At the very least, the deportation of these groups should not be prioritized. We should use a new framework for handling the Central American refugee crisis. We need to remedy the fact that the United States created a due process nightmare out of a humanitarian crisis. I then assess whether Trump has now assumed the title of deporter-in-chief over his predecessor. This includes an assessment of how Trump's enforcement actions compare with his predecessors – including how he not only has continued the mistreatment of UACs, but also wants to make the process even more challenging.

In the Epilogue, I discuss how disruption of immigration enforcement is occurring on different fronts and why various forms of disruption are critical during these times. I also provide my personal thoughts on why this resistance is so important.

In the Afterword, I provide a summary of particularly harsh Trump administration policies implemented in the late Spring and Summer of 2018. The policy of separating migrant children from their parents at the border shocked the American public, attracting widespread criticism. At the same time, the attorney general announced that migrants fleeing domestic or gang violence would not longer be eligible for asylum, set.

PART I

Clinton and Bush Lead the Way for Obama

1

Nightmarish ICE Enforcement Tools

Over the past quarter century, the Immigration and Naturalization Service (INS) or, after 9/11, Immigration and Customs Enforcement (ICE) has engaged in immigration enforcement actions that, in my view, go far beyond what is necessary under the law. These efforts have crossed the line between what is necessary in enforcing the immigration laws and over-zealous tools that wreak unnecessary havoc on communities and lack a common sense of humanity and decency. In this chapter, I summarize a handful of INS and ICE enforcement tools and priorities that raise the eyebrows of decent-minded observers.

1.1. OPERATION GATEKEEPER

Beginning in 1994, the Clinton administration implemented Operation Gatekeeper, a strategy of "control through deterrence" that involved constructing fences and militarizing sections of the southern border that were most easily traversed. But instead of deterring migrants, Gatekeeper forced migrants to shift their entry choices to the treacherous terrain of the desert and the mountains. The number of entries and apprehensions did not decrease, but the number of deaths due to dehydration and sunstroke in the summer or freezing in the winter dramatically surged. In 1994, fewer than 30 migrants died along the border; by 1998, the number was 147; in 2001, 387 deaths were counted; and in 2007, 409 died.[1]

The San Diego Sector of the DHS Border Patrol covers the section of the United States–Mexico border that historically has been the preferred site of entry for those

---

[1] California Rural Legal Assistance Foundation, Charts on page 191 of *Defining America Through Immigration Policy*; Frontera NorteSur, *2008 Migrant Death Count*, July 8, 2008, available at: http:// newspapertree.com/news/2630-2008-migrant-death-count

entering the United States without inspection.[2] This sector contains sixty-six miles of international border.[3] Tijuana, Mexico's third largest city, lies directly south of San Diego, California, the sixth largest city in the United States.[4] A smaller Mexican city, Tecate, is situated in the eastern end of the sector.[5]

In 1994, over 450,000 apprehensions of illicit border crossings were made in the San Diego sector. This number far surpassed the sectors with the next highest apprehension: Tucson (139,473) and McAllen, Texas (124,251). In the period prior to the end of 1994, undocumented border crossers in the San Diego sector commonly entered in the western part of the sector near the city of San Diego. Often, many of these individuals traveled through private property, and some were even seen darting across busy freeways near the international border inspection station. Most of the illicit crossers entered along the fourteen-mile stretch from Imperial Beach (at the Pacific Ocean) to the base of the Otay Mountains.[6] Most of the region involves "easy terrain and gentle climbs," where the crossing lasted only ten or fifteen minutes to a pickup point.[7] Even individuals who were apprehended and turned back across the border were just as likely to attempt reentry in the westernmost part of the sector at that time.[8]

These highly visible border crossings resulted in tremendous public pressure on the INS to act. Residents of San Diego complained. Anti-immigrant groups demanded action. Politicians decried lack of border control. President Clinton responded to the outcry in his State of the Union address on January 24, 1995, signaling a renewed get-tough policy by "mov[ing] aggressively to secure our borders by hiring a record number of border guards" and "cracking down on illegal hiring."[9] Facing reelection in 1996, administration officials hoped that renewed enforcement efforts against undocumented aliens would shore up Clinton's support among voters in California, who overwhelmingly passed the anti-immigrant Proposition 187 in 1994.[10]

Operation Gatekeeper was one of several operations that resulted from the Clinton administration's commitment to a new aggressive enforcement strategy for the Border Patrol, with INS Commissioner Doris Meissner approving a new

---

[2] Gustavo De La Vina, *U.S. Border Patrol San Diego Sector Strategic Planning Document*, April 29, 1994, at I.

[3] Ibid., at 3.

[4] Ibid.

[5] Ibid.

[6] Border Patrol, *Operation Gatekeeper: 3 Years of Results in a Glance*, 1997.

[7] Ibid.

[8] INS Fact Sheet, *Frustrating Illegal Crossers at Imperial Beach and Moving the Traffic Eastward*, October 17, 1997.

[9] *Clinton Vows More Immigration Enforcement, Bills Introduced in Congress*, 72 Interpreter Releases 169, January 30, 1995.

[10] *Clinton Will Seek Spending to Curb Aliens, Aides Say: Political Balancing Act*, NY Times, January 22, 1995, at AI; Matthew Jardine, *Operation Gatekeeper*, 10 Peace Rev. 329, 333, 1998.

national strategy in August 1994.[11] The heart of the plan relied on a vision of "pre-vention through deterrence," in which a "decisive number of enforcement resources [would be brought] to bear in each major entry corridor" and the Border Patrol would increase the number of agents on the line and make effective use of tech-nology, raising the risk of apprehension high enough to be an effective deterrent.[12] The specific regional enforcement operations that resulted included (1) Operation Blockade (later renamed Hold the Line), which commenced in September 1993 in the Greater El Paso, Texas areas; (2) Operation Gatekeeper, which commenced in October 1994, south of San Diego, California; (3) Operation Safeguard, which also commenced in October 1994 in Arizona; and (4) Operation Rio Grande, which commenced in August 1997 in Brownsville, Texas.[13] The idea was to block tradi-tional entry and smuggling routes with border enforcement personnel and physi-cal barriers.[14] By cutting off traditional crossing routes, the strategy sought to deter migrants or at least channel them into terrain less suited for crossing and more con-ducive to apprehensions.[15] To carry out the strategy, the Border Patrol was to con-centrate personnel and resources in areas of highest undocumented alien crossings, increase the time agents spent on border-control activities, increase use of physical barriers, and carefully consider the mix of technology and personnel needed to con-trol the border.[16]

In the San Diego sector, efforts would be concentrated on the popular fourteen-mile section of the border beginning from the Pacific Ocean (Imperial Beach) stretching eastward.[17] Steel fencing and bright lighting were already in place in sections of this corridor, erected in part with the assistance of the US military.[18] Yet because of the persistent traffic of undocumented entrants along this corridor, phase I of Gatekeeper concentrated on increasing staffing and resources along the fourteen-mile area.[19]

As the INS implemented its national border strategy, Congress supported these efforts; between 1993 and 1997, the INS budget for enforcement efforts along the southwest border doubled from $400 million to $800 million.[20] The number of Border Patrol agents along the southwest border increased from 3,389 in October 1993 to 7,357 by September 1998 – an increase of 117 percent.[21] State-of-the-art

---

[11] US Border Patrol, *Border Patrol Strategic Plan: 1994 and Beyond-National Strategy*, July 1994.
[12] Ibid., at 6.
[13] Petition on the Inter-American Commission on Human Rights of the Organization of American States, Feb. 9 1999, at 16, n.4.
[14] *National Strategy*, at 6–9.
[15] Ibid., at 7; US General Accounting Office, *Illegal Immigration: Status of Southwest Border Strategy Implementation* 3, May 1999 (1999 GAO Report).
[16] Ibid.
[17] Ibid., at 1, 4, 8.
[18] Ibid.
[19] Ibid., at 8.
[20] INS Fact Sheet, *Operation Gatekeeper: New Resources, Enhanced Results*, July 14, 1998.
[21] 1999 GAO report, at 7.

technology, including new surveillance systems using electronic sensors linked with low-light video cameras, infrared night-vision devices, and forward-looking infrared systems for Border Patrol aircraft, were installed.[22]

Operation Gatekeeper buildup was impressive. Before Gatekeeper, the San Diego sector had 19 miles of fencing. By the end of 1999, 52 miles were fenced. Half of this fencing ran from the Pacific Ocean to the base of the Otay Mountains. Fourteen miles contained primary fencing (a 10-foot wall of corrugated steel landing mats left over from the Vietnam War). Two backup fences, each 115 feet tall, were constructed. The first backup fence was made of concrete pillars, the second of wire mesh with support beams. Both are topped with wire. Almost 12 miles of this stretch are illuminated by stadium lights. Some fencing was erected on sections of the Otay Mountains, as well as around various East San Diego communities along the border.[23] The Department of Defense's Center for Low Intensity Conflicts along with the Army Corps of Engineers provided guidance to INS on the development of Gatekeeper features.[24]

In all, 73 miles of fencing was erected on the 2,000-mile border. The 66-mile San Diego sector had 72 percent of it, as well as 54 percent of the illumination.[25] The 144-mile long San Diego and El Centro sectors were provided with almost a third of the Border Patrol agents stationed on the southwest border.[26]

In implementing its national strategy beginning in 1994, the INS made a key assumption about its "prevention through deterrence" approach: "alien apprehensions will decrease as [the] Border Patrol increases control of the border."[27] In other words, the INS anticipated that as the show of force escalated by increasing agents, lighting, and fencing, people would be discouraged from entering without inspection so that the number of apprehensions naturally would decline. The Border Patrol predicted that within five years, a substantial drop in apprehension rates border-wide would result.[28] The deterrence would be so great that "many will consider it futile to continue to attempt illegal entry."[29]

[22] Statement of Michael A. Pearson, Exec. Assoc. Commissioner for Field Operations, Immigration & Naturalization Service, Sept. 24, 1999 (hereinafter "Pearson Statement"), at 5.

[23] Letter from Claudia E. Smith to Mary Robinson, Nov. 19, 1999.

[24] Ibid.; 1999 GAO Report, at 12.

[25] November 19, 1999 letter to Mary Robinson. In contrast, in areas other than San Diego, the construction was not as significant. The El Centro sector covers 72 miles of the border and is sparsely populated on the United States side and has only 7 miles of fence – all of it between the contiguous border cities of Calexico and Mexicali. Arizona has 17 miles of fencing – 6 in the Yuma sector and 9 in the Tucson sector. That fencing was erected exclusively in the towns and cities. Texas has the Rio Grande River and 7 miles of fencing from El Paso/Ciudad Juarez area – 2 miles of primary and 5 of secondary.

[26] Claudia E. Smith, *Operation Gatekeeper Report*, May 10, 2000, at 17–18.

[27] US Border Patrol, *Border Patrol Strategic Plan: 1994 and Beyond – National Strategy*, July 1994 (hereinafter "National Strategy"), at 17.

[28] Letter from Claudia E. Smith to Mary Robinson, Sept. 30, 2000.

[29] *National Strategy*, at 23.

The assumptions and predictions were not borne out. Apprehension levels did not decline. While apprehension levels for the San Diego and El Paso sectors were considerably lower in 1998 than in 1993 (e.g., 531,689 apprehended in San Diego in 1993 compared to 248,092 in 1998), the apprehension levels surged in El Centro, Yuma, and Tucson during the same period (e.g., from 92,639 to 387,406 in Tucson; from 30,508 to 226,695 in El Centro; and from 23,548 to 76,195 in Yuma).[30] From 1994 to 1999, the statistics for total apprehensions along the southwest border actually increased by 57 percent.[31] The number of apprehensions for fiscal year 2000 was 1.64 million, which was an all-time high.[32] So after Gatekeeper sealed the western-most section of the border, apprehensions in San Diego declined, but crossers moved east, and overall apprehensions actually increased substantially.

Thus, migrants ultimately were not deterred by Gatekeeper, but began looking for other areas to penetrate the border instead. However, the new areas of travel were risky; they were more dangerous and life threatening. Given the challenges, more migrants turned to costly smugglers to help them cross the border.

The tragedy of Operation Gatekeeper is the direct link of its prevention-through-deterrence strategy to an absolutely horrendous rise in the number of deaths among border-crossers who were forced to attempt entry over terrain that even the INS knew to present "mortal danger" due to extreme weather conditions and rugged terrain. Before Gatekeeper began in 1994, crossers were just as likely to make their second try at the westernmost part of the sector; but that changed very quickly. By January 1995, only 14 percent were making their second try near Imperial Beach. The illicit border traffic had moved into "unfamiliar and unattractive territory."[33]

The death statistics are revealing. In 1994, 23 migrants died along the California–Mexico border. Of the 23, 2 died of hypothermia or heat stroke and 9 from drowning. By 1998, the annual total was 147 deaths – 71 from hypothermia or heat stroke and 52 from drowning. Figures for 2000 followed this unfortunate trend, when 84 known casualties resulted from heat stroke or hypothermia. In spite of the aid of smugglers, the new routes were simply too dangerous for many border-crossers and death of migrants surged. The number of migrant deaths increased six times from 1994 to 2000; a number that could be attributed to Operation Gatekeeper's pushing surreptitious entries toward treacherous eastward routes.

From 2007 to 2013, over 2,000 known migrant deaths occurred along the Mexico–Arizona border. In the first seven months of 2017, 232 migrants died crossing the border from Mexico – a 17 percent increase over the same period in 2016.[34] This number is significant, because unauthorized border crossings are actually

[30] Ibid., at 18–20.
[31] Rosenberg Foundation, *Changing Environment*, Nov. 22, 2000, at 11.
[32] 1999 GAO report, at 17–18, 20.
[33] November 19, 1999 letter to Mary Robinson.
[34] Amanda Holpuch, *Migrant deaths at US–Mexico border increase 17% this year, UN figures show*, The Guardian, Aug. 5, 2017.

decreasing.[35] Many more bodies likely go unfound, and of the ones that are found, many go unidentified.

1.2. BUSH ICE RAIDS

On a cold, raw December morning in Marshalltown, Iowa, Teresa Blanco woke up to go to work at the local Swift meat packing plant. Hundreds of others across town were doing the same thing, in spite of the miserable mixture of sleet, mist, and slush that awaited them outside their front doors. As they made their way to the plant the workers, who were from Mexico, did not mind the weather.

Unfortunately, the workers' day turned into a nightmare soon after they reported for work. Not long after the plant opened, heavily armed agents from the US Immigration and Customs Enforcement agency (ICE) stormed onto the scene. Pandemonium broke out. The workers panicked; many began to run; others tried to hide, some in dangerous and hazardous areas. As the ICE agents began rounding up all the workers, they ordered those who were US citizens to go to the cafeteria. Noncitizens were directed to a different section of the plant. Agents shouted out instructions for documented workers to form one line, and undocumented workers to form another. If an agent even suspected a citizen to be undocumented, the agent would instruct the person to get into the undocumented line. More than one individual was told, "You have Mexican teeth. You need to go to that line [for undocumented persons] and get checked."

The nightmare was only beginning. Although supervisory ICE agents carried a civil warrant for a few individuals, the squad demanded that all plant employees be held, separated by nationality. That included US citizen workers who were interrogated and detained. No one was free to leave – even those who carried evidence of lawful status or proof that they were in the process of seeking lawful permission to remain. Each was interrogated individually. The process took the entire day, and no one was permitted to make a phone call until later in the day. By the end of the day, ninety were arrested, but hundreds, including citizens, had been detained for hours. The entire community was shaken to its core.

That morning of December 12, 2006, coincided with the feast day of Our Lady of Guadalupe, a holy day of special significance to Mexican Catholics. The Marshalltown raid was one of six massive military-style raids on Swift & Company meatpacking plants across the nation's heartland. Hundreds of federal ICE agents in riot gear, armed with assault weapons, also descended upon plants in Cactus, Texas; Greeley, Colorado; Grand Island, Nebraska; Worthington, Minnesota; and Hyrum, Utah.

ICE was there to execute arrest warrants for a handful of named workers – less than 1 percent of the workforce. The sheer number of ICE agents on the scene

---

[35] Ibid.

and the manner in which the operation was conducted made clear that the execution of those warrants was not the government's real purpose. Rather, the raids seemed designed to ramp up the number of arrests, capturing the headlines on the evening news as if to make an example of the workers. In total, ICE rounded up nearly 13,000 workers – the vast majority of them US citizens – holding them against their will for hours.

US citizen Melissa Broekemeier worked at the Swift plant in Marshalltown for more than eight years. But the "longest day [she] ever worked was on December 12, 2006." Broekemeier described her experience on the day of the Swift raid this way:

> I, like all my coworkers that went to work that day … we were instructed by our supervisors to finish up … and report to the cafeteria, where we were inspected, and our private lives were scrutinized by ICE agents as if we were illegal convicts…
>
> The power that runs our machines should have been shut off first, but it was not…
>
> The Federal government jeopardized our safety and health without care. We were overlooked. We were ignored. We were treated like criminals. We were not free to leave.

The Swift plant raids became emblematic of the enforcement strategies utilized by ICE under the Bush administration.

A different ICE raid in Stillmore, Georgia, the Friday before Labor Day weekend in 2006, evoked outcry from local residents who labeled the ICE action as nothing short of "Gestapo tactics." Descending shortly before midnight, ICE agents swarmed the area, eventually arresting and deporting 125 undocumented workers. Most of those rounded up were men, while their wives fled to the woods to hide with children in tow. In the weeks after the raid, at least 200 more immigrants left town. Many of the women purchased bus tickets to Mexico with their husband's final paycheck.

The impact underscored how vital undocumented immigrants were to the local economy of Stillmore. Trailer parks lay abandoned. The poultry plant scrambled to replace more than half its workforce. Business dried up at local stores. The community of about a thousand people became little more than a ghost town. The operator of a trailer park that was raided, David Robinson, commented, "These people might not have American rights, but they've damn sure got human rights. There ain't no reason to treat them like animals."

Local residents witnessed the events, as ICE officials raided local homes and trailer parks, forcing many members of the community out of Stillmore. Officials were seen stopping motorists, breaking into homes, and there were even reports of officials threatening people with tear gas. Witnesses reported seeing ICE officials breaking windows and entering homes through floorboards. Mayor Marilyn Slater commented, "This reminds me of what I read about Nazi Germany, the Gestapo coming in and yanking people up."

Bush's ICE returned to Iowa in April 2008, when one of the largest immigration raids in US history took place in the small Midwestern town of Postville, Iowa. Postville represents the quintessential American melting pot in a community with a population of roughly 2,600 people. The community houses a mix of Hasidic Jews, who originally moved to Postville to open up a kosher meatpacking plant, working alongside immigrant workers from Mexico and parts of Central America who staff the plant, along with other residents, including descendants of German Lutheran migrants. The raid occurred at the kosher meat plant, Agriprocessors, Inc., the largest employer in town, and one of the largest in northeastern Iowa. Here, ICE seized over 400 undocumented workers, including 18 juveniles.[36]

Agriprocessors employed approximately 970 workers, 80 percent of whom were believed to have fraudulent identification.[37] After the raid both Agriprocessor and the entire Postville community were in recovery mode, and the company brought in a skeleton crew from New York to meet their staffing needs. Community residents observed the sudden drop in business and worried about the town's future. Postville is home to many Latino businesses, and in the days after the raids many storefronts posted signs in Spanish reading "closed."[38] Postville Mayor, Robert Penrod speculated on the effect of a possible Agriprocessor plant closure upon the town, estimating that "two-thirds of the homes here will sit empty [and] 95% of downtown business ... will dry up."[39]

Like other communities, the school system also felt the immediate impact of the raids. The local school district estimated that 150 of the 220 students from immigrant families were absent the day after the raid.[40] The Catholic Church became a refuge for the local immigrant population. One local nun, Sister Kathy Thrill, of nearby Waterloo where the detainees were being held at a local fairground, spoke out against the raids. She participated in an effort to collect donations for the affected families but noted the fear in the community. Many residents heard a story of someone who was stopped while shopping at a local Wal-Mart, and tales like these scared many families into hiding. Sister Thrill also spoke of her own apprehension as she

---

[36] Antonio Olivio, *Immigration raid roils Iowa Melting Pot*, Chicago Tribune, May 18, 2008, available at: www.chicagotribune.com/news/nationworld/chi-iowa-plant-raidmay19,0,3571577.story

[37] Ibid.

[38] *Raids Could Make Postville a Ghost Town*, KAALTV.com, May 14, 2008 available at: http://kaaltv.com/article/stories/S443938.shtml?cat=0

[39] Ibid.

[40] Mary Ann Zehr, *Iowa School District Left Coping with Immigration Raid's Impact*, EDWEEK May 20, 2008, available at: www.edweek.org/login.html?source=http%3A%2F%2Fwww.google.com%2Fsearch%3Fhl%3Den%26client%3Dfirefox-a%26channel%3Ds%26rls%3Dorg.mozilla%253Aen-US%253Aofficial%26hs%3Di5G%26q%3DImmigration%2Braids%26btnG%3DSearch&destination=http%3A%2F%2Fwww.edweek.org%2Few%2Farticles%2F2008%2F05%2F21%2F38immig.h27.html&levelId=2100&baddebt=false

got word of possible checkpoints set up by ICE officials while she was en route to deliver donated items to families.[41]

One witness to the effects of the ICE raid in Postville labeled the government strategy "criminal," as the women were made to wear restrictive "humiliating GPS bracelets" while caring for their children, and hundreds of women and children were faced with the threat of being left "homeless and starving."[42]

1.3. SECURE COMMUNITIES

Under the ICE Secure Communities program, which Obama's DHS expanded, deportations were greatly facilitated. As part of normal enforcement practices, state law enforcement agencies, who fingerprint individuals, submit those fingerprints to a state identification bureau. The prints are then routed to the Federal Bureau of Investigation (FBI) to ascertain whether there are any outstanding warrants for the individual. But under Secure Communities, the fingerprints are automatically sent by the FBI to ICE's immigration database to initiate an immigration status background check; if there is a "hit" or there is a question as to someone's legal status, the FBI sends a message to various departments within ICE, and the law enforcement agency is also informed. ICE then determines whether to order the local police to hold the person for pick-up by ICE. All too often, victims of crimes, minor offenders, and even crime witnesses have been swept up by Secure Communities. Reports that domestic violence victims have been rounded up because of Secure Communities are common. More than one-third of individuals arrested under Secure Communities have a US citizen spouse or child; Latinos comprise 93 percent of individuals arrested through Secure Communities, even though they are only about 75 percent of the undocumented population.[43]

The Secure Communities initiative was intended to focus on serious criminals. Yet, the vast majority of individuals removed as a result of Secure Communities referrals were noncriminal or low-level offenders. Additionally, DHS has taken a strict position on Secure Communities accessing all fingerprints submitted to the FBI by local law enforcement officials even without the permission of state and local officials. In fact, Secure Communities casts a wide net, scooping up the fingerprints of everyone not born in the United States whether or not they pose a criminal risk. For example, an abused woman in San Francisco worked up the courage to call police, but was arrested when the police saw a "red mark" on the alleged abuser's check. While the charges against her were dropped, her fingerprints had already

---

[41] Jayne Norman, *Immigrants feel distress, shock, nun says*, Des Moines Register, May 21, 2008, available at: www.desmoinesregister.com/apps/pbcs.dll/article?AID=/20080521/NEWS/805210358

[42] Jonah Newman, Minneapolis, Letter to the Editor, New York Times, June 3, 2008.

[43] Aarti Kohli et al., Secure Communities by the Numbers, 2011.

been forwarded to ICE under the Secure Communities program, and she faced deportation.[44] This case was an exact replica of one that occurred in Maryland.

1.4. SILENT RAIDS

Soon after Janet Napolitano took over as Secretary of the Department of Homeland Security (DHS) in 2009, she made clear that the gun-toting ICE raids of the Bush era did not fit into her enforcement strategy.[45] That turned out to be true for awhile. Instead, she would be targeting employers who hired undocumented workers.[46]

The targeting of employers is presumably based on enforcing employer sanctions laws that have been on the books since the Immigration and Control Act of 1986 (IRCA). However, the Obama administration's focus-on-employers-rather-than-workers strategy in fact falls squarely on the shoulders of the workers. Immigration raids at factories and farms were replaced with a quieter enforcement strategy: sending federal agents to scour companies' records for undocumented immigrant workers. "While the sweeps of the past commonly led to the deportation of such workers, the 'silent raids,' as employers call the audits, usually result in the workers being fired, although in many cases they are not deported."[47] The idea is that if the workers cannot work, they will self-deport, leaving on their own. However, they actually do not leave because they need to work. They become more desperate and take jobs at lower wages.[48] Given the increasing scale of enforcement, this can lead to an overall reduction in the average wage level for millions of workers, which is, in effect, a subsidy to employers. Over a twelve-month period, ICE conducted audits of employee files at more than 2,900 companies.[49] "The agency levied a record $3 million in civil fines [in the first six months of 2010] on businesses that hired unauthorized immigrants, according to official figures."[50] Thousands of workers were fired.[51]

Employers say the audits reach more companies than the work-site roundups of the Bush administration, forcing businesses to fire every suspected undocumented worker on the payroll – not just those who happened to be on duty at the time of a

---

[44] Lee Romney and Paloma Esquivel, *Caught in a Very Wide Net: A Federal Deportation Program Snares Many Noncriminals and Low-Level Offenders*, Los Angeles Times, Apr. 25, 2011, at A1.

[45] *Secretary Seeks Review of Immigration Raid*, New York Times, Feb. 26, 2009, at A19, available from: www.nytimes.com/2009/02/26/washington/26immig.html

[46] *Secretary Seeks Review of Immigration Raid*, New York Times, Feb. 26, 2009, at A19, available from: www.nytimes.com/2009/02/26/washington/26immig.html

[47] Julia Preston, Illegal Workers Swept from Jobs in "Silent Raids," N.Y. TIMES, July, 9, 2010, at A1, available at: www.nytimes.com/2010/07/10/us/10enforce.html.

[48] Ibid.

[49] Ibid.

[50] Ibid.

[51] Ibid.

raid – making it much harder to hire other unauthorized workers as replacements. As such, auditing is highly effective in getting unauthorized workers fired.[52]

Whether the Obama or Bush administrations, or the Clinton administration before them, actually want to stop migration to the United States or imagines that this could be done without catastrophic consequences is doubtful. More likely, the workers are being used as pawns. The very industries they target for enforcement are so dependent on the labor of migrants that they would collapse without it.[53] Instead, immigration policy and enforcement consigns those migrants to an "illegal" status, and undermines the price of their labor. Enforcement is a means of managing the flow of migrants and making their labor available to employers at a price they want to pay.

In 1998, the Clinton administration mounted the largest sanctions enforcement action to date, in which agents sifted through the names of 24,310 workers in forty Nebraska meatpacking plants[54] sending letters to 4,762 workers, saying their documents were insufficient to permit residency, forcing over 3,500 from their jobs.[55] Mark Reed, who directed "Operation Vanguard," claimed it was really intended to pressure Congress and employer groups to support guest worker legislation.[56] "We depend on foreign labor," he declared. "If we don't have illegal immigration anymore, we'll have the political support for guest workers."[57]

1.5. TARGETED ENFORCEMENT OPERATIONS

Unfortunately, the Obama administration's commitment to not engaging in Bush era-type raids was impermanent. For example, in New Orleans in 2013, ICE began waging war on the Latino immigrant community, using raids with suspicious racial effects. The circumstances of the raids were every bit as disturbing as Bush raids.

In the summer of 2014, I spoke with two men in ICE detention who were swept up in a raid at an auto-body shop under the so-called Criminal Alien Removal Initiative (CARI). On May 13, Wilmer and Yestel were arrested when ICE conducted a sweeping workplace raid of a Latino auto shop in a heavily Latino suburb of New Orleans. Yestel and Wilmer told me how ICE agents and local police surrounded the auto shop, blocking off all exits and grabbing all Latinos in sight, including workers and customers, men and women. Wilmer was a mechanic at the shop who was working on repairs, while Yestel was a customer who just happened to

---

[52] Ibid.

[53] Ricardo Sanchez, Bush's Immigration Proposal Keeps Industry in Cheap Labor, SeattlePI.com, January 30, 2004, available at: www.seattlepi.com/opinion/158609_ricardo30.html

[54] David Bacon, The Political Economy of Immigration: Reform the Corporate Campaign for a US Guest Worker Program, Multinational Monitor, Nov. 2004, available at: multinationalmonitor.org/mm2004/112004/bacon.html

[55] Ibid.

[56] Ibid.

[57] Ibid.

be at the shop getting his car repaired. After being detained, their fingerprints were processed with a high-tech machine in the back of the ICE van. Both men were then arrested, and neither had seen their homes or partners for weeks.

Under CARI, ICE squads – sometimes accompanied by local police – have been raiding apartment complexes, grocery stores, laundromats, Bible study groups, parks, and anywhere else Latinos might gather. The officers make stop-and-frisk type arrests based on racial profiling and indiscriminate mobile fingerprinting. The raids make daily routines such as going to buy groceries or bringing the car to get repaired a terrifying task that can lead to deportation.

While the CARI program name suggests that "criminals" were the target, in fact these raids were racial profiling-based area sweeps. Wilmer Irias Palma and Yestel Velasquez were arrested because they had prior deportation orders – they had no criminal records, not even traffic tickets. Wilmer and Yestel arrived in New Orleans after Hurricane Katrina to help with the reconstruction. Both men did demolition and clean-up, exposed to hazards and surrounded by chemicals. The waste smell was awful, and they often got sick and developed skin rashes. Many Latino workers they knew suffered serious injuries on the job. Some workers died. Still, Wilmer and Yestel were happy to help rebuild the city and aid its economic growth. They, like other Latinos, settled in New Orleans and started families. They were happy that former residents were able to return to the city and live with dignity after so much destruction. Now, the Latino workers who made that possible felt hunted and treated like trash.

In November 2013, brave immigrant workers and community leaders exposed the destructive CARI community raids in a protest. Shortly after their arrest in May, Yestel and Wilmer courageously came forward to expose the ongoing ICE raids. They filed a civil rights complaint with the Department of Homeland Security Office for Civil Rights and Civil Liberties, calling for an end to the DHS raids. While their civil rights complaint was pending, ICE promised that their removal would be stayed for a year, but they would, however, remain in detention. During their interviews with DHS civil rights officials, Yestel and Wilmer were shackled under ICE surveillance.

Three years earlier in July 2011, ICE announced a Prosecutorial Discretion Policy promising that upstanding residents like Yestel and Wilmer, engaged in protecting civil rights, would not be enforcement priorities. Under that policy, Yestel and Wilmer ought to have been granted immediate release from detention, as witnesses and victims participating in a civil rights investigation. As whistleblowers to unseemly official actions, they should have been encouraged and protected.

Instead, in a shocking development less than twenty-four hours after Yestel and Wilmer participated in a Washington, DC, civil rights briefing by telephone, ICE revoked their stays of removal and announced that they would be deported within days. ICE directly and spitefully retaliated against Yestel and Wilmer for speaking out about civil rights. Eventually, Wilmer was indeed deported, but Yestel was allowed to stay for another year in an inexplicable split decision. Whatever result, this kind of retaliation creates a chilling effect that goes far beyond the individuals involved.

The fact that these types of ICE raids continued during the Obama Administration is deeply troubling. That ICE would retaliate against immigrant civil rights leaders for exposing abuse is even more disturbing. ICE's vengeance raised the concern that this civil rights crisis was not an isolated product of a rogue office in the Deep South, but rather a product of Obama's national deportation policies. The administration continued its record-breaking deportation pace, and as a result of CARI, Louisiana had the highest per capita deportation rate in the country, as well as the highest per capita rate of immigration arrests of any non-border state. The raids, detentions, and deportations showed that the administration was either incapable of addressing rampant civil rights violations by its own agents, or was willing to turn a blind eye to a rogue agency in exchange for record-setting deportation numbers.

The CARI program was only the tip of the iceberg. Soon after news of the CARI program in New Orleans broke out, immigrants and community advocates around the country reported significant increases of individuals detained as "collateral" arrestees during similar raids. This increase was especially acute in places like New York, Philadelphia, Wisconsin, Washington, Alabama, Massachusetts, Florida, and Illinois. Reports from Georgia and Connecticut also documented sharp increases of collateral arrests of record-free individuals under the pretext that ICE was looking for people with old criminal convictions or prior deportation orders. In places like Arizona, local organizers reported that these home raids and collateral arrests had been ongoing for a long time.

However, ICE officials did not label these policies "raids." Instead, in its terminology, ICE conducted "targeted enforcement" operations to arrest "priority" individuals who present a danger to the public. On the ground, however, there was little difference. As implemented by ICE, "targeted enforcement" looked very much like a raid. In a targeted enforcement operation, ICE staked out a single home, apartment building, business, or – in some cases – an entire neighborhood in search of its target. Along the way, ICE agents requested identification from anyone they encountered, often arresting and placing individuals who were not the stated target of the operation in deportation proceedings. A variety of branches of ICE, including Fugitive Operations teams, conducted the operations under the direction of the local Field Office Director.[58] These operations were not limited to businesses. In the words of one-day laborer organizer in New Orleans:

---

[58] Bill Ong Hing, *Civil Rights Abuse: Evil Nature of Obama Deportation Machine in New Orleans*, IMMIGRATIONPROF BLOG, Aug. 7, 2014, available at: www.lawprofessors.typepad.com/immigration/2014/08/civil-rights-abuse-evil-nature-of-obama-deportation-machine-in-new-orleans.html

Before ICE used to round people up in the community. Now, they go to people's houses. They show them a picture of a person they usually don't know. Even if the person isn't there, everyone in the house still gets fingerprinted using the biometric machines. The only difference is ICE makes sure to show people a photograph so that they can say it is targeted enforcement and not a raid.[59]

To make matters worse, ICE retaliated against community organizers and immigrants who advocated for improved conditions, a moratorium on removals, or protection of rights of those in custody. An Arizona advocate reported that "In retaliation for organizing, ICE has denied people's visitation rights, gone out of their way to keep people in detention even when granted bond, and even put people's family members in solitary confinement."[60] Organizers in Tacoma, Washington working with immigrants who participated in a detention center hunger strike reported similar retaliation against families of those who led these actions. Family visits [were] often reduced to ten or twenty minutes.[61]

1.6. REMOVAL OF LAW PERMANENT RESIDENTS WITHOUT A FAIR HEARING

When President Obama announced his expansive actions in November 2014 granting deferred action and employment authorization to undocumented parents of US citizens, he emphasized that deportation would be focused on "felons, not families."[62] While this is a catchy phrase, its flaw is obvious:

> "People with felonies have families too," said [Abraham] Paulos, whose organization Families for Freedom advocates for families who've been separated by criminal deportation. "That's a false binary [Obama] is setting up," said Tia Oso, the Arizona organizer for the Black Alliance for Just Immigration. Oso pointed out that because blacks in the [United States] are already targeted by the War on Drugs and racial and ethnic profiling by police, partnerships between law enforcement and immigration authorities mean that black immigrants are in detention and criminal deportation proceedings at a rate five times their actual presence in the [United States] undocumented community.[63]

Rithy Yin was a baby when his family fled the killing fields of the Cambodian Khmer Rouge, that took his father's life, and entered the United States as a refugee. In a Seattle inner city neighborhood "plagued with drugs and gang violence," Rithy

[59] Ibid.
[60] Ibid.
[61] Ibid.
[62] Julie Pace, *Immigration: Obama seeks to focus efforts on 'felons, not families,'* Associated Press, Nov. 20, 2014.
[63] Julianne Hing, *Who Will Lose Under Obama's Executive Action?*, Colorlines, Nov. 21, 2014.

"turn[ed] to the streets to find acceptance," and he was in state prison by the age of eighteen.[64] While serving his entire ten-year sentence, Rithy "grew up," completing his GED, working in the prison ministry, and providing moral support to new inmates.[65] However, on his release from prison, Rithy was greeted by an ICE deportation order, despite having grown up in the United States alongside his mother, siblings, and their families, being wholly unfamiliar with Cambodia.[66]

Many other Cambodian refugees who have committed crimes have been deported or face the prospect of removal.[67] All paid the price of their crimes by serving their time in prison, but unlike US citizens, they face the additional punishment of banishment, even though they have strong evidence of rehabilitation and remorse. Once classified as an aggravated felon (usually for being sentenced to a year or more in prison), their long residence in the United States and the effect of deportation on their families is irrelevant in deportation proceedings.

Consider Lundy Khoy. Lundy is facing deportation because of the US immigration law zero-tolerance policy toward aggravated felons. Lundy was born in a Thai refugee camp after her parents fled the genocide in Cambodia. When she was a one-year-old, she and her family came to the United States as refugees. Lundy and her parents were granted lawful permanent residence status when Lundy was in kindergarten, but they never filed for citizenship through naturalization because of the expense. In 2000, when Lundy was a 19-year-old freshman at George Mason University, she was stopped by a bicycle cop who asked if she had any drugs. She answered honestly and told the officer that she had seven tabs of ecstasy, but that they were not all for her. She was arrested for possession with intent to distribute. On the advice of her lawyer, she pled guilty[68] to spare her family the expense and embarrassment of a trial. She was sentenced to five years in prison.

Although Lundy was released and placed on probation after serving only a few months in prison, her conviction is an aggravated felony for deportation purposes. In the spring of 2004, Lundy arrived at a regularly scheduled probation appointment to show off her college report card. When she stepped inside the office, she was greeted by her probation officer and several Immigrations and Customs Enforcement agents who were targeting removable agents on active probation. She was instructed to hand over possessions and stand spread eagle against the wall, she was then handcuffed and transported to Hampton Roads Regional Jail in Portsmouth, Virginia.

---

[64] Clayborn D. Tolliver, Jr., *One the president's action does not help*, The Hill, Nov. 26, 2014.

[65] Ibid.

[66] Ibid.

[67] Bill Ong Hing, Detention to Deportation – Rethinking the Removal of Cambodian Refugees, 38 U.C. Davis. L. Rev. 891 (2005).

[68] Guilty pleas on advice of counsel are, of course, common. In *Padilla* v. *Commonwealth of Kentucky*, 559 U.S. 356 (2010), the Supreme Court ruled that criminal defense attorneys must advise noncitizen clients about the deportation risks of a guilty plea. When the law is unambiguous, attorneys must advise their criminal clients that deportation "will" result from a conviction. When immigration consequences are unclear or uncertain, attorneys must advise that deportation "may" result.

Given her aggravated felony conviction, an immigration judge ordered that Lundy be deported without hearing evidence of her childhood in the United States, current family situation, her educational pursuits, or her perfect cooperation during her probation. Lundy remained in ICE custody for nine months while the United States attempted to deport her to Cambodia. However, due to Cambodia taking its time in issuing travel documents for Lundy, ICE has released her pending receipt of those documents.

Now in her 30s, Lundy is trying to lead a normal life as she awaits her fate. Having been born in a Thai refugee camp and lived in the United States since the age of one, she finds it hard to imagine being removed to Cambodia, a country with which she has no familiarity or family ties; all her relatives live here. She is now trying to complete her bachelor's degree, works full-time as a college enrollment counselor and volunteers for local charities, including Habitat for Humanity and the Boys and Girls Club. Had Lundy been born in the United States (like her two siblings) or if her parents had become naturalized citizens before Lundy turned 18, she would not be on the deportation list.

Lundy lives in Washington, DC, a few blocks from her younger sister, Linda, who is only eighteen months younger, but is a US citizen because she was born after the family arrived in the United States. The two are inseparable. They grew up sharing a bed and a bedroom, until Lundy started college. Linda is Lundy's most ardent supporter. They cook together, go out together, laugh together, and cry together; they think of each other as soul mates. They share intimate details about each others' lives. Linda joins Lundy in speaking out about current deportation policies, and the two are working with community-based organizations in Washington, DC, and Philadelphia to seek a legislative solution for those in a similar position to Lundy. When Lundy is feeling depressed or worried, Linda provides emotional support to bring Lundy back from those lows. Linda cannot imagine what her life would be like if Lundy was deported to Cambodia.

We have a glimpse of what Lundy Khoy would accomplish with a second chance, as she continues working as a college counselor, pursuing her degree, and engaging in volunteer work. Instead, she awaits a deportation notice, foreclosed of an opportunity to plead for a second chance. Many deported noncitizens are removed to countries where they have virtually no ties. That is what Lundy fears. However, the federal courts are not in a position to intervene, because any noncitizen convicted of an aggravated felony is subject to deportation from the United States without statutory relief.

Of course, the deportation of so-called criminal immigrants who deserve a second chance is not limited to Cambodian refugees. Every day DHS deports lawful permanent residents from all over the world who have committed crimes. More often than not, family separation results, as US citizens, lawful resident parents, spouses, and children remain.

The thought, or perhaps lack of thoughtfulness, behind some deportations is numbing. For example, when I heard about the deportation of Tatyana Mitrohina, the circumstances were hard to fathom.

Tatyana was born in Russia in 1978. She was born with multiple health problems, including heart defects. Both hands are small and partially deformed. She has a similar problem with her feet. Her parents abandoned Tatyana immediately after birth, and she spent the first ten years of her life in hospitals, rehabilitation facilities, and at a boarding school for disabled children without contact with her parents. She underwent several surgical procedures to correct her birth defects, but the abnormalities of her hands and feet were never fully corrected.

As with most children, these first ten years of Tatyana's life had profound impact on her emotionally and psychologically. She had multiple caregivers and had no one to whom she felt attached. She felt rejected and abandoned by her biological family. When asked about the effect this period of her life had on her, Tatyana explained: "I didn't like to be touched, I couldn't stand to be touched or hugged."[69] A psychologist who evaluated Tatyana observed: "Ms. Mitrohina demonstrates a range of psychopathology frequently observed as a sequel of early neglect, abandonment and institutionalization, emotional rejection, and physical trauma."[70]

When she was about seven years old, after she was released from the hospital, Tatyana's maternal grandmother took responsibility for her. At the time, Tatyana was unaware that she had a family. A year or so later, her father began to visit, and about three years later, he decided to bring Tatyana back into the family.[71]

Her father brought Tatyana home to live with family because that made the family eligible for a better apartment in Russia. The atmosphere in the home was hostile, chaotic, and filled with conflict.[72] Tatyana's mother was opposed to her return and was openly hostile and critical of Tatyana. Tatyana was constantly beaten by both parents.[73] Her parents continually told her that she was "inadequate and worthless."[74] The psychological evaluation reported a "history of neglect, physical and verbal abuse as a child and one attempted molestation between the age of 8 and 10."[75]

The tense home-life led to the disintegration of the family and her parents divorced when Tatyana was twelve. Her father departed, and Tatyana was left with her mother who did not want her. So when Tatyana turned fourteen, her grandmother, who had legal custody, signed adoption papers. Oldrich and Ruth Gann of Sonoma,

---

[69] Psychological Evaluation of Tatyana Mitrohina (2007) (hereinafter "Evaluation"), at 4.

[70] Evaluation at 9.

[71] Removal Proceedings of Tatyana Mitrohina, Transcript of Record (2007) (hereinafter "Transcript"), at 10–11.

[72] Evaluation at 4.

[73] Evaluation at 6.

[74] Julianne Hing and Seth Wessler, *When an Immigrant Mom Gets Arrested*, Colorlines Magazine, July–August, 2008, at 23.

[75] Evaluation at 6.

California, who were 68 and 63 years old, respectively, at the time, adopted Tatyana and brought her to the United States in 1993.

Tatyana had difficulty adapting to her new family. She constantly felt that she could not live up to her adoptive parents' expectations.[76] Her dislike of being touched or held persisted into her late teens. She had difficulty addressing her new parents as "mom" and "dad."[77] To Tatyana, the relationship was a "mismatch" and she did not get along with her adoptive parents from the start.[78]

Concerned with the conflict, Tatyana's adoptive parents had her evaluated by a psychologist. The psychologist prescribed medication, and her parents threatened to send Tatyana back to Russia if she did not take the medication. Tatyana did not appreciate the psychological treatment and argued with her parents; her parents, who often called the police after these altercations erupted.[79] Tatyana felt trapped and became depressed and angry. After an argument in 1999 led to a call to the police, Tatyana was so upset that she kicked her adoptive father in the leg in front of the police officer.[80] Tatyana was taken into custody, but charges were later dismissed.

In 2000, while still living with her adoptive parents, Tatyana threatened to kill herself. She was not arrested, but was taken to a mental health facility for three days. She eventually moved out of her parents' house.[81] Since then, Tatyana's adoptive father has passed away and she has not maintained contact with her adoptive mother.

After moving out, Tatyana rented a room from a young man with whom she later became emotionally involved. She soon noticed that he mistreated his six-year-old son. On one occasion when the child was complaining about a stomach pain and the father refused to do anything, Tatyana called an ambulance. After that, the landlord was abusive toward her for eighteen months. In 2002, after an argument in which Tatyana kicked him several times, he called the police, and she was arrested and pled guilty to a misdemeanor battery. Tatyana received thirty-six months formal probation, was ordered to pay fines and fees, complete a 52-week batterer's program, maintain employment, and complete community service.[82] She successfully completed all the terms of her sentence.

Tatyana held a variety of jobs in the United States and attended junior college. She worked at the Sonoma Market, Baskin Robins, and provided care for the elderly through an agency, losing all these jobs because of anger management problems.[83] She worked for a time caring for elderly residents at an assisted living facility. Tatyana

---

[76]   Ibid.

[77]   Transcript at 18, Evaluation at 4.

[78]   Transcript at 18.

[79]   Transcript at 19.

[80]   Ibid.

[81]   Transcript at 20.

[82]   Probation Report (2007) (hereinafter "Report"), at 2.

[83]   Decision of the Immigration Judge (Memorandum and Order), December 4, 2007 (hereinafter "IJ Decision"), at 2.

admitted that she had kicked an elderly patient three or four times while working at this facility. The patient did not report the incident because she suffered from Alzheimer's Disease. Tatyana also took classes at a junior college over a two-year period from Spring 2005 to Spring 2007.[84]

In 2005, Tatyana became pregnant by a man named John Carter Goode. The baby was born on October 17, 2005. Although Tatyana tried to get him involved, the father of the child was never involved in the child's life. Tatyana had no one to rely on for financial help or other assistance in the child's upbringing.[85] Her probation officer noted that Tatyana lacked "a support system for parenting and when she needs a break, she has been unable to secure a reliable babysitter."[86] Although Tatyana was eventually convicted of child abuse, the child protective services investigator observed that the child was "healthy, had suffered no long-term injury, and appeared to be slightly advanced for his chronological age."[87] When her son was a year and a half old, Tatyana got a job at Metro PCS, a wireless phone company, in an attempt to get off of welfare assistance. She lost that job when she was arrested in June 2007.[88]

On June 26, 2007, when the child was just under two years old, the child spilled some water and then grabbed a roll of paper towels to clean up the mess. He scattered paper towels all over the floor. According to a presentence report:

> Mitrohina then grabbed the victim, took him to the bedroom, and threw him on the bed to give him a "time out." She then began to slap the victim with her hands, on his head and legs, approximately ten times. Mitrohina stated: "I was yelling at him like he was 20," even though she knew he could not understand. The defendant explained that she did not stop when she should have, and left a bruise and mark on his face. Victim John Doe was screaming and crying as she hit him.
>
> Mitrohina commented that the instant matter was not the first time she slapped victim John Doe, but indicated that it was the worst because it left a mark. She said she would become angered when John Doe, as a newborn, "threw up" or "pooped" too much. She admitted that she had been hurting victim John Doe since he was born, and had become more physical with him as he grew older. At times, she slapped him and threw him on the ground. She also admitted that approximately one year earlier, she had hit John Doe in the face and caused a large, visible bruise under his eye.[89]

Tatyana then took her child to a day care center, explained to an employee that she had become frustrated with her son at home and had struck him with her bare

---

[84] Transcript at 14.
[85] Transcript at 21.
[86] Report at 7.
[87] Report at 5.
[88] Report at 5.
[89] IJ Decision at 2–3.

hands. She left the child at the day care and went to her job. The child was visibly bruised on his left temple. A county worker interviewed Tatyana later that day, noting that she "did not cry, and appeared very cold and nonchalant about the abuse. She was only concerned about being arrested and not about the condition of her son, and never once asked if he had gone to the hospital or if he was alright."[90]

As a result of this incident, the child was removed from Tatyana's care, and child abuse charges were brought. Tatyana pled guilty and was sentenced to 120 days in jail and four years on probation. Ultimately, she was only required to serve about a month in jail. A probation officer who interviewed Tatyana while she was in custody noted that she was very remorseful and forthcoming throughout the interview, noting that she "has struggled with shame and guilt while in custody, and has spent much time in introspection."[91] When she was first taken into custody, Tatyana was very upset and she cried a lot. The mental health staff in the county jail determined that she was likely suffering from depression, perhaps due to a chemical imbalance in her brain. So she was prescribed Zoloft.[92] Zoloft is an antidepressant drug, used to treat depression, obsessive-compulsive disorder, panic disorder, anxiety disorders, and post-traumatic stress disorder (PTSD).[93]

While in jail for the child abuse conviction, Tatyana was on a "no mix" status, and was unable to avail herself to counseling and other resources normally offered to inmates. In spite of that status, she sought to participate in anger management correspondence courses.[94] She took responsibility for her actions and was remorseful. She was committed to doing whatever was required to successfully reunite with her son.[95] She testified, "My baby is first in my life now. I know I need to get help myself in order to take care of my baby."[96]

The child was placed into foster care and became the subject of juvenile court proceedings.[97] In early October 2007, the juvenile court ordered that family reunification services be offered to Tatyana. The court's goal was to reunify Tatyana with her child. Tatyana was ordered to participate in a number of different services, including counseling and domestic violence programs.[98] The problem was that by then, Tatyana was in ICE custody, unable to comply with the juvenile court's order.

If Tatyana had been a US citizen, after her month in jail, she would have been released from custody. However, she was a lawful permanent resident alien who now had committed a deportable offense. So ICE officials took custody of Tatyana

[90] IJ Decision at 3.
[91] Report at 3.
[92] Transcript at 47–8.
[93] *Zoloft*, Dec. 21, 2017, available at: www.rxlist.com/zoloft-drug.htm
[94] Report at 4.
[95] Report at 4; Transcript at 34, 36–7.
[96] Transcript at 45.
[97] Report at 7.
[98] Letter from Jennifer Hall, Child Welfare Services, Nov. 2, 2007, Exhibit 4.

upon her release from jail and kept her in custody pending removal proceedings. By the time her removal hearing took place, she had been in custody for four months.[99]

Tatyana wanted to abide by the juvenile court's mandate because she had the utmost desire to resolve her personal problems and regain custody of her son. Being out of ICE custody would have given her the opportunity to straighten out, and have a chance at reunifying with her son. If she had been able to do that, her legal position in the deportation case would have been far different.

In determining whether Tatyana merited a favorable exercise of discretion, the immigration judge felt that he had to balance the positive factors in Tatyana's case against the negative ones to determine whether the granting of relief was "in the best interests" of the country.[100] In choosing to interpret the balance unfavorably and conclude that Tatyana was not deserving of a waiver, the judge used the following reasoning:

> There are factors about the respondent's life that evoke genuine sympathy. She has to live her life with visibly deformed hands. She spent her first seven years in a hospital, and was essentially abandoned by her birth parents. She was in an abusive relationship, and she testified that the father of her child has never played any meaningful role in his life. In addition, if the respondent is removed to Russia, she may find it difficult to support herself, and has no real family to rely upon. She also points out that if she is removed her son will grow up as an orphan, in much the same way she did. She wrote letters to the sentencing judge in the Superior Court and to this court, expressing her remorse for what she has done and vigorously arguing that she will not break the law or hurt her son again. Sonoma County, where the most recent offense occurred, has ordered respondent (if she is released) to participate in a number of counseling programs in order to see whether respondent can be reunited safely with her child.
>
> Balanced against those factors, however, is the fact that respondent has repeatedly decided to address her frustrations and disappointments with violence. She assaulted her stepfather, her ex-boyfriend[,] an elderly disabled patient who was entrusted to her care, and on many occasions her very young child. She said she got physical with this baby "a few times a month." She hit him in the face and caused a bruise under his eye. She threw him on the bed and beat him while he screamed. She struck him in the temple, an extraordinarily dangerous act, and did so with such force that it caused visible swelling and bruising. The victim was only twenty months old.
>
> This was not an isolated incident, but a repeated response to situations of stress. The difficulty is that no person can eliminate situations of stress from their lives, and this pattern of behavior gives this court grave concern that the respondent may act in a violent or dangerous way in the future. Of particular concern is the fact that not only has the respondent assaulted able-bodied adults, but highly vulnerable

[99] Transcript at 21.
[100] IJ Decision at 3–4.

persons, namely the elderly patient at the nursing home and, with frequency, her small child.

The respondent's most recent psychological evaluation revealed that she had gone through a course of anger management in 2002 along with psychotherapy on a weekly basis, but that she had resisted previous therapeutic interventions. She "perceived parenting instructions as an intrusion and interference with her doing things her own way." The psychologist who interviewed her found "a chronic angry undercurrent during the interview as well as some difficulty with an overly idiosyncratic way of perceiving. She [respondent] tended to distort reality to meet her needs or misidentify the salient aspects of a situation. It wasn't at the level of psychosis, but was at a level that would significantly interfere with her ability to accurately perceive and cope with everyday life and interactions." She had no symptoms of underlying neurological impairment, but "evidenced very little insight regarding her thoughts, feelings and behaviors." The report states that persons with respondent's psychological profile have "a tendency to act out in an impulsive, aggressive manner, display poor judgment, and do not seem to learn from their experiences." Such persons "often agree to treatment to bring about an outcome they desire or avoid some consequences, but are likely to terminate their participation in interventions before they can have an effect." The report concludes "[o]verall, the prognosis for Ms. Mitrohina benefiting from services is poor."

...

After considering all relevant factors, this Court finds that the negative factors far outweigh the positive in the present case. The respondent has not shown that it is in the best interests of the community that she remain in the United States. Indeed there is a real concern that she is a danger to others.

One of the more troubling aspects of the immigration judge's decision is that his deportation order was effectively a family law decision to sever the parent–child relationship. The denial of Tatyana's cancellation application foreclosed her from following the reunification conditions of the state court, thereby making termination of the relationship a fait accompli. The sad irony is that had we been able to hit a pause button on the removal proceedings and release Tatyana to follow the reunification plan (parenting classes, anger management, mental health medication), and if she had been able to regain custody of her son or at least make clear progress, the outcome of the deportation case might have been different once the hearing resumed. The immigration judge's decision blocked these possibilities, even though he lacked the necessary family law expertise to make such conclusions.

Unlike the Immigration Court, the state Superior Court was acting in one of its areas of expertise in conjunction with the probation department. In making their determination, the probation officer and state court made their choices; taking into account Tatyana's criminal history, they concluded that offering reunification services was appropriate. This is important because terminating parental rights is a grave matter, and the state's main concern is the best interest of the child. Significantly, reunification services are not to be provided if a parent is suffering from a mental disability that renders him or her incapable of utilizing those services.

In essence, the Immigration Court decided not to defer to the expertise of the state court, instead making its own decision – without the benefit of experience or special expertise, determining that it was in the best interests of Tatyana's child to be taken from Tatyana permanently.

Tatyana was born in Russia with heart defects and deformed hands. She was rejected by her parents for many years, spending her infancy in hospitals and institutions. Later she was abused by her parents, then abandoned by them. She immigrated to the United States as a young teen, adopted by US citizens. After more than a decade, she had a child of her own, whom she abused. Tatyana was diagnosed with mental illness. Although she was convicted of child abuse, the state court recommended medication, counseling, and a chance to regain custody of her child. But ICE took over, and Tatyana was removed from the country. The parent–child relationship was severed.

1.7. REVISIONS TO CREDIBLE FEAR STANDARDS

As the surge in UACs began in early 2014, United States Citizenship and Immigration Services (USCIS), whose asylum office handles asylum cases, revised its lesson plan to officers on how to determine whether asylum applicants who make it to the border meet the credible fear screening standard.[101] The new credible fear standards were quite misleadingly and inappropriate. The language and tone instructed asylum officers to impose a burden on applicants not only beyond screening purposes, but appeared to surpass the standard for asylum established by the Supreme Court in *INS* v. *Cardoza-Fonseca*.[102] In fact the actual screening standard should be more deferential than the actual standard for asylum.

As the lesson plan correctly pointed out, the function of credible fear screening is "to quickly identify *potentially* meritorious claims to protection and to resolve *frivolous* ones with dispatch ... If an alien passes this *threshold-screening* standard, [the] claim for protection ... will be further examined by an immigration judge."[103] This is consistent with the statutory structure. Under INA § 235(b), if "the alien indicates either an intention to apply for asylum ... or a fear of persecution, the officer shall refer the alien for an interview by an asylum officer." Then if the asylum "officer determines at the time of the interview that an alien has a credible fear of persecution ... the alien shall be detained for further consideration of the application for asylum." Thus, the credible fear process clearly is a screening process for potentially

---

[101] Lesson Plan Overview, February 28, 2014 (hereinafter "Lesson Plan"), available at: http://cmsny.org/wp-content/uploads/credible-fear-of-persecution-and-torture.pdf; Catholic Legal Immigration Network, *USCIS Amends Credible Fear Lesson Plans*, available at: https://cliniclegal.org/resources/uscis-amends-credible-fear-lesson-plans

[102] 480 U.S. 421 (1987).

[103] (emphasis added) (Lesson Plan at 11), citing Immigration and Naturalization Service, Regulations Concerning the Convention Against Torture, 64 Fed. Reg. 8478, 8479, Feb. 19, 1999.

meritorious asylum claims versus frivolous ones. Structurally and explicitly, the alien certainly does not need to establish the asylum claim at this point; a potentially meritorious claim at this juncture is all that is necessary.

Thus, the standard and burden for credible fear – a threshold screening stage – must be lower than establishing an actual meritorious claim for asylum. At this credible fear review, the asylum officer can only screen out frivolous claims.

Since the standard for credible fear is structurally less rigorous than the standard for asylum, in order to adequately appreciate and grasp the correct credible fear standard, one must know what the standard is for asylum. In order to qualify for asylum, the applicant must meet the definition of refugee set forth in INA § 101(a)(42), by establishing "a well-founded fear of persecution." In *INS* v. *Cardoza-Fonseca*, the Supreme Court explained the well-founded fear standard: "So long as an objective situation is established by the evidence, it need not be shown that the situation will probably result in persecution, but it is enough that persecution is a reasonable possibility" in order to qualify for asylum. In fact, "10% chance of [persecution may be sufficient to establish] well-founded fear ... [I]t is enough that persecution is a reasonable possibility." Clearly, the applicant is not required to prove that it is more likely than not he or she will be persecuted.[104] The applicant is not required to establish by a preponderance of the evidence that he or she will not be persecuted. In fact, the Supreme Court's holding in *Cardoza-Fonseca* requires a very low standard of proof for asylum. This makes sense, given the humanitarian purpose of asylum and what is at stake if an incorrect decision denying asylum is made. In essence, the benefit of the doubt is given to the applicant. An "applicant for asylum has established a well-founded fear if he shows that a *reasonable person* in his circumstances would fear persecution."[105]

Thus, since we know that the asylum standard is low, requiring only a "10% chance" or a "reasonable possibility" of persecution, we know intuitively that the credible fear screening hurdle must be even lower. Instructions suggesting anything more are therefore incorrect and misguided. Therein lies the problem with the Lesson Plan, whose tenor, format, and content suggests too high a burden for credible fear.

Here are some examples of specific problems with the Lesson Plan:

- Throughout the text, the Lesson Plan points out that credible fear of persecution means that there is a "significant possibility" that the alien can establish eligibility for asylum. However, this is done without regular

---

[104] Prior to *Cardoza-Fonseca*, the Supreme Court held that the "preponderance" or "more likely than not" standard of persecution did apply to the "clear probability" standard for withholding of deportation. *INS* v. *Stevic*, 467 U.S. 407 (1984). *Cardoza-Fonseca* provided the Supreme Court the opportunity to explain for the first time that the well-founded fear standard for asylum was intended to be more generous than the withholding standard; the two provisions were located in two different parts of the Immigration and Nationality Act.

[105] See *Matter of Mogharrabi*, 19 I&N Dec. 439 (BIA 1987).

acknowledgment and reminder that the threshold for establishing eligibility for asylum, i.e., well-founded fear, is relatively low compared to other burdens of proof such as preponderance of the evidence, or beyond a reasonable doubt. Without that reminder or acknowledgment, the reader is left with the words "significant possibility" which connote a high burden. In fact, it is a burden that requires less than a 10% likelihood of persecution.

- The Lesson Plan contains this guidance:

> The applicant bears the burden of proof to establish a credible fear of persecution or torture. This means that the applicant *must produce sufficiently convincing evidence that establishes the facts of the case*, and that those facts must *meet the relevant legal standard*. (emphasis added)

The italicized language suggests an incorrect standard as it suggests that each and every fact must be established by convincing evidence. That language suggests the inapplicable preponderance standard. That standard is not even required for asylum, so it certainly cannot be the proper standard for credible fear, which should be much lower.

- Citing INA § 208(b)(1)(B)(ii), the Lesson Plan says that the applicant's testimony is sufficient only if "credible, is persuasive, and refers to specific facts." This part of the Lesson Plan goes on:

> Therefore, the terms "persuasive" and "specific facts" must have independent meaning above and beyond the first term "credible." An applicant may be credible, but nonetheless fail to satisfy his or her burden to establish the required elements of eligibility. "Specific facts" are distinct from statements of belief. When assessing the probative value of an applicant's testimony, the asylum officer must distinguish between fact and opinion testimony and determine how much weight to assign to each of the two forms of testimony.

This statement and citation to INA § 208(b)(1)(B)(ii) comes under the specific part of the Lesson Plan labelled: "V. BURDEN OF PROOF AND STANDARD OF PROOF FOR CREDIBLE FEAR DETERMINATIONS." This is a serious error. In fact, INA § 208(b)(1)(B)(ii) falls in the section of the Immigration and Nationality Act that pertains to the burden of proof for asylum, not credible fear. Thus, the lesson plan incorrectly instructs that the same burden of proof for asylum applies to credible fear. The clear incorrect lesson to the reader is that the credible fear applicant must meet an eligibility requirement that in fact does not apply.

Recognizing credible fear is not a grant of asylum. It merely recognizes that the person has shown a significant possibility that that the applicant can meet the less-than-preponderance standard for asylum before an immigration judge. As such, the credible fear standard is quite low. A credible fear finding simply gives the person a chance for a fair hearing in an Immigration Court. Credible fear requires less than a one in ten chance that persecution is likely – something that the new Lesson Plan failed to teach.

Those who come to our borders seeking asylum deserve fair treatment. The entire content of the Lesson Plan needs to be reconsidered so that asylum seekers are treated fairly at this screening stage. If they meet the correct, contextualized credible fear standard, they should be allowed to make a case for asylum in front of an immigration judge where all the nuances of asylum law can be fairly evaluated. Given the likely manifestations of PTSD, complications in assessing credibility, possible problems with translation, and other logistical challenges, the screening function of credible fear determinations is most correctly viewed as one of deference to the applicant.

1.8. FAMILY SEPARATION

Felipe Calderon is not unlike many natives of Mexico who are living in the United States without official documentation. Calderon was born in 1955 in a small town in the state of Guanajuato, Mexico. He grew up poor, often lacking food, clothing, and housing. He attended the local elementary school through the third grade – the highest level of education the hometown elementary school offered. He then attended three more years of school in a town five kilometers away, walking two hours each way as the family could not afford to pay the school transport costs. As the eldest child, he had to stop school and begin work aged eleven to help put food on the table.

Calderon's hometown – Valle de Santiago – only had about five hundred residents, and the only work available was in the agricultural fields. Some years later, his father decided to try his luck in Mexico City to earn more money. Calderon and two of his brothers, who also left school at an early age to help supplement the family income, remained in Valle de Santiago to work in the fields. In 1975, the entire family moved to Mexico City to join their father, where Calderon found work in a stationery store earning minimum wage – more than what he made in the fields.

Shortly thereafter, Calderon met Laura Gomez and fell in love. After three years of dating, they decided to get married and start a family. Even after marrying, Calderon still felt an obligation to help his parents and siblings with expenses, so he continued to share part of his salary with them. His dream was to build a house with his wife and raise children in an environment where they could obtain a good education – an environment very different from his own childhood. Unfortunately, the couple learned that Laura was unable to have children, but they nevertheless continued to strive for their dream of earning enough money to build a home. However, good work became difficult to find and the cost of living was climbing.

Like so many others, Calderon looked to the United States to pursue his dream. In 1985, he entered with his father-in-law, looking for work in Oakland, California.

He soon found work as a potato packer for a produce company earning only $120 per week. Six months later, he found a better job working the graveyard shift from 11pm to 7am in the kitchen of a Holiday Inn (later purchased by Hilton Hotel). Calderon worked the graveyard shift for ten years. By working hard, Calderon was given the opportunity to work the day shift, and he maintained that shift until August 2007, when he was arrested by ICE. Although the pay was modest, the job provided medical benefits. In addition to working at the hotel, Calderon worked part time at a pizza parlor to supplement his income. In total, he averaged a 68–72-hour working week to provide for his family's needs. When the Board of Immigration Appeals (BIA) ruled against him in 2010, Calderon had worked in the hotel kitchen for almost twenty-five years.

After his first trip to the United States, Calderon returned to Mexico a couple of times. His last visit was in 1987 with his first wife Laura, after which he resided in the United States continuously. In September 1993, they decided to buy a house in Oakland, with the idea that they would adopt a child in future. Both continued working, but in 1994 Laura began getting sick. Her illness became so debilitating that after a while she had to stop working. Doctors discovered a problem affecting Laura's lungs and heart, which caused her to suffer a great deal. Sadly, Laura died in January 1995.

The loss of Laura changed Calderon completely. He was alone in the United States. This was a painful period for him, having lost his wife of seventeen years. He did not want his parents or siblings to come to the United States because of the difficulties and dangers of crossing the border. Calderon took refuge in his work; he also played baseball to take his mind off the tragedy.

After some time, his friends suggested that Calderon look for a new partner so he would not be alone. He was doubtful that he could find someone who would understand his situation and state of mind. However, a couple he knew told him about another friend whose spouse had also passed away. They told Calderon about Juana, who was now alone with two young children and also needed companionship. Calderon was interested in meeting Juana, especially because she had two children.

Calderon and Juana were introduced and they eventually married in March 1996. He treated Juana's two children Donaldo and Lorena like his own; they were quite young when he became their stepfather. They felt so fortunate to have been brought together when each was in such great pain and need. They truly felt that they were brought together through divine intervention.

However, ICE arrested Calderon in 2008 while working in the hotel kitchen and placed him in removal proceedings. At his deportation hearing, Calderon applied for cancellation of removal, and his attorney introduced strong supporting documents from Calderon's friends and neighbors that describe him as a humble, caring, and well-respected member of the community. Calderon and his second wife were successfully integrated into the community and had established strong roots.

Calderon was a good neighbor, a good worker, and a regular churchgoer. He was the godfather to a disabled boy, and participated in church and community events. Reverend A.M., executive director of a local church organizing group, noted that Calderon and his family "participated in many community activities in our organization ... [W]e are grateful for their leadership, responsibility, and commitment to the community."

Calderon's commitment to the community extended beyond religious boundaries. Mr. L. A., a union representative, wrote that Calderon "has been an active Union member ... for 22 years. He has always helped his co-workers with problems, attended Union meetings, and worked together with management to resolve any issues as they came up." Calderon was also deeply involved in PTA meetings, school activities, and community athletic and cultural programs. Other parents in the community expressed, "Mr. [Calderon] is an active, honest, respectful, and quietly supportive member of our community soccer programs. He and his wife are truly role models for his children as well as their teammates." Calderon's service to the community through many outlets has made him a role model for other children and adults. For example, parents in the community have described Calderon as "a very responsible person, dedicated to the well being of his family, deeply involved in community and family activities, PTA meetings, school reunions, and church issues." The PTA Council President expressed, "I feel strongly that Mr. [Calderon] is a stabilizing factor in our community. We need more men like him, who are loyal and loving to their families." Another Berkeley parent noted:

> [Y]ear after year, [Calderon] volunteered with me in events held for the local church and Berkeley Unified School District where our children attended. As part of his nature, [Calderon] goes out of his way to motivate our Latino population and even organizes cultural celebrations at our church and local senior centers.

The evidence was strong enough for the immigration judge to grant Calderon's application for cancellation, but the government appealed, and the Board of Immigration Appeals reversed on the grounds that the "Immigration Judge erred in concluding the respondent met his burden in establishing the requisite hardship." The BIA felt that neither US citizen children "suffered from any health issues," or "showed compelling educational needs." Regarding Lorena, the BIA held the possibility that she "may not be able to complete her college education" due to Calderon's removal not constituting an "exceptional and extremely unusual hardship." Nor did the evidence regarding their third child, Felipe Jr. establish for the BIA that he would "suffer hardship which is substantially beyond what would ordinarily be expected as a result of the respondent's removal."

A month prior to Calderon's removal, I asked the local ICE director to grant deferred action to Calderon based on prosecutorial discretion instructions from the ICE director in Washington, DC. His response was a flat rejection:

> The June 17 and August 18 memos and announcements from D.C. didn't say anything new that I have not already been doing; they didn't change anything; they didn't change my marching orders; 25 years residence doesn't mean anything; [Calderon] just happened to be under the radar. The public expects us to enforce immigration laws. No one has told me the [Calderon] case is a low priority case; resources have always been expended on these kinds of cases. I also won't consider an extension of time for him to attend [Lorena]'s graduation. If I did that, then what about the next kid?

The local ICE director's attitude during the Obama era is emblematic of typical unsympathetic, enforcement-only-minded ICE officers, who can be found throughout the country. As we will see in Chapter 6, President Donald Trump has taken full advantage of those officers, unleashing their fury.

PART II

Obama's Shame

2

Deporting Unaccompanied Children

2.1. INTRODUCTION

When they were young children, Luis and Marta found themselves without their mother.[1] Their mother, Maria, did not want to leave Luis and Marta behind, but like so many mothers in El Salvador who could not remain home, she had little choice. Remaining with her children in El Salvador would have amounted to a death sentence. Luis's father subjected Maria to constant domestic violence, not unlike what so many other women faced in a country ravished with unconscionable levels of femicidal violence. So, like countless other women in strikingly similar situations, Maria had to make the gut-wrenching decision to leave her children behind in search of refuge and an uncertain future. She chose to save her own life while leaving behind the life she so desperately hoped to have with her children. "I left them in God's hands," says Maria.

Years later, Luis and Marta are now much like any other San Francisco Bay Area high school students. After facing threats of their own in El Salvador, they too were forced to flee to the United States, retracing their mother's footsteps and joining her in California. They now find themselves in the care of the Immigration and Deportation Defense Clinic at the University of San Francisco, after arriving in the United States as unaccompanied minors and immediately being placed in deportation proceedings.

"Mommy, come for me." Maria shares with the clinic staff how she was tormented by her children's pleas to reunite every time she called home; the desperation in their voices haunted her. She urgently longed to hug them, over the many years they were apart. She often thought about taking the chance – to dare to look death squarely in the eyes – and returning to El Salvador so that should she could hold her

---

[1] Pseudonyms have been used for Luis, Marta, and other family members.

55

children again. But her fear of the threat to her own life back home kept her from returning; it was an unbearably difficult position to be in.

When she left El Salvador, Maria left Luis and Marta with her sister and father. Luis' father, Gustavo, never wanted anything to do with Luis when Maria was still in El Salvador. However, shortly after Maria left El Salvador, Gustavo and his violent gang-affiliated family began threatening to kidnap Luis and to harm or kill Maria's family. At the same time, Luis was getting older and the gangs were watching. Little by little, they recognized Luis as a prime recruit – young, abandoned, and vulnerable; he presented a perfect target.

Daughter Marta was targeted for a related purpose. At school, she came to know a charming young man named Jesus. Handsome, engaging, and friendly, Jesus captivated Marta and for a minute, filled the hollow void she had been longing to fill for years. They say love is blind. Although all the signs were there, Marta shut her eyes to the warnings from everyone around her who tried to caution her – "Jesus is a *mara*." Marta was being recruited as a gang "girlfriend."

Eventually there was nothing anyone could do for them. Marked by one of the gangs, MS-13, Luis and Marta had nowhere to go and nowhere to hide. Facing the same violent threats as their mother, countless other mothers, and countless other children left behind by their mothers, Luis and Marta fled the country. Although the hope of reuniting with their mother sustained them, the only thing certain about what lay ahead was a dangerous journey through Guatemala and Mexico, followed by an uncertain reception and future in the United States. Would they even get to the United States alive? Even if they did, would they be allowed to stay? Would they just end up being deported anyway? If deported back to El Salvador, would MS-13 be right there waiting for them when they returned? In spite of these uncertainties, the potential gang violence was too much, so in the middle of the night, they fled.

Luis and Marta are only two of the tens of thousands of narratives of unaccompanied minors (UACs) who have been forced to risk their lives in search of protection from unspeakable violence that has ravished Central America for many years. In the summer of 2014, their numbers surged, and UACs began seeking the protection of the United States at the southern border. The Obama administration's response was disappointing.

2.2. CAUGHT OFF GUARD

The number of UACs – specifically those fleeing the Northern Triangle – had been rising steadily since 2011. In fiscal year 2014, the Department of Homeland Security (DHS) apprehended more than four times the number of UACs (about 73,700) than in fiscal year 2011 (about 17,100). This was a staggering figure, since many UACs traveled hundreds if not thousands of miles under extremely dangerous conditions – on foot or on top of trains through deserts and a hostile territory in Mexico – just to reach the United States in search of refuge. Along the way, UACs are vulnerable to robbery, assault, sexual assault, human trafficking, exploitation, and other crimes at the hands of government or private actors.

The Obama administration should not have been caught off-guard by the surge of children arriving at the southern border. In its 2012 report to Congress, the Department of Health and Human Services (HHS) acknowledged the existence of "a rapid, unanticipated, and unprecedented increase in UAC referrals from the DHS." In a separate report on its activity in 2012, the Office of Refugee Resettlement (ORR) said it served a total of 13,625 children for the year – more than double the number in 2011, and far exceeding the 8,200 projected. As referrals to ORR doubled again in 2013, the administration projected that the number of UACs that would be referred to ORR for placement would more than double again to 60,000 in 2014.

Thus, unaccompanied minors reaching the southern border was not a new phenomenon when the numbers spiked in 2014. According to data, the large majority of UACs were Mexican through 2011, with a few thousand each year traveling from the so-called Northern Triangle countries of El Salvador, Guatemala, and Honduras. However, in 2012, the number of children from the Northern Triangle that were apprehended at the southern border surpassed 10,000 – ultimately reaching a staggering 51,705 in 2014. The 2016 numbers for Guatemala, El Salvador, and Honduras nearly reached the 47,000 mark, as violence in those countries continued to rank among the highest in the world.

The sharp increase in 2014 generated tremendous media coverage and speculation by elected officials and others about the root causes of the seemingly sudden influx. However, many of the explanations were overly simplistic. Some claimed that the surge resulted from immigration reform promises or administrative reforms in enforcement that sent encouraging signals to Central Americans, suggesting that they may enjoy a "de facto amnesty" if they only manage to make it across the United States–Mexico border. Others said that children were being drawn to the United States by rumors that the Obama administration would grant special protections for migrant children – in reference to the Deferred Action for Childhood Arrivals (DACA) program announced in 2012 that, in fact, did not apply to recent arrivals.

In reality, as we will see in Chapter 4, the problem was – and remains enormously – complex. For example, through interviews with UACs themselves, the Women's Refugee Commission found that their migration arose out of longstanding, complex problems in their home countries – in particular, the growing influence and power of gangs and drug cartels and their strategy of targeting youth for recruitment. In addition, corruption within police forces, gender-based violence, rising poverty, and continuing unemployment were also found to be factors driving UACs to flee their countries. All this is consistent with the stories that staff and students in the University of San Francisco School of Law Immigration and Deportation Defense Clinic have heard from our clients. The same report found that over 77 percent of those interviewed stated that violence was the main reason that children such as themselves were fleeing their countries.

Honduras, which has been the largest country of origin of UACs, has become one of the most dangerous countries worldwide. In 2011, Honduras became the country with the highest murder rate in the world. By 2015, neighboring El Salvador was given the dishonor of that claim. What the entire region has in common is that children are at a greater risk of gang violence. A separate report by the nonpartisan Congressional Research Service reported that 48 percent of children apprehended by US border officials have said that they experienced serious harm or had been threatened by organized criminal groups or state actors in their countries of origin. In addition, more than 20 percent reported to have been subjected to domestic abuse.

To further illustrate the severity of the conditions in the Northern Triangle, according to the University Institute on Democracy, Peace and Security at the National Autonomous University of Honduras, 920 Honduran children were murdered between January and March of 2012. In El Salvador, gangs have increasingly targeted children in schools, resulting in El Salvador having one of the lowest school attendance rates in Latin America. The United Nations High Commissioner for Refugees (UNHCR) reported that common motives of organized criminal groups who target children in the region are to coerce children into prostitution, and to force children into working as assassins, lookouts, and drug mules. In fact, drug traffickers may target children within their home country and then subsequently force them to traffic drugs into the United States. Since these children are often left to fend for themselves while traveling to the United States alone and are desperate to escape death in their home countries, they are faced with no choice but to carry drugs or work for drug cartels in order to successfully cross the border.

Gang and drug trafficking actors in Central America do not simply target young boys. Young girls are also being recruited to smuggle and sell drugs in their home countries, under the threat of gang rape as a means of forcing them to comply. For the gangs in the region, age is of no concern; girls as young as nine years old have been targeted for rape and sexual assault. Gangs also use the threat of rape as a tactic to gain money through extortion and kidnapping in order to fund their operations.

The surge of UACs that started in 2014 clearly tracked the rising threat of gang violence in Honduras, Guatemala, and El Salvador. Luis and Marta are part of the ongoing story of violence affecting young boys and young girls.

2.3. THE RESPONSE

Instead of greeting the children with the sympathy and services they deserve, the Obama administration's response to the influx of unaccompanied minors was to prioritize their deportation. After detaining them at the border, officials funneled UACs into detention facilities operated by the ORR throughout the country. Deportation proceedings were then immediately initiated. Prior to the 2014 surge, UAC deportations were not a priority; back then after their release from ORR custody, their removal hearings might be set years down the line. With little sympathy for the trauma and fear that drove the UAC surge, the new response was said to be needed to deter further asylum seekers at the southern border.

Those caught in the snare of the new deportation regime included individuals like Alberto and Juana. This is Alberto's declaration that was eventually submitted in support of his asylum claim once he was released from ORR custody and found representation with our immigration clinic.

Declaration of Alberto, 2015

1. My name is Alberto. I was born in 1996 in Agraria Pensamiento, Colomba Costa Cuca Quetzaltenango, Guatemala.
2. In the community where I was born, people suffer from malnutrition, and they lack money and food. It is a community that is very far from the city, near the mountains. The means of transportation are very few because the roads to get to the community are made of dirt and rock, which makes it more difficult to go to the town to buy things for the kitchen or buy medicine when you get sick.
3. The majority of the people work in the fields cutting coffee, firewood, or beans. But the money that you earn is very little and the work is very difficult because you work all day under the sun from 6 am until 5 pm earning 800 quetzals a month, which is around $100, barely enough for food.
4. Growing up, my mom took my brothers to cut coffee when they didn't go to school. I couldn't work because I was very little, but my mom would carry me while working. My brothers and my mom would work all day and at the end of the day we would take firewood to the house so that we could cook our food. I started helping to work too as soon as I could carry anything, like at four years old. Many times we had to work all day under the sun and without eating because we had very little money. In the winter when it rained we had to work without caring that it was raining but we had to do it so that my brothers could afford to study.
5. My dad worked very far in the city. He worked in construction because he was a builder. The city was seven hours from where we lived so my dad would only come home every fifteen days to see us and to leave a little bit of money for our expenses. Then he had to return early the next day to the city to continue to work.
6. I lived in the same community since my birth until I was about five years old. Then we had to move to Quetzaltenango, which is the principal city in the department.
7. The reason for the move was that my dad and my mom found work in a school because food prices in our community were rising more every day and we didn't have enough money. Sometimes we were only eating one or two

times a day and we didn't eat enough. We were left without money to pay the water and the electricity, so when the night came, we were left in the darkness. We also had to go to the river for water.

8. That is why we left our community to live in Zone 3 in Quetzaltenango. In Quetzaltenango, my dad had a job as a gardener and my mom as a cleaner at the school. We all lived in a small room that was provided to us. I started school there, from grades one to three, but then they took away my parents' jobs because there was a change of the personnel.

9. After my parents lost their jobs, we moved to a small house in Zone 8 where we had to pay 1,000 quetzals every month. I enrolled in a public school where I studied from grades four to five. In total, I studied for three years at the public school in Zone 8 because I failed the first year because I didn't have the money to buy the books that the school required me to have.

10. Then I went to another school where I completed sixth grade. Then I transferred to another school where I couldn't finish the year for lack of money because my dad fell from a construction site and couldn't work for almost six months. In the meantime, I covered for him so that he could keep his job. Later, I studied at yet another school at night to be able to finish another grade.

11. The next year we moved to another house in Zone 8. Zone 8 is known as a completely gang-controlled zone in the city.

12. In Zone 8, we attended Catholic mass on Thursdays and Sundays for support, yet this became hard with the gangs harassing me. They would shout at me insultingly that the area was Barrio 18 territory.

13. In Zone 8, there were a lot of gang members specifically from the gang, 18. The house we moved into had a big 18 graffiti mark. The gang started slipping notes under our door demanding we pay "taxes" since we were in their territory. The people in the community did not want to walk outside or go to school until the police patrol passed by slowly. Most children did not go outside since gangsters threatened any kids that were in the street. When trucks passed by selling food and products from the back of their trucks, we bought from them so that we would not be in danger of patrolling gangsters on the street. Nearly all store [owners] had to pay taxes to the gangs or were murdered. It was not safe to go to the store or be out in the streets.

14. The gang likes to expand by recruiting young poor males between age ten to twenty-five years. At this age boys are strong enough to survive an 18-gang initiation beating. I think they prefer students because they think students will follow their orders. The ones who appear alone are the ones who get targeted the most.

15. The Mara 18 walked down the street with tattoos all over their bodies greeting the police insultingly to show them that they run the show. The gangsters made deals with bus drivers to rob all the passengers [using] buses with everything planned and well organized.

16. The gangsters hung out at the soccer field to watch the youth play soccer. I played soccer with a group of friends from [my area] and they started messing with us. My friend, Eddie, a member of the team, was 22-year-old back in 2012. His father started living with his other wife outside of the neighborhood, so Eddie lived with his mother alone without an adult male breadwinner or a stable home.

17. Eddie was first to be attacked and beat up badly for refusing to join the gang. Afterward, he hid at his mother's house and we stopped playing soccer because the gangsters were always at the field and looking for him. Eddie was afraid because they threatened to kill him if he did not join the gang,

18. One day, in February 2012, Eddie was jumped [on] and beaten up badly for not joining the gang. He was beat up even worse because he tried to defend himself. This time, he went to the police and filed a police report. The police entered Zone 8 to interview everyone about the incident. The gangsters heard of the police investigation. Then they found him on the way home and shot him through the ribs. He died two days later at a local hospital. His brothers, a couple of years older than me, fled to their relatives in other cities a couple of days later because they feared for their lives too.

19. For me, things got worse because the gangs then started to threaten me when they would see me. They would offer me drugs. When I would encounter them on the street, they would corner me and would tell me that I was the next one to join their gang.

20. My first incident happened sometime around January 2012. I was walking home from night school on the street, when I noticed gangsters with tattoos. They yelled at me, "who are you, you belong to a gang?" I said, "No, I am a student." They told me to join their gang because they had a nice life with drugs and beef. I said, "I don't like drugs." They reminded me that I was in Mara 18 territory, so I had to join "or else." I told them that I don't mess with those things and they said, "if you want to be a man and have a good life, join us. Think about your decision or you know what happens to you ..." They pushed me around, but I just walked away without answering them. Afterwards, I tried to avoid them every time I saw them. I would run or I would hide as fast as I could.

21. The second incident happened a couple of weeks later. I was walking to an evening class when they cornered me to ask me if I had made a decision. I walked around them and they stepped in front of me and hit me in the chest hard with a metal pole. They said, "Answer now!" They said that they were getting bored waiting for my response. They told me, "What is wrong with you *pendejo* [colloquial insult], everything will be good and chill with us." They told me that this rough treatment happened because I didn't want to join them and that it was going to get worse. They gave me a bit of time to think, and then let me walk away.

22. After these events, I rarely ever walked to school or took the bus. My boss from the bakery where I was working picked me up at 4am at my house in his truck and dropped me at school afterwards. Then my older brother would pick me up from night school in his car. After Eddie died I was afraid of things getting worse.

23. In August 2013, a school friend, Marcos, joined the gang after they gave him the choice of joining or death. After joining he always had drugs and bullets in his backpack and talked about the gang 18, being initiated and the cool life of the gang. He informed us how the robberies, murders, and bus assaults were all pre-organized with even bus drivers cooperating. In September, his mom came to school looking for him, but he had disappeared. I never heard of him again. He is probably dead for talking too much.

24. The third encounter occurred later in 2013. My brother could not take me to school by car so I had to walk. I was crossing the street to the bus to go to an evening class when a gangster stepped in front of me and pushed me backwards. Then five others appeared from the alleys around the bus stop. One yanked my backpack and shoved my shoulders. They told me to make my decision and contribute to the gang. One opened my backpack and shoved a bag of drugs in it that I was instructed to share with my classmates. They said that the drugs were tasty and that I should try. I said, "I don't do drugs." One drew a knife and shouted that I had to choose between death and joining them and then repeated that my task was to share the drugs with my classmates. I told him "no because I would get in trouble." He told me to do it "or else." I was afraid and only wanted to study so when I got onto the bus with the backpack, I left the bags of drugs on the bus.

25. The fourth time occurred around January 2014. I was getting on the bus to go to night class because I again did not have a ride. The gangsters yanked me off the bus. They all came out of the alleys and jumped on top of me and one put a knife to my throat. I started to cry because they were calling me names and threatening to kill me. Sucha, the gang leader was there with a tattooed 18 on his forehead. He told me, "look *cabron* [colloquial insult] we are tired of you being alive. The next time that we see you, you either join us or you die *pendejo* [colloquial insult]." Then they nearly beat me to death. They beat me for several minutes. They kicked me as a group with all they had. Afterwards, Sucha said, "next time it will be the last time."

26. The last time I saw the gangsters was February 6, 2014. I was getting off the bus from work when I saw a gangster in an alley. I started walking through a cornfield to avoid them, but they saw me and started yelling and chasing after me. I ran and circled back through the field. As I left the field, another group of gangsters threw a muddy rock that hit me in the face as I ran by. I heard shots into the air, but I kept running because they wanted to kill me for sure. I looked back and saw Sucha holding the gun. They did not catch me because

they were drugged and slow and struggled to hold up their baggy pants. Sucha yelled that he was going to kill me for sure.

27. As I ran into my house, my four-year-old niece and mother hugged me. A bit later, the gangsters arrived outside throwing stones at the windows and roof. They were yelling, "you run fast but men don't run." They called me "*hijo de puta* [colloquial insult]" and "*maricon* [colloquial insult]." Sucha yelled, "you are dead if you ever leave your house again." My mother and niece were crying with fear and we were afraid that they would break into our house and kill us.

28. That night, we talked about sending me to the United States to save my life. Also, I recalled how Eddie was killed, so I knew I had to get out now.

29. On February 9, my bakery boss and my brother drove me to the plaza to meet with a guide to leave for the United States for good.

We turn now to Juana's story. After Juana made her way to our clinic for assistance, this psychological evaluation was submitted on her behalf.

Psychological Evaluation of Juana, 2015

Juana was born in 1996. At the time of this evaluation she is 19 years old. She grew up in the city of Chalchuapa, El Salvador, where her parents still live. Juana's father worked for the highway department until around five years ago when he suffered a stroke. Since then he has not been able to work. Juana's mother works for a funeral home business and is the only wage earner for the family.

Juana is the youngest of three children. Her sister is six years older than Juana and lives in Santa Ana, El Salvador, which is about nine miles from Chalchuapa. Since arriving in the United States, Juana has been living with her 30-year-old brother and his family in California. She recently graduated from high school.

The neighborhood where Juana's family lives in Chalchuapa is occupied by many gang members from the Barrio 18 and Mara Salvatrucha gangs. Juana would see groups of gang members in the neighborhood and would ignore them or say "hi," and keep walking away from them.

There also were gang members hanging around the secondary school Juana attended for ninth grade. The students knew they were gang members because they all had tattoos. The 18th Street gang was the one that controlled the neighborhood around the school. Even though there was a police station near the school, the police did not do anything to keep the gang from bothering and frightening the students.

Juana walked to school and home again, a distance of around two to two-and-a-half miles. She often had to walk past groups of gang members as she left school. Among the students it was known that boys could be threatened and killed if the gang demanded that they join the gang and they didn't comply.

It was common knowledge also that if a girl was conscripted into the gang she had to have sex with one or more of the guys in the gang. Many girls and women from the gangs were murdered, as were others who tried to resist the gangs' demands. Juana had friends, both male and female, who were threatened by gangs. An older cousin of Juana's moved away from the area when gangs were demanding money from her and threatening to cut her young son's fingers off. She has not been in touch with family members since she fled.

In early August 2014, gang members near the school began harassing Juana and her friends when they were leaving school at the end of the day. The leader of the gang complimented Juana on her looks and told her she should be a girl in their gang. She didn't respond and kept walking home. Soon after that, when she was walking alone, she had to pass a group of six of the men. Three of them approached her and asked her for money and she gave them $2. One took out a pistol. They asked her to join the gang and said she should have sex with one of them. If she didn't, they said they would kill her by cutting her to pieces. They said they would give her time to decide and would meet her in the same place in a week.

Around three or four days later, the same men approached Juana again and asked what she had decided about joining the gang. She told them to give her a few more days to tell them. After that she stopped attending school. Her parents decided that the only way to keep her safe was to send her to California to live with her older brother.

Juana was one of the youngest of a group of travelers led out of El Salvador by a guide ("coyote"). Part way through the journey, she joined a different guide after the first one began approaching her for sex. The second *coyote* did not accompany her as far into California as she had been led to expect. Instead, he abandoned her and another girl in an uninhabited area. They did not know where they were or what to do. They started walking, and after a long time, they came to a highway, where immigration officers picked them up.

Alberto's and Juana's stories are common. Gang and domestic violence serve as the impetus for the flight of countless other young boys and girls like Luis, Marta, Alberto, and Juana. Their experiences of perilous journeys through Mexico are also all too familiar. While the most recent chapters in their lives include the joy of being granted asylum, skipping ahead to what could be labeled a happy conclusion would be simplistic and short shrift the unnecessary challenges they, and others in similar shoes, face after their arrival at the US border.

Between 2009 and 2014, over 90 percent of UAC apprehensions (186,233) occurred along the southern border, 75 percent of which were apprehended specifically in the Rio Grande Valley of Texas or near Tucson, Arizona. Most of these southern border apprehensions involved children between sixteen and seventeen years old. Three-quarters were males and about 97 percent were either from El

Salvador, Guatemala, Honduras, or Mexico – in fact, almost half were Mexican nationals. Generally, the flow of Mexican UACs remained constant.

The spike in UAC apprehensions in 2014 was primarily the result of an increase in UACs from violence ravished El Salvador, Guatemala, and Honduras. Thus, in the spring and summer of 2014, at the height of the increase in UAC apprehensions, the White House directed DHS to establish a unified interagency response to be led by DHS's Federal Emergency Management Agency (FEMA), to provide humanitarian services to UACs including housing, general care, medical treatment, and transportation. Unfortunately, the response was marred with complications and controversy.

The majority of UACs encountered at the border are apprehended, processed, and initially detained by Customs and Border Protection (CBP) – the division of DHS charged with border enforcement. UACs – at least those from non contiguous countries, such as El Salvador, Guatemala, or Honduras – are placed into removal proceedings in immigration court. After being apprehended by CBP, CBP must transfer custody of unaccompanied minors to the HHS and its ORR within seventy-two hours.

2.4. THE MATRIX OF GOVERNMENT AGENCIES

UACs who are caught at the border generally interact with a number of federal agencies. The CBP and Immigration and Customs Enforcement (ICE) both play roles in the apprehension, processing, temporary detention, and care of UACs who attempt to enter the United States without inspection. CBP agents usually apprehend UACs (and others crossing the border) without proper documentation and detain them for ICE. ICE is responsible for transferring UACs, when appropriate, to HHS or repatriating UACs to their countries of nationality or country of last habitual residence. HHS's ORR then works with DHS to place UACs in one of many shelters located throughout the country. For UACs who are not repatriated, ORR identifies "qualified sponsors" in the United States who are able take custody of the children and care for them while they await immigration proceedings. Qualified sponsors are adults who are suitable to provide for the child's physical and mental well-being and have not engaged in any activity that would indicate a potential risk to the child. All sponsors must pass a background check before a child is released to their custody. The process has not always proven to be reliable.

The proper treatment of UACs is governed by federal law. Under the Trafficking Victims Protection Reauthorization Act of 2008 (TVPRA), CBP agents first make a determination as to whether a child is truly "unaccompanied." The Homeland Security Act of 2002, which transferred responsibility for detained children to HHS, defined the term "unaccompanied alien child" to mean a child who has no lawful immigration status in the United States; has not attained 18 years of age; and who has no parent or legal guardian in the United States, or no parent or legal guardian in the United States available to provide care and physical custody. Although many of the children may already have family inside the United States, the practice by DHS classifies children as unaccompanied "if neither a parent or legal guardian (with a court-order) is with the juvenile at the time of apprehension, or within a geographical proximity" to care for the juvenile. According to interviews conducted with DHS officials in 2006, "if a parent or legal guardian is not present to provide care (or cannot be present within a short period of time), that child is technically considered unaccompanied and processed accordingly."

Under the TVPRA, after CPB or ICE apprehends a UAC, a CBP or ICE official must interview each child and collect personal information – such as the child's name, country of nationality, and age – within 48 hours of apprehension. Officials then evaluate each child to determine whether he or she meets certain criteria signifying that additional steps may have to be taken to ensure the child is safe from harm. TVPRA requires that, except in exceptional circumstances, UACs must be transferred to the care and custody of ORR within seventy-two hours of determining a child is a UAC.

Mexican and Canadian UACs do not have the same rights. The TVPRA imposes different rules for UACs from these contiguous countries. UACs who are Mexican and Canadian nationals are evaluated on a case-by-case basis, and thus are not necessarily entitled the right to be turned over to ORR. Officials may allow a Mexican or Canadian child to withdraw his or her application for admission to the United States and return to his or her country of nationality or country of last habitual residence without further removal proceedings. That process is followed if after screening it is determined: (1) the UAC is not a victim of a severe form of trafficking in persons; (2) there is no credible evidence that the UAC is at risk of being trafficked if repatriated; (3) the UAC does not have a fear of returning to his or her country owing to a credible fear of persecution (i.e., expresses no asylum-type fear); and (4) the UAC is able to make an independent decision to withdraw the application for admission to the United States and voluntarily return to the country of nationality or last habitual residence. UACs originating from contiguous countries must be screened within 48 hours of apprehension.

If not all four of the screening criteria are satisfied, TVPRA requires the US officials to follow the same process for Mexicans and Canadians established for UACs from non contiguous countries, i.e., mandatory transfer to ORR within seventy-two hours of determining they are UACs. Thus, UACs originating from contiguous countries are not allowed to remain in the United States to apply for asylum if DHS asserts that the four screening criteria were satisfied. When DHS concludes that a UAC should be transferred to ORR, ORR is notified, and DHS then transports the UAC to a shelter where ORR has space to accommodate the child. For UACs who have been cleared for repatriation back to Mexico or Canada, typically CPB physically transports the child to the border port of entry, where custody of the child is then transferred to Mexican or Canadian officials.

There is some concern over whether DHS is capable of accurately determining how long UACs have been in ICE custody, which affects the determination whether UACs are being transferred to ORR within the 72-hour limit established by TVPRA.[2] The *Flores* Agreement, discussed in greater detail in Section 2.8, requires the collection of information on all UACs placed in removal proceedings and who have remained in DHS custody for more than seventy-two hours.[3] Discrepancies in DHS data have appeared, and information was found missing in 13 percent of cases audited.[4]

In March 2009, CBP issued a memorandum containing policies and procedures that Border Patrol agents and other DHS officers are required to follow when screening UACs regardless of nationality. Consistent with TVPRA requirements, the memorandum states that DHS officials must transfer all UACs from countries other than Canada or Mexico to ORR shelters. In addition, the memorandum established separate procedures to screen UACs from Canada and Mexico to determine whether they too should be transferred to an ORR shelter or should instead be repatriated. Specifically, agents and officers were directed to assess the four criteria set forth in the TVPRA for each unaccompanied Mexican or Canadian child when determining whether to repatriate the child. DHS agents and officers are instructed to use a form (Form 93) for the screening of a Mexican and Canadian child. This form prompts agents and officers to ask questions to facilitate the determination as to whether the child has a fear of returning to Mexico or Canada, and to determine if the child may be the victim of human trafficking. A separate form (Form I-213) is used to document, among other things, the results of the screening process, such as any expressions of fear by the child. The child's responses are statutorily required to be documented for the purpose of determining whether to repatriate the Canadian or Mexican child. Thus, whether a Mexican or Canadian child is transferred to ORR custody or repatriated is entirely contingent upon the child's responses to the questions contained within Form 93.

It's important to note that the TVPRA had a non controversial history of bipartisanship. While the 2008 version was the first to introduce a specific language on the immigration treatment of UACs, the TVPRA dates back to 2000, when the original Trafficking Victims Protection Act (TVPA) was first enacted into law. The December 2008 TVPRA reauthorization was by unanimous consent in the Senate and voice vote in the House, then signed into law by President George W. Bush.[5] The 2008 TVPRA codified (section 235) the process for the treatment of all UAC in the United States and established the "special rules" for children from "contiguous countries" (Mexico and Canada). Section 235 was based on previously proposed legislation

---

[2] Unaccompanied Alien Children: Actions Needed to Ensure Children Receive Required Care in DHS Custody, July 14, 2015 (hereinafter "GAO"), at 46.

[3] Ibid., at 47.

[4] Ibid., at 48.

[5] Lozaro Zamora, Unaccompanied Alien Children: A Primer, Bipartisan Policy Center, July 21, 2014.

that also passed the Senate by unanimous consent, in the Unaccompanied Alien Child Protection Act of 2005 (UACPA).

The 2008 TVPRA provisions sought to address concerns that children apprehended were not being properly protected nor adequately screened to determine whether they should be returned to their country of origin. Similar concerns in the 1980s and 1990s about the former Immigration and Naturalization Services (INS) led to several lawsuits against the government, one of which resulted in a settlement agreement known as in the *Flores* Agreement of 1997, which established regulations for the humane detention and treatment of children. Several years after the implementation of the agreement, the Homeland Security Act of 2002 (HSA) again addressed the treatment of children and transferred responsibility for UACs from DHS to the ORR within the HHS. The *Flores* Agreement and its controversy is covered in Section 2.8.

2.5. THE EVIL MANIFESTATIONS OF PRIORITIZING UAC REMOVALS

The Obama administration's response of prioritizing the deportation of UACs came under heavy scrutiny for a variety of reasons. First, the conditions in the detention facilities raised many concerns for the safety and well-being of UACs in ORR custody. Second, the creation of hurry-up "rocket dockets" in Immigration Courts throughout the country made it incredibly difficult for UACs to secure legal representation in deportation proceedings, resulting in the deportation of more than 7,000 unrepresented UACs within the first several months. For example, from July 18, 2014 to October 21, 2014, 11,392 fast-tracked master calendar (preliminary) hearings were held; 1,542 children were ordered deported at that time, and 94 percent of these UACs had no counsel.[6] Beyond the serious due process concerns over the unfairness of the proceedings, many of the children were murdered upon their return to Central America. The fact that federal agencies also were severely underresourced exacerbated the problematic reaction to the influx. As a result, the expedited procedures implemented in reaction to the influx in new cases ultimately derailed the application of proper legal standards used to screen asylum seekers upon arrival.

Take the initial screening of UAC arrivals. The screening process is very problematic. For example, even though the TVPRA requires that all non-Canadian and non-Mexican children be transferred to ORR, the Government Accountability Office (GAO) has found that many UACs apprehended crossing the border without inspection and those apprehended at border points of entry are improperly repatriated. The screening of Mexican UACs also has raised serious concerns. The GAO found that the Border Patrol was inconsistent in its assessment of: (1) children's ability to make independent decisions; (2) credible

---

[6] David Rogers, *Many child migrants lack lawyers*, Politico, Nov. 6, 2014.

fear of persecution; (3) whether children were victims of severe trafficking; and (4) the risk of being trafficked upon return to their countries of origin (in other words, the entire screening process).[7]

For example, with regard to the ability to make independent decisions, agents and officers are not provided indicators or suggested questions on how to make that assessment. Agents and officers are given guidance that they should generally assume that UACs who are fourteen years of age or older are able to make an independent decision about returning to their countries of nationality and those under age fourteen are generally unable to make an independent decision. However, these presumptions may be overcome after consideration of such factors as the child's intelligence, education level, and familiarity with the US immigration process. It turns out that not all agents and officers are even aware of these policies and presumptions. As such, agents and officers frequently repatriate Mexican UACs under the age of fourteen if the Mexican consulate is able to locate a family member in Mexico or when the Mexican consulate provides approval for repatriation. That is a serious problem, because the determination of whether a Mexican UAC in the United States merits international protection is the responsibility of DHS, not the Mexican government – the potential persecutor. Failure to take such responsibility could have serious consequences for the life, safety, and well-being of the child. After reviewing DHS apprehension data, the GAO concluded that agents and officers did not understand or follow the policy regarding Mexican UACs under age fourteen, resulting in a 95 percent repatriation rate of this group.[8] Furthermore, during the screening process, Border Patrol agents often fail to consistently document the basis for their decisions to repatriate Mexican UACs as required.[9] For example, in one particular case, a Mexican UAC was screened to have been "emotionally distraught" and "unable to speak clearly." Nevertheless, the agent repatriated the child without documenting the reason for deciding that the child was able to make an independent decision.[10]

Other related findings by the GAO are worrisome. The GAO has been troubled by agents and officers who report that Mexican UACs repatriated generally have not understood the options available to them that would allow them to remain in the United States while awaiting removal proceedings.[11] The GAO also found that Border Patrol agents and other DHS officers do not make consistent decisions about whether Mexican UACs have what is known as a "credible fear" of persecution if they are repatriated to Mexico.[12] As noted above, the Border Patrol is supposed to transfer Mexican and Canadian UACs to ORR if they have a credible fear

---

[7] GAO, at 22–3.
[8] Ibid., at 24.
[9] Ibid., at 26.
[10] Ibid.
[11] Ibid.
[12] Ibid., at 27.

of persecution to allow them to remain in the country, at least for the time that it takes to pursue an asylum claim. In the same vein, the GAO has also found that agents and officers do not have a good understanding of what types of fears warrant transferring UACs to ORR. Agents often make wildly different screening decisions when presented with similar responses to credible fear questions. For example, in one case, a child claimed a fear of repatriation because her grandmother had abused her, and the agent transferred the child to ORR. However, in two other cases, sisters told the interviewing agent that their aunt had mistreated them and the agent chose to repatriate the siblings. In another case, a child claimed that he was fearful of gangs and transnational criminal organizations in his hometown, and the interviewing agent decided to transfer him to ORR. However, in two other cases, a child claimed fear of gangs and another claimed fear of violence in Mexico, but the DHS agents decided to repatriate both children. Border Patrol officials have acknowledged that by law, agents should transfer Mexican UACs to ORR when the children claim a credible fear of persecution or torture. Disturbingly, most agents and officers interviewed by UNHCR investigators stated that it was not their job to assess a child's fear of returning to his or her country. Some officials also stated that their definition of fear requires that the fear of persecution or harm must be inflicted directly by the government and that UACs who fear gangs or cartels are to be categorically repatriated;[13] in fact, that is a clearly erroneous understanding of the law.

Not surprisingly, nongovernmental organizations (NGOs) have expressed concern that CBP is the "wrong agency" to screen children for signs of trauma, abuse or persecution. The public justice group Appleseed issued a report finding that CBP screening, "as a practical matter ... translates into less searching inquiries regarding any danger [children] are in and what legal rights they may have." The report also expressed concern that the United States–Mexico repatriation agreement has been geared toward "protocols of repatriations logistics," rather than best practices for child welfare.

In spite of many serious concerns with Border Patrol's handling of UACs, after a visit to a Border Patrol facility in Arizona in July 2014, where more than 900 UACs were held at the Nogales Placement Center, some Border Patrol agents were recognized by the GAO for helping US government public health volunteers provide basic care to UACs. This included helping children as young as two or three years old to eat and bathe. Border Patrol officials supplemented food supplied by a FEMA contractor with food purchased separately using Border Patrol funding. In addition, some Border Patrol agents had purchased items such as toiletries, toys, and other supplies with personal funds, and some officers entertained UACs by playing games with them.[14]

---

[13] Ibid., at 28–9.
[14] Ibid., at 40–1.

The manner in which CBP and ICE agents determine the age and eligibility of a child that is being considered for release to the custody of ORR is problematic in other ways. For example, many of the I-862 charging documents, Notices to Appear (NTAs), often contain typographical errors, e.g., wrongly spelled names and incorrect birthdates. If the border patrol officer or ICE agent makes a mistake while writing down something as simple as a birth date, if gone unnoticed, the error can affect the child's ability to be released from ICE detention and transferred to ORR for attempted reunification with a family member.

2.6. BORDER PATROL *HIELERAS*

The conditions under which UACs are initially detained in CPB holding facilities, before being transferred to ICE or ORR for further processing has been the focus of great controversy. Upon arrival and apprehension by Border Patrol officers, children and adults alike are placed in the infamous CPB holding cells with notoriously atrocious conditions. In these facilities, detainees spend one to several nights in holding cells before they are turned over to ICE or ORR – if screened and deemed to be a UAC – or to ICE for longer-term housing if they are accompanied. Detainees have come to refer to the Border Patrol holding cells as *hieleras* or "iceboxes" because of their extremely cold and unsanitary conditions. According to a federal lawsuit challenging the propriety of these facilities, immigrants are "stripped of outer layers of clothing and forced to suffer in brutally cold temperatures."[15] Once in a *hielera*, detainees are not provided with blankets, instead they are only provided with lightweight Mylar blankets. Detainees that I met at a family detention center in Dilley, Texas, in December 2017, continued to describe similar experiences at *hieleras*, although by then, the Trump administration added another larger early detention processing center detainees call *la perrera* – the dogpen.

The *hielera* cells are overcrowded and known for poor nutrition and hygiene conditions. The rooms often hold up to a hundred or more unrelated adults and children; all – including the children – are often forced to sleep standing up or not at all. Commonly, an *hielera* cell has only two toilets for everyone to use and no waste baskets in the stalls which results in people having to throw used sanitary napkins on the floors. In one particular *hielera* in McAllen, Texas, mothers sleep in the bathroom with their babies in their arms. Detainees are typically provided only two meals – bread with ham and a juice box. Apples were eventually added to the daily diet – one of the only items that children could stomach. The lights are kept on at all times for security reasons and operational necessity, making it difficult to sleep.

According to government officials, what the detainees describe as "iceboxes" are holding rooms constructed of "impervious materials that can be easily cleaned and

---

[15] Jorge Rivas, *These unsealed photos offer rare peek inside Border Patrol's notorious 'Ice Box' detention cells*, Fusion, June 29, 2016.

are hygienic." The government claims that the temperature is maintained at a "comfortable temperature," but concede that detainees who "are not accustomed to air conditioning at times find it cooler" than they are used to. Mylar blankets are necessary in order to provide cost-effective, sanitary bedding that does not require routine laundering or risk of transmitting communicable diseases such as lice or scabies. As for the lack of trashcans, officials claim that they are not provided out of fear that they may be used as weapons.

The Women's Refugee Commission recorded the testimony of many who suffered through these conditions:

> Carmen was apprehended by Border Patrol crossing the river with her five-month-old daughter Lily. She was placed into a cell with no dry clothes or blankets for her or the baby. Carmen requested something to keep the baby warm since it was so cold in the cell and all she had was wet clothing. The agents refused. By morning Lily was turning blue.[16]

The rooms were all filthy and smelled terrible:

> There was garbage on the floor of all of the cells and no trash bins. The only time the cell was cleaned during [one detainee's] detention was by several inmates who had been offered an extra burrito in exchange for cleaning the cell. Even after that cleaning, the cell was filthy and littered with trash. In one cell, there was no toilet paper. In the last cell, in which 130 people were held, one of the three toilets did not work, and men had to wait in line to use the remaining two. The foul smell was overpowering.[17]

After Kaitlin Talley visited the Dilley facility with the University of San Francisco School of Law Immigration and Deportation Defense Clinic in the Fall of 2015, she reported the following:

> *Some of the most shameful reports of the conditions women and children experienced after being detained were during their detention at the temporary holding centers located right by the border and operated by the Customs and Border Protections (CBP). These are the centers where the women and children are held before being transferred to Dilley or Karnes. They are also the same centers that have gained the nicknames "the ice box" and "the [dog] pound" or "la hielera" or "la perrera" as the women call them in Spanish.*
>
> *Women I spoke to complained about CBP officials who yelled at them angrily and seemingly without reason. Others said the officials separated them form their children for the entirety of their stay in the temporary detention without telling them if they would see their children again. Other women said the border officials had told them*

16 *Women's Refugee Commission, Forced from Home: The Lost Girls and Boys of Central America,* 2012. https://womensrefugeecommission.org/component/zdocs/document/844
17 Ibid.

that they are liars and criminals and they will never be able to stay here legally. They told them that their children will never be able to go to school; that their family will not ever be allowed to work in the Unites States.

Further complaints included having to sleep on cold concrete floors, [in a] room kept at very cold temperatures with the air conditioner on, refusing to give the women and children blankets, keeping the lights on all night, the women of one cell having to share one cup to drink out of, and children and women who had wet their pants because the officials would not let them go to the bathroom.[18]

Ned M. Juri-Martinez, another student who visited the Dilley facility with the University of San Francisco School of Law Immigration and Deportation Defense Clinic in the Fall of 2015, reported the following:

Many women spoke of a lack of sufficient food and water while being held in the "hieleras," often times for over a day and multiple days in some cases. In reviewing English-only transcripts of their initial interviews at the border or in the "hieleras," scores of women declared to me that they had answered affirmatively to having a fear of being returned to their countries, yet the transcripts of the initial questioning reflected a false negative response to this question. When I asked if anyone even bothered to translate the contents of the transcript, not a single one stated to me that it had been.

For those able to endure the egregiously inhumane tactics employed in the hieleras, they are transferred to the Dilley facility were there have been additional reports of abuses such as a gross lack of adequate healthcare, which is especially critical since many women and children catch colds and sometimes pneumonia from their time in the freezing hierleras. Many desperate mothers expressed to me their concern for the health of their child or themselves. They expressed how their illnesses are not taken seriously at the on-site infirmary, and they are forced to dangerously endure high fever and other ailments. One particular women had an open sore on her chest that was bleeding out. When she sought medical attention, she was patched up but was not provided with any medicine for pain or to ward-off infection.[19]

The following are excerpts from the statements of persons who have been subjected to the appalling conditions in *hielera* holding cells in the Border Patrol's Tucson Sector. Attorneys representing the plaintiffs and class members in *Doe v. Johnson* interviewed approximately seventy-five individuals detained in Tucson Sector Border Patrol holding cells prior to filing the class-action lawsuit challenging these conditions as unconstitutional and in violation of CBP's own standards. The former detainees were held in cells located at all eight of the Border Patrol Stations located within the Tucson Sector. These accounts represent experiences in 2014 and 2015.

[18] Kaitlin Talley, 2L and Legal Volunteer with the University of San Francisco School of Law, Immigration and Deportation Defense Clinic, Fall 2015.

[19] Ned M. Juri-Martinez, Legal Volunteer with the University of San Francisco School of Law, Immigration and Deportation Defense Clinic, Fall 2015.

2.6.1. *Overcrowding*

- *I was placed in a cell that was about 15 feet by 20 feet … [T]here were about 30 to 35 people in the cell. We were like cigarettes stuffed in there … [T]he second station … was worse! The cell was a bit bigger but there were about 60 men in there or more… The benches and the floor were covered with men sitting, standing, or lying down. To get around you had to walk on the benches and jump from bench to bench to avoid stepping on people … Sleeping here was horrible. It was so crowded we just had to lay any way we could, sometimes on our sides, so we could fit more people. If you moved, someone else would take your spot. – C.V.J.*
- *There were approximately 50 women and their children in the cell in Arizona … There was not enough room for everyone to lie down and some kids had to sleep near the toilet. If you got up, you would not have a space to sit when you came back. At times I was able to lie on the floor, but other nights it was so crowded that I had to sleep sitting up or kneeling. – M.E.*
- *I saw a "maximum capacity" sign outside the room that indicated forty people was the maximum number the cell could hold … Over time, more people arrived until there were close to sixty people in the cell. With that many people, there was no room to move and people were lying on the floor, including in the bathroom. – J.C.C.O.*

2.6.2. *Freezing temperatures*

- *The temperature in the cell was very, very cold … as hard as I tried I could not get warm. I now understand why dogs sleep in a little ball, to keep warm, but I couldn't even keep warm by doing that. We did ask the guards to change the temperature but the guards didn't change it. – V.H.R.G.*
- *We were not able to sleep all night because of the cold. At one point my six-month-[old] daughter did fall asleep briefly and I laid her down on the cold concrete floor. She was able to sleep a little bit but she was shivering from the cold as she slept. – G.F.G.*
- *The cold made me sick. I felt like I had a fever. My body hurt and I had a headache. My lip started blistering as well. – M.J.L.M.*
- *It was so cold [in the cell], I had a severe headache and backache … The Border Patrol agents took my sweater from me … so all I was wearing was a short sleeve shirt … I tried to curl up on the floor and huddle with some of the other women … but I was not able to get warm. During the night, I would wake up often and walk around the cell to try to warm myself up. – V.R.A.*

2.6.3. *Intolerable sleeping circumstances*

- *They detained me around midnight ... and we were kept in the van for more than twenty-four hours. The agents drove around with us and then parked overnight while we slept in the van. There were five us in the van ... The van was cold and they didn't give us covers ... There was very little room in the van for the five of us and we were crowded in the space, especially when we tried to lie down to sleep.* – J.B.C.
- *There were no beds in the cell and we were not provided any blankets or other bedding. My daughter tried to sleep on the bench and I sat up so that she could at least rest her head on my lap ... I was not able to sleep at all because my daughter would have fallen off the bench if I had moved.* – B.C.L.
- *There were no beds in the cell and we were not provided any real blankets, they only gave us an aluminum sheet. I had to try and sleep standing. I gave my place on the concrete floor to another man who was hurt ... I did not sleep all night because I was standing. I was one of 15 people standing that night.* – F.M.E.
- *I was kept in this cell for 76 hours. I spent three nights in this cell. There were no beds in the cell and we were not provided any blankets or other bedding. I had to try and sleep on the concrete floor. Some people had to sleep in the bathroom because there was not space for everyone to lie down ... It was very difficult to sleep because the floor was so hard and because there were so many people.* – J.B.C.
- *I had to try to sleep on the floor but I still could not sleep because of the cold. It was like trying to sleep on ice.* – M.R.Z.D.
- *It was also difficult to sleep because we were called out four times for interviews over the course of the night. One of those times we had to wait five and half hours ... we had to stand for those five and half hours. We were already tired from walking in the desert and I was exhausted from standing and holding my daughter for so long.* – G.F.G.
- *It was also difficult to sleep because the guards would talk with us or hit the windows to get our attention. The light was always on so it was also hard to sleep.* – M.J.L.M.

2.6.4. *Intolerable Sanitation*

- *There was one sink but no soap or towels. Most people had spent a lot of time in the desert and were very dirty, but it was impossible to really wash your hands or clean yourself after using the toilet. The conditions became disgusting with so many people packed into a cell in this way.* – N.G.P.

- *There was one sink in the cell but it did not work. There was also no soap or paper or cloth towels. It was impossible to wash your hands or clean yourself after using the toilet.* – J.A.M.B.
- *The smell was so bad because we could not shower. People had been trying to cross the desert for days and we all smelled. It was awful, just very ugly.* – C.V.J.
- *For the first 19 hours in detention, the agents did not give me any diapers for my one-and-a-half-year old daughter. She dirtied her diaper and had to spend the whole night with a dirty diaper.* – N.M.M.
- *I did not receive enough diapers for my daughter. When we asked for more, the agents would say "wait, wait, there aren't any." They would only give us two diapers per child in the morning and sometimes another at night. This was particularly a problem when a child had diarrhea, like my daughter had.* – M.E.
- *While I was detained, I had my menstrual period and so did a few other women. Each of us were only given two sanitary pads each day. This was not enough and other women shared their unused pads with me. When we asked the guards for more pads, we were denied and told that there were no more.* – V.R.A.
- *There were approximately 50 women and their children in the cell … There was one toilet in the cell. There was one sink attached to the toilet.* – M.E.
- *[T]here were close to sixty people in the cell … There was not enough toilet paper for everyone. When we ran out of toilet paper, the guards did not bring us more right away, sometimes we had to wait for hours or more.* – J.C.C.O.
- *There were between 30 to 40 other people in the cell … There was one toilet in the cell.* – N.G.P.
- *There was no waste bin in the cell so the trash was piled in the corner of the room. Toilet paper was thrown on the floor. The odor was awful because some kids had diarrhea and the mothers did not have soap to wash their hands after cleaning them or changing their diapers. The cell was cleaned once a day but we still had no way to wash our hands.* – M.E.
- *The cell was very dirty for our entire time there. There were diapers, toilet paper and other trash strewn around the bathroom area when we arrived. No one came to clear the cell and the smell was terrible. We were not able to clean because there was no trash can.* – G.F.G.

2.6.5. Nutritional Problems

- *We were not given food until Saturday afternoon [after being detained the night before]. In order to eat the first night, we found some crackers that were lying on the ground and left over from the other families. We divided the crackers amongst the four children in the cell but my son kept crying and saying that he wanted food.* – M.V.H.

- When I arrived, they said they had already fed the rest of the detainees so I was not given food. They did not even give me food the next day before transferring me ... They also did not give me food in the second cell nor was there any water container. At that point I had not eaten for almost two days. – J.A.M.B.
- When we were detained we were already hungry and tired. We had not eaten for an entire day and a half ... We were given something to eat twice a day. The food consisted of only crackers and juice. It was very little food and my son and I were very hungry ... My son cried because he was hungry. – D.G.B.
- I was seven-months pregnant ... I spent a total of 24 hours in a cell ... The whole time I was [there] we were only given snacks twice. These snacks were crackers and juice. It was not sufficient for me and I was extremely hungry. – Y.R.P.L.
- I was hungry the entire time ... We would be given a small burrito, crackers, and a small juice. But sometimes we wouldn't even get the burrito. Sometimes they would bring us food in the middle of the night when we were sleeping and it would be very cold by the time people woke up. Burritos would lie on the cold ground during the night. When we asked for more food, it was never given. The food was never enough, and I was very hungry. – N.G.P.
- The only food we received was a packet of crackers and an orange, which we were given once daily. I was extremely hungry and exhausted the entire time I was detained. – R.V.M.
- We ate the food the first time it was given to us because we were very hungry but it gave us diarrhea and made my daughters vomit. We also noticed that the juices were already expired. – D.G.M.
- One time some of us received burritos in tortillas that had gone bad and were black all over. We did not eat the burritos because they had gone bad. – G.H.S.
- There was no water cooler in our cell so we were not able to drink water for the entire first day ... We had to ask several times for water and only on our second day did they bring us a water cooler. We were all very thirsty because we had not had sufficient water. – D.G.B.
- [W]e were kept in the van for more than twenty-four hours ... They did not give us food or water that whole time. I was already thirsty and hungry because I had not had water for an entire day. In fact, I had turned myself in because I was out of water. I asked for water and they responded that they did not have any. – J.B.C.
- There was a water container in the cell, but no cups. We would run out of water often because there were so many people and the guards would not listen when we asked for more. We could only drink the smallest amount to get by. – N.G.P.
- There was one sink in the cell but it did not work ... There was no drinking water in the cell. I was not able to drink water for the [16 hours I was in this cell]. – J.A.M.B.
- We were not given water and there was no water container ... I saved my extra juice for my [three-year-old] daughter because she was thirsty. We had to ask

permission to go outside to the water containers, but there was no cup ... so we
were not able to drink the water. I was very thirsty. – F.E.G.G.

- *There was a water container in the cell ... but no cups ... I asked for a cup and the*
  agent said that they would not give out cups and I would have to squat down to
  drink the water as it fell out. – I.V.L.G.

2.6.6. Lack of Basic and Emergency Healthcare

- *[After being treated for a broken ankle], I was released from the medical facility*
  with prescription medication for the pain. But Border Patrol agents took those
  pills from me. While I was in detention, I yelled from the pain and begged for
  the pills. But the agents refused to give them to me. Only once in my entire time
  in detention was I allowed to take my prescription ... I felt like I was going to die
  because the pain was so bad. I could not breathe.– Y.R.P.L.
- *I told a guard that ... I was sick and he said "I am not a doctor." He said*
  that even if he had pills he wouldn't give them to me ... [A] guard took [my
  medicine] away and said he wouldn't give them [back] to me. I was taking
  medication for an ovarian cyst ... I was supposed to take the medicine for five
  days but had only taken two or three days of the medicine when I was detained.
  – M.J.L.M.
- *The agents ignored me when I tried to tell them that my [20-month-old] daughter*
  was sick. When they finally answered me, they said that they could not give her
  the medicine that I had for her in my belongings. They would not do anything
  else for her. – M.E.
- *I take medicine for a heart ailment, I have heart problems, I get attacks where*
  my ... left arm goes numb. I have a prescription for this ailment. I take three pills
  twice a day. I did not have this prescription with me when I was picked up ...
  I told the agents I had this heart ailment but the agents told me that they could
  not prescribe anything there. – F.M.E.
- *During my time in detention, I would have liked medical treatment for a large,*
  deep gash ... on my chest ... But when I showed it to an agent he said nothing.
  I didn't bring it up again because they don't listen, they get mad just by us talking.
  – L.C.V.M.

2.6.7. Physical and Emotional Abuse

- *[The agents] said that if we made too much noise they would take our food ...away.*
  They said that if even one person made [a] loud noise they would punish us all.
  So we tried to stay as quiet as possible because we were worried that our food
  would be taken away. – J.A.M.B.

- We asked the guards to change the temperature but they would not ... Instead, the guards told us that if we did not keep quiet they would make it even colder. – C.V.J.
- When I was screaming in pain, I was told not to cry because I was just going to be deported to Guatemala and there was nothing I could do. – Y.R.P.L.
- I am currently five-months pregnant. When I arrived at the Border Patrol station, I told the agents I was pregnant, but the agents were very hostile and did not believe me. They insulted me and poked my stomach and said there wasn't anything there. – J.S.M.P.
- While I was detained ... a male Border Patrol agent told me that if I didn't sign the documents he showed me that I would be detained longer. Then the same agent took a picture of me with his cell phone and he said he was going to send it to the Zetas [a powerful and violent criminal organization in Mexico]. When I asked why, the agent told me it was because I did not want to give him information about drugs. But I did not know what he was talking about because I did not have drugs or anything like that. By saying all of this, he forced me to sign documents I did not understand. – F.M.E.
- I told [the agents] I was seeking asylum and that I wanted to see a judge, but the agents told me I was just here to work and that I didn't have the right to see a judge because I broke the law. They had me sign a lot of other papers without explaining to me what they were. – M.L.L.L.
- One of the agents told me that they were going to take away my [six-year-old] son. They said that my child would stay in the United States and they would deport me. I said that I did not want to be separated from him. The agents responded that the United States didn't want any more Guatemalans ... I signed various documents that I did not understand. I asked the agent to explain the papers but they just said "sign" ... [and] that I did not have the right to know whether or not they were my deportation papers ... While I was detained I was very sad and afraid that the agents would take away my son. I cried because of my situation. My son was also crying. – A.V.M.

2.6.8. Restrictions on Outside Communication

- I asked for a phone call to the consulate and they said that I could not make the call. I said that it was my right to talk to the consulate and they said that we didn't have rights there and would have to wait until the consulate visited. – J.A.M.B.
- I asked for a phone call. I was told that we could not make a phone call, and that we were all just going to be deported. Other people ask[ed] for phone calls too. They were told that the consulate is not the person in charge, the guards were the people in charge and they were going to be deported. – Y.R.P.L.

- *I asked to use the phone to call my family and was told that I could not make any phone calls at all and was never allowed to make one phone call ... I was never informed that I had a right to call the Mexican consulate. –* C.V.J.

The lawsuit filed by a group of civil and immigration rights groups resulted in a preliminary decision by the federal judge to disclose photos of the *hieleras*. The group included the American Immigration Council in Washington, D.C., the National Immigration Law Center in Los Angeles and the American Civil Liberties Union of Arizona.[20]

2.7. ORR FACILITIES

Getting transferred to ORR custody from ICE custody is qualitatively important. As we will see in Chapter 3, the conditions in ICE's adult and family detention centers across the country are atrocious. In contrast, while not perfect, by and large UACs have had relatively positive experiences while in ORR custody. ORR has housing centers in Chicago and New York and many other communities to where UACs are transferred from border states like Texas. Those ORR facilities provide a safer, more stable, and more open environment free from many of the abuses so often documented in ICE facilities. ORR provides classroom instruction for the children, including instruction in math, reading, spelling, and physical education. They also have Spanish-speaking ESL (English as a Second Language) teachers who provide basic English instruction, as well has greater access to healthcare.

Once transferred to the care and custody of ORR, its officials are responsible for housing and caring for the child unless the child can be released to family or a qualifying sponsor who will care for the child while their immigration case proceeds. Like Juana and Alberto, once DHS officials are satisfied that they are truly unaccompanied minors, the children are required to be transferred out of CBP or ICE custody to an ORR facility.

ORR operates about 100 permanent shelters located mostly near the United States–Mexico border. However, because of the sudden influx of children after the spring and summer of 2014, three additional temporary shelters with approximately 3,000 beds were opened on military bases in California, Oklahoma, and Texas. Preliminary plans for an additional 1,000-bed facility in the town of Lakewood, Colorado, were scrapped in early 2016 after it was revealed that the project – a conversion of a warehouse – would have cost almost $37 million to complete. Nevertheless, new facilities were set up to accommodate more UACs in places such as Homestead, Florida, and the Holloman Air Force Base in New Mexico.

---

[20] Jorge Rivas, *These unsealed photos offer rare peek inside Border Patrol's notorious 'Ice Box' detention cells*, Fusion, June 29, 2016. *See also Flores* decision, at 16–18, available at: www.documentcloud.org/documents/2179157-flores-order.html

Once in ORR custody, the treatment of UACs is regulated by statute. The TVPRA lists the following guidelines and protections for processing and care of UACs post-apprehension:

- **Notification**: HHS must be notified within 48 hours upon the apprehension of an UAC.
- **Transfer**: Except in the case of "exceptional circumstances," UACs should be transferred to HHS no later than seventy-two hours after the child is determined to be "unaccompanied."
- **Safe Placement**: UACs must be promptly placed in the "least restrictive setting possible" while awaiting a court hearing. (Usually this means placement with a parent, relative, or other sponsor in the United States. If no sponsor can be found, ORR retains custody, which may mean placement in a shelter or foster home.)
- **Suitability Assessment**: The child may not be placed with a qualified sponsor until HHS determines that the proposed sponsor is capable of providing for the child's physical and mental well-being. At a minimum, HHS is required to verify the custodian's identity and relationship to the child.
- **Legal Orientation**: HHS must work with the Executive Office for Immigration Review (EOIR) to ensure that custodians receive legal orientation presentations.
- **Access to Counsel**: HHS must try to ensure that UACs have access to pro bono legal counsel.
- **Child Advocate**: UACs should be provided access to an advocate.

While UACs are in government custody, the government is required to meet certain minimum requirements for care and custody, as stipulated by TVPRA, the 1997 Flores Agreement, and DHS regulations. Taken together, these instruments require that at a minimum, DHS must:

- Maintain custody of UACs in the least restrictive setting appropriate to the children's age and special needs, provided that such setting is consistent with the need to protect the child's well-being and that of others, as well as with any other laws, regulations, or legal requirements;
- Provide safe and sanitary facilities, as well as facilities with adequate temperature control and ventilation;
- Provide UACs with access to drinking water and food as appropriate, emergency medical care, and toilets and sinks;
- Generally separate UACs from unrelated adults and adequately supervise UACs;
- Provide specialized training for care and custody of UACs to government personnel who have substantive contact with UACs; and
- Transfer UACs to HHS within seventy-two hours of apprehension, except in exceptional circumstances.

UACs are automatically placed in formal removal proceedings and will ultimately appear in immigration court to fight their deportation. At the same time, the guidelines require that – for those UACs that do remain in government custody – ORR must find the least restrictive setting possible while they wait for their immigration case to conclude.

Before the 2014 surge, the immigration process took many months or even years due to backlogs in the immigration court system. According to the Transactional Records Clearinghouse (TRAC), in June 2014, the total number of immigration cases in the backlog stood at 375,000 cases, including 41,640 minors who were awaiting court dates. At the time, TRAC also estimated the average waiting time for all cases (not just child cases) was 587 days. As Table 2.1 illustrates, many children arriving at the southern border were from Honduras, Guatemala, and El Salvador. They could not be quickly screened and sent back to their countries of origin in the same manner as their Mexican and Canadian counterparts. When the 2008 TVPRA was enacted, only about 3300 UACs were being apprehended from Honduras, Guatemala, and El Salvador. However, by fiscal year 2014, more than 51,000 UACs from those three nations had been apprehended.

The unprecedented spike in the number of apprehended children strained the government's ability to house, place, or process UACs in accordance with TVPRA provisions; more resources or a shift in approach was needed. In June 2014, while under immense pressure to respond to the crisis, President Barack Obama submitted an emergency supplemental request to Congress, asking for $3.7 billion to manage the crisis at the border with further resources.[21] In a letter to Congress, the White House also asked for "additional authority to exercise discretion in processing the return and removal of unaccompanied minor children from non-contiguous countries like Guatemala, Honduras, and El Salvador."[22]

Thus, problems related to custody do not end after UAC status is verified and ORR steps in. During the summer of 2014, the sudden rush of UACs at the United States–Mexico border overwhelmed the ORR. As the number of children increased, the government had staffing problems and started running out of space to accommodate the UACs. ORR began paying millions of dollars to outsource its responsibility to private companies to operate facilities. Southwest Key, for example, is a company that bills itself as one of the largest providers of services for unaccompanied children in the United States. The company operates more than twenty-five

[21] White House Fact Sheet: Emergency Supplemental Request to Address the Increase in Child and Adult Migration from Central America in the Rio Grande Valley Areas of the Southwest Border, July 8, 2014, available at: www.whitehouse.gov/the-press-office/2014/07/08/fact-sheet-emergency-supplemental-request-address-increase-child-and-adu

[22] Letter from the President – Efforts to Address the Humanitarian Situation in the Rio Grande Valley Areas of Our Nation's Southwest Border, June 30, 2014, available at: www.whitehouse.gov/the-press-office/2014/06/30/letter-president-efforts-address-humanitarian-situation-rio-grande-valle

TABLE 2.1. Unaccompanied alien children encountered by fiscal years 2009–2015, 2016 (October 1, 2015–December 31, 2015)

Country	FY 2009	FY 2010	FY 2011	FY 2012	FY 2013	FY 2014	FY 2015	FY 2016
El Salvador	1,221	1,910	1,394	3,314	5,990	16,404	9,389	17,512
Guatemala	1,115	1,517	1,565	3,835	8,068	17,057	13,589	18,913
Honduras	968	1,017	974	2,997	6,747	18,244	5,409	10,468
Mexico	16,114	13,724	11,768	13,974	17,240	15,634	11,012	11,926
Total	19,418	18,168	22,101	24,120	38,045	67,339	39,399	58,819
w/o Mex	3,304	4,444	3,933	10,146	20,805	51,705	28,387	46,893

Source: www.cbp.gov/newsroom/stats/southwest-border-unaccompanied-children/fy-2016 (last accessed on December 19, 2017). There are also separate charts for family units on the website.

shelters across fifteen cities in Texas, Arizona, and California, serving thousands of children each day.

In addition to government and privately run facilities, other large organizations like the US Conference of Catholic Bishops and Lutheran Immigration and Refugee Service ("LIRS") have worked with the federal government, overseeing smaller community-based and residential care. Kimberly Haynes, Director for children's services at LIRS explained, "[m]any organizations that began working with these children have been historically faith-based organizations that have extensive immigrant and refugee resettlement experience and a long history of working with ORR, as welcoming the stranger is a large component of faith-based response to any vulnerable individuals to provide support, assistance, and help."[23]

As the number of arriving UACs continued to grow, a larger public bidding process was implemented to recruit more organizations to contribute to the effort of accommodating the children. As part of a $350 million commitment, ORR invited providers to submit proposals to care for UACs. The announcement explained that the majority of UACs were expected to remain in government custody between thirty to thirty-five days, but often the length of stay varies significantly. In order to qualify, applicants must provide case management services, education, counseling, and medical services. Religious organizations were some of the most enthusiastic respondents to the call for help. The Archdiocese of Chicago, for instance, announced that it would offer to help shelter the children. Although many communities and organizations reached out to aid the effort, others stood in opposition. In July 2014, communities such as Murrieta, California, and Oracle, Arizona protested the arrival of buses carrying UACs to facilities in their community, some carrying signs with phrases such as "Return to Sender" and "Send 'em to Coyote Obama."[24]

Although many UACs will end up in ORR facilities for some duration of time, of the approximately 68,000 UACs who were apprehended at the border in 2014, more than 43,000 were released to live with qualifying sponsors, usually parents or relatives residing in the United States. The children can remain with sponsors while their cases are being processed. The majority of children residing with sponsors are in states where immigrants have traditionally settled, like Texas, New York, California, and Florida. A large number of children have also been sent to less obvious states such as Maryland, Virginia, Georgia, and Louisiana.

However, in releasing UACs to caregivers, the ORR has come under immense scrutiny. In January 2016, news broke that in 2014, government agencies released some children to human traffickers and abusers. Some children were forced to live and work in dangerous conditions. At the time, ORR was under increased pressure to process and release the children, and adjusted its policies to expedite the process.

---

[23] Rebecca Kaplan, Shelters for child border-crossers aren't all government-run, CBS News, Aug. 1, 2014.
[24] Halimah Abdullah, Not in my backyard: Communities protest surge of immigrant kids, CNN, July 16, 2014, available at: www.cnn.com/2014/07/15/politics/immigration-not-in-my-backyard/

Although ORR has since taken steps to tighten its screening and oversight measures, these tragic events were the focus of intense Senate scrutiny. During one Senate
Homeland Security and Government Affairs Subcommittee on Investigations hearing, the Senators grilled officials from ORR and HHS on the adequacy of their
efforts and policies to protect unaccompanied children. The subcommittee also
released a detailed report noting that the trafficking incidents were "likely prevent-
able" because HHS failed to run background checks on all adults in households
of petitioning sponsors as well as on secondary caregivers. In addition, the agency
failed to visit any of the sponsors' homes and failed to realize that a group of sponsors
was accumulating multiple unrelated children. The subcommittee found that in
addition to the incidents reported by the media, thirteen other cases were identified
involving post-placement trafficking of UACs and fifteen more with serious trafficking indicators.

At the Senate hearing, Mark Greenberg, Acting Assistant Secretary at HHS, and
Robert Carey, Director of ORR, explained that in the wake of the scandal, ORR put
in place measures to ensure the safety of the children upon release. In their written
testimony, they stated:

> Potential sponsors for unaccompanied children are required to undergo back-
> ground checks and complete a sponsor assessment process. ORR has recently
> enhanced its policies, requiring additional checks for sponsors and others who are
> likely to come into contact with the child post-release. All potential sponsors and
> individuals identified in the sponsor care agreement must complete a criminal
> public record check, based on the sponsor's name and address, and a sex offender
> registry check. Additionally, a fingerprint background check is required whenever
> the potential sponsor is not a parent or legal guardian.

However, several Senators were quick to point out that many of the new enhance-
ments were announced just days before the hearing, and they were skeptical about
whether concrete action would have taken place if the hearing had not been
announced.

Representatives from the US Committee for Refugees and Immigrants (USCRI),
the Ohio Department of Jobs and Family Services, and Lutheran Immigration and
Refugee Services (LIRS) also testified before Congress. LIRS, a nongovernmental organization with a history of providing services to unaccompanied children for
ORR, outlined important recommendations for ORR and Congress. For example,
ORR should have contingency funds so that in periods with higher than average
arrivals of UACs or refugees, ORR could provide adequate bed space and services
in a timely fashion. In addition, LIRS recommended that ORR also ensure that all
children have access to post-release services and that all children receive at least one
home visit to check on the child's well-being following release. That recommendation was emphasized as a means of preventing secondary trafficking incidents.

Some ORR decisions on the release of children to parents or adult caregivers have been controversial. According to immigration attorney Joanna Gaughan, in one case, ORR refused to release a child to the care of the child's mother because the mother was undocumented and in the United States under a prior removal order. There was no question that the mother was fit to care for her child. In a second case, a mother was in removal proceedings, and ORR refused to release the child until the mother retained an immigration attorney to assist in her proceedings.

Many arriving children are not given the benefit of the doubt and foreclosed from ORR treatment under questionable circumstances. Consider the declarations of these children:

Declaration of Manuel Rosales

I, Manuel Rosales, declare and state the following:

1. I am 16 years old. I first arrived in the United States in June 2016.
2. After I was detained near the Mexican border, I was initially placed in Homestead, a shelter in Miami. I stayed there for approximately three weeks.
3. About a month later, I was transferred to a staff secure facility in Texas. My understanding was that I was transferred for drawing gang symbols in a bathroom at the shelter. Although I had not drawn the gang symbols, I had provided the pencils that the youths who drew them had used. I took responsibility for drawing the symbols because I did not want to have trouble with those kids later, as they were all bigger than me.
4. I stayed at the staff secure facility for almost two months. I was then transferred to NOVA, a facility in Alexandria, Virginia, that I believed was a jail. I understood that I had been transferred there primarily because staff had seen a video in which I was making gang symbols while I was talking to another staff [member] from El Salvador. I am not a member of a gang, but we had been discussing how the gangs had treated us in El Salvador. I was never given an opportunity to explain this before I was transferred.
5. When NOVA closed, I was transferred to Shenandoah Valley Juvenile Center. I was not told that I was being transferred to a secure facility for any reason other than the fact that NOVA was closing. I had not had any behavioral problems at NOVA during the three weeks prior to the transfer.
6. I have been detained at Shenandoah since December 2016.
7. I had been told by my case manager that if I was good for 30 days, I could be transferred to another, less-secure facility.
8. I had good behavior for the first two months that I was at Shenandoah. I did not get involved in any fights with other kids or staff.
9. After 30 days had passed with no behavioral issues and no mention of a transfer, I was surprised. After 60 days had passed with still no word on a possible transfer, I became extremely frustrated.

10. Since I had arrived at Shenandoah, I had spent most of my time in Charlie and Delta Pods, but some of the kids in those pods had tried to pick fights with me. I asked to be transferred to Alpha Pod because it seemed to me that the kids in that pod had gotten involved in fewer fights. I did not realize at the time that Alpha Pod was where kids with behavioral problems were usually placed.

11. Shortly after I was placed in Alpha Pod, I was pressured by another youth to become involved in a fight with staff. He told me that if I did not participate, he would have me beat up. Because of his threats, I became involved in a fight in the gym with several of the kids from Alpha Pod and several staff members. After this incident, I was locked in my room for two days and placed in handcuffs for 10 days.

12. A few weeks after this incident, I was approached by another group of youths and urged to initiate a fight with a staff member, and I agreed.

13. I became involved in these fights out of both fear for what would happen to me if I did not do so and disappointment that my good behavior had not resulted in a transfer.

14. I have not had any other incidents with staff since those two incidents, but I have been involved in a few fights with other residents.

15. I have had good behavior for the past 39 days, but I have not received any information about a possible transfer or review of my case.

Declaration of Juan Martinez

I, Juan Martinez, declare and say the following:

1. I am 17 years old. It's four months until I turn 18. I'm from Honduras. I am currently being held at Shenandoah Valley Juvenile Hall in Virginia. I have been detained here for six weeks or so. I have not been told how much longer I will be detained.

2. I came to the United States to save my life from the "*maras*" and assassins in Honduras. Also because an older woman was harassing me there, and to be with my mom, who currently lives in Texas. In my country I never had problems with the police. The "*mara*" forced me to leave my studies because they were looking for me at school to get me to join them. So I have no choice but to leave my country.

3. On August 22, 2016, I entered the United States by the border with Reynosa, Mexico. I had walked alone for 16 hours on a dry field, thirsty and hungry, when I was arrested by the Border Patrol. They put me very roughly inside in a big and long truck and they took me to the immigration facility where I stayed for about two days. Then they moved me to what we call "*la hielera*" (the freezer). We were like 20 people in one room, we were packed tight. I stayed

there for about three days. There was not enough room for us to lie down, no mattresses or anything. There were small children enduring the cold, until I took off my shirt to lend it to a young boy. Then they sent me to *"la perrera"* (the dog kennel). I spent two days there, and then they took me to IES House Norma Linda in Brownsville, Texas.

4. They treated us well in Norma Linda. I only had one problem there, with another young man being detained. He was homosexual, and I began to feel uncomfortable. I reported him to my counselor. I told the counselor I did not want problems with him or anyone. I think she took it the wrong way, that I wanted to hit the young man or something. About a week later, I was transferred to Southwest Key in Brownsville, Texas. I was at school in Norma Linda one day, when they suddenly came to me and said, "Juan, you're leaving. Pack your things." I thought I was going to go with my mom, but I was informed in the car that I was going to another shelter. I was asking them why. They answered that I could not be in that program because I had too many reports. I asked them, "what reports?" because I was never warned that there were reports against me. They gave me no more explanation or opportunity to defend myself. I started to cry because I was frustrated and also because I did not think it was right that I was suddenly moved.

5. Life in Southwest Key was more complicated. The staff shouted at us with insults, insulting us, calling us *"putos"* or *"apurense culeros."* A staff [member] there gave a pen to one of my partners to get a tattoo. There, too, I watched as they grabbed the minors brutally, throwing them to the ground. I managed to avoid that abuse by taking great care of myself.

6. I spent approximately four months at Southwest Key. Around the second month, my mom moved from Kansas to Texas to be closer to me. She found a house, which is said to be very nice, to receive me. They continued to take long making the decision to let me live with her. According to her, the government did a study of the home, and everything went well.

7. Around February of this year, I was transferred to BCFS, another secure place in California, where I stayed until October, more or less. In California I was scolded from time to time for using bad words, and for other small things, but never was I warned that they were going to move me because of bad behavior. One day I had a disagreement on the soccer field. A staff member approached me suddenly. I was surprised and without thinking I reacted, but I was accused of beating him. About two days later, suddenly at four in the morning the supervisor came to tell me that they were going to move me to another program. And that is how I arrived at Shenandoah. They gave me no hearing or opportunity to explain my side of the facts. I was given no alternative but to accept the transfer to high security.

8. Shenandoah is a jail, though the staff speak to us better than in Southwest Key. However, life here is very difficult. We wear prison uniforms that smell bad

and cause me an allergic itch. Sometimes it becomes a little difficult not to get into trouble with our cellmates. There is not much to do, and one spends a lot of time [being] bored. Normally, we spend almost 13 hours and 45 minutes locked in our rooms, and even longer if there are problems with the behavior. We are divided into five or six pods, with a limit of 10 young people per pod. They punish us for what young people do in another pod, and that's not fair. There are four staff that can take care of us: two in the morning and two in the afternoon. Of the four who take care of us, almost always only one, who works the morning, speaks Spanish. So it is very easy that there are misunderstandings among the young people and the staff.

9. To date, I have had only one hearing before an immigration judge, in Texas. The judge explained to me my rights and that they were going to give me another court date, and that if I did not arrive with a lawyer the deportation order would be more likely. After two or three weeks from arriving in Shenandoah, I spoke to a lawyer for the first time since I've been locked up. Neither Texas nor California gave me a lawyer. Lawyers came to talk about our rights, but none to represent me.

I declare under protest to tell the truth that all the information I have provided here is correct and complete, I am aware of the legal consequences of declaring falsehoods before the authority.

July 11, 2017, Staunton, Virginia.

2.8. *FLORES* SETTLEMENT ISSUES

For those children that are not released by ORR to adult caregivers, the conditions of custody in ORR-sponsored shelters must meet certain standards. The special conditions afforded to children from non contiguous countries stems from litigation. In 1997, as part of a case titled *Flores* v. *Meese*, a pivotal settlement was reached concerning the treatment of children in immigration detention. The settlement stipulated that children waiting for a determination of removal or relief must be placed in the "least restrictive setting." This agreement was intended to protect the rights of minors in immigration custody and ensure their well-being. Under the settlement, UACs are to be released to the care of their parents or other family members whenever possible, and if not, they are to be placed in foster homes or licensed facilities. These purportedly child-friendly licensed facilities are to be operated in accordance with age-appropriate policies and programs.

Flores was filed in 1985 by two human rights legal advocacy organizations on behalf of Plaintiff Lisette Flores and other children held by immigration authorities in the United States District Court for the Central District of California. After years of litigation, an agreement was reached between the plaintiffs and the government providing that juveniles who are not released to adult caregivers must be placed in juvenile care facilities that meet or exceed state licensing requirements for the provision of services to dependent children. As part of the settlement, the government is also required to report annually to the court approving the agreement on its compliance with the terms of the agreement. The government also must report semiannually to the plaintiffs on its compliance and provide data about the juveniles in immigration custody longer than seventy-two hours.

Aside from the conditions of the facilities, the *Flores* agreement also provides that federal authorities can release children to other "responsible adults." For a number of years prior to *Flores*, the issue of releasing UACs was apparently handled on a regional, ad hoc basis, with some immigration offices releasing UACs not only to their parents but also to a range of other adults and organizations. In 1984, responding to the increased flow of UACs into California, the Western Regional Office of the Immigration and Naturalization Service adopted a policy of limiting the release of detained minors to "a parent or lawful guardian," except in "unusual and extraordinary cases," whereby the child could be released to "a responsible individual who agrees to provide care and be responsible for the welfare and well-being of the child."[25] In *Flores*, The District Court invalidated the regulatory scheme on unspecified due process grounds, ordering that "responsible adult part[ies]" be added to the list of persons to whom a juvenile must be released and requiring that a hearing on release to a qualifying relative before an immigration judge be held automatically whether or not the juvenile requests it.

2.9. PRIORITIZING UAC REMOVALS VIA "ROCKET DOCKETS"

The importance of assuring that UACs are released to responsible adult caregivers goes beyond the obvious concerns for their safety and well-being. The caregivers must also guide the child through their removal proceedings; an especially critical task given what a child in removal proceedings is up against. However, as the number of UACs swelled in 2014, the White House feared that the border crisis would undermine its hopes for larger immigration reforms. Instead of treating the flow as a humanitarian crisis, the Obama administration regarded the challenge as a political crisis. Thus, as soon as a UAC was apprehended, deportation proceedings were swiftly initiated.

The White House issued a directive to immigration judges in June 2014 to accelerate the arraignment process for UACs. To show greater toughness, judges were instructed to give top priority to the UAC cases with the goal that each child would be arraigned within twenty-one days of being turned over to the courts. In the summer of 2014, the EOIR, the division within the Department of Justice which houses the immigration courts, adopted a new policy with respect to prioritizing cases for

---

[25] See *Flores v. Meese*, 934 F. 2d 991, 994 (CA9 1990) (quoting policy), vacated, 942 F. 2d 1352 (CA9 1991) (en banc).

adjudication. The stated goal of this new policy was to "focus the department's immigration processing resources on recent border crossers" (i.e., individuals who arrived on or after May 1, 2014).

Under the policy, the immigration courts were instructed to prioritize the following cases: (1) unaccompanied children who recently crossed the southwest border; (2) families who recently crossed the border and are held in detention; (3) families who recently crossed the border but are released on "alternatives to detention"; and (4) other detained cases. As a result, immigration courts now schedule a first hearing for UACs within twenty-one days of the court's receiving the case.[26] Given the speed at which these cases progress, the expedited child dockets were referred to as "rocket dockets." The concern with this strategy was that as a consequence, children on rocket dockets were provided with less time to find attorneys before immigration courts moved forward with their cases – and, as a result, would be required to explain why they should not be deported without the help of an attorney. If they were unable to handle the situation, unrepresented children would be ordered removed or required to "voluntarily" depart from the United States. Thus, their otherwise meritorious defenses against deportation would never be adequately presented before an immigration judge.

In addition, given the rapid pace of the twenty-one-day scheduling of preliminary hearings, many children were ordered removed from the United States *in absentia* for failure to attend their first hearings. Adult caregivers who sponsor children in proceedings are responsible for assuring the children attend their hearings, but mistakes can and do happen, through no fault of the child. Children and their caregivers were given as little as three days' notice of their court hearing date, severely limiting their ability to find counsel and often contributing to their failure to attend their hearings. Continuances (periods of time in between hearings) were granted to allow for more time to locate and retain an attorney, but often times continuances are granted for very short periods of time, in some instances as little as a week. As a result, the already fragile and limited network of pro bono lawyers available to take on UAC cases was overwhelmed by the speed of the rocket dockets. In fact, the entire federal immigration system was severely strained – adding to the inherent weaknesses in how agencies prepare and give notice to the children as to when they must appear in court.

Notably, there are two types of notice that are required in the context of removal proceedings. One is the "notice of hearing" that is sent out by the courts to the children. The second is the formal NTA (notice to appear), which is prepared by the

[26] Brian M. O'Leary, Docketing Practices Relating to Unaccompanied Children Cases in Light of New Priorities, Sept. 10, 2014, available at: www.justice.gov/sites/default/files/eoir/legacy/2014/09/30/Docketing-Practices-Related-to-UACs-Sept2014.pdf; Brian M. O'Leary, Docketing Practices Relating to Unaccompanied Children Cases and Adults with Children Released on Alternatives to Detention in Light of the New Priorities, March 24, 2015, available at: www.justice.gov/eoir/pages/attachments/2015/03/26/docketing-practices-related-to-uacs-and-awcatd-march2015.pdf

DHS and originates when the child is first apprehended at the border. The courts' hearing notices are sent out by regular first-class mail, not as registered letters. Given the twenty-one-day timeframe and confusion over where the children had relocated with adult caregivers, there have been frequent complaints of families learning of the court dates too late or not at all – nevertheless receiving *in absentia* orders of removal for failing to appear.

Problems also have arisen with the timeliness and accuracy of NTAs, which are filed to the immigration courts by DHS and must be served on the child or the assigned guardian. DHS is required to show "clear, unequivocal, and convincing evidence" that proper notice has been given when proceeding *in absentia* – without the child present. However, in these scenarios, this standard often times has not been met. In a letter to DHS, the California-based pro bono law firm Public Counsel said it had found repeated cases in which the underlying NTA filed with the court by DHS had been prepared improperly. The letter read, in part:[27]

> DHS is filing NTAs with [the courts] which fail to reflect compliance with the regulations and case law governing children's cases. And DHS is moving for *in absentia* removal orders against children using these NTAs. This failure has devastating consequences for children.

Many judges were mindful of these problems, and the record in these cases show that some judges insisted on more than one hearing to allow time for a second notice to be sent out. However, in many cases, a quick *in absentia* removal order became an easy way to clear the crowded dockets. Whatever the Obama administration intended, the government's own lawyers were in the courtroom and party to these actions. For the children, the end result put them further behind the eight ball. That's because the legal procedures are highly technical for reopening an immigration case once it has been decided *in absentia*. And any young respondent – already without a lawyer – is worse off than before. As veteran immigration attorney Lindsay Toczylowski put it, "it would be virtually impossible for a child – or an adult for that matter – to handle [reopening a case] without hiring an attorney." "You have to file the motion to reopen. The case would be re-calendared; you would also have to show good cause why your case should be reopened. It's just virtually impossible without an attorney helping you. I can't imagine the child being able to do that without an attorney trained in immigration law." Coordinated efforts by service providers to respond to the rocket dockets in many parts of the country helped, but the stress and pressure on these providers was immense. They simply could not provide all the representation that was needed.

By July 22, 2014, Dana Leigh Marks, President of the National Association of Immigration Judges, sent a letter to Senator Harry Reid, then Senate Majority

---

[27] David Rogers, *Under 16 and ordered deported–with no lawyer*, Politico, Nov. 18, 2015.

Leader, and Senator Mitch McConnell, then Senate Minority Leader, expressing "serious concerns" about immigration judges' caseloads and the use of expedited procedures in children's cases. In the first thirteen months, nearly 2,800 removal orders were issued by immigration judges for children who were afforded no defense lawyer and only a single hearing. In at least 40 percent of these cases, the defendant was sixteen or younger. From mid-July 2014 through August 31, 2015, the data show that at least 392 children, all fourteen or younger and without defense counsel, were ordered removed after a single hearing before an immigration judge. The total jumps to 1,150 when fifteen- and sixteen-year olds – also without counsel and afforded just one hearing – are counted. Adding seventeen-year olds, under the same circumstances, brings the number to 1,883. The full universe including eighteen-year olds reached 2,797, all ordered removed with no lawyer and a single hearing.

The swiftness of the process underscores the "get tough" approach taken by the White House as it scrambled to respond to the flood of border crossings. The record of swiftly removing young, vulnerable individuals undercuts Obama's promise of compassion for those caught in what he himself had initially described as a humanitarian crisis exacerbated by the poverty and violence in Central America. There was one special concern regarding the large number of cases in which immigration judges issued removal orders *in absentia* for young children who had no attorney and failed to show up at their first court hearing. The initial hearings, known as master calendar hearings, are typically described as only an arraignment for the child respondent. However, in the cases when the children failed to show, these otherwise purely arraignment style hearings were ultimately less an arraignment and more a one-stop, trial-and-sentencing proceeding resulting in a deportation order.

Within the administration, there were signs of misgivings about the forces set in motion by the president's directive and the need to do something to rectify the inequities shown in the data. More special juvenile dockets were established with a greater emphasis on training for the presiding judges. And the EOIR began a new effort in the summer of 2015 to reach out to those children who were most quickly ordered removed and try to educate their families about how the cases might be reopened. The Obama administration insisted that rocket dockets were never intended to be more than a first step in the deportation process and that judges were free to grant any number of continuances while the child's family attempted to find a lawyer and prepare a defense. But the data plainly show that the opposite occurred for thousands who became casualties of the White House's directive. Certainly, as the flow of border crossings has slowed and more attorneys have become available, the level of legal representation has improved significantly. Nevertheless, the outcome and evidence of due process varies significantly when comparing one immigration court to the next around the country.

While a law student at the University of San Francisco School, Monica Valencia, who is now a fellow in the school's deportation defense clinic, volunteered with the San Francisco Immigration Court's Attorney of the Day program. The program is designed to provide a volunteer attorney who will enter a single appearance for unrepresented respondents at master calendar hearings. Typically, the volunteer attorney helps unrepresented respondents by seeking a continuance of their case in order to find a permanent attorney. On one particular day, Valencia helped organize and prepare children that had been placed on rocket dockets and were scheduled to appear before an immigration judge. Following her experience, Valencia wrote:

> The most disheartening part about working in Immigration Law is the disproportionate numbers of undocumented immigrants who go without legal representation ... Before I began to observe the proceedings on this day, I participated in conducting a quick "Know Your Rights" briefing in the waiting area and I also helped gather information of those that did not have legal representation. The Attorney of the Day (AOD) then reviews the information gathered and talks with each person individually. The AOD is usually an attorney who volunteers to represent persons in the proceedings who do not already have representation, but it is only for that day. After that, each person must find their own attorney. Maria is 11-years-old and she traveled to the United States alone from Guatemala. She didn't really understand what was happening or what was about to take place; all she knew is that she had to be present in the courtroom on this day. She handed me her Notice to Appear and said, "Can you be my lawyer?" I explained to her that I was not an attorney and gave her a resource packet of organizations and pro bono attorneys that provide free legal assistance. She hardly looked at me after that. You could tell that she was scared. In giving her that packet, I knew that it would be difficult for her to find a pro bono attorney to take her case because of backlogs that non-profit organizations are experiencing. Those organizations do not have the resources or bodies to provide free legal services to everyone. In that moment, I felt like a liar. The reality for many undocumented children is that they will have to appear in court and represent themselves pro se. That is, if they do not find an attorney to effectively advocate for them and seek out legal remedies, they will have no choice but to face the immigration judge and the government attorney on their own. How can this be okay in our American system of justice? First, children and other undocumented immigrants I encountered do not speak English and do not understand the immigration process in its entirety. I don't understand the process completely myself, and I am a law student, so how can a three-year-old, a seven-year-old, or even an eleven-year-old understand? Even though they are afforded an interpreter, it takes a knowledgeable legal advocate to battle it out in court. What then of the children who have to defend themselves and protect their interests against an educated judge and a well-trained government attorney? What ever happened to an equal balance? This type of arbitrary procedure perpetuates a bully-effect – where the bigger, meaner wolf attacks the defenseless and wins.

3

Family Detention Centers

Creation, Conditions, and Continued Detention

3.1. INTRODUCTION

The 1980s witnessed a dramatic increase of Cuban, Haitian, and Central American children (accompanied and unaccompanied) and refugees to the United States. Most children were released to a parent or guardian, but many others were held in border detention facilities and tent shelters where access to legal assistance, health care, and education was foreclosed.[1] In 1996, the US Congress and President Bill Clinton enacted major changes to US immigration law and policy, including the Illegal Immigration Reform and Immigrant Responsibility Act that adversely affected migrant families. These changes created an "expedited removal" process and expanded the categories of persons subject to mandatory detention.[2]

As noted in Chapter 2, after more than a decade of litigation, including a Supreme Court decision upholding the right of the federal government to detain migrant children,[3] attorneys representing detained children reached an agreement with the federal government in 1997 over the conditions under which the children could be held. The *Flores* settlement resulted from negotiations over the Immigration and Naturalization Service's (INS) detention policies toward the influx of unaccompanied migrant children in the 1980s.[4] The agreement set national standards

---

[1] American Bar Association, *Defending Liberty Pursuing Justice, Commission on Immigration, Family Immigration Detention: Why the Past Cannot be Prologue*, American Bar Association (July 31, 2015). Available at: www.americanbar.org/content/dam/aba/publications/commission_on_immigration/FINAL%20ABA%20Family%20Detention%20Report%208-19-15.authcheckdam.pdf.

[2] Ibid.

[3] *Reno v. Flores*, 507 U.S. 292 (1993).

[4] The Flores Settlement Agreement, Case No. CV 85-4544-RJK(Px). Available at: http://web.centerforhumanrights.net:8080/centerforhumanrights/children/Document.2004-06-18.8124043749. Some of the agreement's terms have been codified at 8 CFR §§236.3, 1236.3. For cases culminating in the settlement agreement, see *Flores v. Meese*, No. 85-4544-RJK(Px)(CD Cal. Nov. 30, 1987); *Flores v. Meese*, No. 85-4544-RJK(Px)(CD Cal. May 25, 1988); *Flores v. Meese*, 934 F.2d 991 (1990); *Flores v. Meese*, 942 F.2d 1352 (1992); *Reno v. Flores*, 507 U.S. 292 (1993).

regarding the detention, release, and treatment of all children in INS custody. The guidelines require that juveniles be held in the "least restrictive setting appropriate to their age and special needs, generally in a non-secure facility licensed to care for dependent, as opposed to delinquent, minors."[5] Furthermore, "juveniles [must] be released from custody without unnecessary delay to a parent, legal guardian, adult relative, individual specifically designated by the parent, licensed, program, or alternatively, an adult seeking custody deemed appropriate by the responsible government agency."[6] Today, the settlement extends to migrant children held with the Department of Homeland Security (DHS) and Health and Human Services' Office of Refugee Resettlement (ORR).

Treatment of migrant children who are accompanied by a parent is different. They are considered part of a family unit. Despite the *Flores* settlement, in March of 2001, immigration authorities continued to increase available detention spaces for families and opened the Berks County Family Residential Center ("Berks") in Pennsylvania. The purpose of the Berks facility was to temporarily detain migrant families undergoing administrative immigration proceedings and those subject to mandatory detention.[7]

After the September 11, 2001 terrorist attacks, the federal officials made further changes to immigration law enforcement and family detention policies. In 2002, Congress passed the Homeland Security Act, created the DHS, and established Immigration and Customs Enforcement (ICE) within the DHS to be in charge of immigration enforcement.[8] These post-9/11 policies expedited removal proceedings and disproportionately impacted and separated families and certain asylum seekers crossing US borders.

In 2005, the Bush administration decided to deny the *Flores* protections to refugee children traveling with their parents, taking the position that *Flores* applied only to unaccompanied migrant children. Instead of adhering to the general policy favoring release, the administration began to incarcerate hundreds of families for months at a time. Officials opened the T. Don Hutto Family Detention Center near Austin, Texas, and within a year, the American Civil Liberties Union (ACLU) filed a lawsuit over the facility's conditions. Young children were forced to wear prison jumpsuits, live in dormitory housing, use toilets exposed to public view, and sleep with the lights on. No schooling was provided.

Given the situation, a federal judge in Texas denounced the administration's actions as a violation of the *Flores* settlement: "The court finds it inexplicable that defendants have spent untold amounts of time, effort and taxpayer dollars to establish the Hutto family-detention program, knowing all the while that *Flores* is still in

5   Ibid.
6   Ibid.
7   American Bar Association, *Defending Liberty Pursuing Justice.*
8   Ibid.

effect." The Bush administration avoided a final ruling in the case by promising to improve conditions at Hutto, but maintained its position that children in the family detention were not entitled to the *Flores* protections.[9] In response to the lawsuit and criticism over the restrictive settings at Berks and Hutto, ICE agreed to "utilize Hutto as a placement of last resort, improve the physical plant and its policies and procedures so it was less like a prison, professionalize the workforce, regularly review detainees' eligibility for reassignment to less restrictive settings, and adopt transparent operating standards."[10]

Soon after President Barack Obama took office in 2009, his administration discontinued family detention at Hutto, leaving only the Berks facility to house refugee families in exceptional circumstances. For other refugee families, the Obama administration returned to a policy of "catch and release" while awaiting removal proceedings. Concern that such families would abscond was not significant, because the data showed that nearly all those released with some form of monitoring will appear for their hearing.[11] Taking further steps to reduce reliance on detention and make ICE more effective, the DHS conducted a comprehensive assessment of detention policy and practices in early 2009.[12]

However, in 2014, just five years later, all this changed, and the goal of reducing reliance on detention largely disappeared. When the number of refugees from Central America spiked in the summer of 2014, the Obama administration abruptly announced plans to resume family detention. As the two tables illustrate, family units entering (usually a mother and a child) represent significant numbers. Once again, women and children ended up in immigration detention facilities – in New Mexico and Texas – that operate like prisons in every sense of the word.

These facilities are owned and operated by private prison companies. Involving private prison corporations is exceedingly problematic, as they are indeed in the business of punitive incarceration – that is what they know and do best. Companies like Corrections Corporation of America (CCA) – renamed CoreCivic in 2017 – also have a long-standing record of disregarding inmate safety and violating federal laws, and the ACLU reported rampant human rights violations at CCA's immigrant detention facilities even prior to the 2014 refugee surge.[13]

The immigration detention industrial complex has become a lucrative extension of the prison industrial complex. In 2013, CCA, which is publicly traded on the

9 Wil S. Hylton, *The Shame of America's Family Detention Centers*, NY Times, February 4, 2015. Available at: www.nytimes.com/2015/02/08/magazine/the-shame-of-americas-family-detention-camps.html?_r=0.
10 American Bar Association, *Defending Liberty Pursuing Justice*.
11 Hylton, *The Shame of America's Family Detention Centers*.
12 American Bar Association, *Defending Liberty Pursuing Justice*.
13 Taylor Wofford, *The Operators of America's Largest Immigrant Detention Center Have A History of Inmate Abuse*, Newsweek (December 20, 2014). Available at: www.newsweek.com/operators-americas-largest-immigrant-detention-center-have-history-inmate-293632. Am. Civil Liberties Union, *see below* note 16.

TABLE 3.1. Apprehensions by fiscal year at southern border

	FY 2013	FY 2014	FY 2015	FY 2016
Unaccompanied children	38,759	68,541	39,970	59,692
Family units	14,855	68,445	39,838	77,674
Individuals	360,783	342,385	251,525	271,504
Totals	414,397	479,371	331,333	408,870

TABLE 3.2. Family unit* apprehensions by fiscal year and country

Country	FY 2015	FY 2016
El Salvador	10,872	27,114
Guatemala	12,820	23,067
Honduras	10,671	20,226
Mexico	4,276	3,481
Totals	38,639	73,888

*Note: Family unit represents the number of individuals (either a child under eighteen years old, parent, or legal guardian) apprehended with a family member by the US Border Patrol.
Source: www.cbp.gov/newsroom/stats/southwest-border-unaccompanied-children/fy-2016

New York Stock Exchange, boasted $1.69 billion in total yearly revenue and $473 million in gross yearly profit.[14] If the United States stopped mandatory detention of immigrants, companies like CCA would suffer a major financial crisis. They have spent millions lobbying Congress and DHS for harsher immigration laws in order to build their business and increase profits.[15] This detention scheme has resulted in the commodification of immigrants, including children. For-profit prison management fosters a ripe environment for human rights abuses that violate a number of rights, including the rights to health, food, water, counsel, and even life; when CCA inevitably cuts corners to save money, especially women and children suffer degrading conditions.

The Obama administration's termination of the "catch and release" border policy and its renewal of family detention created tragic results. Most of the women and children are held in detention and are eventually deported. They are treated

[14] Investor Relations, Corrections Corp. of Am., Annual Income. Available at: http://ir.correctionscorp.com/phoenix.zhtml?c=117983andp=irol-fundIncomeA (last visited February 1, 2015).
[15] Chris Kirkham, *Private Prisons Profit from Immigration Crackdown, Federal and Local Law Enforcement Partnerships*, Huffington Post (November 26, 2013). Available at: www.huffingtonpost.com/2012/06/07/private-prisons-immigration-federal-law-enforcement_n_1569219.html. Azadeh Shahshahani, *The 'sunk costs' of a profit-driven prison system*, AlJazeera (May 29, 2012). Available at: www.aljazeera.com/indepth/opinion/2012/05/20125261128124469344.html.

like prisoners, confined to barracks, subject to room checks, provided substandard access to medical care, nutrition, and psychological treatment, and are not provided adequate due process.

Given the fast-track removal process to which DHS came to subject all northern triangle children and their mothers beginning in 2014, detention of these family units severely affects proper access to due process protections under US law.[16] Coupling immediate removal procedures with detention is wrongheaded given the vulnerabilities of this group that include "symptoms of Post-Traumatic Stress Disorder, cognitive infirmities, or other mental health impairments."[17] DHS now deports the vast majority of noncitizens without ever bringing them before the immigration court.[18] Fast-track removal processes, like expedited removal and reinstatement of removal, put deportation decisions directly in the hands of enforcement agents and often deny asylum seekers the chance to present valid claims in court.[19]

Many factors contribute to the due process failures of expedited removal and reinstatement of removal, including: (1) the fact that those processes rely on initial screenings by Border Patrol Officials who are often inaccurate in their assessments, ignore expressions of fear, and/or provide noncitizens with insufficient information about their rights and responsibilities; (2) threshold eligibility determinations for asylum and other protections take place rapidly in jail-like facilities many miles from major cities and pro bono legal and mental health resources; and (3) the government does not guarantee necessary legal counsel at its expense, preventing individuals subject to removal from a fair chance to present their claims.[20]

Ned M. Juri-Martinez is one of several students from the University of San Francisco School of Law Immigration and Deportation Defense Clinic that we sent to volunteer at detention centers. He noted the following due process problems at the facility in Dilley, TX:

> The frustration of due process begins immediately upon arrest. Once in immigration custody, the women and children are often separated and interrogated separately. One woman spoke of how she was forced to watch in horror from across the room while an ICE agent used verbally abusive tactics on her adolescent daughter to try to get a false declaration of having no fear of returning to her country of origin. At this point in the process, many women are asking about their reasons for coming to the United States. If an individual expresses a fear of returning to their country of origin, they are supposed to be processed for a preliminary assessment

[16] CARA Family Detention Pro Bono Project, *CARA OCRCL Complaint: Ongoing Concerns Regarding the Detention and Fast-Track Removal of Detained Children and Mothers Experiencing Symptoms of Trauma*, American Immigration Lawyers Association (March 29, 2016). Available at: www.aila.org/advo-media/press-releases/2016/cara-crcl-complaint-concerns-regarding-detention.

[17] Ibid.

[18] Ibid.

[19] Ibid.

[20] Ibid.

of their claim during a credible or reasonable fear interview before the asylum office. However, if the individual availing herself to the protection of US authorities happens to be from a contiguous country such as Mexico, such individuals can be removed immediately. The policy for Mexicans is a major due process concern for Mexican nationals with otherwise valid asylum claims.

For others, once in custody, many women spoke of being interrogated under freezing conditions without the presence of an attorney. Many women spoke of ICE agents lying to them to try and coerce them into signing for their deportation. The women are often told lies that they have no rights in the United States so they might as well go back.[21]

3.2. ARTESIA DETENTION CENTER CONDITIONS

In summer 2014, when the southwest border of the United States experienced a "surge" of Central American migrants fleeing violence, the Obama administration responded with swift policy changes. Rather than following standard practice and releasing those apprehended at the border from custody for removal proceedings to be initiated at a later date, ICE responded by locking up families, women, and children – most of whom were asylum eligible and fleeing countries where their lives were at risk. Although media attention was focused on the more than 67,000 unaccompanied minors, the 2014 surge included more than 60,000 women with children from Central America. The Artesia Detention Center in New Mexico opened in June 2014 in order to supplement the necessary additional family detention capacity that the Berks facility in Pennsylvania was unable to accommodate after the catch and release policy was abandoned.

Human rights violations quickly mounted up. Numerous violations were soon documented by organizational monitors and attorneys who visited Artesia. They reported poor living conditions, harm to children from prolonged detention, and due process concerns and obstacles to asylum seekers.

3.2.1. *Poor Living Conditions*

The poor living conditions at the Artesia Detention Center resulted in severely detrimental physical and psychological effects on detainees. According to Detention Watch Network, the detained children were often sick with fevers; many contracted chicken pox. They were rarely provided appropriate medication or medical treatment. The detained children were lethargic and inactive; they were not playful and were often very quiet the entire day. Some detained children hardly ate at all. Detainees slept eight to a room, with little room to exercise and nothing for the

[21] Ned M. Juri-Martinez, Legal Volunteer with the University of San Francisco School of Law, Immigration and Deportation Defense Clinic, Fall 2015.

children's stimulation. The institutional cafeteria food was unfamiliar to the detainees, who were accustomed to tortillas, rice, and chicken. Many children refused or could not eat, which worried their parents. One Salvadoran woman described the effect of detention on her two-year-old daughter: "She's been so upset during the two weeks we've been here that I notice her losing weight. She just won't eat."[22] Detainees were not provided with any process for reporting inadequate conditions or abuse in the detention facility. In legal terms, the facility did not comply with conditions set forth in the *Flores* settlement.

3.2.1.1. Misery, Suffering, and Dangerously Poor Health

Many attorneys and paralegals who volunteered to meet with detainees at Artesia documented the misery suffered by the women and children. Allegra Love, who previously had worked at the Mexico and Guatemala border noted: "[In my past experience] I had seen kids in all manner of suffering, but this was a really different thing. It's a jail, and the women and children [many under the age of six] are being led around by guards. There's this look that the kids have in their eyes. This lackadaisical look. They're just sitting there, staring off, and they're wasting away. That was what shocked me most."[23] Attorney Maria Andrade saw "[g]aunt kids, moms crying ... losing hair, up all night," while Lisa Johnson-Firth, said: "I saw children who were malnourished and were not adapting. One seven-year-old just lay in his mother's arms while she bottle-fed him." Mary O'Leary, an attorney who volunteered three times at Artesia, recalled: "I was trying to talk to one client about her case, and just a few feet away at another table there was this lady with a toddler between two and four years old, just lying limp. This was a sick kid, and just with this horrible racking cough."[24] On her first visit to Artesia as a volunteer paralegal, Vanessa Saldivar says. "I just stopped, and all I could hear was a symphony of coughing and sneezing and crying and wailing ... a big outbreak of fevers ... sent an infant into convulsions." Volunteer attorney Christina Brown saw "[k]ids vomiting all over the place, [p]neumonia, scabies, [and] lice."[25]

Another pro bono attorney, Helen Lawrence, who traveled to assist detainees in Artesia observed:

Most of the children had coughs, some had sores on their faces, one kid had a growth on his face. There have been chicken pox outbreaks here, leading to quarantines. Many of the children who are old enough to be weaned from bottles have

---

[22] Human Rights Watch, US: *Halt Expansion of Immigrant Family Detention; Problems with Detaining Children Evident in New Mexico Center* (July 29, 2014). Available at: www.hrw.org/news/2014/07/29/us-halt-expansion-immigrant-family-detention.
[23] Hylton, *The Shame of America's Family Detention Camps.*
[24] Ibid.
[25] Ibid.

regressed to bottles. Some moms reported their children were sleeping for distressingly long hours. I read medical records of a five-year-old reporting to the clinic
here that expressed that his level of pain was between 7 to 8 on a scale of 10.

We heard that some of the little boys have started to pretend they are ICE agents,
mimicking them at count (when the guards count the detainees to confirm that
everyone is still there).

Another disturbing observation from our team is how quiet the kids are in Artesia.
All day we are surrounded by them either in our consultation area in the detention
center or in court. They all seem so sedated and [have] low energy. I spent two days
working with one mother and her sixteen-month-old. The child's face was always
tear-stained and yet he never made a peep or fussed.[26]

In a declaration by attorney Daniel Rodgers, most of detainees he met in Artesia
(twenty-five to thirty women) were "in a state of despair," and the poor health of their
children was overwhelming. No medicine was provided for their sick children, and
the meat they were provided to eat was inedible. He also heard accounts of physical
abuse by ICE guards. The detainees did not have basic knowledge of asylum or
expedited removal rights.[27]

Ana, a Honduran asylum-seeker, and her daughter were held at Artesia for more
than five months. Ana's daughter got sick and lost weight rapidly. Her volunteer
attorney, Rebecca van Uitert, of Chicago's Mormon Church, said doctors who visited Artesia threatened drastic measures after seeing how emaciated Ana's daughter
became. According to Van Uitert, "They were like, 'You've got to force her to eat,
and if you don't, we're going to put a PICC line in her and force-feed her.'" Ana's
daughter "[S]tarted to cry and cry."[28]

3.2.1.2. Schooling

The *Flores* settlement requires that regular schooling for children in detention must
be provided. However, visitors who were given access to Artesia were troubled by
what they saw. For example, the mayor of Artesia, Phillip Burch, paid several visits to
the facility, but the classrooms were always empty. He "was told that children were
attending classes," but during his visits, he never saw "the children actually in class."
When members of the New Mexico Faith Coalition for Immigrant Justice, toured
the compound, all they saw was an empty school. They were told that the school
was temporarily closed. Detainees told their lawyers that the school was never open
on a regular basis. They recalled that for a few weeks in October 2014, classes were
offered for an hour or two per day, but were never in session in November.[29]

---

[26] Email from Helen Lawrence, Esq., October 22, 2014.
[27] Declaration of Bill Ong Hing (pertaining to Artesia conditions), August 17, 2014 (hereinafter "Hing
      Declaration"), paragraph 11.
[28] Hylton, *The Shame of America's Family Detention Centers*.
[29] Ibid.

3.2.1.3. *Flores* Violations

The various ways in which Artesia failed to comply with the *Flores* settlement were reported by the Lutheran Immigration and Refugee Service[30]:

¶ (1)   Of the Flores settlement, proper physical care and maintenance, suitable living conditions, food, appropriate clothing, and personal grooming items:
Children are held in restrictive, jail-like settings with little privacy and lack familiar, nutritional food, often leading to weight loss in children.

¶ (2)   Appropriate medical and dental care:
Most children are either unable to access medical services or lack adequate treatment

¶ (3)   Individualized needs assessments:
Children do not receive psycho-social or educational assessments, nor have they received any family reunification screening.

¶(11)   Segregation of minors from unrelated adults:
Customs and Border Patrol (CPB) has improved, but yet still routinely separates related children from their parents or adult family members.

¶(11)   Treatment with dignity, respect, and concern for the particular vulnerability of children:
Children in CPB custody are cared for by CBP agents rather than individuals with specific child welfare expertise. Treatment can range from special consideration to abusive treatment.

¶(11)   Visitation and contact with family members:
Children have inadequate visitation access and lack of contact with family members who may be looking for them.

¶(12)   Safe and sanitary facilities:
Numerous complaints filed by UAC's and their families on CBP violations relating to these issues.

¶(14)   Legal services:
Many children in family detention have an independent claim to asylum but lack resources to know their rights and lack access to legal representation. ICE has deported many families without allowing children hearings before an immigration judge, denying these children due process.

¶(24d) Right to notice of rights:
CPB routinely only has a copy of the English version of the I-770 form. The form is often inadequately explained to children.[31]

[30]   Lutheran Immigration and Refugee Service, *Flores Settlement Agreement and DHS Custody*. Available at: http://lirs.org/wp-content/uploads/2014/12/Flores-Family-Detention-Backgrounder-LIRS-WRC-KIND-FINAL1.pdf.

[31]   Ibid., at 3–6.

After voluminous complaints and a lawsuit, the Artesia facility was closed. Although ICE shuttered the Artesia facility in December 2014, a new facility in Dilley, TX was opened and the Karnes, TX center expanded soon thereafter. In July 2015, federal Judge Dolly M. Gee decided that the DHS's continuing policy of detaining children and their mothers violated the 1997 *Flores* settlement – the guidelines regarding when and in what manner immigrant children can be detained – and ordered the government to comply with the settlement within ninety days. The government had asserted that *Flores* did not apply to accompanied children. The Ninth Circuit Court of Appeals agreed with Judge Gee that the *Flores* settlement applied to all children in custody – including those accompanied by a parent.[32] And although the Court of Appeals disagreed with Judge Gee that the *Flores* agreement created an affirmative right of release for parents in detention centers, the Court of Appeals did not dispute her critique of the conditions faced by mothers held at the detention centers in Texas:

> With evidence in the form of declarations, Plaintiffs contradict aspects of the Defendants' rosy account of the conditions in the centers and contend that they are not acceptable. (*See, e.g.*, P's First Set, Exh. 12 ["J_H_M Decl."] ¶¶ 10, 11 ["There are no classes for my children here; we are told they will start the 29th of this month … We are not permitted visits without family members."]; Ps' First Set, Exh. 14 ["M_F_S Decl."] ¶ 9 ["My two sons have both been ill since we arrived in Artesia. They had fever and coughs for about a week, and were also vomiting and diarrhea [sic] … The doctor told me they didn't have medicine for them and that they should just drink water. More recently medicine arrived, and now both are getting better."]).[33]

3.2.2. *Lack of Due Process*

Women and children detainees in Artesia were subjected to serious due process concerns. First, their access to attorneys was severely limited. Second, the manner in which asylum cases were handled was extremely problematic.

3.2.2.1. Access to Counsel

Women and children in immigrant detention centers are not likely to know their legal rights under United States and international law, and accessing legal counsel is very difficult. Incarcerated criminal suspects in the United States have the right to government-funded counsel. Although the women and children in private immigration centers are detained in an environment that thoroughly resembles

[32] *Flores* v. *Lynch*, 828 F.3d 898 (9th Cir. 2016).
[33] *Flores* v. *Johnson*, July 24, 2015. Available at: www.documentcloud.org/documents/2179157-flores-order.html.

incarceration, they do not have the same right, despite the United Nations High Commission on Refugees' (UNHCR) guidelines providing that counsel should be available to immigration detainees.[34] Women and children in Artesia experienced many barriers to effective legal counsel. First, the facility was located three-and-a-half hours from Albuquerque – the closest major city. That meant close to an eight-hour roundtrip drive for an attorney attempting to reach a client at Artesia. But that assumes that an attorney was available for the detainee. The remoteness of Artesia created a huge obstacle in a detainee's ability to obtain legal representation in the first place, exacerbated by the fact that the right to appointed counsel is not a guaranteed right in immigration proceedings.

Human Rights Watch investigated the access to counsel problems at Artesia. Although detainees were given a short list of legal service programs that were hours away, none of the programs had the capacity to represent the hundreds of detainees at the facility. Fearing the prospect of having to go unrepresented, one Honduran woman worried: "I need to find a lawyer but it seems impossible. I will die if I am sent back to my country."[35] Human Rights Watch discovered an odd connection between perceived misbehavior, punishment, and the access to counsel. After children were accused of allegedly vandalizing toilets, guards cut off telephone access to all of the detainees in one of set of barracks for an entire day. Human Rights Watch complained: "Group punishment that affects access to lawyers and family communication is a dangerous response for childish misbehavior."[36]

Volunteer attorneys and interpreters at Artesia also observed problems with telephone access:

> Access to telephones was inadequate. Detainees were forced to pay for landline calls or forced to ask officers to make "emergency" calls, which were often denied, even for calls to consulates to obtain important documents ... Detainees had to ask for an officer's approval to make calls, but decisions on whether to grant permission were arbitrary and also varied from officer to officer ... Calls were often monitored – including calls to attorneys.[37]

Even when attorneys were able to be present at the facility, the attorney–client relationship was repeatedly challenged with red tape throughout the asylum process. The declaration of attorney Philip Smith described repeated requests to meet with his client prior to a hearing. However, the ICE officer took the client directly to the review video hearing room without affording the attorney time to speak with

---

[34] Human Rights Watch, *US: Halt Expansion of Immigrant Family Detention*.

[35] Ibid.

[36] Ibid.

[37] Expose and Close: Artesia Family Detention Center, New Mexico, Detention Watch Network, September 2014. Available at: www.detentionwatchnetwork.org/sites/detentionwatchnetwork.org/files/expose_close_-_artesia_family_residential_center_nm_2014.pdf. [hereinafter Detention Watch Network].

his client. Smith found the room, but the immigration judge said that the attorney could not appear, and he was escorted out of room. Smith witnessed numerous women and children who asked to speak with a volunteer attorney, only to be told that they were not on the list and got turned away. Smith (and attorneys in other declarations) noted that he was never permitted to have a cellphone at the detention facility. This prevented him from contacting relatives to confirm or request information. It also prevented him from contacting an offsite office to obtain file information in order to find out if documents had arrived, or to coordinate representation for upcoming hearings or interviews. He also was not permitted to have his iPad at the facility. This prevented access to online research or to his cloud-based client document management system.[38]

3.2.2.2. Credible Fear Interviews and Asylum Hearings

Advocates reported serious due process issues regarding the manner in which asylum cases were being handled in Artesia. Concerns were raised about how officials were conducting credible fear interviews (CFIs) (discussed more fully in Chapter 1). These screening interviews determine whether an asylum seeker will have her claim heard before an immigration judge, so the consequences of a problematic interview are substantial. Officials were, in fact, applying an erroneously high standard of review to determine credible fear.[39] Detainees often were not able to tell their entire story to the asylum officer during the CFI because the officer said there was not enough time to do so. Other women did not understand questions asylum officers posed to them.[40] Not surprisingly, problems surfaced with asylum hearings being conducted remotely via video teleconferencing, such as problems with understanding what was being said in addition to technical issues. Further, women were often required to talk about horrendous experiences in front of their children, resulting in a reluctance to provide details of their past experiences that could be key to their asylum claims.

One of volunteer attorney Daniel Rodgers' clients said that her CFI was conducted with her two young sons present; one child was a product of rape and she could not talk openly about what happened with the officer in front of her son. The attorney assisted this client in a review of the negative credible fear finding. A video hearing was conducted with an immigration judge in Arlington, VA. However, the

---

[38] Hing Declaration, paragraph 12.

[39] In *INS v. Cardoza-Fonseca* (1987), the Supreme Court explained the well-founded fear standard: "So long as an objective situation is established by the evidence, it need not be shown that the situation will probably result in persecution, but it is enough that persecution is a reasonable possibility" in order to qualify for asylum. In fact, "10% chance of [persecution may be sufficient to establish] "well-founded fear … [I]t is enough that persecution is a reasonable possibility." Hing Declaration, paragraph 7.

[40] Declaration of Kelly Miller (pertaining to Artesia conditions), August 15, 2014.

attorney was not allowed to speak during the hearing – a restriction experienced by several attorneys.[41]

According to Clara Long, a researcher with Human Rights Watch:

> A woman isn't going to want to discuss severe trauma or violence, including sexual violence and abuse, in front of her children. Compelling a woman to discuss that trauma in front of her children is not merely cruel, but could hurt her chances to get the protection she may desperately need ... In its guidelines on international protection for child asylum claims, the United Nations refugee agency, UNHCR, recommends separate and confidential interviews for all family members to give each an opportunity to discuss any independent claims for protection. UNHCR has also found that a lack of confidentiality could hinder the ability of women to fully access asylum procedures and recommended that "a confidential personal interview, that is gender and culturally sensitive, should be guaranteed in the asylum process, to help ensure access."[42]

Clearly, the awkward logistics imposed on families where children were able to hear their mother's testimony about personal violence was not conducive to bringing out full and complete testimony. The situation chilled the women from coming forward with the full story. A special, quiet, and trusting environment is necessary to hear full stories of potential or past persecution. Even the presence of infants can distract and affect the outcome of CFIs because of the distractions created to the mothers. Foreign nationals with little formal education have a difficult time communicating about technical concepts like "particular social group" (a basis for asylum) or even domestic violence.

3.2.2.2.1. CONSEQUENCES OF PROBLEMATIC CREDIBLE FEAR INTERVIEWS. By August 2014, the faulty CFI process at Artesia was clear: The fate of many asylum seekers was adversely affected by due process problems associated with the CFI, including a generally detrimental shift in approval rates for CFIs, and a specifically bad effect on trafficking victims. The Artesia credible fear approval rates dropped markedly. For example, from June 27, 2014 (when the Artesia facility opened) through August 7, 2014, positive credible fear determinations were made in 34–49.5 percent of the cases depending on the country of origin. In contrast, in the early months of the 2014 fiscal year, positive credible fear determinations were made in over 80 percent of the cases nationwide. Reviewing the declarations of attorneys representing clients in Artesia and reading sample CFI records revealed that the low credible fear grant rates were attributable to new standards or guidelines that were being followed.[43]

---

[41] Hing Declaration, paragraph 11.
[42] Human Rights Watch, *US: Halt Expansion of Immigrant Family Detention.*
[43] Hing Declaration, paragraph 9.

Attorney Lynly S. Egyes raised serious concerns for many of the women who had been ordered deported – who were actual victims of trafficking but USCIS had fail to identify during CFIs. Government interviews apparently failed to ask the right questions. Shockingly, the supervisor of detention said it was the detainee's responsibility to speak up and say that she was a victim of trafficking. However, in the experience of Egyes and others, it is quite rare for a victim to know the word "trafficking" and how that would relate to a case. Egyes asked about filing a stay of removal with the supervisor's office who repeated over and over that they would be denying any stay requests filed.[44]

3.2.2.3. Explicit Bias and Presumption of Ineligibility

In Artesia, ICE officers worked with a mindset that revealed a general presumption against the asylum claims of women and children. To volunteer attorney Shelley Wittevrongel the constant threat of deportation at Artesia was palpable. Consular officials from the northern triangle countries were on hand to interview detainees in order to get documentation ready for deportations. Sometimes women and children were removed from the dorms in the middle of the night and ordered onto buses for deportation. On one particularly chaotic day, Wittevrongel asked to see a supervisor. Officer Henry Davila came out and shouted to everyone in the room, "I want you to know that all of these people are going to be deported" and "our job is to get them deported and there's maybe one in 1,000 entitled to stay in the United States, and the rest are going to go." The explicit bias in this statement was apparent. Most of the women and children that Wittevrongel interviewed, in fact, had valid credible fear and asylum claims. ICE officials delayed attorney access to detainees. The children were required to attend their mothers' CFIs. This practice was extremely distracting and concerning to mothers who were dealing with complex questions and telephonic interpretations with frequently faulty connections.[45]

Volunteer attorney Stephanie Izaguirre spoke with fifteen women detained at Artesia. All indicated that they had requested to speak with an attorney prior to their CFIs, but were never told that there were lawyers available to consult with. Izaguirre offered a Know your Rights flyer to a woman to share with other detainees. But the woman said that she was "scared" to take a flyer and that she was not "allowed" to have a flyer. She said that an ICE officer had screamed at another woman who had tried to pass the flyer out to other detainees. Izaguirre and other attorneys learned that CFIs were often scheduled with no notice to the women or the attorneys who represented them. She observed a CFI that was conducted in a manner that was not conducive to her client's ability to explain why she feared returning to El Salvador. When she discussed her fear of gangs in El Salvador, the asylum officer seemed

[44] Ibid., paragraph 14.
[45] Ibid., paragraph 15.

impatient and began to rush through the interview. The client was not afforded the opportunity to explain. The asylum officer's demeanor throughout the interview was dismissive. When the client's daughter asked to speak and started to explain something, the officer interrupted her and told her he did not need to hear the story. The atmosphere revealed an absence of any sense of objectivity in the process.[46]

Attorney Elizabeth A. Ferrell raised the issue of posting bonds for detainees who wanted to be released – especially those who had demonstrated credible fear of persecution. However, the officer who was in charge of bond requests said he was not granting bond because he felt that the women and children in the Artesia facility were all going to be deported anyway. He was surprised that one of Ferrell's clients had a positive credible fear determination. He still maintained that it was his job to "move these people through here." Credible fear finding did not matter to him; he simply would not consider bond for anyone.[47]

Stephanie Taylor, an attorney who represented clients at another ICE facility in 2014, noted that she had "seen a huge uptick in the number of denials at the CFI stage" in the summer during the surge. More interviews were being completed over the phone. She also noted a lack of objectivity. Interviews began being "conducted in an adversarial manner, and many of the officers are openly hostile or skeptical from the start." Asylum officers used "Form I-213, which contains a record of any statements an individual made when apprehended at the border, to challenge credibility."[48]

3.2.2.4. No Bond Policy

Under the Immigration and Nationality Act (INA), unless a noncitizen is a suspected terrorist or has been convicted of certain types of crimes, the person is subject to mandatory detention and is not eligible for release on bond.[49] However, when Artesia opened, release on bond was not something readily available to the detainees – the vast majority of whom had no criminal convictions and who certainly were not terrorists. Vanessa Saldivar who first visited as a volunteer then returned to coordinate pro bono attorney assistance at Artesia provided this insight:

---

[46] Ibid., paragraph 16.
[47] Ibid., paragraph 17.
[48] Ibid., paragraph 18.
[49] The circumstances that trigger mandatory detention under INA § 236(c), 8 U.S.C. § 1226(c), includes persons who are inadmissible for having committed an offense described in INA § 212(a)(2) [e.g., crimes of moral turpitude (CIMT) and drug offenses]; persons who are deportable for having committed any offense in INA § 237 (a)(2)(A)(ii) [multiple CIMTs], 237(a)(2)(A)(iii) [aggravated felony], 237(a)(2)(B) [drug offense] 237(a)(2)(C) [firearms offenses], or 237(a)(2)(D) [crimes related to espionage]; persons who are deportable under INA § 237(a)(2)(A)(i) [has been convicted of a crime of moral turpitude that was committed within five years of admission] and has been sentenced to a term of imprisonment of at least one year; and persons who are inadmissible under INA § 212(a)(3) (B) or deportable under INA § 237(a)(4)(B) [involved in terrorist activities].

Upon arrival, we immediately began meeting with detainees and preparing them for their upcoming CFIs. For those who had already received a negative decision, we accompanied them to their review hearings before an immigration judge. Low and behold, the rate of CFI approvals skyrocketed, allowing us the space to develop and implement our release strategy. However, this is where we encountered the government's no bond policy.

After a credible fear was established, we began to move forward with bond hearings. We didn't expect it to be difficult to establish that women and children were not a flight risk or a danger to the community, but we were sorely mistaken. The government submitted 49 pages of evidence supporting their request for no bond for every single family detained in Artesia. Evidence consisted of declarations from DHS officials, media articles, and reliance of Matter of D-J-,[50] [a 2003 decision by Attorney General John Ashcroft directing that all undocumented migrants from Haiti who arrive by boat and are apprehended in the United States must be detained without bond while their asylum claims are adjudicated. The decision relied in part on the argument that the surge of Haitians implicated national security interests] ... [T]he following arguments were made [by the government]:

1. A "no bond" or "high bond" policy would be a deterrent for future migration.
    a. "According to debriefings of Guatemala, Honduran, and Salvadoran detainees, the high probability of a prompt release, coupled with the likelihood of low or no bond, is among the reasons they are coming to the United States. I have concluded that implementation of a 'no bond' or 'high bond' policy would significantly reduce the unlawful mass migrations of Guatemalans, Hondurans, and Salvadorans." (Declaration of Philip T. Miller, Assistant Director of Field Operations for Enforcement and Removal Operations.)
2. Allowing detainees to bond out would undermine the integrity of the border.
    a. "Allowing detainees to bond out would have indirect yet significant adverse national security consequences as it undermines the integrity of our borders." (Declaration of Philip T. Miller, Assistant Director of Field Operations for Enforcement and Removal Operations.)
3. These families were part of a mass migration and mass migrations are a threat to national security.
    a. "Violent extremists or criminals can hide within this larger flow of migrants who intend no harm ... and combating illegal migration and human smuggling requires significant HSI resources which necessarily must be diverted from other investigative priorities." (Declaration of Traci A. Lembke, Assistant Director of Investigative Programs, Homeland Security Investigations.)
    b. "In determining whether to release on bond undocumented migrants who arrive in the United States by sea seeking to evade inspection, it

---

[50] 23 I&N Dec. 572 (A.G. 2003).

is appropriate to consider national security interests implicated by the encouragement of further unlawful mass migrations and the release of undocumented alien migrants into the United States without adequate screening." (In re D-J)

Our volunteer attorneys submitted their own evidence and made several of their own arguments in support of an order releasing our clients on their own recognizance or with bond of $1,500, the minimum established by INA 235(a). Some of the following arguments were made:

1. Client is not a flight risk.
    a. Using Matter of Patel,[51] declarations, and testimony from our clients and their family members in the United States we established that our clients had family ties and support in the United States and this would help ensure that they attended future hearings.
2. Client is not a danger to the community.
    a. Attorneys highlighted that detainees had no criminal history and the average age of a minor detained in Artesia was six years old.
3. Matter of D-J does not apply.
    a. The project argued that there was no national emergency. In Matter of D-J-, the opinion applied only when there was a declared National Emergency and a mass migration. The National Emergency in Matter of D-J- concerned the use of Haiti as a staging ground for terrorist activity from Pakistan but in the case of Central American migration, there wasn't a National Emergency declared by the President.

It was a long battle but eventually we did start to win bonds. At first, they were upwards of $25,000 but we kept fighting and they got down to $1,500. We were also able to get some families released on their own recognizance. By the time Artesia shut down in December [2014], almost all of our clients had been released.[52]

3.2.2.5. Due Process Conclusion

By August 2014, Artesia's widespread due process violations were evident. Representation is key to adequate preparation for CFIs, especially when the interview environment is not conducive to speaking about past threats, persecution, or abuse. Competent attorneys take the time to explain credible fear and help clients understand the importance of raising certain subjects. Without this consultation, asylum officers and immigration judges may not elicit vital information. In the absence of representation, given the humanitarian purpose of asylum, detention facilities should create an atmosphere that is friendly, open, and warm. A hostile environment

[51] Int. Dec. 2491 (BIA 1976).
[52] Email reflection from Vanessa Saldivar, February 8, 2018.

to potential asylum applicants is antithetical to the nation's obligations and responsibilities under international refugee protocols.

Unfortunately, the situation at Artesia was chaotic and rushed. This environment was not conducive to gathering information calmly and fully. Asylum officers were rushing through interviews. Instead, they should have been encouraged to take the time to ask all necessary and relevant questions. Officers did little to develop a good, trusting atmosphere, conducive to direct communication with applicants. Applicants were not comfortable telling very personal stories free of distraction and with assurances of confidentiality.

Individuals who were victims of trafficking or domestic violence faced particular challenges. Often, they do not self-identify without relevant, sensitive, and searching questions aimed to uncover such abuse. The CFI outlines used by officers at Artesia did not satisfy those needs.

Applicants who expressed a fear that gangs had targeted them or their families or who feared domestic violence should presumptively meet the credible fear standard. Given emerging case law, a person who expresses such fear has a strong enough possibility of qualifying for asylum to be allowed to apply under CFI standards. Fear of gang violence and recruitment is definitely sufficient to meet the CFI standard. However, that was not the practice at Artesia.

The higher negative CFI determinations at Artesia in 2014 indicated that new restrictive guidelines were being followed that violated the humanitarian principles and purposes embodied in the asylum provisions of the INA.[53]

3.2.3. *Artesia Closure*

As a result of verified complaints about inadequate access to legal counsel, a policy of high bond or no bond for children and their mothers, inadequate detention conditions, non compliance with the stipulations of the *Flores* Settlement, and disparities in the average national rate of credible fear findings, the Artesia Detention Center closed in December 2014. However, the Obama administration soon opened an additional family detention center – the South Texas Family Residential Center in Dilley, TX, and expanded the Karnes County Residential Center in Karnes City, TX. These ICE facilities are operated by subcontracted private prison companies, with profit-driven models that subject the detained women and children to atrocious cost-cutting conditions.

3.3. KARNES COUNTY RESIDENTIAL CENTER CONDITIONS

In August 2014, the Karnes County Civil Detention Center (Karnes), previously a male-only facility located 100 miles south of Austin, TX, was renamed Karnes

53 Hing Declaration, paragraphs 20–4.

County Residential Center and converted into an immigrant detention center for women and children fleeing from Central American countries. The detainees were thereafter referred to as "residents," and the guards "resident advisors."[54] Following its conversion, Karnes held 531 women and children, but by December 2014 the facility expanded by an additional 626 beds, increasing its capacity to 1,158 women and children.[55] Despite the euphemisms, the Karnes facility continues to operate as a for-profit prison; the country's second largest private prison corporation, GEO Group, Inc. manages the Karnes facility.[56]

3.3.1. *Prison-Like Conditions*

An American Bar Association inspection team described Karnes as a twenty-nine acre "secure lockdown detention center, run with a rigid schedule, including set meal times, wake-up and lights-out times, and multiple counts and room checks during the day and night. The facility is not licensed for the care of children, and the guards are not trained to address either the needs of mothers or children seeking asylum or trauma survivors."[57] The Karnes facility guards, who are predominately male, "have free access to the detention cells and the women and children at any and all times, day or night."[58] A reasonable person confined to this environment would not likely characterize herself as a "resident," but indeed as a prisoner.

In her 2015 opinion regarding *Flores* and other class members' motion to enforce the 1997 *Flores* agreement at the ICE family detention centers, Federal Judge Dolly Gee highlighted several problems. For example, evidence presented by the plaintiffs demonstrated that the facilities are indeed "secure" in nature, which violates the *Flores* agreement's requirement that care facilities that house children must be non secure:

> The Karnes City facility is a large block building, which appeared to have only one entrance. To enter, my colleagues and I were required to deposit our cellphones in a metal locker, exchange our driver's licenses for visitor's badges, pass our personal items through an X-ray machine, and walk through a metal detector. We were then directed to a sally port, which comprised two heavy metal doors with a small room between. We passed through one door, it closed behind us; we were then directed

[54] Chris Sadeghi, *Karnes Immigrant Detention Center Softens Its Image*, KXAN-TV (July 31, 2014). Available at: http://kxan.com/2014/07/31/karnes-immigrant-detention-center-softens-its-image/.

[55] Ibid.

[56] American Bar Association, *Defending Liberty Pursuing Justice*.

[57] Ibid.

[58] Mexican American Legal Defense and Educational Fund (MALDEF), *MALDEF and Other Groups File Complaint Detailing Sexual Abuse, Extortion, and Harassment of Women at ICE Family Detention Center in Karnes City*, MALDEF (September 30, 2014). Available at: www.maldef.org/news/releases/maldef_other_groups_file_complaint_ice_family_detention_center_karnes_city/.

to display our visitor's badges to a guard behind heavy glass; the second door was opened, we walked through, and we reached the interior of the facility.

The Karnes facility is constructed of concrete block. A staff member stated the facility had been designed to house adult male prisoners ... In the central open area I saw neither a direct view nor access to the outside: It was effectively surrounded by the high block walls of the facility itself, denying those inside any means of ingress or egress except via the secure entrance I earlier described. Facility staff stated that children detained at Karnes have never been permitted outside the facility to go to the park, library, museum, or other public places. Children attend school exclusively within the walls of the facility itself. Detainees, including children, are required to participate in a "census" or head-count three times daily.

...

Defendants do not dispute that the facilities are secure. Nor have Defendants argued that this provision is not a material term in the Agreement. Plaintiffs present evidence that secure confinement can inflict long-lasting psychological, developmental, and physical harm on children regardless of other conditions ... Plaintiffs also proffer evidence that the children at [Karnes] specifically "are suffering emotional and other harms as a result of being detained."[59]

3.3.2. *Lack of Adequate Medical Attention*

ICE has failed to provide adequate medical care to mothers and children held in detention facilities. Immigrant rights organizations have submitted complaints to the DHS Office for Civil Rights and Civil Liberties (CRCL) and the DHS Office of the Inspector General (OIG) on these issues. The complaints include detailed, sworn declarations of several detainees supporting the medical care claim.[60] Three disturbing personal narratives describe Karnes' utter disregard for the severe physical and mental health issues associated with women or children, with incarceration itself, and with fleeing violence:

Yaniret

Yaniret is a twenty-four-year-old mother fleeing threats of death in her native Honduras. Yaniret was detained with her five-year-old daughter, Cecilia, at Karnes for fifty-two days. Yaniret and her daughter suffered with inadequate medical treatment and indignity at Karnes that left her feeling powerless, eventually resulting in self-harm. In early May, Yaniret took her daughter to the clinic at Karnes because she noticed her daughter had a strange vaginal secretion. The doctor at Karnes told Yaniret he would take a swab from the outer areas of little Cecilia's vaginal lips, but

---

[59] *Flores v. Johnson*, July 24, 2015. Available at: www.documentcloud.org/documents/2179157-flores-order .html.

[60] American Immigration Lawyers Association (AILA), *Deplorable Medical Treatment at Family Detention Centers*, AILA, July 30, 2015. Available at: www.aila.org/advo-media/press-releases/2015/ deplorable-medical-treatment-at-fam-detention-ctrs.

instead shoved a probe deep into her vagina. Cecilia screamed in pain. The same day, Yaniret and her daughter were taken to a clinic outside of the detention center. The doctor who examined Cecilia wrote a prescription for antibiotics for Cecilia's infection. Back at Karnes, however, Yaniret was never able to access these prescribed antibiotics for Cecilia. She felt very upset about how little power she had over the health of her daughter.

At the end of May, GEO staff members took Yaniret and Cecilia to a different outside doctor to examine her infection. Cecilia refused to be examined, crying and hysterical, because she was traumatized from the first doctor's rough handling and shoving of a probe into her vagina. In the first week of June, Yaniret spoke with a woman from the Honduran consulate who later accompanied Yaniret and Cecilia to another outside clinic. The doctor confirmed that Cecilia needed medicine and wrote a second prescription. Back at Karnes, however, Cecilia never received the prescribed medication. Several times Cecilia was told that she would be able to leave without a bond and several times ICE or GEO officials rescinded this offer. When Yaniret spoke with a journalist and showed her a diaper of Cecilia's secretion that was untreated, GEO staff members denied her food. Yaniret also spoke out when Congressional officials visited Karnes. Soon after this, she was assigned to another ICE deportation officer and her bond was set at $8,500, an amount Yaniret was unable to pay. As her daughter suffered in detention, Yaniret felt that "ICE and GEO were taking away my ability to be a mother." She was unable to obtain a new pair of shoes from GEO when little Cecilia's shoes wore through at the sole, and was forced to send Cecilia to school in socks. At one point, GEO staff members threw food at Yaniret. Feeling powerless and depressed, Yaniret resorted to self-harm. She fainted and was put in isolation in the medical unit. She was stripped naked against her will, wearing only a heavy green jacket. Yaniret asked the doctor to speak to her attorney and he responded that she could not talk to anyone. Yaniret remained in isolation, but could hear her daughter crying from a room nearby. The same doctor later referenced Yaniret cutting herself in front of her five-year-old daughter, understandably not something that Yaniret wanted little Cecilia to know.

Yessica

Yessica fled Honduras with her fifteen-year-old son and fourteen-year-old daughter to seek protection in the United States. In Honduras, a transnational criminal organization threatened and beat her son in an effort to convince him to join their organization. The same entity killed Yessica's uncle because he was critical of the gangs, cutting out his eyes and teeth when they murdered him. Yessica was then assaulted by a gang; collaboration between the gangs and the police put her at further risk.

Yessica never had an opportunity to undergo a psychological evaluation while she was detained at Karnes from October 2, 2015 to November 3, 2015. Yessica's fifteen-year-old son, having been beaten and threatened by gangs, also manifested symptoms of trauma, waking up at the detention center in the middle of the night with nightmares. Her son and daughter also began to refuse to eat while they were detained. Yessica received a negative credible fear determination, which an immigration judge later affirmed. Although a private attorney not affiliated with the CARA Project [Catholic Legal Immigration Network, the American Immigration Council, the Refugee and Immigrant Center for Education and Legal Services, and the American Immigration Lawyers Association, collectively known as CARA pro bono attorney program] attended Yessica's review, he never met with her prior to the hearing or prepared her in any way. On the same day that the immigration judge affirmed Yessica's negative determination, she almost threw herself off a balcony at the detention center. When she finally met with CARA staff just a day before she was deported, Yessica told them that she had heard voices in her head telling her to throw herself off the balcony so that she would be freed.

Although both Yessica and her son manifested symptoms of trauma, they were never treated for these symptoms; they also never received a psychological evaluation during their month-long detention at Karnes. They were deported back to Honduras on November 3, 2015.[61]

Detainees' health problems are not only often left untreated or improperly attended to, but psychological trauma also is ignored throughout the asylum hearing process.

Penelope

Penelope fled her native El Salvador after suffering domestic violence for eight years at the hands of her partner and receiving threats from a powerful transnational criminal organization. Penelope met her abusive partner when she was eighteen years old, and for years she suffered physical, verbal, and emotional abuse. Her partner regularly hit, slapped, and punched her, and routinely told her she was "worthless." He even beat her when she was pregnant with his child, injuring her back.

On one occasion, he beat her so badly that her head started bleeding, and since then she has had persistent migraines. On other occasions, Penelope's partner hit her so hard that she was knocked unconscious. He also raped her throughout the relationship.

Dr. Susanna Francies, a licensed clinical psychologist, conducted a psychological evaluation while Penelope was detained. She diagnosed Penelope with posttraumatic stress disorder (PTSD), chronic, with dissociative features, and reported that Penelope manifested the following symptoms:

> Significant avoidance symptoms, such as trying to forget about a bad time, avoiding people and places that remind her of a traumatic event, trying not to think of upsetting events in the past, and blocking out memories.

[61] Ibid.

Dr. Francies also reported that Penelope suffered "feelings of anxiety and shame," and never told anyone what happened to her. Dr. Francies explains that Penelope also suffered from dissociative symptoms of PTSD, which include:

> [F]eeling like you are in a dream, 'spacing out,' and feeling like things aren't real. [Penelope] also reports: not feeling like your real self, having trouble remembering details of something bad that happened, and feeling like you are watching yourself from far away.

Dr. Francies explains that prior to her arrival in the United States, Penelope never explained the abuse she suffered, "as it was a source of shame." Dr. Francies concluded that Penelope's:

> [C]oping style may have helped [Penelope] to endure severe ongoing abuse, but it has interfered with her ability to advocate for herself in the form of disclosure of her trauma history. This is a common phenomenon among immigrant survivors of abuse, especially when sexual abuse is involved.

During her CFI, Penelope did not feel comfortable disclosing the intimate details of her domestic violence history to the male asylum officer. In her declaration, she states that she did not understand some of the asylum officer's questions and had a hard time explaining herself. Unrepresented at the immigration judge's review of her negative credible fear determination, Penelope again found it difficult to explain herself. Penelope finally connected with CARA Project attorneys, who have since filed two requests for reconsideration with the asylum office, both of which were denied without any explanation.

Penelope and her six-year-old son were detained at Karnes from October 14 until their transfer to Berks on November 14. Only after attorneys filed a writ of habeas corpus on Penelope's behalf were she and her son released from Berks on November 24, 2015.

Penelope's pro bono attorney is submitting a third request for reconsideration in the hope that Penelope will finally have the chance to disclose the story that she is ready and able to recount now that she is no longer in detention.[62]

In another case reported by Andrea Guttin, an associate attorney with Human Rights First, a small child of one asylum seeking family held in Karnes suffered from a life-threatening brain tumor that went untreated while she and her mother were detained.[63] These complaints are emblematic of the DHS's failure to provide

[62] Ibid.
[63] Candice Bernd, *Call to Close "Deplorable" Private Detention Center for Immigrants Made, as Expansion Planned*, Truthout, September 23, 2014. Available at: www.truth-out.org/news/item/26358-call-to-close-deplorable-private-detention-center-for-immigrants-made-as-expansion-planned.

adequate medical care for the mothers and children held in the Texas detention centers.[64]

3.3.3. *Lack of Adequate Food and Water*

Detainees have reported that the food served at the Karnes center is "practically inedible" and children in detention have suffered "significant weight loss."[65] Furthermore, the fact that Karnes County, TX sits atop an active, fracking drilling site creates a major problem; this means that water used at the detention center has to be "heavily chlorinated," and causes stomach issues for the women and children.[66] ICE flippantly argues that instead of going to the cafeteria, women are free to purchase food and water from the commissary. However, this is not a viable option; detainees do not have the money to spend. Consider the fact that some women can work at the center and earn $3 a day, but a bottle of water costs $2.50.[67]

3.3.4. *Hunger Strike*

In April of 2015, seventy-eight women in the Karnes Detention Center went on a five-day hunger and work strike to demand better food and medical care; they also demanded release from the Karnes facility.[68] All the women had been interviewed by ICE officials and established a credible fear of persecution, but were either not given an opportunity to post bond for release or the bond amount set was unrealistically high. In a letter written to ICE, the women addressed the fact that they had been held for as long as ten months, and pledged to reject any detention facility services until their asylum cases had been approved and their families released.[69] The letter, translated from Spanish to English, read: "We have come to this county, with our children, seeking refugee status and we are treated like delinquents. We are not delinquents nor do we pose any threat to this country."[70]

In response to the strike, ICE officers took away communications privileges, threatened deportation, and even tried to intimidate some women by saying that

---

[64] American Immigration Lawyers Association (AILA), *Deplorable Medical Treatment at Family Detention Centers*.

[65] Sameera Hafiz, *No Place for Mothers and Children-A Dispatch from the Karnes Family Detention Center in Texas*, We Belong Together (April 26, 2016, 11.10am). Available at: www.webelongtogether.org/news/no-place-for-mothers-and-children-a-dispatch-from-the-karnes-family-detention-center-in-texas.

[66] Esther Yu-Hsi Lee, *Mothers and Children Allegedly Locked in A Dark Room for Protesting Detention Conditions*, Think Progress (April 5, 2015). Available at: http://thinkprogress.org/immigration/2015/04/05/3642880/karnes-hunger-strike/.

[67] Ibid.

[68] Ibid.

[69] Amanda Sakuma, *Hunger Striking Immigrant Moms and Kids Allege Retaliation*, MSNBC (April 3, 2015). Available at: www.msnbc.com/msnbc/supporters-allege-retaliation-against-hunger-striking-moms-and-kids.

[70] Ibid.

they would lose custody of their children.[71] Three families were placed in the "medical infirmary," which acted as a solitary confinement cell.[72] The medical infirmary was a dark room. The lights would only turn on when they were forced to eat.[73]

ICE denied that a hunger strike took place and maintained that solitary confinement does not exist in the family detention facilities.[74] However, according to a 2011 ICE handbook, "Any detainee who does not eat for 72 hours shall be referred to the medical department for evaluation."[75] The handbook also provided instructions that in the event of a hunger strike, detainees could be kept in isolation.[76] Alex Friedman, Human Rights Defense Center's (HRDC) associate director, asked GEO corporate officials about reports of the hunger strike and was told that there had been no hunger strike. Instead, the executive claimed that some women were involved in a "boycott of dining facilities."[77]

Later that month, three Central American mothers who participated in the hunger strike filed a federal lawsuit against ICE Director Sarah Saldaña and the GEO Group. The suit was brought on behalf of all the women who went on hunger strike and those who acted in solidarity with the strikers. In their federal complaint, Delmy Cruz, Polyane Oliveira, and Lilian Rosado alleged that they were retaliated against for protesting their incarceration and the deplorable conditions at Karnes.[78]

In seeking an end to their incarceration, the women also alleged that ICE and GEO Group officials confined hunger-strikers separately, keeping them out of sight during a media tour of the prison camp. Under the pretext that they had a court hearing in a videoconference room, the women were ordered to the room expecting to speak with an immigration judge. In fact, no hearing occurred; the women were simply confined to the room until reporters visiting the detention compound departed.[79]

3.3.5. *Sexual Abuse*

Within a few weeks of opening, on September 30, 2014, the Mexican American Legal Defense and Educational Fund (MALDEF) filed a complaint to DHS

[71] Lee, *Mothers and Children Allegedly.*
[72] Ibid.
[73] Ibid.
[74] Ibid.
[75] Ibid.
[76] Ibid.
[77] Candice Bernd, *Mothers Sue Prison Company, ICE for Alleged Retaliation at Karnes Family Detention Center*, Truthout, May 1, 1015. Available at: www.truth-out.org/news/item/30533-hunger-striking-mothers-sue-private-prison-company-ice-for-alleged-retaliation-at-karnes-immigrant-family-prison.
[78] Ibid.
[79] Ibid.

regarding sexual abuse of women in DHS custody at the Karnes facility.[80] At least three of Karnes facility GEO employees were suspected of removing female detainees from their cells late in the evening and during early morning hours for the purpose of engaging in sexual acts with them in various parts of the facility. Additionally, the sexual abuse included calling detainees their "*novias*" or "girlfriends," using their power and position to request sexual favors in exchange for money, promise of assistance with pending immigration cases, or shelter upon release.[81] Guards also allegedly kissed, fondled, and/or groped female detainees in front of other detainees, including children.[82]

Human Rights First and other legal groups filed similar complaints alleging sexual abuse, extortion, and harassment of the women and children detained at Karnes.[83] In spite of the huge number of allegations, the DHS Office of Inspector General (OIG) conducted a two-month investigation and determined that no sexual misconduct occurred at the detention center.[84] The problem is that the conclusion was based on interviews with guards and detainees who feared deportations if they reported abuse.

In contrast, a Frontline investigation revealed that few of the more than 170 complaints filed against guards by immigration detainees for sexual abuse over the course of four years were ever even investigated by DHS.[85] This raises serious questions about the Inspector General's finding in favor of GEO Group following his Karnes investigation. This also raises concerns that biased oversight perpetuates impunity among corrupt administration and invisibility of the plights of women and children in detention. Without guaranteed access to legal counsel, many detainees do not even bother to report their abuse. Additionally, lack of adequate supervision can result in sexual abuse of young children by older minors in detention who are troubled.[86]

Unfortunately, the Obama administration excluded immigration detention centers from proposed rules to comply with the Prison Rape Elimination Act (PREA); the administration's final PREA rules were released in 2011.[87]

[80] Mexican American Legal Defense and Educational Fund (MALDEF), *MALDEF and Other Groups.*
[81] Ibid.
[82] Ibid.
[83] Bob Owen, Seeking Asylum in Karnes City, Texas Observer (February 2, 2015). Available at: www.texasobserver.org/seeking-asylum-karnes-city/.
[84] John Roth, *Investigative Summary-GEO Group Incorporated Detention Facility, Karnes City, Texas,* Office of the Inspector General (January 7, 2015). Available at: www.scribd.com/doc/254974212/OIG-mga-010715.
[85] Wofford, *The Operators of America's.*
[86] Melissa del Bosque, *As Feds Lock Up More Immigrant Families, Abuse Allegations Grow,* The Texas Observer (November 4, 2014). Available at: www.texasobserver.org/growing-number-abuse-cases-immigrant-family-detention-facilities/.
[87] Catherine Rentz, *How Much Sexual Abuse Gets "Lost in Detention"?,* Frontline, October 19, 2011. Available at: www.pbs.org/wgbh/frontline/article/how-much-sexual-abuse-gets-lost-in-detention/.

3.3.6. *Lack of Due Process*

The lack of due process for detainees at Karnes has been evident as well. Inadequate access to legal counsel has been serious. Detainees who have valid asylum claims are not provided with sufficient information about the process for pursuing asylum. Interviews with asylum officers are rushed. Some detainees were threatened with separation of their family if certain documents were not signed, including waivers of hearing rights and accepting voluntary deportation.[88]

3.3.7. *Karnes, Conclusion*

By any measure, the detention facilities in Karnes, TX, are prison-like, and not conducive to family health and well-being. Inadequate right to counsel, inedible food, little respect for asylum claims, and sexual assault have been constant themes. The conditions are shameful.

3.4. DILLEY SOUTH TEXAS FAMILY RESIDENTIAL CENTER CONDITIONS

In December 2014, the Obama administration closed Artesia and opened the South Texas Family Residential Center (Dilley) as a replacement family detention center for women and children. Dilley is a fifty-acre secure detention facility located in Dilley, TX, seventy miles southwest of San Antonio. Dilley has a 2,400-bed capacity,[89] and is estimated to cost $260 million per year.[90] The Dilley facility is not only the biggest family detention center in the United States, but also is operated by the biggest for-profit private prison company, the CCA (renamed CoreCivic in 2017).[91] That's unfortunate. CCA previously ran the Hutto detention facility, which was shut down in 2009 due to its rampant human rights violations.[92]

3.4.1. *Prison-Like Conditions*

As with Karnes County Residential Center, the name "South Texas Family Residential Center" misrepresents the fact that Dilley is a detention facility. Dilley was founded on the premise: *If you come here, you should not expect to simply be*

---

[88] Bernd, *Call to Close.*

[89] American Bar Association, *A Humanitarian Call to Action: Unaccompanied Children in Removal Proceedings,* American Bar Association (June 3, 2015). Available at: www.americanbar.org/content/dam/aba/administrative/immigration/UACSstatement.authcheckdam.pdf.

[90] Carl Takei, *The South Texas Family Residential Center is No Haven. It's an Internment Camp,* The Marshall Project (May 21, 2015). Available at: www.themarshallproject.org/2015/05/21/the-south-texas-family-residential-center-is-no-haven#.zFmxID9C2.

[91] Ibid.

[92] Julia Preston, *Detention Center Takes Toll on Immigrants Languishing There,* New York Times (June 14, 2015). Available at: www.nytimes.com/2015/06/15/us/texas-detention-center-takes-toll-on-immigrants-languishing-there.html?_r=0.

released.[93] Officials claim that Dilley is more like a residential facility because it includes schoolrooms for the children, a doctor and dentist office, more lounge space, and a beauty salon where the detained women can earn $1 a day for styling hair.[94] However, a reasonable person held in Dilley is not likely to consider the facility as merely a place of "residence" while awaiting her asylum hearing, but rather as a place of incarceration.

The "residential center" is owned by a private prison, structured like a prison, and operated like a prison. A high fence and security cameras encircle the fifty-acre facility, that prevent the "residents" from escaping. As with regular prisons, visitors must go through metal detectors and follow a strict security process at entry. Three times a day, the detainees have to go through a head count; bed checks are taken at night frequently. The mothers and children are not fooled – they know that the guards are guards, not residential "supervisors."[95] Barrack-like structures offer no privacy; a single room holds as many as twelve people from unrelated families.[96] At 5:30 am, guards wake up the children by shouting and with lights. There are no toilets or showers inside the housing units, only communal restrooms.[97] Women and children detained inside the fences of Dilley are forced to share living spaces with strangers, line up for meals, share public restrooms, respond to roll call, and adjust to ever-changing rules and regulations with the guards.[98] Not much had changed, even on my personal visit to Dilley in December 2017.

3.4.2. *Lack of Adequate Medical Attention*

Instances of poor medical care at Dilley have been amply recorded, similar to the complaints cited at Karnes;[99] additionally, a formal complaint filed by the CARA Family Detention Pro Bono Project reveals cases of inept clinicians and substandard or inappropriate medical treatment at Dilley.[100] Further, over a two-month period

[93] *Statement by Secretary of Homeland Security Jeh Johnson Before the Committee on Senate Appropriations*, Department of Homeland Security, July 10, 2014. Available at: www.dhs.gov/news/2014/07/10/statement-secretary-homeland-security-jeh-johnson-senate-committee-appropriations.

[94] Preston, *Detention Center Takes Toll.*

[95] Takei, *The South Texas Family Residential Center.* After a Fall 2015 visit to Dilley, Kaitlin Talley, Legal Volunteer with the University of San Francisco School of Law, Immigration and Deportation Defense Clinic, stated: "*At Dilley, some mothers reported that the detention center staff would come into their room at night, turn on the lights and shine flashlights in their faces, and even yank the blankets off the sleeping mothers and children to count everyone.*"

[96] Ibid. (Takei)

[97] Ibid.

[98] American Bar Association, *Defending Liberty Pursuing Justice.*

[99] American Immigration Lawyers Association (AILA), *Deplorable Medical Treatment at Family Detention Centers.*

[100] American Immigration Lawyers Association, *Complaint: ICE's Continued Failure to Provide Medical Care to Mothers and Children Detained at the South Texas Family Residential Center*, American Immigration Lawyers Association (October 6, 2015). Available at: www.aila.org/advo-media/press-releases/2015/crcl-complaint-family-detention/cara-jointly-filed-a-complaint.

in the summer of 2015, ABA investigators heard from women and counted seventy-four additional instances of medical care complaints at Dilley.[101] Horrific personal narratives describe CCA personnel's apathy regarding the severe physical and mental health issues associated with women and children and their experiences fleeing violence.

3.4.2.1. Women's Issues with Lack of Adequate Medical Attention

The most common complaints regarding women's health at Dilley identify: (1) barriers to obtaining their own medical records; (2) excessive wait times to see a doctor – and if a patient had to give up waiting, often to put her child to sleep, she was forced to sign a declaration stating that she refused medical care; (3) inability to procure necessary medication; and (4) ICE's failure to understand the nature of trauma experienced by asylum seekers, particularly those who have experienced sexual abuse or assault, often results in erroneous credible fear determinations. Some specific examples of these problems are revealing:

Jessica
When Jessica was forced to flee Honduras, she had been recently diagnosed with breast cancer. At Dilley, Jessica went to the clinic to try to speak to a doctor about her medical concerns. After waiting for five hours, in pain, in a cold room, clinic staff told Jessica that the doctors were there to see the children and there was nobody there to see her. She did not receive any pain medication. That night, a staff member told Jessica that a specialist would attend to her the next day. The following day, Jessica inquired at the medical clinic about the specialist, but an officer and a nurse confirmed that there was no specialist and sent her back to her room without any medicine. The next day Jessica had a headache so painful that she was vomiting, but having lost hope in the clinic, she decided not to return to attempt to seek treatment because she did not want to wait in the cold room and be turned away again. Jessica suffered from vomiting for nine days, non-stop. When she first started vomiting, she waited to see the doctor for six hours without being seen. She returned, after seven days of vomiting, and waited seven hours to see the doctor. Jessica lost thirteen pounds since being detained.

Lillian
Lillian fled Honduras after a gang beat her ten-year-old daughter and threatened both of their lives. She arrived at Dilley with ten-year-old Rosa on June 3, 2015. After a six-hour bus journey and waiting eleven hours to be showed to her room, Lillian got on her knees to pray, but around 8 pm she fainted. She awoke in a hospital, receiving intravenous fluids and oxygen ... Returning to Dilley at 4 am, she was transported directly to the medical clinic, where she handed over the papers

---

[101] American Immigration Lawyers Association (AILA), *Deplorable Medical Treatment at Family Detention Centers.*

she received at the hospital. Lillian was returned to her room with sleeping medication and woke up later that day to see the doctor. Lillian asked the doctor for her medical records and the doctor told her that she "did not need them" because the medical results were "fine."

Lillian felt light headed and dizzy for the next five days until she fainted again on June 30. She awoke in the medical facility at Dilley, unable to speak or move. Lillian remembers medical personnel pounding her chest repeatedly and telling her to stay awake. For a week afterwards, Lillian's chest was swollen and bruised and little Rosa applied cream to her mother's chest.

During this same incident on June 30, in an attempt to give Lillian intravenous fluids, two medical personnel pricked Lillian with a needle seven times and laughed each time they were unsuccessful locating a vein. Lillian cried out in pain for them to stop. Despite her request for them to stop, the women continued and found a vein in her other hand and inserted a tube with fluids. Lillian was then wheeled on a stretcher to an ambulance, where the Emergency Medical Technician (EMT) immediately took out the tube and showed Lillian that the needle was bent, saying "look what they did to you," telling her that the two women did not know how to insert the tube. When Lillian was brought back to Dilley, she saw a doctor who asked for the hospital paperwork. The doctor threw the papers on top of a black bin on the floor by a desk. Lillian asked if she could keep the papers because she may need them and tried to pull the papers out of the bin. The doctor then seized the papers, placing them behind her computer out of Lillian's reach. Lillian explained to the doctor that she was still having severe headaches, the right side of her face would become swollen, her right eye red, her left arm felt like pins and needles, and her hand had become pale with purple spots on the palm. The doctor told Lillian she needed to see a psychologist.

...

Lillian's concerns for Rosa are mounting. Rosa has asked her mother why they cannot leave and asked "what if we die? Can we leave then?" Only ten years old, Rosa has told her mother that she will never forget this experience. Distraught and overwhelmed about the effects of detention on Rosa, Lillian went to the bathroom intending to slit her wrists with a razor. After this event, Lillian met for the fourth time with the psychologist. After disclosing her suicide attempt to the psychologist, Lillian and Rosa were held in isolation for three days. Rosa cried and begged to leave the room but the psychologist told her that she had to stay with her mother. Rosa was bored, angry, and sad in isolation and Lillian felt immense guilt for separating Rosa from the other residents in the facility because of her depression and suicide attempt.

A doctor visited Lillian when she was in isolation, telling her he wanted to talk to her about test results revealing a "black shadow" in the upper right side of her face, where her headaches originate. He explained that they wanted to do tests in the morning and would be drawing a lot of blood. Lillian asked why she needed tests when the other doctors had told her that the previous test results had been fine and the doctor said, "I don't know why they didn't explain the results earlier." The doctor examined Lillian and found extreme pain on the left side of her body, near her womb. He told Lillian that he would order a prescription for her and that the next day she would have blood drawn. No one showed up the next day to draw blood. A psychologist came the next day and inquired about the blood tests, and when the psychologist realized the tests had not occurred, she told Lillian the blood would be taken the next morning. Again, the next morning, no tests were performed.

Francisca

Francisca's appendix was removed on June 14 and she was transferred back to Dilley the same day ... Following the surgery, she was running a high fever and constantly vomiting. She sought medical attention at the clinic, arriving at 9 am and was forced to wait for five hours to see a nurse, who told her to return to her room and drink water ... Eventually, as her symptoms increased, she returned to the clinic and upon arrival fainted from exhaustion and sickness. She woke up in a bed and was told to go [to her room] and drink water.

Melinda

Melinda is a twenty-year-old mother who fled a lifetime of abuse in El Salvador ... Melinda arrived at Dilley with a broken hand after a gang kidnapped, raped, and beat her constantly for five days. She fled after the gang threatened to kill her after she sought treatment at the hospital. On arrival at Dilley Melinda showed officials her broken pinky finger, sticking out to the left of her hand. Officials told her that it did not matter, that nothing was wrong, and that she should drink some water ... The doctor did not examine Melinda, but looked at her hand, told her nothing was wrong, and that she should drink water. Melinda continues to experience pain in her hand. She is unable to move two of her fingers and they are bent in the wrong direction. She has extreme pain in her wrist and hand and has trouble sleeping and writing.

Sofia

About a month before she left Guatemala, Sofia sought medical attention for a urinary infection and a hemorrhaging ulcer in her uterus. The Guatemalan doctor advised Sofia that these symptoms could be an indication of cancer and directed her to return to for a follow-up visit. Sofia was forced to leave Guatemala before her follow-up appointment. When she arrived at Dilley, she told a doctor about her ongoing stomach pain, infection, and possible uterine cancer. The doctor told Sofia that they could not treat her at Dilley, took a urine sample, but did not examine her[102] ... As of October 2, 2015, nearly a month after her arrival at Dilley, Sofia remained detained and did not know whether she has cancer.

Suzanne

When she was detained at the border, Suzanne was not allowed to take a shower and developed a urinary tract infection. Although she was given medication to treat

[102] Although the population at Dilley consists entirely of mothers and children, there was reportedly no gynecologist on staff at STFRC as of September 30, 2015.

the infection, her condition has not improved. When Suzanne raised this with a doctor on September 25, she was told to drink water and continue taking the medication.

Brenda
Breda fled El Salvador because gang members shot her twice in the stomach and back. Following the shooting, she underwent surgery in El Salvador, but continues to suffer pain because of the damage to her ribs and intestines. On September 27, six days after her arrival at Dilley, Brenda saw a doctor. Although she told the doctor about her constant discomfort and intense pain, the doctor did not prescribe any pain medication or advice on pain management. Sometimes when her pain is very intense, Brenda has trouble taking care of her young daughter, who, in turn, becomes anxious when she sees her mother in pain.

Cristina
Before fleeing El Salvador, Cristina took daily medication, Enalapril, to manage her high blood pressure. Six days after her arrival at STFRC, on September 25, Cristina saw a doctor for the first time. Cristina informed the doctor about her condition and her need for medication. The doctor said that she would find out if the medication was available at Dilley and that a nurse would come to check Christina's blood pressure on a daily basis. As of October 2, Cristina had heard nothing about the medication, and no one had checked her blood pressure. When Cristina attempted to go to the clinic to follow up, a guard turned her away, even after she explained her situation, because she did not have an appointment. Cristina has now been without her medication for more than three weeks and is experiencing chronic headaches, constant fatigue, and blurred vision. She has difficulty taking care of her four-year-old daughter in this condition.

Sara
Sara fled El Salvador with her three children, ages nine, ten, and twelve after receiving death threats from a powerful transnational criminal organization, the MS-13, in her home town. Sara was raped by the brother of an MS-13 member; when her rapist died shortly thereafter, his mother blamed Sara for his death and vowed to kill her. Her family has informed her that MS-13 members continue to look for, and threaten to kill, her. She fears that she and her children will be killed if they return.

Sara was unable to disclose the sexual assault and subsequent death threats during her CFI due to the trauma she continued to experience. In her declaration, Sara explains:

I live in deep trauma. I'm scared of what could happen to me. I get nervous even thinking about it when I'm alone. I didn't share this information with the asylum officer because of my fear. I don't want to ever have to think about this again. I get really scared talking about it. I just want it to all disappear.

Initially detained on February 10, Sara received a negative credible fear determination from the asylum office on February 17. Appearing before the immigration judge on February 24 for review of her negative determination – during which no attorney participation was allowed[103] – was so stressful for Sara that it triggered a severe migraine. Sara was only able to talk about the fact of her sexual assault and the death threats after the immigration judge affirmed the negative determination. When she was finally able to disclose these facts to her attorney, Sara experienced another debilitating migraine.

Aware of these new facts, her attorneys worked diligently to obtain an independent psychological evaluation to submit as a critical piece of evidence to support her request for reconsideration by the asylum office. No fewer than twelve requests to ICE to obtain clearance for this evaluation delayed the scheduling of this evaluation, and attorneys were forced to submit Sara's request for reconsideration before the evaluation could be obtained. Eventually, Dr. Ricardo Castaneda, a psychiatrist, was able to evaluate Sara and diagnosed her with three psychiatric and cognitive conditions, social phobia, learning disabilities, "dyslexia and Dycaculia that are indicative of cognitive impairment," and PTSD. He specifically found that these "conditions significantly impaired her capacity to comprehend and fully answer questions posed to her by the asylum office and subsequently by the immigration court." As Dr. Castaneda explained, Sara's ability to recount her story to the asylum officer and the immigration judge were impaired by her mental health conditions:

More relevant to her current situation, a review of her history and her mental status makes clear that her initial accounts of her story were significantly impeded by a state of severe social anxiety in the stressful context of the court, where she reports having felt utterly frozen by fear, unable to remember not only her history of sexual and physical abuse but also the death threats made to her by the mother of her former abuser. Such failure to remember traumatic events is consistent with the dissociative symptoms of PTSD.

On February 29, Sara submitted a request for reconsideration, including Dr. Castenada's psychological evaluation, to the Asylum Office. This request was denied on March 21. Sara and her three children have now been detained for more than six weeks, initially at Dilley and now at the Berks detention center.

Nessa

Nessa and her eight-year-old daughter were detained on Christmas Eve 2015 after fleeing Guatemala to ensure her daughter's safety. Nessa grew up in an abusive household where her father regularly beat her mother, and at the age of nine, two of Nessa's teenage cousins started to sexually abuse her; the abuse continued until she was around twelve years old. Nessa was later abused and raped by her spouse and the father of her child.

Only after undergoing both a CFI (on January 5, 2016) and review by an immigration judge of her negative credible fear determination (on January 13), which

---

[103] This review took place in front of an immigration judge who, citing the Immigration Court Practice Manual, categorically prohibited the participation of attorneys during reviews of negative credible fear determinations. See Imm. Court Practice Manual Chap. 7.4(d)(iv)(C) (February 2016). ("[T]he alien is not represented at the credible fear review. Accordingly, persons acting on the alien's behalf are not entitled to make opening statements, call and question witnesses, conduct cross examinations, object to evidence, or make closing arguments.")

was ultimately affirmed, did Nessa finally feel able to share with CARA attorneys at the Dilley detention center what she had endured in Guatemala and her deep desire to protect her daughter from the abuse that she had suffered as a child. Dr. Allen Keller conducted a psychological evaluation of Nessa. Dr. Keller diagnosed Nessa with PTSD, explaining that:

Since these traumatic events, [Nessa] describes suffering significant symptoms of emotional distress. She continues to feel a profound sense of shame and humiliation because of these events. She reports continuing to be extremely fearful of men, and fearful of being raped again. She is also intensely focused on fear for the safety of her daughter. She tries to avoid thinking about what happened, and does find solace in prayer. Nevertheless, concern for her daughter's safety is a constant trigger for her of these terrifying memories.

Although Nessa expressed a preference for a female asylum officer to immigration officials before the day of her interview, a male officer conducted her CFI. It was not until midway through the interview that the officer asked whether she felt comfortable with a male officer and whether Nessa's eight-year-old daughter, who knew nothing about her mother's traumatic past, could stay in the room. As Dr. Keller explains, however, these conditions did not make it possible for her to share what she had endured:

It is my professional opinion that there is clinical evidence explaining why [Nessa] did not reveal critical details of her trauma history, notably a history of rape and sexual assault, during her Credible Fear Interview. Furthermore, as noted above, she was very uncomfortable talking about anything related to her sexual assault with me. As such it is unrealistic to expect that she would or should have revealed her rape and sexual assault during her Credible Fear Interview given the circumstances, including a male Asylum Officer.

Dr. Keller explains further:

Based on my professional experience of more than twenty-five years interviewing, evaluating, and caring for survivors of severe trauma, including victims of sexual assault and rape, it is not uncommon, even under the best of circumstances for individuals to not be immediately forthcoming about these details. It is my professional opinion that the circumstances of the interview were not only far from ideal, but were such that it is predictable that [Nessa] would not reveal this very private information during the credible fear interview.

Nessa submitted a request for reconsideration to the asylum office on January 17, including Dr. Keller's psychological evaluation diagnosing her with PTSD and explaining how her symptoms impeded earlier sharing of the trauma she had endured. Nessa's own sworn declaration, submitted with the request for reconsideration, explains:

I did not tell the asylum officer or the Immigration Judge about what happened to me when I was growing up or with my ex-husband. I was embarrassed and ashamed to tell anyone about the abuse I have suffered. This is the first time I am telling anyone ever about this abuse. It's been very difficult for me.

The request for reconsideration also included a sworn affidavit from Professor Judith Herman, explaining the effects of incestuous abuse, along with articles addressing issues of rape, memory, trauma, and stress.[104] Despite all this, USCIS denied Nessa's request for reconsideration on January 19. The very next day, January 20, Nessa and her daughter were deported.

3.4.2.2. Children's Issues with Lack of Adequate Medical Attention

The most common complaints regarding children's health at Dilley identify: unnecessary vaccinations; the fact that "drinking more water" and using Vicks Vaporub was the cure-all medical treatment regardless of the illness – be it fever, diarrhea, vomiting, or coughing; blanket diagnoses like "allergies" and "just a virus going around"; and weight loss. Other issues cited include inability to procure both medicine and corrective eye glasses for preexisting conditions. And children, like their mothers, experienced excessive wait times to see a doctor, and if a mother had to give up on waiting to put her child to bed, she was forced to sign a form stating that she refused medical care.

Time and time again, testimonials highlight that children were forced to receive vaccinations, despite the fact that many mothers carry proof of prior vaccination. Mothers and children would be awoken at 5 am and taken to a location where they would wait up to five hours for the vaccinations. Following the vaccination, many children became sore or ill from the shots, experiencing vomiting, high fever, and terrible coughing. Clinic staff would not do anything for an ill child following vaccinations. In one situation, a nurse followed up a few days after vaccinations to see if any children had developed fevers, because it turned out that the children had received an adult dose of one of the vaccines. One child, Oscar, was eating very little and developed a problem with his eyes. He cried and rubbed his eyes, unable to sleep. When his mother, Irena, took him to the clinic, the doctor said his eye problem was viral and had nothing to do with the vaccinations.

Other examples of medical care abuse and children include:

Melinda and her son
Melinda sought medical treatment for her son, who had recently turned four in detention, who was vomiting with a fever. After six hours of waiting to see the doctor, the doctor told Melinda that her son should drink water and that he should see a psychologist because there was nothing physically wrong with him. A second time, Melinda took her son, who again was vomiting with a fever, to the clinic. She was advised that she would have to wait for six hours, which she knew would only make her son sicker, so she left, after being forced to sign a form saying that she refused medical attention for her son. Melinda's son became so sick that he virtually stopped eating. She did not feel like she could take him to the clinic because

---

[104] Oliver T. Wolf, Stress and Memory in Humans: Twelve Years of Progress? 1293. *Brian Research* 142–154 (2009); Jenkins et al Learning and Memory in Rape Victims with Posttraumatic Stress Disorder. *American Journal of Psychiatry* 155(2) (February 1998).

she did not think she would get help and would only be told to have her son drink water. Her son wakes up from his sleep coughing. When she arrived at Dilley, her son weighed fifty pounds and now weighs only thirty-nine pounds.

Jocelyn and Luis
Jocelyn fled from her native El Salvador when gangs targeted and threatened her. She was detained at Dilley with her two-year-old son, Luis, for more than two months. During her detention, Luis had diarrhea for fifteen days that was not treated. Jocelyn sought medical attention for him for at least seven consecutive days and each day she was turned away after a six- or seven-hour wait. She only saw a nurse once and was told just to have her son drink water. Her son also had ball of flesh on his arm which was bleeding and secreting puss and the doctors did not do anything about this. At Dilley, her son cried from the pain in his arm.

Carolina and Grace
Carolina's three-year-old daughter, Grace, became sick with a fever, diarrhea, vomiting, coughing, and clutched her ear in pain. Carolina took Grace to the medical clinic, where she waited for more than five hours to see a nurse. The nurse examined Grace and said she looked dehydrated and like her eardrum had exploded. After examining Grace, a doctor concluded that she had either a virus or an infection that would go away in two to three weeks. The doctor prescribed Vicks Vaporub. Since that appointment, Grace has lost weight and is still sick. Carolina has not returned to the medical clinic because the doctor made it clear that they would not do anything to help.

Mariana and Silas
Prior to fleeing Honduras, Mariana's four-year-old son, Silas, experienced hair loss and a problem with his right eye. His hair loss has intensified in detention; his right eye is swollen, red, and painful, and tears continuously flow from that eye. On September 14, 2015, Mariana tried to get medical help for her son at Dilley. A doctor at the clinic did a vision test and told Mariana that Silas's problems were probably due to allergies. The doctor indicated further that a specialist would be required to treat Silas's hair loss. Another doctor told Mariana that the problem seemed urgent and that she should take her son to see a specialist immediately after they were released. Silas and his mother have already been detained for three weeks, and he is still not receiving the care that he needs.

Johanna and Andres
Johanna's four-year-old son, Andres, was diagnosed with anemia when he was an infant. In El Salvador, he received regular medical treatment. Upon arriving at Dilley, sometime on or around August 27, 2015, Johanna told the medical staff that her son needed assistance. As of September 24, 2015, Andres had not received medical care, despite Johanna's repeated efforts to seek help for her son. Andres complains of pain in his head, his lips turn purple, and he shakes from being cold, even in the heat of South Texas. He vomits, is constantly fatigued, and does not play with other children.

Suzanne and Emilia

Suzanne's nine-year-old daughter Emilia suffers from tachycardia, an excessively fast heartbeat. When Suzanne took Emilia to see a doctor on September 28, she experienced a four-hour wait. Because the doctors went to lunch before attending to Emilia, Suzanne missed her scheduled legal appointment and her children missed lunch. When Suzanne asked a nurse if she could leave the clinic to get lunch for her children, the nurse advised that the doctors were on their way. However, Suzanne and her children then waited another two hours. When a doctor finally arrived, he informed Suzanne that he would refer Emilia to a cardiologist, but Emilia has not yet seen a specialist and to Suzanne's knowledge, as of October 5, no appointment has been scheduled. Emilia continues to experience chest pain.

3.4.2.3. Psychological Considerations: Women and Children

Not surprisingly, study after study demonstrates that the negative mental health consequences of detention are particularly acute for children, asylum seekers, and other vulnerable populations.[105] Detention re-traumatizes survivors of violence,[106] and access to legal counsel and mental health services is sharply limited.[107] The risks posed to children's health by detention can be immediate and long lasting.[108] The March 2016 CARA complaint in particular highlighted the fact that many detained families suffer from PTSD, anxiety, depression or other emotional or cognitive disorders. The complaint demanded that the OCRCL (Office for Civil Rights and Civil Liberties) and the OIG (Office of Inspector General) conduct a complete investigation into the physical and physiological impact of family detention and mothers.[109] The plaintiffs wanted the investigation to pay "particular attention to

---

[105] *See*, e.g., Australian Human Rights Commission, *The Forgotten Children: National Inquiry into Children in Immigration Detention* (2014). Available at: www.humanrights.gov.au/sites/default/files/document/publication/forgotten_children_2014.pdf; Jon Burnett, et al. *State Sponsored Cruelty, Children in Immigration Detention*, Medical Justice (2010). Available at: www.statewatch.org/news/2010/sep/uk-medical-justice-statesponsored-cruelty-report.pdf; *see also* Guy J. Coffey, et al. *The Meaning and Mental Health Consequences of Long-Term Immigration Detention for People Seeking Asylum*, Social Science & Medicine 70, 2070, A430 (2010); Masao Ichikawa, et al. *Effect of Post Migration Detention on Mental Health Among Afghan Asylum Seekers in Japan*, The Australian and New Zealand Journal of Psychiatry 40, 341 (2006); Allen S. Keller, et al. *From Persecution to Prison: The Health Consequences of Detention for Asylum Seekers*, Physicians for Human Rights and The Bellevue/NYU Program for Survivors of Torture (2003). Available at: http://physiciansforhumanrights.org/library/reports/from-persecution-toprison.html (describing the traumatic effects of detention on adults).

[106] *See* Rachel Kronick, et al. *Asylum-Seeking Children's Experiences of Detention in Canada: A Qualitative Study*, American Journal of Orthopsychiatry 85, 287, A1788 (2015); see also Keller, *From Persecution to Prison* at 1638–9.

[107] Craig Haney, *Conditions of Confinements for Detained Asylum Seekers Subject to Expedited Removal*, Rep. on Asylum Seekers in Expedited Removal, US Commission on Int'l Religious Freedom 178 (February 2005). Available at: www.uscirf.gov/reports-briefs/special-reports/report-asylum-seekers-in-expedited-removal.

[108] CARA Family Detention Pro Bono Project.

[109] Ibid.

the capacity of mothers and children who are suffering from trauma and other psychological or cognitive disorders to have a meaningful opportunity to present their claims during the credible fear process."[110] Given the difficulty that mental healthcare providers face in accessing individuals in family detention, as well as the sensitive nature of these cases, the examples discussed in CARA's complaint represent only a fraction of those experiencing trauma in, and as a result of, family detention.

3.4.2.3.1. PSYCHOLOGICAL COERCION. The conditions at Dilley visit tremendous physical and psychological stress on detainees. The emotional pressure can result in decisions and actions that are essentially not voluntary. Ned M. Juri-Martinez, a second-year student at University of San Francisco School of Law, visited the Dilley facility with the USF Immigration and Deportation Defense Clinic in the Fall of 2015. He observed the following:

> The degrading and coercive treatment is clearly intended to psychologically tax women to their physiological brink with the hope they will abandon their claims, sign for their deportation, and spare the system the trouble of having to grant them their basic due process right to have their claim heard.[111]

The coercive effects of the environment at Dilley contribute to the overall problems of detention and the toll that the conditions place on the detainees.

3.4.3. *Lack of Due Process*

Due to substantial due process concerns at Dilley, the CARA complaint urged "DHS to significantly curtail its use of expedited and reinstatement of removal, which currently account for more than 80 percent of DHS removals each year."[112] Mothers detained with their children suffer from "symptoms of trauma or cognitive impairment," rendering the questionable procedures particularly unfair and detrimental. The case accounts collected by the CARA volunteers supported the allegations that "many extremely vulnerable individuals, including children, are deported without having a meaningful opportunity to present valid claims for relief."[113]

In addition to due process issues resulting from detainees' PTSD, logistical hurdles created other due process violations. At Dilley, Mohammad Abdollahi, advocacy director with Refugee and Immigrant Center for Education and Legal Services (RAICES) described how ICE arbitrarily capped the capacity inside the legal staff trailer at 60. He charged that the Obama administration's claims of providing

[110] Ibid.
[111] Juri-Martinez, Legal Volunteer with the University.
[112] CARA Complaint.
[113] Ibid.

detainees with access to legal services were "a complete sham."[114] Furthermore, indigenous detainees at Karnes reported that their asylum interviews were conducted in Spanish, even though ICE officials know that Spanish is not their first language.[115]

3.4.4. *Dilley Conclusion*

Although the Dilley facility was opened with the hope and promise that the humanitarian and due process problems of Artesia were remedied, unfortunately, the same problems persisted at Dilley. The prison-like facilities are rife with problems pertaining to healthcare, access to justice, sanitation, lack of education programs for children, and mistreatment of legitimate asylum seekers.

The conditions in Karnes and Dilley have caught the attention of some Congressional leaders. During the summer of 2015, eight House Democrats toured the Karnes County Residential Center and the South Texas Family Residential Center in Dilley. They were appalled and called on the Obama administration to close the two facilities, describing the conditions as "troubling" and likening the incarcerated families to interned Japanese-Americans who were held in camps during World War II.[116] The Obama administration did not budge. In 2016, three Democratic presidential hopefuls – Hillary Clinton, Bernie Sanders, and Martin O'Malley pledged to shut down the ICE family detention centers if elected.[117] However, both facilities remain in operation today.

3.5. OTHER CONSIDERATIONS REGARDING IMMIGRATION DETENTION

3.5.1. *Continued Detention and High Bonds*

Given the humanitarian purposes of asylum, asylum seekers should be released on minimal bond when they present no significant flight risk, no danger to community, and have no criminal record. However, when asylum seekers meet those requirements *and* also have no resources to post bond – which is often the situation in asylum cases – immigration judges should use their discretion to grant release on conditional parole, in other words without bond. The INA, 8 U.S.C. § 1226(a), which governs the detention of individuals pending resolution of their removal cases, expressly authorizes immigration judges to exercise discretion and release a noncitizen on a "bond of at least $1,500 ... *or conditional parole.*"

[114] Candice Bernd, *"Reforms" to Family Detention Centers Aren't Enough, Say Families and Advocates,* Truthout, July 3, 2015.
[115] Bernd, Call to Close.
[116] Bernd, *"Reforms."*
[117] David Nakamura, *Clinton's Stance on Immigration Is a Major Break from Obama,* Washington Post, March 10, 2016.

However, ICE and the immigration judges relied heavily on a deterrence rationale to not exercise conditional parole authority. Instead, they continued to detain families during proceedings even after asylum applicants receive favorable decisions following government screening interviews.[118] Individuals and families fleeing the violence in the Northern Triangle who asked immigration judges to review their detention conditions consistently ran into strict resistance based on a deterrence rationale. ICE attorneys opposed release aggressively and argued that a "no bond" or "high bond" policy was necessary to significantly reduce the "unlawful mass migration of Guatemalans, Hondurans, and Salvadorans."[119] So the opposition had little to do with whether the bond was necessary to ensure that applicants would appear at their hearings. The opposition revealed a bias against legitimate asylum seekers.

When Polyane Oliveira, one of the hunger-striking mothers at Karnes, was issued an $8,000 bond, the RAICES and family friends raised the money quickly because, according to Oliveira's husband: "We didn't want to wait too much [to pay the bond], because, you know, that's what [ICE does]. They set up a bond and then take it away."

Advocates were convinced that the setting of bond at unreasonable rates caused the attempted suicide of two mothers at Karnes. Lilian Yamileth, a teenaged mother, was found in a bathroom unconscious after she had cut her wrists. Yamileth's former partner in Honduras raped and threatened to kill her, and she feared that he would kill her if she was deported. Unfortunately, she was deported, and her advocates never heard from her again. Another mother attempted suicide after ICE imposed an $8,500 bond, which her family was unable to afford. She was subsequently separated from her child and isolated in a medical unit. Fortunately, her representatives were able to obtain her release.[120]

In 2015, the ACLU filed a class action complaint challenging the immigration courts' policy of uniformly denying requests for conditional parole in *Rivera v. Holder*.[121] The court held that detention without the opportunity to seek release on conditional parole from the immigration judge unquestionably violates the INA. Individuals who are deemed suitable for release, but cannot post bond, suffer continued, prolonged, and unnecessary detention. Release on own recognizance, as an alternative to monetary bond, ensures that indigent and low-income individuals, who become vulnerable to unnecessary detention based merely on lack of resources, are not discriminated against. Without this form of release, individuals who pose no flight risk or danger whatsoever remain detained simply because they cannot post a minimum of $1,500 bond.

[118] American Bar Association, *Defending Liberty Pursuing Justice.*
[119] Ibid.
[120] Bernd, *"Reforms."*
[121] American Civil Liberties Union, *Rivera v. Holder*, American Civil Liberties Union (January 26, 2015). Available at: www.aclu.org/cases/rivera-v-holder?redirect=immigrants-rights/rivera-v-holder.

3.5.2. *Licensing*

On February 21, 2016, the Berks County Residential Center license expired because it was not operating as a child residential facility.[122] Under the same reasoning, immigration reform advocates are continuing to push the closure of both federal immigration family detention centers in Karnes and Dilley, TX.

Court challenges have exposed the flaws behind the government's position in defending the family detention centers. The *Flores* settlement required that if the government holds child migrants, they must be held in a licensed child residential facility. Given what has become evident about the family detention centers in Texas, the efforts of a private prison company to depict its Texas family detention facility as a family prison with a day-care facility have been temporarily blocked by a judge in Texas.

Even though child-care licenses were granted to immigrant detention centers in South Texas, Travis County Judge Karin Crump issued a restraining order preventing the Texas Department of Family and Protective Services (DFPS) from granting a second license to the CCA, the company that runs the Dilley compound. This order followed news that DFPS granted a child-care license to the federal immigration detention center in Karnes, managed by GEO Group. GEO group, worth about $1.8 billion, has contributed nearly $1.5 million to various Texas political campaigns – Republican and Democrats alike – since 2011, and was awarded the child-care license.[123]

The government has not established a humane way to detain families – perhaps because detention simply is inhumane. The human costs of family detention are not acceptable. Before 2014, those individuals and families who were not detained under the "catch and release" policy actually appeared at their hearings. ICE used a case management system that addressed its interest in tracking asylum seekers and ensuring their appearances at hearings; inflicting the trauma of detention simply is unnecessary.[124] Detention and fast-track removal processing is also wholly unnecessary.[125] The families should simply be issued Notices to Appear (NTA) and placed

[122] Laura Benshoff, *Pa. Revokes License of Berks County Immigrant Detention Center*, News Works (January 30, 2016). Available at: www.newsworks.org/index.php/local/harrisburg/90588-pa-revokes-license-of-berks-county-immigrant-detention-center.
[123] Mary Ignatius, et al., *Immigrant Detention Centers Are Not Day Cares*, Truthout, May 28, 2016. Available at: www.truth-out.org/opinion/item/36183-immigration-detention-centers-are-not-day-cares.
[124] CARA Family Detention Pro Bono Project.
[125] Brief of Immigrants Rights Organizations as *Amici Curiae* in Support of Plaintiffs-Appellees and in Support of Affirmance of District Court Judgement, *Flores v. Lynch*, No. 15-56434 (9th Cir. February 23, 2016) (explaining that detention is not required in summary removal proceedings and that prior to the summer of 2014, the government processed claims of accompanied minors and their mothers without the use of summary proceedings). Available at: www.aila.org/infonet/ca9-amicus-brief-in-flores.

into regular removal proceedings using the same scheduling and processing as other allegedly deportable immigrants; that was the process prior to 2014.[126]

3.6. INTERNATIONAL HUMAN RIGHTS CONSIDERATIONS

3.6.1. *Background*

As we will see more fully in Chapter 4, Latin American women and children of the Northern Triangle are entering the United States through Mexico to escape violent situations at home.

> In [Central America], the most violent region in the world and with the highest levels of child homicide, the protection of children from violence is put at risk on a daily basis; and it is compounded by high levels of inequality and social exclusion, lack of opportunities, the widespread use of arms, the presence of organized crime and gangs, and a culture of impunity. For many children [in this region], life is defined by two words: fear and pain.[127]

When these children reach the United States and get detained, they are often put into private for-profit immigrant detention centers, where many will continue to suffer both tangible and structural violence.

Pursuant to the General Assembly's resolution 56/138, an in-depth study on violence against children addressed alternative care institutions and correctional detention facilities.[128] The study found that the impact of institutionalization goes beyond the experience by children of violence, and that long-term effects can include severe developmental delays, disability, and irreversible psychological damage. Private detention centers that house migrant children – even those with their mothers – are neither alternative care institutions nor correctional in nature; they comprise a unique set of attributes that require safeguards for protecting children from violence. This under-recognized distinction contributes to the invisibility of violence endured by these children.

The United Nations Committee Against Torture expressed grave concern about the use and expansion of family detention for undocumented migrant families with

---

[126] In regular removal proceedings, legal counsel is permitted to play an active role and immigration judges have authority to prescribe safeguards where necessary to protect an individual's due process rights. *See Matter of* M-A-M-,25 IandN Dec. 474 (BIA 2011) (holding that if an individual Respondent in immigration court proceedings manifest indicia of incompetency, the immigration judge must undertake an inquiry to determine whether the Respondent is competent for the purposes of immigration proceedings, and, if not, the immigration judge must evaluate appropriate safeguards).

[127] U.N. Special Rep. of the Sec'y-Gen. on Violence Against Children, SRSG Marta Santos Pais calls for the effective protection of children from violence in the Americas (December 15, 2014). Available at: http://srsg.violenceagainstchildren.org/story/2014-12-15_1201.

[128] Independent expert for the U.N. study on violence against children, *Rep. of the independent expert for the U.N. study on violence against children*, U.N. Doc. A/61/299 (August 29, 2006).

children who have reached the United States.[129] The Committee was highly critical of the prison-like settings for children. Along with expressing serious concern about the substandard conditions of the facilities, the Committee was also troubled by the use of solitary confinement and evidence of sexual violence committed by staff and other detainees. In its Concluding Observations, the Committee recommended that the United States halt the expansion of family detention and progressively eliminate its use completely.[130]

3.6.2. *Legal Standards Governing Immigration Detention*

3.6.2.1. Arbitrary Deprivation of Liberty

Children in immigrant detention centers are being arbitrarily deprived of their liberty, in violation of the Convention on the Rights of the Child (CRC) and other treaties. Although the United States is not party to the CRC, the treaty's provisions have risen to the level of customary international law which apply to all nations. Customary international law results from a "general and consistent practice of states followed by them from a sense of legal obligations."[131] As such, the United States is obligated to act generally and consistently with these provisions.[132] The United Nations Committee on the Rights of the Child has stated:

> In application of article 37 of the Convention and the principle of the best interests of the child, unaccompanied or separated children should not, as a general rule, be detained. Detention cannot be justified solely on the basis of the child being unaccompanied or separated, or on their migratory or residence status, or lack thereof.[133]

According to the Global Survey by the Special Representative of the Secretary General on violence against children, thousands of children – including those detained by the United States – are deprived of their liberty as a first option rather than the last.[134] These children do not belong in prison-like facilities that publicly criminalize them and also make them feel as if they are criminals. They pose no security risk, and are especially vulnerable. They arrive to countries traumatized

---

[129] U.N. Comm. Against Torture, Concluding observations on the combined third to fifth periodic reports of the U.S., ¶ 9, 1276-1277th Sess., November 20, 2014, CAT/C/USA/CO/3-5 (December 19, 2014).

[130] Ibid.

[131] American Law Institute, *Restatement of the Law, Third, the Foreign Relations Law of the United States.* St. Paul, MN: American Law Institute Publishers, 1987. §102(2).

[132] Silke Sahl, *Researching Customary International Law, State Practice and the Pronouncements of States regarding International Law*, NYULawGlobal.org, June/July 2007.

[133] U.N. Comm. on the Rights of the Child, General Comment No. 6: Treatment of Unaccompanied and Separated Children Outside their Country of Origin, ¶ 18, 39th Sess., May 17–June 3, 2005, CRC/GC/2005/6 (September 1, 2005).

[134] U.N. Spec. Rep. of the Secretary General on violence against children, *Toward a world free from violence; Global survey on violence against children*, ¶40, (October 2013).

from the violence they are seeking to escape, and from the trauma of their journey to the border. Similarly, Human Rights Watch notes:

> Jailing immigrant children is hardly in their best interest. Cost-effective, humane, and reliable alternatives to detention are used around the world and have been found to benefit government and the community, as well as children.[135]

Alternatives can include electronic monitoring or supervised release, in which the head of the family checks in regularly with authorities.[136]

In 2007, the ACLU reached a landmark settlement with ICE, which was the result of lawsuits brought on behalf of twenty-six immigrant children detained with their parents at Hutto Center, a CCA facility that was shut down in 2009. Prior to this settlement, children were required to wear prison uniforms, were allowed very little time outdoors, and guards would discipline children by threatening to separate them from their parents. Hutto also had employed a "count system," which forced families to stay in their cells for twelve hours a day.[137]

3.6.2.1.1. STRUCTURAL VIOLENCE AND DISCRIMINATION. In the United States, immigration charges now make up half of all federal arrests, and drug offenses rank second at 15 percent.[138] The United States' "war on drugs" normalized the prison industrial complex and violent police actions toward African Americans in urban inner cities. Now, the post-9/11 "war on terror" is normalizing the immigration detention industrial complex and violent police action toward Latino migrants at the United States–Mexico border. What began as a heightened focus on detaining undocumented immigrants in the interest of curbing terrorism quickly transformed into mass incarceration regardless of whether or not those being detained actually posed a threat to national security. And just as African American children have been absorbed into the former scheme, Latin American immigrant children are now within the latter. Creating immigrant detention centers meant for children normalizes and condones a framework of violence and discrimination against migrant children.

These children suffer structural violence – chronic, historically entrenched political-economic oppression, and social inequality. They face symbolic violence, the internalized humiliations and legitimations of inequality and hierarchy. They experience everyday violence, the daily practices of violence on a micro-interactional level: interpersonal, domestic, and delinquent. In short, under this

---

[135] Human Rights Watch, US: *Halt Expansion of Immigrant Family Detention*.
[136] Ibid.
[137] ACLU, *ACLU Challenges Prison-Like Conditions at Hutto Detention Center* (March 6, 2007). Available at: www.aclu.org/immigrants-rights-racial-justice-prisoners-rights/aclu-challenges-prison-conditions-hutto-detention.
[138] Mark Motivans, Fed. Justice Statistics, Bulletin, January 2015 (US Dept. of Justice Bureau of Justice Statistics).

regime, the United States at the very least has created an "experience that normal-izes petty brutalities and terror at the community level and creates a common sense or ethos of violence."[139] Normalizing this violence of detention concurrently nor-malizes discrimination, in violation of Convention on the Elimination of all forms of Racial Discrimination.

3.6.2.2. Degrading Treatment

3.6.2.2.1. HEALTH CONCERNS. Poorly maintained private facilities foster substand-ard living conditions that threaten the health of those in detention. The ACLU has reported CCA detainee complaints of temperature extremes, overcrowding, facili-ties running out of hygiene products, and detainees being given used underwear.[140] Food was spoiled, meager, and provided at irregular times; the water was non-potable.[141] At Hutto, children with skin infections were not treated until they bled from the rash.[142] One child who was frequently vomiting was not allowed medi-cal attention unless the staff saw the vomit.[143] Detainees experienced unreasonable delays in receiving medical care and in the case of people with mental disabilities, punitive rather than care-oriented treatment was given. Lack of adequate medical care also caused unnecessary deaths.[144]

3.6.2.2.2. SEXUAL ABUSE. Sexual abuse of detainees occurring in immigration facil-ities has been widely reported. Women in Karnes, the family detention center owned and operated by the private prison corporation GEO Group, reported ongoing and substantial sexual abuse by male staff.[145] The DHS inspector general stepped in, but cleared Karnes of all allegations.[146] However, an investigation by Frontline revealed that few of the more than 170 complaints filed against guards by immigration detainees for sexual abuse over the course of four years were ever even investigated by DHS,[147] questioning the DHS investigation's finding in favor of GEO. This raises

[139] Philippe Bourgois, The Continuum of Violence in War and Peace: Post-Cold War Lessons from El Salvador, in *Violence in War and Peace*, 425–6 (Nancy Scheper-Hughes and Philippe Bourgois eds., Blackwell Pub., 2004).
[140] Am. Civil Liberties Union *Prisoners of Profit: Immigrants and Detention in Georgia* (2012) (hereinafter "Am. Civil Liberties Union").
[141] Ibid.
[142] Crossing the Border: Immigrants in Detention and Victims of Trafficking: Hearing Before the Subcomm. on Border, Mar., and Global Counterterrorism of the Comm. on Homeland Sec., H.R., 110th Cong., 110–16 (2007).
[143] Ibid.
[144] Am. Civil Liberties Union, at 27, 108–9.
[145] Marisa Taylor, *Immigrant Women allege sexual abuse at detention center*, AlJazeera America (October 9, 2014). Available at: http://america.aljazeera.com/articles/2014/10/9/family-detentioncenterabuse.html.
[146] Julia Preston, *Report Finds No Evidence of Abuse at Immigration Center in Texas*, New York Times (February 6, 2015). Available at: www.nytimes.com/2015/02/07/us/report-finds-no-evidence-of-sexual-abuse-at-texas-immigration-detention-center.html.
[147] Wofford, *The Operators of America's*.

concerns that biased oversight perpetuates impunity among corrupt administration and invisibility of the plights of women and children in detention. Without guaranteed access to legal counsel, many detainees do not even bother to report their abuse. Children's status as an especially vulnerable group at particularly high risk for sexual abuse also is concerning. The lack of adequate supervision and oversight at these facilities can result in sexual abuse of young children by troubled older minors in detention.[148]

3.6.2.2.3. IMMIGRATION WORKERS. The Human Rights Council has called upon States to ensure proper training of all persons working with children, including prison staff, immigration and border control agents. This includes persons working on legislation and policies relevant to the rights of the child, including anti-discrimination policies, alternatives to detention, and child-sensitive counseling and communication skills.[149] Relatedly, the Organization of American States Declaration on violence and exploitation of children calls for the reduction of secondary victimization. The focus is on behaviors and attitudes of social service providers who are insensitive or who tend to engage in victim-blaming, and actions that traumatize victims of violence who are being served by these agencies.[150]

These issues are relevant to US immigration family detention centers run by private companies. For example, CCA's record of abusive treatment is not entirely confined to its detainees, but also extends to its employees. CCA cuts corners to increase profits by maintaining dangerously low staff-to-detainee ratios, reducing employee benefits and salaries, and not providing adequate staff training.[151] Many employees have sued CCA over issues such as unreasonably long work hours, no overtime compensation, poor pay, denial of meal breaks, and forced work with no compensation.[152] The ACLU has reported verbal and physical abuse of detainees and retaliatory behavior from guards, including placing detainees in segregation.[153] This may be a reflection of CCA's mismanagement of its own workers. In light of CCA's negligence in training and supervision of its employees, the fact that misconduct and violence often ensue is not surprising.

---

[148] del Bosque, *As Feds Lock Up More Immigrant Families*.

[149] Human Rights Council Res. 25/6, Rights of the child: access to justice for children, 25th Sess., March 3–28, 2014, A/HRC/RES/25/6, ¶ 6 (April 14, 2014).

[150] Org. of Am. States [OAS], Declaration on violence against and exploitation of children, 2nd Plenary Sess, June 4, 2014, OAS Doc. AG/DEC. 76 (XLIV-O/14) ¶ 12 (June 10, 2014). Available at: www.oas.org/en/sla/docs/AG06712E04.pdf.

[151] Grass Roots Leadership, The Dirty Thirty: Nothing to Celebrate About 30 Years of Corrections Corp. of America 3 (2013).

[152] Ibid.

[153] Am. Civil Liberties Union.

3.6.2.3. Right to Counsel

Children in immigrant detention centers are not likely to know their rights under United States and international law, and accessing legal counsel is difficult for them. Incarcerated criminal suspects in the United States have the right to government-funded counsel. Although children in private immigration centers are detained in an environment that thoroughly resembles criminal incarceration, they do not have the right to appointed counsel, despite UNHCR's guidelines that counsel should be available to immigration detainees.[154] The remoteness of many immigrant detention centers in the southwestern borderlands makes it difficult for pro-bono attorneys to reach the facilities with any kind of frequency or longevity.[155] Most of the children are forced to navigate the convoluted US legal system on their own, a system that US-born English-speaking adults find difficult to comprehend.

US courts of appeals have repeatedly recognized that an immigrant facing removal from the United States should be allowed sufficient time to find and hire an attorney. The "rocket docket," however, impedes upon this right. The rocket docket is a product of the US Department of Justice's attempt to deal with the large number of Central American migrants, many of whom are unaccompanied minors, fleeing their homes to seek refuge. US immigration courts were directed to "fast track" the cases of the more recent arrivals. The problem with this system is that those individuals who are being fast-tracked do not have enough time to obtain effective legal counsel.

Statistics demonstrate that children who have legal representation are far more likely to be awarded asylum than those who are forced to represent themselves.[156] The rocket docket also means that these non criminal children's cases are prioritized over all other immigration cases, thus delaying cases that are already pending. Judge Dana Leigh Marks, President of the National Association of Immigration Judges complained that interrupting the rest of the docket to fast track the removal of these children made little sense because their claims would require more, rather than less, time.[157]

3.7. CONCLUSION

The negative health and psychological effects of detention on children and families are obvious. After conducting a series of interviews with women and children who had passed their CFIs and had just been released from detention facilities, the

---

[154] Human Rights Watch, US: *Halt Expansion of Immigrant Family Detention.*

[155] Hylton, *The Shame of America's Family Detention Camps.*

[156] Jayashri Srikantiah, *The Immigration Rocket Docket: Understanding the Due Process Implications,* Stanford Lawyer (August 15, 2014). Available at: https://stanfordlawyer.law.stanford.edu/2014/08/the-immigration-rocket-docket-understanding-the-due-process-implications/.

[157] Ibid.

Unitarian Universalist Service Committee had little trouble identifying necessary reforms. Its psychological study published in 2015 called for an end to family detention, the decriminalization of the asylum process, and mandated trauma training for DHS and ICE agents, border patrol, prison contractors, and attorneys alike.[158]

The report found that the conditions in detention centers not only contributed to mental illness and trauma, but are also correlated to children's physical sickness, such as weight loss, and complications from inadequate treatment of fevers, burns, and rashes. The study points to evidence that detaining children can result in long-term health problems caused by extreme anxiety, self-harm, depression, suicidal thoughts, regressions in development, PTSD, weight loss, and other illnesses. Most of the mother and children asylum seekers in detention had already survived past traumas, but detention was demonstrated to exacerbate the fear, isolation, hopelessness, and anxiety from which they already were suffering. After dangerous journeys in which many face violence and exploitation, these vulnerable migrants are subjected to humiliation and made to feel like criminals by Border Patrol and ICE agents, and their internalization of these terrifying encounters "leaves them with lasting psychological scars."[159]

The use of family detention centers needs to end. The Obama administration's 2014 decision to start detaining families apprehended at the border contributed to the fact that more individuals were deported during his presidency than under any other previous US president. Despite a dark history of the effects of immigration detention on families, the Obama administration opened more family detention centers, continuing the deprivation of fundamental due process and human rights to women and children. The physical conditions of the family detention centers create long-lasting mental and psychological trauma for women and children. The situation is a violation of the *Flores* settlement – at least as applied to children – because the detention centers are not properly licensed to care for children and do not constitute the least restrictive setting.

Central American migrant women and children are not criminals; they are survivors. Continuing to detain women and children who risk their lives to escape fear and persecution from their former country is inhumane. We should not be treating them like prisoners and holding them in prison-like structures. Using family detention centers in this context and in this manner is a disgrace. In years to come, the nation will look back at what we have done with embarrassment and great regret.

[158] Amber D. Moulton, *No Safe Haven Here: Children and Families Face Trauma in the Hands of US Immigration* (2015).
[159] Ibid., at p. 8.

4

Country Conditions

Why Women and Children Flee the Northern Triangle

4.1. INTRODUCTION

As we have seen in the previous two chapters, since 2014 the flood of women and unaccompanied children migrating to the United States has raised considerable concerns by government officials as well as immigrant rights advocates.[1] While the Department of Homeland Security's (DHS) response is couched in terms of an immigration enforcement challenge, the crisis represents urgent human rights, human development, refugee, and humanitarian challenges to human rights advocates.[2] Overwhelmingly, the women and unaccompanied minors are coming from El Salvador, Guatemala, and Honduras – a region in Central America known as the "Northern Triangle."[3] Researchers and journalists have documented how corrupt officials, gang members, traffickers, and even family members take advantage of the vulnerable population through abuse, violence, and exploitation.[4] Chapter 4 provides an overview of the conditions in the Northern Triangle in order to better understand the reasons why women and children are fleeing.

In 2016, out of 188 countries assessed, El Salvador, Guatemala, and Honduras were ranked 117, 125, and 130, respectively, on the global Human Development Index, which calculates and ranks countries on life expectancy, education, and national income per capita.[5] The "Medium Human Development" of all three

---

[1] Congressional Research Service, *Unaccompanied Alien Children: Demographics in Brief*. September 24, 2014.

[2] Karen Musalo, Lisa Frydman, and Pablo Ceriani Cernadas, *Childhood and Migration in Central and North America: Causes, Policies, Practices and Challenges*. February 2015.

[3] Ibid., at 35.

[4] See, e.g., I. Ahn (2014). Feminist justice and the case of undocumented migrant women and children: a critical dialog with Benhabib, Nussbaum, Young, and O'Neill. *Journal of Global Ethics*, 10(2), 199–215.

[5] United Nations Development Programme (UNDP). (2016). Human Development Index.

countries fall between Botswana and São Tomé and Príncipe.[6] All three have a life expectancy of at least seventy-one years and have at least ten expected years of education or schooling. That data alone do not explain the influx of asylum seekers, primarily unaccompanied minors and women, migrating from these countries. After all, few individuals are fleeing from neighboring Nicaragua, a country with a high poverty and ranking of 124 on the global Human Development Index.

Violence, extreme poverty, and family reunification are the central factors that cause children and adolescents to leave Honduras, Guatemala, and El Salvador.[7] In particular, crime, gang threats,[8] and other forms of violence are among the strongest determining causes for flight (amounting to more than 60 percent). Extreme poverty also plays a fundamental role.[9] So, unaccompanied minors and women from the three countries clearly are fleeing gang and other criminal violence, domestic violence, as well as poverty.

4.2. GANG VIOLENCE AND OTHER CRIMINAL ACTIVITY COMBINED WITH THE LACK OF POLICE POWER AND *MANO DURA* POLICIES

Two reports commissioned by the United Nations High Commissioner for Refugees (UNHCR) – Children on the Run[10] and Women on the Run[11] – detail the motivations behind the decision to migrate from the Northern Triangle. While violence, persecution, poverty, family reunification, and the search for employment can be the principal motivators of migration by women and unaccompanied children, the reports present a complex tapestry of interrelated causes for migration.[12]

During the summer of 2013, UNHCR researchers interviewed more than 400 unaccompanied children between the ages of twelve and seventeen from El Salvador, Guatemala, Honduras, and Mexico to learn from the children why they

---

[6] Ibid.

[7] Musalo, *Childhood and Migration in Central and North America*, at 41.

[8] Youth gangs in this area has been around for decades, but during the civil wars and other conflicts of the 1980s they drew little attention from the authoritarian regimes. See Thomas Bruneau. Pandillas and Security in Central America. *Latin American Research Review*, 49(2), 2014 152–72.

[9] *See generally* E. Kennedy (2014, July). No Childhood Here: Why Central American Children are Fleeing their Homes. Retrieved from: www.immigrationpolicy.org/sites/default/files/docs/no_childhood_here_why_central_american_children_are_fleeing_their_homes_final.pdf. (last accessed May 2, 2016).

[10] UNHCR. (2014). Children on the Run: Unaccompanied Children Leaving Central America and Mexico and the Need for International Protection. Retrieved from www.unhcrwashington.org/children. (last accessed May 2, 2016).

[11] UNHCR. (2015). Women on the Run: First Hand Accounts of Refugees Fleeing El Salvador, Guatemala, Honduras, and Mexico. Retrieved from www.unhcrwashington.org/womenontherun. (last accessed May 2, 2016).

[12] *See generally* J. Bhabha (2014). *Child Migration & Human Rights in a Global Age*. Princeton: Princeton University Press.

decided to leave their country of origin.[13] The research was conducted to "ascertain whether the surge in unaccompanied and separated children from El Salvador, Guatemala, and Honduras to the United States reflects an increase in children from these countries with international protection needs."[14] In total, 313 boys and 91 girls who had entered the United States during or after October 2011, were asked six questions:

1. Why did you want to leave your country?
2. What was the most important reason?
3. Were there any other reasons? What were they?
4. Did anyone make you suffer at some point in your country or in your home?
5. Did anyone hurt you at some point in your country or in your home?
6. Were you in danger at some point in your country or in your home?[15]

UNHCR conducted similar interviews with women asylum seekers to provide an analysis of why women were fleeing El Salvador, Guatemala, Honduras, and Mexico.[16] The interviews were conducted between August and September 2015 with 160 women, ranging in age from eighteen to fifty-seven.[17] Of those interviewed, 93 percent of the women had passed their credible fear interviews – the first step in accessing asylum procedures in the United States.[18] The remaining 7 percent of women had been granted asylum, withholding of removal, or protection under the Convention against Torture in the United States.

Every woman indicated that she fled her home country in pursuit of protection that she could not receive in her home country.[19] Ninety-four percent of the women interviewed were being held in United States detention facilities at the time of the interview; 25 percent had been in detention for less than one month, 27 percent had

---

[13] "Nearly all of the children from Central America were interviewed while in the custody of the Office of Refugee Resettlement (ORR), the agency within the Department of Health and Human Services to which unaccompanied and separated children apprehended by US immigration authorities are referred for custody and care until the children can be released to the care of adults while such claims for status are pending or after lawful status to remain in the US is granted." UNHCR Children on the Run, at 18.

[14] Ibid., at 21.

[15] Ibid., at 20–1.

[16] "UNHCR sought to interview women aged 18 or older with El Salvadoran, Guatemalan, Honduran, or Mexican nationality. All the women interviewed had most recently entered the United States on or after October 1, 2013. In order to understand women's reasons for flight, UNHCR chose to focus the interviews for this report on women who had passed either a credible or reasonable fear screening with a US asylum officer, or had been granted some form of protection in the United States (such as asylum)." UNHCR, Women on the Run, at 12.

[17] Ibid., at 13.

[18] Ibid.

[19] Ibid.

been in detention for one to three months, and 41 percent had been in detention for more than three months.[20]

In each section below, the answers provided during the interviews with women and children begin the discussion and help illuminate the causes and conditions for the dramatic exodus from these countries of origin.

4.2.1. Gang Violence

A common theme voiced by migrants from all three countries in the Northern Triangle is a rise in violence due to criminal activity and increased territorial control by organized, criminal, armed groups. According to statistics from the United Nations Office on Drugs and Crime, the region is among the most violent in the world,[21] and in the case of El Salvador, the violence is not only high, but is increasing.[22] *Mara Salvatrucha* (MS-13) and *Barrio Diesiocho* or the 18th Street Gang (M-18), the two most powerful gangs in Central America,[23] alongside other groups, engage in brutal killings, assaults, robberies, and widespread extortion.[24] Both the unaccompanied minors and the women interviewed by UNHCR provided graphic details of the gang violence that drove them to leave their homes.

[20] Ibid.
[21] The United Nations Office on Drug and Crime "2013 Global Study on Homicide: Trends, Contexts, and Data." Released on April 10, 2014. Available at: www.unodc.org/documents/gsh/pdfs/2014_GLOBAL_HOMICIDE_BOOK_web.pdf.
[22] "Five Facts About Migration from Central America's Northern Triangle," January 15, 2016. Available at: www.wola.org/commentary/five_facts_about_migration_from_central_america_s_northern_triangle.
[23] Many "Central American gangs originated as re-imports from the United States back to countries of immigrant origin. Lacking legal status and seeing no way forward in the United States, many undocumented youths found solace and support in gangs. The most infamous, *Mara Salvatrucha*, was founded by Salvadorans in the Pico-Union neighborhood of Los Angeles in the mid-1980s. When undocumented gang members were apprehended and deported, gang violence was then exported to El Salvador. Transnational gang networks took hold." D. Massey, Princeton University. "Children of Central American Turmoil and the US Reform Impasse." *Scholars Strategy Network*. Available at: www.scholarsstrategynetwork.org/children-central-american-turmoil-and-us-reform-impasse. In the 1990s, US deportation policy (the Illegal Immigration Reform and Immigrant Responsibility Act, IIRIRA, of 1996) increased the deportation target to any non-citizen, including legal permanent residents of the United States, who was convicted of a crime whose sentence might last longer than a year was subject to be removed from the United States after they had served a full jail sentence. *See* "Youth Gangs in Central America: Issues in Human Rights, Effective Policing, and Prevention," WOLA Special Report November 2006, at 4. *See also* Nancy Morawetz, *Understanding the Impact of the 1996 Deportation Laws and the Limited Scope of Proposed Reforms.* Boston: Harvard Law Review, 2000. vol. 113. In a three-year period (1994–7) this deportation strategy caused the forced migration of more than 150,000 back to their "home country." *See* Youth Gangs in Central America, at 4. *See also* Margaret Taylor and Alexander Aleinikoff. *Deportation of Criminal Aliens: A Geopolitical Perspective.* Washington, DC: Inter-American Dialogue, June 1998.
[24] UNHCR, Women on the Run, at 16. *See also* Clare R. Seelke, *Gangs in Central America*, Congressional Research Service, Publication No. RL34112, 7-5700 (February 20, 2014).

4.2.1.1. El Salvador

A seventeen-year-old student named Alfonso explained that the reason he left El Salvador was due to the gang violence and threats from the gangs, in particular the gang violence associated with the rivalry between the M-18 and MS-13 gangs. According to Alfonso,

> [W]here I studied there were lots of M-18 gang members, and where I lived was under control of the other gang, the MS-13. The M-18 gang thought I belonged to the MS-13. They had killed the two police officers who protected our school. They waited for me outside the school. It was a Friday, the week before Easter, and I was headed home. The gang told me that if I returned to school, I wouldn't make it home alive. The gang had killed two kids I went to school with, and I thought I might be the next one. After that, I couldn't even leave my neighborhood. They prohibited me. I know someone whom the gangs threatened this way. He didn't take their threats seriously. They killed him in the park. He was wearing his school uniform. If I hadn't had these problems, I wouldn't have come here.[25]

Mario was another seventeen-year-old student who left El Salvador due to threats made by gangs. Mario explicitly states, "I left because I had problems with the gangs."[26] With great detail, Mario described the coercive nature of the gangs and the join-or-die choice that teenagers face:

> They hung out by a field that I had to pass to get to school. They said if I didn't join them, they would kill me. I have many friends who were killed or disappeared because they refused to join the gang. I told the gang I didn't want to. Their life is only death and jail, and I didn't want that for myself. I want a future. I want to continue studying and to have a career. That isn't possible when you're in the gang. I didn't want that for my family either. I didn't want my mother to suffer the way mothers of gang members suffer. The more they saw me refusing to join, the more they started threatening me and telling me they would kill me if I didn't. They beat me up five times for refusing to help them. The pain from the beatings was so bad, I couldn't even stand up. They killed a friend of mine in March because he didn't want to join, and his body wasn't found until May. I went to the police twice to report the threats. They told me that they would do something; but when I saw that they weren't doing anything to help, I knew I had to leave. I even brought a copy of the police report I made; but US immigration took it from me and threw it away. They said that it wasn't going to help me in this country.[27]

---

[25] UNHCR, Children on the Run, at 27.
[26] Ibid., at 32.
[27] Ibid.

But gang violence and threats are not just targeted at teenage boys in El Salvador. Martiza underscores that teenage girls, some as young as fifteen like Martiza, are victims of abusive and fatal gang violence. She vividly explained:

> I am here because the gang threatened me. One of them "liked" me. Another gang member told my uncle that he should get me out of there because the guy who liked me was going to do me harm. In El Salvador they take young girls, rape them, and throw them in plastic bags. My uncle told me it wasn't safe for me to stay there. They told him that on April 3, and I left on April 7. They said if I was still there on April 8, they would grab me, and I didn't know what would happen. I also wanted to come because I was excited about seeing my mother. But I was also sad about leaving my grandmother. My mother's plan was always for the four of us – her, my two sisters and me – to be together. But I wasn't sure I wanted to come. I decided for sure only when the gang threatened me.[28]

Martiza also highlighted a consistent theme throughout the interviews that many unaccompanied children and adolescents left their country of origin for numerous reasons and they struggled with the conflict they felt in deciding to leave.

Of the women interviewed in 2015, many described worrying about children they had been forced to leave behind. One El Salvadoran woman, for instance, was not able to bring all her children with her when she fled. "My daughters are still in El Salvador and I worry for their safety," she said. "I worry that they will be killed by the gangs. I took my son and grandson to the United States so they wouldn't be recruited into the gangs, but I couldn't take my daughters as well. I am very worried for them."[29]

4.2.1.2. Guatemala and Honduras

Similar to the experiences of El Salvadorans, David, a sixteen-year-old Guatemalan, and his cousin escaped being tied up and pursued by a nearby neighborhood gang. He explained that:

> [The gang] wanted me to give them money, but what money was I supposed to give them? I didn't have any. They asked me a bunch of questions, like who was my father, and who was my family. I told them my father was dead. They told me to say goodbye because I was going to join my father. They asked me if I knew who they were, if I could identify them. I said "no," because I knew if I said "yes" they would kill me. They held my cousin and me for three hours, tied up. My cousin was able to untie the rope and he helped me untie mine. We heard gun shots and we ran. They kept looking for us, but we escaped.[30]

[28] Ibid., at 34.
[29] UNHCR, Women on the Run, at 22.
[30] UNHCR, Children on the Run, at 35.

And on the unavoidable violence associated with gangs, Kevin explained that his "grandmother wanted me to leave. She told me: 'If you don't join, the gang will shoot you. If you do join, the rival gang will shoot you – or the cops will shoot you. But if you leave, no one will shoot you.'"[31]

Finally, Nelly, a young Honduran woman, said: "The gangs treat women much worse than men. They want us to join as members, but then women are also threatened to be gang members' 'girlfriends,' and it's never just sex with the one; it's forced sex with all of them. Women are raped by them, tortured by them, abused by them."[32]

Thus, in all three countries, there is a constant fear of gang violence. The children and women described the fear of being killed, having loved ones killed, of being raped, getting recruited into the gangs themselves, and having no place of safety. They made the decision to leave their country because they feared for their lives.

4.2.2. Mano Dura *Policies, Lack of Police Power, and Corruption*

The women and minors described their personal encounters with gangs in their countries as reasons for seeking asylum in the United States. El Salvador, Guatemala, and Honduras all have relatively recently transitioned to democratic states and stress the importance of police reform and the rule of law.[33] And in recent years some of these policies and strategies have been implemented specifically to combat the gang violence.[34]

Unfortunately, some of these policies were inspired by the zero-tolerance policies implemented in several North American states and cities that focused more on penalizing wrongdoers rather than on preventing the wrongs from occurring. The indiscriminate policies enacted via special laws, executive acts, and the revisions of criminal codes have allowed the police and different law enforcement agencies to

---

[31] Ibid., at 36.

[32] UNHCR, Women on the Run, at 16.

[33] The armed conflicts that raged across the region during the Cold War officially ended two decades ago.

[34] Beginning in the 1990s, all three countries began the process of demilitarization and democratization. According to the Washington Office on Latin America, reform and professionalization of police was a central element of the transition to a more democratic state. Reform of the police and security forces was written into the 1992 Peace Accord in El Salvador, and the 1995 Peace agreements in Guatemala. With the end of the "contra war" in Nicaragua, and the peace agreement in El Salvador, the space for reform began to emerge in Honduras, as well, and a slow reform process began there in the early 1990s, in which police and security forces were separated, and a process of police reform and professionalization began. The police reform process in Central America were generally intended to: (1) Separate police and security forces, and delineate clearly the mandates and appropriate roles and sphere of each in a democratic society; (2) Subject police practice to a system of internal controls and rules, preventing arbitrary detentions, the abuse of detainees or suspects, the excessive use of force, and extra-judicial actions by the police; (3) Strengthen the investigation capacity of the police, particularly of detective unites, thus reducing the likelihood that police would resort to coercive practices or forced confession in order to solve crime; and (4) Reduce and control police corruption. *See* Youth Gangs in Central America, at 8.

round up, incarcerate, and prosecute gang members and any youth suspected of criminal activity.[35]

As a result, these *mano dura* (iron fist or strong hand) polices have blurred the line between the military and police forces. These repressive strategies include mass detentions of youth for the crime of gang membership, relaxed evidentiary standards, and harsh prison sentences.[36] The following sections will explain how, in effect, *mano dura* has undermined the progress these countries had made in the rule of law and police reform, and has transformed the gangs from neighborhood youth gangs into international, highly organized gangs.

4.2.2.1. *Mano Dura* Laws

In July 2003, El Savadoran President Francisco Flores enacted a *mano dura* law known as *Ley Antimaras*. This law aimed to facilitate the detention and prosecution of suspected gang members based on the newly defined felony of "illicit association" and gang membership.[37] Through this new law, the police could use the presence of tattoos, hand signals, some dress codes, and physical appearance as evidence of gang membership.[38]

Also in 2003, the Honduran President, Ricardo Maduro, revised Article 332 of the Penal Code to make gang members subject to prosecution for membership in a criminal organization, regardless of whether they or their group had been convicted of any crime.[39] Honduran police acted in similar fashion to their El Salvadoran counterparts, jailing children who happened to be dressed like gang members.[40]

Although formal legal measures were not enacted in Guatemala, the police implemented suppression plans based on arbitrary interpretations of the existing laws. The police jailed youth they suspected of gang membership, detained them with little legal basis, and indicted them for drug possession.[41]

4.2.2.2. The Effect of the *Mano Dura* Laws

After the initial implementation of these strict, no-tolerance laws, homicide rates began to decrease. However, within two years the homicide rates reached and then exceeded the pre-*mano dura* rates. The unintended consequence of jailing thousands of young gang members is that the state created an incubator for new gangs, and gang membership flourished.

[35] Bruneau Pandillas and Security in Central America., 161.
[36] Youth Gangs in Central America, at 3.
[37] Bruneau, Pandillas and Security in Central America., 161.
[38] Ibid.
[39] Ibid.
[40] Ibid.
[41] Ibid.

It was within the prisons that dozens of members from widespread regional *clicas* of the same gang were first able to establish contact with each other, recognize that their gangs consisted of a myriad of uncoordinated groups, and work together to develop more structured organizations. Incarceration enabled gang members to function as a sort of permanent assembly in which they could debate, make pacts, and decide on structures, strategies, and ways to operate that had to be observed by the members of all the *clicas*. This was made even easier, in part, by the decision of the authorities to separate prisoners according to their gang affiliation to cut down on intergang violence within the prisons. The broad-brush laws, by sweeping up gang members from several countries, also facilitated communications and connections at the international level among gang members.[42]

The increase in gang organization and violence, due in part to the *mano dura* policies, has affected the security of individuals at every level of society in the three countries. These are the societies from which the unaccompanied minors and women migrated. Thomas Bruneau, Professor Emeritus of National Security Affairs at the Naval Postgraduate School, has analyzed the effects of gangs on security in the following way:

At the citizen security level the pandillas [street gangs] are a serious threat in that they rob, extort, kill and generally threaten large sectors of the population, especially those in poorer sections of larger cities. At the public security level they are also a security threat in that they halt public transportation routinely, to demonstrate their power, by killing the drivers, as they have periodically in Guatemala City and San Salvador. In one notorious case in the Barrio of Mejicanos in El Salvador on June 21, 2010, members of the 18th Street gang doused a bus with gasoline, burning alive the passengers. Through their extortion of businesses in the bigger cities, they also challenge public security. As there is an identified tendency for the pandillas to resemble organized crime, at the level of national security they also should be considered a threat in El Salvador, Guatemala, and Honduras, which remain fragile democracies with relatively poorly articulated political institutions and very tentative popular support.[43]

4.3. VIOLENCE AGAINST WOMEN AND CHILDREN

A second type of violence has plagued the citizens of the Northern Triangle: gender-motivated violence against women. This type of violence includes domestic (or intra-familial) violence and sexual violence. The interviews of the unaccompanied minors reveal that young men also have been victims of domestic violence.

---

[42] Ibid. *See also* Jose Miguel Cruz. Government Responses and the Dark Side of Gang Suppression in Central America. In *Maras: Gang Violence and Security in Central America*, edited by Thomas C. Bruneau, Lucia Dammert, and Elizabeth Skinner, 137–58. Austin: University of Texas Press; 2011.

[43] Bruneau, Pandillas and Security in Central America, p. 165.

However, violence against women for gender-motivated reasons is a dire reality in the three northern triangle countries and is a considerable factor in the decision to migrate and seek asylum in the United States. While some studies have collected and disseminated data on violence, problems persist in fully understanding the true nature and extent of these deadly acts.[44]

Available accounts and data reveal that the escalation of lethal violence targeting women in El Salvador, Guatemala, and Honduras is the result of a confluence of factors. These factors range from the increased militarization of the state and society in response to drug wars, which directly affect or even target women, to the persistent *machismo* culture.[45] The fact that men act with impunity is a substantial obstacle to the prevention, prosecution, and punishment of these crimes of violence. The absence of judicial redress contributes to the perpetuation of the cycle of violence.[46] Inefficiency and bias in the justice system, confusion by judicial actors over the applicability of laws, and lack of access to counsel, shelters, and other support contribute mightily to the problem.[47] The women interviewed by the UNHCR in 2015 described "prolonged instances of physical, sexual, and psychological domestic violence, for which authorities provided no meaningful help. Unable to secure state protection, many women cited domestic violence as a reason for flight, fearing severe harm or death if they stayed."[48]

4.3.1. *Guatemala*

A rape survivor from Guatemala described constant and debilitating abuse. "My husband abused me verbally and physically on a regular basis. He kept me locked in the house. I wore my hair pulled back, and sometimes he would grab my hair,

---

[44] "Limited availability and accessibility of sex-disaggregated data stems largely from poor reporting practices, an absence of standardized definitions and coding, underreporting, and insufficient resources for training and data collection in relevant state and non-state agencies." Geneva Declaration on Armed Violence and Development: Global Burden of Armed Violence 2015: Every Body Counts, p. 88.

[45] Ibid. See also NWI (Nobel Women's Initiative). 2012. *From Survivors to Defenders: Women Confronting Violence in Mexico, Honduras and Guatemala.* Available at: http://nobelwomensinitiative.org/wp-content/uploads/2012/06/Report_AmericasDelgation-2012.pdf?ref=18. (last accessed May 12, 2016). See also HBS (Heinrich-Böll-Stiftung). 2013. *Feminicide: A Global Phenomenon: From Madrid to Santiago.* Brussels: HBS. Available at: www.boell.eu/sites/default/files/feminicide_3_.pdf. (last accessed May 13, 2016).

[46] Geneva Declaration on Armed Violence and Development, p. 93. See also HBS (Heinrich-Böll-Stiftung). 2013. *Feminicide: A Global Phenomenon: From Madrid to Santiago.* Brussels: HBS. Available at: www.boell.eu/sites/default/files/feminicide_3.pdf>. (last accessed May 13, 2016).

[47] Karen Musalo and Blaine Bookey. Crimes without Punishment: An Update on Violence Against Women and Impunity in Guatemala. *Hastings Race and Poverty Law Journal*, 10. Summer 2013, 265–292.

[48] UNHCR, Women on the Run, at 25.

shove my face near the fire, and ask 'Are you fine here?' Or he would hold a knife to my neck and ask the same thing. I had to respond 'yes.' To me, this is not a life."[49]

A Guatemalan woman, whose partner was abusive, emphasized intrinsic links between the domestic violence she experienced and the violence in her neighborhood: "Twice, I saw the gang kill two young men who approached the block. My ex required me to watch ... it was a way of making me more afraid, weaker. How they screamed and begged for their life, I can't forget it."[50]

A sixteen-year-old, Lucia, described another example of grave domestic violence:

> I had problems with my grandmother. She always beat me from the time I was little. That's why I went to live with my boyfriend – and because I was lonely and sad. But after we had been living together for about a month, my boyfriend also beat me. He beat me almost every day. I stayed with him for four months. I left because he tried to kill me by strangling me. I left that same day.[51]

Guatemala explicitly outlaws violence against women and has sought to prevent such violence before it occurs. However, despite these efforts, Guatemala continues to experience high levels of violent deaths of women.

According to a Guatemalan attorney and leading expert on gender discrimination in Guatemala, "it is widely accepted [in Guatemala] that a man has the right to abuse his partner. Women are expected to endure such violence, because it is viewed as 'normal.' The abuse stems from a culture that places a man at the top of a hierarchy granting him control over all aspects of a woman's life, from her economic situation, to her politics, to her sexuality. Women are commonly viewed as the 'daughters' of their husbands, and as such, women must obey their partners. This idea furthers women's dependence on their violent partners."[52]

Guatemalan women are not only controlled by their husbands or partners, but they also often lack support from their families and communities in the process. In Guatemala's "community-oriented society, family members, the church, and other community members exert significant influence over a woman's decision to participate in the legal process, and they often pressure women not to file complaints against intimate partners."[53]

In the rare situations when women contact the criminal justice system, there are important considerations that affect whether a woman would press charges against her abuser and try to break the cycle of violence before death occurs. The first factor

[49] Ibid., at 25–6.
[50] Ibid., at 25.
[51] UNHCR, Children on the Run, at 35.
[52] *Declaration of Guatemalan attorney Elisa Portillo Nájera, leading expert on gender discrimination in Guatemala and the resulting violence that stems from this discrimination.* February 3, 2012, available at: http://cgrs.uchastings.edu/sites/default/files/Elisa_Portillo_Najera_Affidavit.pdf (last accessed September 11, 2015), at 4.
[53] Ibid.

is the economic dependency of the woman to her abuser. When women do not feel safe on their own or have economic independence, they are not likely to pursue cases. When women do take the courageous step of making a criminal complaint, prosecutors often fail to diligently undertake "the necessary investigation because either they do not see violence against women as a serious problem that warrants their attention, or they express disbelief of women's stories and subject them to 'veracity tests.'"[54] These are some of the barriers that women face when they consider seeking judicial redress and protection from their abuser. Given the options, little wonder that the interviews reveal that many women have made the decision to flee their country to escape being further victimized at home.

4.3.2. *El Salvador and Honduras*

The interlocking fates of gang violence, domestic violence, and the lack of safety or protection from the police were revealed in the interviews of women interviewed in 2015. Many of their abusive partners were members or associates of criminal armed groups. The women stated that "because these groups were often the highest powers in their neighborhoods, they did not believe the government could protect them. 'My husband was connected with the *maras*. When he abused me, I knew there was nowhere I could go,' said Claudia from El Salvador. 'There is no way to escape them.'"[55]

Another woman from El Salvador endured escalating levels of physical and sexual violence for years. "He'd demand that I have sex with him, and sometimes I did not want to. And he'd then take me by force. He said I was his," she explained. "He'd throw the table, the utensils ... Sometimes he put the iron to me, hit me with a belt, cut me. I have scars. But I always took it. He'll hit the wall with his fists until his fists bleed. He has so much anger and so much hurt. This scares me. I really think he'll kill me now. He's so violent."[56]

One Honduran woman fled to the United States after years of abuse escalated to the point that her husband nearly killed her. "He severely beat her many times, often in front of her young children. Yet one incident stood out in her mind. On this evening, the woman's husband came home drunk and she did not want to be near him, so she slept on the sofa. 'In the middle of the night, I felt like water was falling on me. I woke up and he was urinating on my face and body.'"[57] The machismo behavior by men in these countries is a horrifying display of the systemic lack of respect for women.

---

[54] Musalo and Bookey, Crimes without Punishment.
[55] UNHCR, Women on the Run, at 25.
[56] Ibid., at 26.
[57] Ibid.

Reminiscent of similar reports from Guatemala, when women finally chose to go to the police and seek protection from the legal authorities, one El Salvadoran woman recalled that she was "standing in front of the police, bleeding, and the police said, 'Well, he's your husband.'" Another El Salvadoran woman stated: "One time the police came to our home, but they said that because this was a case of domestic violence, we could resolve it between ourselves. I do not have confidence in the police."[58]

Severe domestic violence on children is also common. Angelo revealed that his "father would get mad at me and beat me all the time. Sometimes he would beat me with a belt every day. My mother couldn't really defend me because he would beat her, too."[59]

Finally, the combination of being subjected to domestic violence and a longing to reunite with his mother, compelled twelve-year-old Oscar to flee:

I left because I wanted to be with my mother. I miss her a lot. My grandmother mistreated me. She was mean to me. She told me to leave the house, but where was I supposed to go? The only place I could go was here. She forced me and my siblings to work. I couldn't stand to be there anymore.[60]

According to the Geneva Declaration on Armed Violence and Development, violence against women in El Salvador and Honduras has been increasing over the past several years, and the two nations are now ranked number 1 and 2 in average female homicide rates. They each experience more than ten female homicides per 100,000 women.[61] The rate for El Salvador (14.4 per 100,000 women) is more than double the base rate (or average across all other counties) for the category (6.0 per 100,000).[62] Honduras is second with a rate of 10.9 homicides per 100,000 women.[63] The staggering data of homicides against women are consistent with the fact that both countries also rank highest in terms of overall homicide rates, with seventy-three persons killed per 100,000 population in Honduras and fifty-nine in El Salvador – particularly high mortality rates due to intentional violence.[64] The level of lethal violence affecting women in El Salvador surpasses the overall rate of male and female homicides in some of the forty countries with the highest rates worldwide, such as Ecuador, Nicaragua, and Tanzania.[65]

Since 2011, when the Geneva Declaration group made its last report, Honduras has had the largest increase in the rate of female homicide, followed by El Salvador.

[58] Ibid.
[59] UNHCR, Children on the Run, at 28.
[60] Ibid., at 26.
[61] Geneva Declaration on Armed Violence and Development, p. 94.
[62] Ibid., at p. 93.
[63] Ibid.
[64] Ibid., at p. 93–4.
[65] Ibid., at p. 93.

One correlation is clear: Countries that experience a high volume of narco-trafficking – such as El Salvador, Honduras, and Mexico – are also plagued by rising female homicide rates. That has prompted human rights activists to redub the "war on drugs" the new "war on women."[66] As noted above, the *mano dura* interventions, designed to improve security and combat drug-related violence, can have the opposite effect, inadvertently increasing insecurity among the civilian population, and particularly among women.[67] Women are targeted as "drug mules," executed as an evil public message to the authorities to desist from combating drug trafficking, or killed to settle accounts with rival gangs.[68]

4.4. POVERTY

On the surface, poverty certainly contributes to migration from El Salvador, Guatemala, and Honduras. However, the strong interplay between poverty and gang membership and the violence that stems from that membership is more relevant. Experts note that "[m]ost *mareros* [gang members] suffer from poverty, unstable family backgrounds, a lack of educational, social, or professional outlets, or some combination of these factors ... For marginalized youths, gang membership offers a steady cash flow, a sense of status and belonging, and, for men, access to women."[69] Therefore, poverty may be a root cause for many gang problems and related violence.

One unaccompanied minor interviewed, seventeen-year-old Mauricio, spoke about extreme poverty and rationalized that, "if they really do want to know how hard life is down there, they should go see it. There are kids who don't make it past five [years old] because they die of hunger. Their parents can't work because there are no jobs.

---

[66] Ibid, at p. 94. See also Fox, Edward (2012). 'Honduras' New Human Trafficking Law Faces Enormous Challenges.' InSightCrime. 13 June. Available at: www.insightcrime.org/news-analysis/honduras-new-human-trafficking-law-faces-enormous-challenges

[67] Geneva Declaration on Armed Violence and Development, p. 94. See also Carlsen, Laura (2012). 'Mexico: The War on Drugs Is Becoming a War on Women.' Open Democracy. 16 April. Available at: www.opendemocracy.net/5050/laura-carlsen/mexico-war-on-drugs-is-becoming-war-on-women

[68] Geneva Declaration on Armed Violence and Development, p. 96. See also Fox, Edward (2012). "How the Drug Trade Fuels Femicide in Central America." InSightCrime. 12 July. Available at: www.insightcrime.org/news-analysis/how-the-drug-trade-fuels-femicide-in-central-america. See also Giacomello, Corina (2013). *Women, Drug Offenses and Penitentiary Systems in Latin America.* IDPC Briefing Paper. October. Available at: http://dl.dropboxusercontent.com/u/64663568/library/IDPC-Briefing-Paper_Women-in-Latin-America_ENGLISH.pdf. See also IRIN. 2014. Women Paying Price of Latin America Drug Wars. 15 April. Available at: www.irinnews.org/report/99944/women-paying-price-of-latin-america-drug-wars

[69] Hal Brands, *Crime, Violence, and the Crisis in Guatemala: A Case Study in the Erosion of the State,* May 2010, Strategic Studies Institute, available at: www.uscrirefugees.org/2010Website/5_Resources/5_4_For_Lawyers/5_4_1%20Asylum%20Research/5_4_1_2_Gang_Related_Asylum_Resources/5_4_1_2_4_Reports/Hal_Brands_Crime_ViolenceandtheCrisisinGuatemala.pdf (last accessed September 12, 2015).

Just give us a chance. Let us better ourselves so we can be something better than what we are today."[70]

In El Salvador, the majority of the population is young, with 63.7 percent under the age of 30.[71] The percentage of underweight children and adolescents is 5.5 percent, and the percentage of those with chronic malnutrition is 19 percent. Among children and adolescents whose mothers lack an education, the percentage of those underweight is 15.7 percent and of those with chronic malnutrition is 36.6 percent.[72]

Guatemala, one of the most marginalized countries in the world, has a population of approximately 15.4 million, almost half of whom are children and adolescents, with more than 17 percent under five years of age. According to the National Survey on Living Conditions in 2011, 53.7 percent of the population lives in conditions of poverty, while 13.3 percent lives in conditions of extreme poverty. The statistics for 2012 reveal that 19 percent of children aged between seven to fourteen years work in the labor market, with the highest rate of child labor in rural areas.[73] According to the United Nations Development Program, while children under the age of five suffer from chronic malnutrition, the average educational level of children and adolescents is a mere four years.[74] The data on malnutrition among children from the indigenous population are significantly higher, reaching 65.9 percent.[75]

Honduras is one of the lowest-income countries in Latin America and the Caribbean, with a poverty rate of 60 percent of households in 2011. Suffering from poverty in rural areas is worse, given severe limitations in the coverage and quality of social services. The rural population, which represents approximately 53 percent of the country's total population, has a level of poverty of 65.4 percent as of 2010.[76] Acute malnutrition affects more than half of the children aged between one and five

[70] UNHCR, Children on the Run, at 24.

[71] PNUD. *El Salvador en Breve*. Retrieved from: www.sv.undp.org/content/el_salvador/es/home/countryinfo/.

[72] Informe sobre Desarrollo Humano El Salvador 2013, Imaginar un nuevo país. Hacerlo posible, Diagnóstico y propuesta, p. 130. Retrieved from: www.sv.undp.org/content/dam/el_salvador/docs/povred/UNDP_SV_IDHES-2013.pdf.

[73] Instituto Centroamericano de Estudios Fiscales (ICEFI), Suecia, & UNICEF. (2012, diciembre). Análisis del Presupuesto General del Estado de Guatemala aprobado para 2013, Enfocado en la niñez y adolescencia y en seguridad alimentaria y nutricional. *Serie de documentos de análisis* ¡CONTAMOS! 12. Available at: www.unicef.org.gt/1_recursos_unicefgua/publicaciones/2012/Contamos12%20Presupuesto2013.pdf.

[74] Programa de las Naciones Unidas para el Desarrollo en El Salvador (PNUD). *El Salvador en Breve*. Retrieved from: www.sv.undp.org/content/el_salvador/es/home/countryinfo/.

[75] Instituto Centroamericano de Estudios Fiscales (ICEFI) & UNICEF. (2011, septiembre). Protegiendo la nueva cosecha, Un análisis del costo de erradicar el hambre en Guatemala, 2012–21. *Serie de documentos de análisis* ¡CONTAMOS! 4. Retrieved from: www.unicef.org.gt/1_recursos_unicefgua/publicaciones/contamos_4.pdf.

[76] PNUD. *Reducción de la Pobreza*. Retrieved from: www.hn.undp.org/content/honduras/es/home/library/poverty/.

years, and average schooling for the population of Honduras is a mere 4.3 years in rural regions and seven years in urban areas.[77]

4.5. GUATEMALA'S GOVERNANCE CRISIS

This section reviews a broader scope of human rights abuses and other factors that are causing women and children to flee Guatemala. Special consideration is given to non-state actors as well as the State's role in permitting, being complicit in, and perpetuating human rights abuses within its borders. The information speaks not only to specific acts, but also to the broad understanding that pervasive and enduring violence and corruption as general matters create an unlivable, intolerable environment, forcing citizens to flee and seek refuge.

According to the 2015 US Department of State Country Report on Guatemala[78]:

> Principal human rights abuses included widespread institutional corruption, particularly in the police and judicial sectors; police and military involvement in serious crimes, such as kidnapping, drug trafficking, trafficking in persons, and extortion; and societal violence, including lethal violence against women.
>
> Other human rights problems included arbitrary or unlawful killings, abuse and mistreatment by National Civil Police (PNC) members; harsh and sometimes life threatening prison conditions; arbitrary arrest and detention; prolonged pretrial detention; failure of the judicial system to conduct full and timely investigations and fair trials; government failure to fully protect judicial officials, witnesses, and civil society representatives from intimidation and threats; and internal displacement of persons because of criminal activities. In addition there was sexual harassment and discrimination against women; child abuse, including commercial sexual exploitation of children; discrimination and abuse of persons with disabilities; and trafficking in persons and human smuggling, including of unaccompanied children. Other problems included marginalization of indigenous communities and ineffective mechanisms to address land conflicts; discrimination on the basis of sexual orientation and gender identity; and ineffective enforcement of labor and child labor laws.
>
> The government cooperated with the UN-backed International Commission against Impunity in Guatemala (CICIG) and took significant steps to prosecute officials who committed abuses. Nonetheless, impunity continued to be widespread. Gangs, organized crime, and narcotics trafficking organizations committed considerable violence; corruption and inadequate investigation made prosecution of such crimes difficult.[79]

---

[77] UNICEF Honduras. *Contexto de país.* Retrieved from: www.UNICEF.org/honduras/14241_16946 .htm.

[78] U.S. Dept. of State, *Guatemala 2015 Human Rights Report,* 2016 (hereinafter "State Department Guatemala Report"), available at: www.state.gov/documents/organization/253229.pdf.

[79] Ibid.

4.5.1. *Government Corruption and Its Effect on Human Rights and Violence Against Women and Children*

Where do victims of crime and violence turn to if not the authorities? For people living in Guatemala – and for that matter, Honduras and El Salvador as well – it is often useless to call upon law enforcement or their government leaders to ensure that the streets in their communities are safe. This lack of safety and protection is rooted in deep-seeded corruption involving top ranking officials and trickling down to local police agencies. While many government officials operate under the control of cartels and gangs, many also participate in criminal activity of their own. "As of early November [2015], the [Guatemalan] Public Ministry reported that at least 602 public officials were arrested during the year for corruption and/or abuse of authority."[80] These included charges such as tax evasion, money laundering, and illicit association, and also included the resignations and arrests of former President Otto Perez Molina and former Vice President Roxana Baldetti.[81] There were also reports that "the government or its agents committed arbitrary or unlawful killings of journalists, human rights activists, political candidates, and trade unionists."[82] Rather than leading the country in a direction of positive reform, they are contributing to the problem.

Brutal physical attacks, death threats, and murder of civil rights activists are some of the more devastating aspects of the criminal activity supported by officials. The number of people who fall victim to the government's efforts to prevent a social uprising is shocking, while little is being done to stop the injustice. A number of nongovernmental organizations (NGOs), human rights workers, and trade unionists reported threats, violence, and intimidation. NGOs assert that the government does little to investigate reports of the violence or to prevent further incidents. NGOs also report that the government uses threats of legal action as a form of intimidation. Local human rights NGO Unit for the Protection of Human Rights Defenders reported nine killings of human rights defenders through August 2015, following seven killings in 2014. The NGO also reported 455 attacks against human rights defenders through November of 2015, compared with 813 attacks in 2014. According to various human rights NGOs, many of the attacks related to land disputes and exploitation of natural resources.[83]

Part of maintaining the status quo means covering up the criminal activity operating from within the government. All too often, journalists pay the price of government cover up by being murdered for exposing the truth. Investigative journalism in Guatemala became increasingly dangerous for journalists and their families in 2015, resulting in harassment, self-censorship, frivolous defamation lawsuits, violence,

---

[80] Ibid.
[81] Ibid., at 12.
[82] Ibid.
[83] Ibid., at 13.

and death.[84] Members of the press reported numerous threats by public officials, and actions by criminal organizations increased journalists' vulnerability. On March 13, 2015, unidentified attackers killed reporter Guido Villatoro as he entered his office; apparently his employer refused to make an extortion payment to a Mara 18 street gang. On March 10, assailants killed reporters Danilo Lopez and Efrain Salazar in the downtown plaza of Mazatenango for their investigative work on corruption and organized crime in several municipalities in the area. The Public Ministry arrested two police officers and several other associates who participated in the killing.

One organization that is responsible for allowing criminal activity to percolate throughout the country's police forces is the PNC National Civil Police (Policía Nacional Civil). The presence of expansive criminal enterprises coupled with an unusually young, indigent, and illiterate general population in Guatemala means that the police force is asked to respond to persistent civilian unrest. However, the lack of resources to property fund and train members of the PNC has resulted in a multitude of mishandling confrontations between civilians and police officers furthering the divide between these groups. In 2015, civilian authorities did not always have effective control over the security forces, and the government did not effectively investigate and punish abuse and corruption within the understaffed, inadequately trained, and insufficiently funded PNC. Police have been accused of "indiscriminate and illegal detentions when conducting anti-gang operations in some high-crime neighborhoods."[85] There is an implied risk that boys and young men who are of gang-recruitment age are therefore being terrorized not only by the local gangs, but also by police who may be illegally profiling them as gang members. Further, "Security officials allegedly arrested and imprisoned suspected gang members without warrants or on fabricated drug charges. There were press reports of police involvement in kidnappings for ransom ... There were no reliable data on the number of arbitrary detentions, although most accounts indicated that police continued to ignore writs of habeas corpus in cases of illegal detention, particularly during neighborhood anti-gang operations."[86]

A disturbing truth is that the organizations enlisted to keep communities safe are themselves engaged in warfare, but it is even more unsettling that very little can or will be done to condemn these wrongdoers for their crimes. There is no lack of complaints filed against members of PNC who commit crimes of humanity against the public, in fact the sheer volume of complaints filed in 2015 is alarming. The Office of Professional Responsibility (ORP) reported receiving 1,215 complaints of police misconduct over nine months in 2015,[87] however, the level of impunity for security forces accused of committing crimes remained high. During the year there were thirty-one complaints of police extortion and 856 for abuse of authority. The PNC

[84] Ibid.
[85] Ibid.
[86] Ibid.
[87] Ibid.

routinely transferred officers suspected of wrongdoing rather than investigating and punishing them. Through November 2015, approximately 210 police officials were arrested. While many claims are brought against members of the PNC, most are ignored or tied up so long in the court system that the complainants never see a sentence served. One reason that organized crime in Guatemala goes unpunished and endures is that members of the judiciary may be either threatened or corrupted into not punishing guilty persons.

> Judges, prosecutors, plaintiffs, and witnesses continued to report threats, intimidation, and surveillance, most often from drug-trafficking organizations. By the end of September [from January the same year], the special prosecutor for crimes against judicial workers received 202 complaints of threats or aggression against workers in the judicial branch, compared with 171 for the same period in 2014 ... The Supreme Court continued to seek the suspension of judges and to conduct criminal investigations of improprieties or irregularities in cases under its jurisdiction. The Judicial Disciplinary Unit investigated 1,047 complaints of wrongdoing through October, held hearings on 445 complaints, and applied sanctions in 161 cases, ranging from written warnings (114 cases) to recommending dismissal (nine cases).[88]

Authorities arrested four PNC agents, accusing them of torturing four detained suspects.[89] As of September 30, 2015, the PNC and ORP accused nine PNC officers of homicide.[90] According to the Public Ministry, there were 133 complaints filed for attacks or threats against journalists and three reported killings through the end of September, compared with seventy-seven complaints and no killings for all of 2014. Some analysts attributed this significant increase to heightened tension and violence directed at the media during election years. The Public Ministry employed a unit dedicated to the investigation of threats and attacks against journalists.[91]

Vigilantism also occurs in Guatemala. Vigilante mobs have attacked and killed those suspected of crimes – often individuals suspected of rape, kidnapping, theft, or extortion. The NGO Mutual Support Group reported that in a nine-month period, twelve were injured and forty-four killed in public lynchings. Many observers attributed the acts to public frustration with the failure of police and judicial authorities to provide justice and security. This vacuum led to the emergence of local citizen security groups. In many instances, PNC agents feared for their own safety and refused to intervene. In one high-profile case, the mayor of the town of Concepcion died after being beaten and set on fire by an alleged vigilante mob that suspected him of ordering a prior attack on his political opponent and relatives.[92]

[88] Ibid.
[89] Ibid.
[90] Ibid.
[91] Ibid.
[92] Ibid., at 23.

4.5.2. *Violence Against Women*

Guatemala's justice system also fails to protect two of its most vulnerable classes of individuals: women and children. A 2012 Small Arms Survey reported gender-based violence at epidemic levels in Guatemala and ranked the country third in the killings of women worldwide. The same year, the UN reported that two women are killed there every day.[93] One of the biggest challenges facing women in Guatemala is the country's deeply rooted patriarchal society. There is "a prevailing culture of machismo and an institutionalized acceptance of brutality against women [that] leads to high rates of violence."[94] Tragically, machismo not only condones violence but places the blame on the victim. For this reason, many crimes against women go unreported and unpunished.

The government's failure to enforce the laws and punish violence against women can be attributed to several factors. It begins with the prevailing machismo mentality that sees women as not having any rights; they are subordinate to their government and to their husbands. "Politicians don't think women are important," says former Secretary General of the Presidential Secretariat for Women Elizabeth Quiroa. "Political parties use women for elections. They give them a bag of food and [women] sell their dignity for this because they are poor."[95]

Guatemalan police also have little training or capacity to investigate sexual crimes against women.[96] Of course, rape is a crime in Guatemala.[97] And in 2008, Guatemala became the first country to officially recognize femicide – the murder of a woman because of her gender – as a crime.[98] However, the government does not effectively enforce these laws. As a result, lack of confidence in the justice system, social stigma, and fear of reprisal often cause victims to not report rape.[99] Nonetheless, and in spite of under reporting, "according to the Public Ministry, there were 11,449 reports of sexual or physical assault through October [2015]. During the same period, there were 527 convictions for sexual or physical assault on women."[100]

Domestic violence is also a serious problem in Guatemala, despite laws prohibiting domestic abuse.[101] Guatemala's law, "allows for the issuance of restraining orders against alleged aggressors and police protection for victims, and requires the PNC to intervene in violent situations in the home."[102] The State Department reports,

---

[93] "Nearly 20 years after peace pact, Guatemala's women relive violence," released by CNN.com, April 7, 2015, available at: www.cnn.com/2015/04/02/world/iyw-guatemala-gender-violence/

[94] Ibid.

[95] Ibid.

[96] Ibid.

[97] U.S. Dept. of State, '*Guatemala 2015 Human Rights Report*', , at 14.

[98] Where women are killed by their own families, released by BBC News, December 5, 2015, available at: www.bbc.com/news/magazine-34978330.

[99] U.S. Dept. of State, *Guatemala 2015 Human Rights Report*, at 14.

[100] Ibid

[101] Ibid., at 15.

[102] Ibid.

however, that, "The PNC often failed to respond to requests for assistance related to domestic violence ... and women's rights advocates reported that few officers received training to deal with domestic violence or assist survivors."[103] Further,

> The government's Program for the Prevention and Eradication of Intrafamily Violence, under the Secretariat of Social Work, reported receiving an average of five calls daily from battered women and children ... The Public Ministry reported 29,128 complaints of intrafamily violence against women and children as of July 31. The government reported 141 convictions in cases of intrafamily violence against women and children as of the end of September.[104]

And although the law stipulates that shelter be provided to victims of domestic violence, there were insufficient facilities for this purpose.[105] Given, the difficulty in finding a safe haven near home, Guatemalan women seek refuge outside the country.

Femicide in Guatemala remains a major problem. According to the State Department:

> Sexual assault, torture, and mutilation were evident in most killings. The government's national forensics agency reported 501 violent deaths of women through the end of August, compared with 507 deaths reported in all of 2014. In 2013 (the latest year for which data was available), authorities convicted 41 individuals for femicide, compared with 18 the year before. NGOs noted the severity of sentences was not always appropriate to the crime.[106]

One federal court has recognized the problem of femicide and domestic violence in Guatemala. The Ninth Circuit Court of Appeals reviewed the asylum claim of a Guatemalan woman who had testified about her fear based on the high incidence of murder of women in Guatemala, and her own status as a Guatemalan woman. She provided the immigration judge with several reports by the Guatemala Human Rights Commission, documenting the torture and killing of women, the brutality of the killings, the non-responsiveness of the Guatemalan government to such atrocities, the countrywide prevalence of the killings, and the lack of explanations for the killings. The immigration court was not impressed with the claim, but the Ninth Circuit disagreed. Given the circumstances, the appellate court said that the agency should not automatically foreclose asylum, because women, in a particular country under these circumstances, could form a particular social group for purposes of asylum.[107]

---

[103] Ibid.
[104] Ibid.
[105] Ibid.
[106] Ibid.
[107] *Perdomo v. Holder*, 611 F.3d 662 (9th Cir. 2010).

4.5.3. *Violence Against Children*

Children have become major victims of physical abuse and sexual violence in Guatemala, in addition to being victimized by gangs. Children, some as young as seven years old, are making the dangerous journey from their homelands to the United States to escape the cycles of poverty and violence. The combination of intra-family violence, sexual exploitation by gangs and other groups, and human trafficking are all significant push factors for unaccompanied child migrants from Guatemala.

The commercial sexual exploitation of children, including sex tourism, remains a problem in the populated areas in Guatemala including, Antigua, Guatemala City, and Solola. The Office of the Human Rights Ombudsman received 477 complaints of commercial sexual exploitation of children between 2009 and October 2015: 413 complaints of child prostitution, 60 for child pornography, and 4 for child sex tourism. Of these cases, only fifteen ended in convictions. Two individuals were arrested for allegedly running a network of bars and restaurants in Peten and Jutiapa that recruited minors to work as waiters and cooks, but instead subjected them to commercial sexual exploitation.[108]

Of course, gangs are the enterprise that takes advantage of the youth. Young asylum seekers testify time and time again that a choice to remain at home was contingent on either joining or dying; little wonder that gang recruitment numbers are stagger-ing. The US State Department reports:

> Criminals and gangs often recruited street children, many of them victims of domestic abuse, for purposes of stealing, transporting contraband, prostitution, and conducting illegal drug activities. According to the Public Ministry and the PNC, approximately 3,000 youths were involved in street gangs. The NGO Mutual Support Group reported 61 minors suffered violent deaths nationwide between January and September [2015]. NGOs dealing with gangs and other youth reported that street youth detained by police were subject to abusive treatment, including physical assaults. A significant number of unaccompanied children attempted to leave the country. Polling indicated a lack of economic and educational oppor-tunity in the country, fear of violence, and family reunification were the primary motivations for migration.[109]

The National Hospital in Guatemala City reports that on average three children a day are treated for injuries related to gang violence, and National Police records show that in the first eight months of 2015, 237 children died as a result of the violence.[110]

Beyond the general exposure to gang violence, children are also targeted for recruitment into the gangs. While the exact reason for why very young children are

---

[108] U.S. Dept. of State, *Guatemala 2015 Human Rights Report*, at 18–19.

[109] Ibid., at 19.

[110] Gangs of Guatemala produce children of violence, released by CCTV America, October 25, 2015, available at: www.cctv-america.com/2015/10/25/gangs-of-guatemala-produce-children-of-violence.

increasingly becoming the primary focus for gang recruitment is difficult to pin-
point, Guatemala's Justice of Ministry points out: "[First], children are innocent
[and] gangs take advantage of that. [Second], a child does not always have the ability to consider the consequences of his actions [and] is easily intimidated. In many
cases, [the child] is told his family will be hurt unless he joins the gang. In addition,
legally, a child cannot be tried as an adult."[111] Gangs throughout the region use
these tactics to build and maintain their criminal enterprises.

Felipe's story is a prime example of the tactics used by gangs to recruit children,
"I was volunteering at a community clinic when a gang member showed up and
tried to force me to join the gang. He became real agitated when I said 'no.' He
threatened to kill everyone in my family and I know he could. Gangs recruit like
a company searching for more employees in order to distribute more product."[112]

In a country where there are limited opportunities and a lack of parental presence,[113] children easily fall victim to the gangs. Miguel's life as a gang member
began when he was just eight years old: "A buddy of mine gave me a gun and told
me I had to defend the neighborhood and I told him I would do it." As a gang member Miguel distributed drugs and extorted money from shop owners. He recalls the
first time he shot a gun, "I don't know what came over me I just grabbed [the gun]
with both hands and felt the impact as I fired it." From that moment on he began
carrying around a 9 mm gun everywhere he went, "I felt like I was the king of the
neighborhood ... I wasn't afraid of anything."[114]

The stories like Felipe's and Miguel's illustrate how strong the influence of gangs
is within these communities and how easily young children can fall into a life of
crime and violence. To avoid that fate, many parents send their children away to
family members in the United States. Often, they can only afford to send one or two
children, leaving the rest of the family behind. The parents who risk their children's
life to the perilous journey know that if their children stay, their chances of survival
as gang members are slim.

Young women and children face yet another threat by staying in Guatemala: the
prevalence of human trafficking. In its 2015 *Trafficking in Persons Report*,[115] the US
State Department reported:

> The [Guatemalan] government identified 673 trafficking victims in 2015 ... how-
> ever, reported data did not specify the types of trafficking experienced. Of the 673
> victims identified, at least 456 were women and girls ... and 217 victims of trafficking

---

[111] Ibid.

[112] Americans for Immigrant Justice. (2014) Children Fleeing Central America: Stories from the Front
Lines in Florida, at 14.

[113] Recruitment, Redemption in the MS-13, released by Samuallogan.com, February 14, 2006, available
at: www.samuellogan.com/articles/recruitment-redemption-in-the-ms13.html.

[114] Gangs of Guatemala produce children of violence, released by CCTV America, October 25, 2015,
available at: www.cctv-america.com/2015/10/25/gangs-of-guatemala-produce-children-of-violence.

[115] U.S. Dept. of State, *Trafficking in Persons Report*, 2016, available at: www.state.gov/documents/
organization/258876.pdf.

were men and boys, including at least 174 men in forced labor ... Officials, however, had difficulty recognizing domestic servitude or other types of forced labor
not involving criminal networks as human trafficking; victims of these forms of
trafficking were unlikely to be identified or referred to protective services.[116]

The report goes on to place Guatemala's record on human trafficking within the
framework of the Trafficking Victims Protection Act (TVPA):

> Guatemala is a source, transit, and destination country for men, women, and chil-
> dren subjected to sex trafficking and forced labor. Guatemalan women, girls, and
> boys are exploited in sex trafficking within the country and in Mexico, the United
> States, Belize, and other foreign countries. Foreign child sex tourists – predomi-
> nantly from Canada, the United States, and Western Europe – and Guatemalan
> men exploit child sex trafficking victims. Women and children from other Latin
> American countries and the United States are exploited in sex trafficking in
> Guatemala. Guatemalan men, women, and children are subjected to forced labor
> within the country, often in agriculture or domestic service, and in the garment
> industry, small businesses, and similar sectors in Mexico, the United States, and
> other countries. Domestic servitude in Guatemala sometimes occurs through
> forced marriages. Indigenous Guatemalans are particularly vulnerable to labor traf-
> ficking. Guatemalan children are exploited in forced labor in begging and street
> vending, particularly within Guatemala City and along the border with Mexico.
> Child victims' family members often facilitate their exploitation. Criminal organi-
> zations, including gangs, exploit girls in sex trafficking and coerce young males in
> urban areas to sell or transport drugs or commit extortion. Some Latin American
> migrants transiting Guatemala en route to Mexico and the United States are sub-
> jected to sex trafficking or forced labor in Mexico, the United States, or Guatemala.
>   The Government of Guatemala does not fully meet the minimum standards
> for the elimination of trafficking; however, it is making significant efforts to do
> so. The government increased trafficking-related investigations, prosecutions, and
> convictions ...
>   The government increased actions to address official complicity in trafficking crimes,
> but it did not convict any complicit officials. The government stripped of official immu-
> nity two judges accused of wrongfully absolving a government official of sex traffick-
> ing. Two officials were arrested for sharing law enforcement-sensitive information with
> organized criminal groups, including those allegedly linked to human trafficking.[117]

Trafficking victims are a highly vulnerable group. Without proper social and legal
reintegration guidelines and services, they are at risk of further victimization.

---

[116] Ibid., at 185.
[117] Ibid., at 184–5. The State Department places countries onto one of four tiers, as mandated by the
  TVPA. The placement is based on the level of action a government has taken to combat trafficking.
  Tier 1 indicates that a government acknowledges the existence of human trafficking, has made efforts
  to address the problem, and meets the TVPA's minimum standards. Guatemala is a Tier 2 country.

The quality of services in remaining government-run shelters remained poor; NGO shelters provided higher quality care and had the capacity to shelter victims as long as necessary to address psycho-social, re-integration, and security needs. Nonetheless, NGO shelter operators expressed concern for victims' safety upon being discharged from shelters. They cited insufficient ongoing case management and reintegration services in government shelters, leaving some victims vulnerable to re-trafficking or retaliation from traffickers – particularly those whose cases involved organized crime groups or public officials ...

Victims residing in government facilities did not receive adequate legal support or witness protection. Prosecutors cited the lack of appropriate protection options for adult victims as a significant impediment to pursuing prosecutions in cases involving adults ... The government ... did not recognize children forced to engage in criminal activity as trafficking victims; officials acknowledged some of these victims may have been prosecuted or otherwise treated as criminals.[118]

In its 2015 trafficking prevention efforts, the Guatemalan government hoped to "reduce the demand for commercial sex, investigating suspects who purchased commercial sex with children," but "made no discernible efforts to reduce the demand for forced labor."[119]

4.6. CONCLUSION

The high levels of violence throughout the Northern Triangle countries of Guatemala, Honduras, and El Salvador continue unabated. That violence has forced thousands and thousands of refugees to flee to the United States to seek protection. The violence has created an ongoing humanitarian crisis.

The violence preys most heavily on women and children. The governments of the Northern Triangle are unable or unwilling to control the gangs that control neighborhoods and lives of the youth. Domestic violence also is uncontrolled, causing palpable fear in the lives of countless women.

[118] Ibid., at 185–6
[119] Ibid., at 186.

5

Challenges to Obtaining Relief

Asylum, Right to Counsel, Due Process, and Mental Health Considerations

Given the opportunity to represent an unaccompanied minor from Central America, an immigration attorney in the United States needs to address several questions: Why did the child flee? What type of relief is this child eligible for? What is the child's current living situation? Is the child attending school? Is the child eating on a regular basis? Is the child suffering from trauma that needs to be addressed? Is the child self-medicating with alcohol or drugs? Who is supporting the child financially and emotionally? Is there a support system in place to help the child acclimatize to life in the United States? These are some relevant and critical inquiries that immigration attorneys and social workers raise when serving the legal, social, and health needs of unaccompanied immigrant children.

Legal representation is critical. One study found that represented children have a 73 percent success rate in immigration court, compared with only 15 percent of unrepresented children. An attorney is especially important for detained immigrants, who can be ten times more likely to succeed in their deportation cases with legal representation. Furthermore, studies show that children who are represented have a much higher appearance rate in immigration court, 92.5 percent versus 27.5 percent for unrepresented children. Appearing in court is important, because an immigration judge has the authority to enter an order of removal against a respondent who does not appear.

For decades, immigration attorneys and paralegals working at community-based organizations (CBOs) have shouldered the burden of representing low-income immigrants from all corners of the globe. The migrants seek counsel for removal defense, but also to become documented, such as through asylum, to obtain work authorization, to apply for other types of visas, to get guidance with naturalization papers, or to sponsor a family member.

The great surge of unaccompanied minors and women arriving from El Salvador, Guatemala, and Honduras in 2014 shifted the paradigm of legal practice for many immigration attorneys and paralegals – especially those working at CBOs. As we saw in the early chapters, as more unaccompanied youth arrived, the Department of Justice and the Department of Homeland Security implemented a scheme of expedited dockets in which the youth were quickly put before an immigration judge to either apply for asylum or special immigrant juvenile status (SIJS) in order to stay in the United States, or suffer the consequences of deportation. Advocates knew that ushering traumatized youth to the front of the line for deportation hearings was an absurd concept, but the practice of expedited youth hearings continued unabated. The expedited system put in place imposed a bias against unaccompanied children (UAC), making it substantively and procedurally challenging for them to prevail.

In response to what came to be known as "rocket dockets," immigration attorneys across the country scrambled to assist as many UACs as possible. In most parts of the country, these attorneys did not see a marked increase in the amount of funding to properly deal with the increased demand for their services, while the government remained fairly ambivalent about the situation on the ground. Already at full capacity, legal services providers stepped up their collaborative efforts in order to represent clients seeking legal representation in deportation proceedings. A few municipalities and local governmental bodies did heed the call for help and provided much-needed infrastructure, funding, and human services to tens of thousands of new arrivals. With the federal government as a stakeholder in immigration enforcement and policy, CBOs frequently asked for help from those at the top in Washington, D.C. Limited AmeriCorps funding for hiring young attorneys by CBOs was provided, but the stipends were too small for those programs in major metropolitan areas. The plight of Central American youth essentially became partisan football that the Obama administration and many members of Congress did not feel was worth the risk of supporting.

Although the Obama administration stated that the priority for enforcement resources would focus on lawful immigrants and undocumented immigrants with criminal backgrounds, disappointingly, Obama officials continued to prioritize the removal of UAC and families arriving from Central America.[1] Even children resettled by the Office of Refugee Resettlement had to initially appear before an immigration judge and possibly an asylum officer, and they often were victimized by an ill-equipped system. As we will see in this chapter, the current immigration laws do not provide for legal representation at government expense to any person, including unaccompanied minors. For many Central American youth who faced a perilous journey to the United States, the choice was straightforward: flee or stay in their

---

[1] American Immigration Council, *A Guide to Children Arriving at the Border: Laws, Policies, and Responses* (June 26, 2015), available at: www.americanimmigrationcouncil.org/research/guide-children-arriving-border-laws-policies-and-responses.

home country and die. They arrive at the US border with hopes of finding a safe haven, but those hopes are frequently dashed because succeeding in the immigration process without a lawyer requires a herculean effort in which most UACs fail.[2]

The initial portion of this chapter is devoted to the complexities of obtaining asylum in order to provide a better sense of the challenges to obtaining this commonly sought relief. The latter part of the chapter is devoted to the importance of having legal counsel and other serious due process needs that UACs and adults with children (AWCs) or family units encounter.

5.2. CHALLENGES OF ASYLUM

Since the surge of 2014, there has been much debate about whether UACs and AWCs fleeing the northern triangle are refugees or simply migrants. A refugee is someone who is outside of his or her country of nationality and is unable or unwilling to return because of persecution or a well-founded fear of persecution on account of race, religion, nationality, membership in a particular social group, or political opinion. An immigrant generally migrates for economic, family, or other reasons. The distinction makes a difference because someone who meets the definition of a refugee qualifies for asylum; and besides asylum, there is very limited legal relief for migrants who enter the country without authorization. In the case of Syria, where millions have been displaced by a devastating civil war, it is widely undisputed that those who have fled are legitimate refugees. However, even as the Obama administration was coming to a close, officials were reluctant to label the Central American exodus a refugee crisis. Publicly, US officials said the Central American migrants are primarily escaping economic hardship in societies with rampant violence and crime perpetrated by drug cartels and organized gangs.[3]

Immigrant and human rights advocates disagree. "The reasons for [the exodus] are quite simple: The root causes of migration have continued unabated – violence in the region, narco-trafficking," according to Wendy Young, president of Kids in Need of Defense. "If you look at displacement around the world, there are more and more situations where nongovernment actors are the sources of violence," Young said. "It may not fit the classic perception of what a refugee is, but it's the same kind of abuse and the same levels of abuse we need to be aware of and offer safe haven to."[4]

This difference of opinion has made the task of obtaining protection through asylum for UACs and AWCs extremely challenging. The challenges to obtaining relief

---

[2] Tina Vasquez, *From Protected Class to High-Priority Target: How the 'System is Rigged' Against Unaccompanied Migrant Children*, Rewire (August 24, 2016), available at: https://rewire.news/ article/2016/08/24/protected-class-high-priority-target-system-rigged-unaccompanied-children/.

[3] David Nakamura, *Flow of Central Americans to U.S. Surging, Expected to Exceed 2014 Numbers*, Washington Post, September 20, 2016.

[4] David Nakamura, *Obama Thanks Mexico for 'Absorbing' Central American Refugees. His Own Administration Wants to Turn Them Away*. Washington Post, September 20, 2016.

are myriad: Strong opposition from the administration, a complex asylum system, the lack of legal representation for migrants to provide assistance in the complicated asylum process, and a lack of understanding on the part of decision-makers that posttraumatic stress can severely affect the ability of asylum applicants to tell a straightforward, cogent, and completely consistent account of what they have gone through.

Even before the 2014 surge, the United Nations High Commissioner for Refugees (UNHCR) interviewed UACs as part of a 2013 study and found that 58 percent of the children raised actual or potential concerns worthy of legal protection.[5] The children experienced personal situations of danger, abuse, or neglect that could have made them eligible to apply for asylum or another form of relief such as SIJS. Unfortunately, this does not mean that 58 percent of the children will ultimately win legal relief even if afforded the opportunity to present their claim. The UNHCR acknowledged that the United States does not interpret its asylum laws as broadly as the UNHCR. The United States is notorious among international observers for making it difficult to win an asylum case, especially given the adversarial Immigration Court system. Although UACs have the right to apply for asylum initially before the Asylum Office in a non-adversarial process, many of the gang recruitment cases are ultimately denied by Immigration Judges and Courts of Appeal, where applicants are met with a rigorous legal standard for asylum.

In order to qualify for asylum an applicant must show that he or she suffered past persecution or has a well-founded fear of future persecution because of race, religion, nationality, political opinion, or membership in a particular social group. If someone presents a fear that is not based on one of these five protected grounds, the claim will be denied, even if credible. That is often what happens with many of the gang-based cases; they are found credible, but the judges hold that the fear is not based on one of the five protected grounds. The past persecution or fear of future persecution must have a nexus with one of the protected grounds.

The primary avenues through which UACs and AWCs can obtain relief in the United States are limited. Under the right circumstances UACs may qualify for asylum and/or SIJS. More infrequently, such individuals may qualify for a U visa as a victim of a crime or a T visa for victims of human trafficking.

The SIJS process is procedurally complex. The first step in requesting SIJS status is generally for the child to obtain a state court "predicate order."[6] The order must contain three specific findings: (1) that the child is declared dependent on the state court or that the child is "legally committed to, or placed under the custody of, an agency or department of a state, or an individual or entity appointed by a state or juvenile court"; (2) that "reunification with one or both of the immigrant's parents is not viable due to abuse, neglect, abandonment, or a similar basis found under

---

[5] United Nations High Commission for Refugees, Children on the Run, March 2014.
[6] 8 U.S.C. § 1101(a)(27)(J); 8 C.F.R. § 204.11(a).

State law"; and (3) that it is not in the child's best interest to be returned to her or his country of origin.[7] The child's advocate must navigate a state's legal system to find the appropriate state court with authority; initiate an appropriate action under state law to trigger jurisdiction; and persuade a state court judge to render judgment in a form that would be sufficient for immigration purposes.[8] A huge problem is that state court practices related to SIJS vary widely from state to state and even from county to county within the same state.[9] Some state courts are outright hostile to the SIJS remedy. For example, courts in Florida are known to error on the side of denying SIJS orders, and according to one practitioner, "if you bring [an SIJS] petition, it will be dismissed offhand" in many counties.[10] Consider this example:

> In October 2015, Lucia, thirteen, was raped and impregnated. When she told her parents, they called her a "cualquiera," or "slut," and tried to send her from their home in Florida back to Guatemala. A case worker had to inform Lucia's parents that they couldn't dispatch their daughter against her wishes to another country. Unable to discard her, Lucia's parents forbade her from reporting her rape to the local police. Instead, they demanded that she extort her rapist. But ICE deported him before he could be blackmailed. Finally, when she was four or five months pregnant, Lucia's parents told her she needed to pay her "debts," so Lucia dropped out of high school and got a job at a plant nursery. At that time, her parents began to charge her $350 a month in rent.
>
> To Lucia's attorney, Rina Gil, her story was an obvious example of parental neglect and abuse, and Lucia, an undocumented minor, should therefore be eligible to apply for a green card under a program called SIJS...
>
> In September 2017, Gil, a staff attorney at Catholic Legal Services in Miami, filed a private petition for dependency, asking the Miami juvenile court to declare Lucia dependent on the state of Florida and therefore not eligible for deportation. Gil knew that for the past few years juvenile judges in Florida had been skeptical of dependency petitions filed by immigrant minors, but she thought that, since the abuse happened in Florida, Judge Cindy Lederman would look compassionately at Lucia's case. Gil had even heard that Lederman was more understanding than other Florida judges "when it comes to immigrant cases."
>
> "I figured – this is a child. She was raped ... She's not in school. She has no one taking care of her. There's no way that you can say that this child was not neglected or abused or abandoned," Gil said.

[7] 8 U.S.C. § 1101(a)(27)(J)(i).
[8] *Cf., e.g., Matter of Marcelina M.-G. v. Israel S.*, 112 AD3d 100 (N.Y. App. Div. 2d Dep't 2013) (granting predicate order; *Matter of Hei Ting C.*, 109 AD 3d 100 (N.Y. App. Di. 2d Dep't 2013) (denying predicate order because child support proceeding insufficient to confer state court jurisdiction).
[9] *See* Immigrant Legal Resource Center, *Frequently Asked Questions in 1-Parent Special Immigrant Juvenile States Cases in California Family Courts*, April 13, 2016.
[10] Ashley Cleek, *Florida Judges Are Turning Their Backs on Abused Young Immigrants*, The Nation, January 22, 2018.

Despite acknowledging Lucia's father's mistreatment, the judge denied her dependency and, with it, her best shot at protection from abuse and deportation.[11]

When the child is fortunate and an appropriate state SIJS order is obtained, the child must then complete and file the appropriate application with US Citizenship and Immigration Services (USCIS).

Although situations vary from case to case, the asylum process usually is more challenging and complex for UACs and AWCs from Central America and Mexico. Asylum is the most common relief sought by UACs and AWCs.[12] In the context of detention centers and fast-tracking, UACs and AWCs face great difficulties in obtaining asylum. Even those fortunate to be out of custody face an uphill battle. Procedurally, the individuals and families have to figure out how and when to apply for asylum, find assistance, prepare applications, find supporting documents specific to the individual, find supporting documents about relevant conditions in the home country, and prepare supporting statements or declarations if possible.

Beyond the procedural challenges, the substance of an asylum claim is very complicated. This is particularly true if the asylum petition involves a claim based on a particular social group, e.g., the person is part of a group being targeted by a particular gang, as is often the case for claims involving Central Americans.[13] Definitively stating the precise contours of a social group claim is complicated even for seasoned attorneys.[14]

5.2.1. *Unaccompanied Children*

The asylum process is different for UACs who entered as part of the surge even when compared with AWCs who entered at the same time.

As reviewed in Chapter 2, Congress passed the William Wilberforce Trafficking Victims Protection Reauthorization Act of 2008 (TVPRA). The act created requirements for the treatment of UACs and crafted substantive and procedural changes for UACs seeking relief from removal. As a result of the passage, Citizenship and Immigration Services division of the Department of Homeland Security (USCIS) now has initial jurisdiction over all asylum applications filed by unaccompanied alien children even if the child is already in removal proceedings.[15] A UAC is "a child who (A) has no lawful immigration status in the United States; (B) has not attained eighteen years of age; and (C) with respect to whom – (i) there is no parent

---

[11] Ibid.
[12] Two other forms of relief are related to asylum: withholding of removal and protection under the Convention Against Torture. The burden for those avenues of relief are higher, although they can be sought more than a year after the person has arrived in the United States.
[13] *See Matter of* W-G-R-, 26 I&N Dec. 208, 209 (BIA 2014) ("Determining whether a specific group constitutes a particular social group under the Act is often a complicated task.").
[14] *Cf.* ibid. at 209–18.
[15] INA § 208(b)(3)(C), 8 USC § 1158(b)(3)(C).

or legal guardian in the United States; or (ii) no parent or legal guardian in the United States is available to provide care and physical custody."[16]

UACs who are encountered at the United States border are apprehended, processed, and initially detained by US Customs and Border Protection (CBP). They cannot be placed in expedited removal proceedings, but regular removal (deportation) proceedings are initiated. In that sense, the children initially are placed in the same process as adults who might be seeking asylum.

The child is interviewed by an asylum officer who is supposed to listen for details of past trauma. Under USCIS guidelines, an asylum officer must conduct "child-appropriate interviews taking into account age, stage of language development, background, and level of sophistication."[17] UACs benefit from initial jurisdiction by the USCIS asylum office. This means that even if the UAC was served a notice to appear (NTA), initiating removal proceedings, before filing his or her asylum application, the UAC may first seek asylum before an asylum officer.

Even while the UAC's application is pending before the asylum office, however, he or she must appear for all scheduled hearings in immigration court. Children whose asylum applications are not granted by the asylum office then proceed to immigration court removal proceedings and must seek asylum relief there.

5.2.2. *Adults with Children and Expedited Removal*

Apprehended adults and children who make up a family unit are typically placed in immigration court removal proceedings if they are apprehended within the United States. This is not necessarily the protocol for individuals who have been apprehended at or near the United States border. In cases where apprehension takes place at or near a border, unauthorized adults with children are commonly placed in expedited removal. In these instances, CBP is supposed to screen individuals by asking questions that might elicit expressions of potential fear if the individuals were to be returned to their home country. Individuals who pass this screening are then referred to USCIS who makes a "credible fear" determination – a decision on whether the individual will be able to request asylum during a removal proceeding before an immigration judge. Otherwise, the persons have to appeal a denial of their credible fear determination to the immigration court.

For close to half the individuals deported from the United States each year, the only legal process they receive is expedited removal. Expedited removal is a summary removal procedure that allows for the deportation of noncitizens without a hearing before an immigration judge and without the right to apply for relief to

---

[16] Homeland Security Act of 2002 § 462(g)(2).

[17] Joseph E. Langlois, *Updated Procedures for Minor Principal Applicant Claims, Including Changes to RAPS*, Interoffice Memorandum (August 14, 2007); and, Joseph E. Langlois, *Implementation of Statutory Change Providing USCIS with Initial Jurisdiction over Asylum Applications Filed by Unaccompanied Alien Children*, Interoffice Memorandum (March 29, 2009).

remain in the United States. During the expedited removal process, an immigration officer – usually an officer with CBP – serves as both the prosecutor and judge, making decisions regarding deportation often within no more than twenty-four hours. A noncitizen has no right to counsel. Only if the person expresses fear of persecution if deported will he or she be given a credible fear interview to determine whether asylum can be sought.

The expedited removal process also applies if the immigration officer determines that: (1) the individual committed fraud or misrepresented a material fact for purposes of seeking entry to the United States; (2) falsely claimed US citizenship; or (3) is not in possession of a valid visa or other required documentation. The determination of whether expedited removal can be used is in the exclusive hands of the immigration officer and subject to minimal judicial review.[18]

5.2.3. *Particular Challenges in the Asylum Process*

Even when individuals pass the credible fear screening and are permitted to apply for asylum, they are definitely not home free. They face a range of hurdles, including these challenges:

5.2.3.1. One-Year Filing Deadline

As part of immigration reform legislation in 1996, Congress created a filing deadline on asylum requests. Asylum applicants now must file an asylum application within one year of entering the United States. This one-year filing deadline does not apply to applicants that are unaccompanied minors.[19] However, all other applicants must file their asylum application within one year of arrival to the United States, or prove that an exception applies.[20]

Beyond the serious problem of missing the opportunity to apply for asylum if the deadline is missed, the pressure of the one-year deadline can create another problem for attorneys trying to help. Experienced representatives know that establishing a relationship with an asylum applicant who may be suffering from Post-Traumatic Stress Disorder (PTSD) can take time. The deadline forces attorneys to come up with something to help the client submit an application in time. The facts and the case theory may not be fully developed, and the attorney has to be careful about including information that may seem contradictory later on when more information is obtained after the deadline has passed.

Exceptions to the one-year deadline are limited. Changed circumstances in the applicant's country of origin can be relied upon, such as a change in government

---

[18] *Smith v. United States Customs and Border Patrol*, 741 F.3d 1016 (9th Cir. 2014).
[19] INA § 208(a)(2)(E), 78 USC §1158(a)(2)(E).
[20] 8 CFR § 208.4(a)(2)(i).

or political power in the home country. Even a change in US asylum law interpretation could constitute changed circumstances that justify filing after the one-
year deadline.[21] Under extraordinary circumstances, the one-year deadline can be
extended as well. Extraordinary circumstances include serious illness, a long period
of mental or physical problems including those caused by persecution or gender
transition. Having a prior attorney who has engaged in ineffective assistance of
counsel on behalf of the applicant could constitute extraordinary circumstances
as well. The application, however, must still be filed within a reasonable period of
time after the changed circumstances or extraordinary circumstances occur in order
to warrant an exception to the one-year bar. Lack of awareness of the one-year deadline is not considered a justification for an untimely filing.

The one-year deadline only applies for asylum applications and not for related
relief, such as withholding of removal or relief under the convention against torture.
However, the standards for those forms of relief are much higher.

5.2.3.2. Post-Traumatic Stress Disorder

Asylum seekers who were threatened or persecuted in their home countries often
suffer mentally, physically, and/or emotionally as a result of what they witnessed or
suffered back home. The injuries suffered by individuals may result in diagnosable
mental disorders including PTSD. PTSD is likely to arise in populations that have
been exposed to "violence, experienced constant fear of physical harm, or those
who were victims or witnesses of serious trauma."[22] Not surprisingly, studies of UACs
from Central America reveal generally high levels of anxiety, depression, and PTSD
that do not dissipate over reasonable time periods.[23]

PTSD symptoms are said to fall into three core categories: intrusive memories, avoidance and numbing, and increased anxiety or heightened emotions.[24]
Individuals suffering from PTSD often experience other mental disorders and are
susceptible to depression and drug and alcohol dependence.

Going through the asylum application process can be a long and daunting experience for applicants with PTSD especially when the process can take months or even
years to complete. In the process, the individual has to delve into emotions and pain

[21] Salgado-Sosa v. Sessions, 882 F.3d 451 (4th Cir. 2018).
[22] Maureen E. Cummins, *Post-Traumatic Stress Disorder and Asylum: Why Procedural Safeguards
Are Necessary*. Journal of Contemporary Health Law and Policy 29 283 (2013). Available at: http://
scholarship.law.edu/jchlp/vol29/iss2/7; citing to Diagnostic Criteria of PTSD, PtsdSupport.net,
available at www.ptsdsupport.net/whatisptsd.html.
[23] Lorna Collier, *Helping immigrant children heal*, Monitor on Psychology. American Psychological
Association 46(3), (2015).
[24] Maureen E. Cummins, *Post-Traumatic Stress Disorder and Asylum: Why Procedural Safeguards
Are Necessary*. Journal of Contemporary Health Law and Policy 29, 283 (2013). Available at: http://
scholarship.law.edu/jchlp/vol29/iss2/7; citing to *Post-Traumatic Stress Disorder (PTSD)*, Mayo Clinic,
available at: www.mayoclinic.com/health/post-traumatic-stress-disorder/DS00246/DSECTION.

that usually are associated with traumatic events. The process is akin to reliving the tragic experience. For example, if the individual was a victim of physical or sexual abuse, in order to do a competent job, the attorney has to ask about the various aspects of the abuse: when did it start; who caused the abuse; what was the abuse; what was said; how many times; what was the response?

PTSD or other mental disorders often make it difficult for applicants to discuss the details of their persecution. Individuals may be hesitant about discussing a traumatic event or resist providing in-depth details. The interview style of attorneys, asylum officers, or immigration judges can affect the manner in which the client responds; the questions can be threatening to survivors of trauma, re-traumatizing, and fear-inducing. Aside from finding it difficult to provide a detailed story, applicants with PTSD can also find it difficult to tell a consistent story of past persecution. Furthermore, individuals who experienced several traumatic events over a period of time may start to blend different incidents together or associate unrelated events with one another.

PTSD-affected storytelling can come across as not credible to attorneys, asylum officers, or immigration judges. So, the client's inability to recount stories accurately can lead to discrepancies in testimony. Good attorneys know that in order to establish credibility, disclosing memory problems or whether the individual suffers from PTSD is critical. Corroboration of these problems by expert testimony – which can be costly – is key to the successful presentation of an asylum case when the client's memory, or ability to testify linearly, may be impaired.

5.2.3.3. Credibility

The asylum applicant's credibility is essential to a successful asylum claim. The Board of Immigration Appeals (BIA) has held that an alien can satisfy the eligibility requirements for asylum when the person's "testimony is believable, consistent, and sufficiently detailed to provide a plausible and coherent account of the basis for his [or her] fear."[25] Immigration judges generally assess credibility by considering the consistency and detail of an asylum applicant's personal testimony.[26]

Provisions of the REAL ID Act enacted by Congress in 2005 affect how credibility is to be assessed. Under the Act, asylum seekers must provide documents to corroborate their asylum claim. If documents are not available, the applicant must explain why they are unavailable or cannot be obtained. Documents that can be used for corroboration include documentary evidence, a detailed written asylum application along with a declaration and oral testimony. The REAL ID Act also makes it easier for an adjudicator to deny a claim based on any inconsistency in the asylum seeker's application or testimony. In making the asylum decision, the adjudicator can

---

[25] *Matter of Mogharrabi*, 19 I&N Dec. 439, at 445 (BIA 1987).
[26] *Matter of Fefe*, Int. Dec. 3121 (BIA 1989).

consider indirect evidence such as an applicant's demeanor, the likelihood that the applicant's account occurred, or consistency in oral and written statements. Under the REAL ID Act, asylum seekers are not presumed to be credible.

The challenge of establishing credibility is illustrated by the BIA's decision in *Matter of A-S-*.[27] In *Matter of A-S-*, the respondent was a twenty-nine-year-old native and citizen of Bangladesh who claimed past persecution and a well-founded fear of persecution on account of his political opinion. At his deportation hearing, the respondent testified that he had joined the Jatiyo Party, the political party of then-President Mohammed Ershad. In 1991 President Ershad was defeated in general elections and thereafter two rival political parties began to search for the applicant in order to kill him in retaliation for his role in the Jatiyo Party.

In making his decision, the immigration judge focused on what he considered inconsistencies between the asylum application and oral testimony. First, during his immigration proceedings the applicant testified that two individuals from rival political parties forcibly entered his house and threatened his parents upon not finding the applicant home at the time. Conversely, his asylum application stated that he was home at the time, but was hiding. Then, the applicant testified that the rival political parties returned to his home a second time, and as he attempted to flee, he was severely beaten in the head with a bamboo stick rendering him unconscious and requiring three weeks of medical treatment. Although the asylum application mentioned this occurrence, the applicant had written that the incident occurred during a different time period. At trial, the applicant described a third incident where the two rival parties again forced themselves into his house and upon discovering that the applicant was not home, physically assaulted members of his family. This incident was not mentioned in the asylum application. The asylum application did however list an occasion in which applicant was at a demonstration and was physically attacked by the police, but he did not offer any testimony about this incident at the deportation hearing. Finally, the applicant testified that a warrant for his arrest had been falsely issued, alleging that he had committed various political crimes. His application included the falsely issued warrant, but indicated that this occurred during a different time period.

Based on these inconsistencies, the immigration judge concluded that the applicant's testimony could not be relied upon, and the BIA agreed. The BIA made specific references to the applicant's inconsistencies and omissions in addition to evidence of his demeanor. The BIA found that the record supported the immigration judge's finding that the applicant testified to dates inconsistent with those in his asylum application and "omitted seemingly important events on his asylum application and while testifying."[28] Although the BIA recognized that applicants who have fled persecution may have trouble remembering exact dates when testifying

---

[27] *Matter of A-S-*, 21 I.&N. Dec. 1106 (BIA 1998).
[28] Ibid., at 9.

before a judge, the BIA felt that in this applicant's case, the dates he provided in his testimony were inconsistent with those listed on his asylum application by more than two years. This two-year discrepancy was a significant period of time to the BIA. Furthermore, the BIA took into account the fact that the applicant integrated three incidents of forced entries into one month. Ultimately, the BIA found that, "while omissions of facts in an asylum application or during testimony might not, in themselves, support an adverse credibility determination, in this case the omission of key events is coupled with numerous inconsistencies, and it is therefore another specific and cogent reason supporting the immigration judge's adverse credibility finding."[29]

With respect to the applicant's demeanor, the BIA found that the immigration judge's "reasonable determination that the [applicant's] very halting and hesitant manner of testifying indicated deception" was strengthened by the judge's "full range of specific and cogent credibility findings."[30] Ultimately, the BIA found that the applicant gave halting and hesitant testimony marked by inconsistencies and omissions hence the immigration judge's "findings regarding the substance of the applicant's testimony provide[d] additional support for the reasonable conclusion that the [applicant's] testimonial demeanor called his credibility into doubt."[31]

The BIA's analysis in *Matter of A-S-* is problematic. Two strong dissenting opinions in the case point to a number of things such as the fact that halting delivery in a formal context can be caused by factors unrelated to untruthfulness. The applicant had testified that he had trouble remembering things, which could be one of a number of plausible reasons for discrepancies in such things as remembering dates. In fact, difficulties in remembering dates are common with respect to victims of persecution or torture. And in a particularly strong warning to attorneys who represent asylum applicants or to adjudicators assessing credibility of asylum applicants who may or may not be represented, BIA Chairman Paul Schmidt noted in his dissent:

> The majority concludes, as reasonable adjudicators perhaps could, that the [applicant] is likely an imposter who has fabricated his claim, or the material portions of it. I, on the other hand, take him for what he appears to me to be: a persecuted individual with a less than perfect memory *who was not properly prepared to testify at his asylum hearing*.[32]

Given what we now know about the effects of PTSD, the BIA position and REAL ID approach to credibility determinations are particularly shortsighted. Professor Carol Suzuki's account of her experience with an asylum applicant who fled persecution in the Sudan is a good example of the wrongheadedness of the BIA's approach.

---

[29] Ibid., at 11–12.
[30] Ibid., at 14.
[31] Ibid., at 15.
[32] *Matter of A-S-* (BIA Chairman Paul W. Schmidt, dissenting) (emphasis added).

The next time I see Mohamed, I ask him a few more questions about the morning he fled his village, to make sure that I have enough detail to adequately explain in the affidavit the level of devastation he experienced at the hands of the Janjaweed. He replies, "When the two other men and I went back to the village the next day to see if there was anything left, we were stopped by two Janjaweed on camels."

At this point in our interview, I stop and check my notes from our previous meetings. The last time we spoke Mohamed said that the attack occurred at the beginning of the day, and today he said that it happened while he was on his way home from work in the early evening. Mohamed told me in an earlier interview that as the Janjaweed set fire to the village, he ran away and did not see any more of the massacre until he returned the next day to look for survivors. Today he said that he ran away as the Janjaweed set fire to the village, and then he sat on a hill and watched the helicopters fly overhead and spray the village with machine gunfire. The story is changing in small increments, and I am confused. "Wait," I say, "last time we talked you said there were four Janjaweed on camels. Were there two, or four?"

Mohamed's story, and its inconsistencies, raise many central and difficult issues attorneys face when representing asylum applicants ... In Mohamed's case, the persecution he suffered in his native Darfur is the basis of his claim of well-founded fear. He must tell a consistent and highly detailed story of his past persecution in order to persuade the asylum officer, who will read his application and interview him, that he is credible and eligible for asylum.

However, the severe trauma an asylum applicant experiences can lead him [or her] to develop [PTSD]. PTSD can profoundly affect the ability to tell consistent and detailed stories of past persecution. An applicant suffering from PTSD may be unable to tell a story that a factfinder would find credible. This is because the applicant cannot tell a story that is consistent and highly detailed such that a factfinder would find it credible. There is an inescapable and cruel paradox evident when one considers the ramifications of PTSD on an asylum claim – those who suffer from PTSD because of their traumatic experiences, and who are deserving of asylum in the United States, may be denied asylum as a direct result of the symptoms of their affliction.

Extensive research has focused on asylum seekers and refugees from countries affected by war and related persecution ... Such individuals may be especially reluctant to divulge experiences of torture and trauma due to their vulnerable political immigrant status. Additionally, PTSD sufferers often suffer from other mental disorders, including depression and drug and alcohol dependence.

The results of the study on Kosovan and Bosnian refugees indicate that the refugee participants had discrepancies in their first-hand accounts. The discrepancies were more likely to involve those details that were peripheral to the experiences than those that made up the central gist of the event. Although a subject was more likely to have accurate recall of central elements of an experience when the experience had a high level of emotional impact on the subject rather than a neutral impact, the subject became less accurate in the recall of peripheral details of the experience. There was no significant difference regarding whether the experience recalled was a traumatic event or a non-traumatic event. Refugee participants with high levels of traumatic stress were more likely to have a greater number of discrepancies the longer the time between interviews. Therefore, discrepancies in recall over time do not necessarily indicate lying. Also, subjects who were depressed and who suffered from PTSD had difficulty recalling central details. Furthermore, the results indicated that the level of detail conveyed in the subjects' response was dictated in part by how the question was worded.

Other studies also show that memory of the details of a traumatic event are not recalled consistently over time. A study of Gulf War veterans, for instance, found that even details that seem immutable, generally objective, and highly traumatic – such as whether a soldier saw other soldiers killed or wounded – often shift or change after two years have passed. In this study, fifty-nine veterans of Operation Desert Storm completed a questionnaire regarding potential traumatic stressors faced by Desert Storm personnel. These subjects were also evaluated for PTSD. The study concluded that subjects with PTSD are more likely to have difficulty remembering details of traumatic events and their stories are more likely to become inconsistent over time. There were inconsistencies in recall of events that were generally objective and highly traumatic in nature. This study found a positive correlation between high levels of PTSD in subjects and inconsistency in memory of traumatic events.

Traumatic memory is stored differently than non-traumatic memory. Unlike explicit memory, traumatic events are stored as implicit memory, which are sensory, emotional, reflexive, or conditioned responses. A person who experiences a traumatic event processes the event in terms of the senses of sight, sound, touch, taste, and smell ... [D]uring the traumatic event, the brain becomes overwhelmed with all of the information it absorbs and stores the information as fragments. These fragments become associated with other, similar memories of possibly unrelated events. Retrieval of the memory of the traumatic event may also retrieve fragments of these unrelated events. A person who has suffered repeated, and similar traumatic events, such as numerous jailings and beatings, may blend the different occurrences together and not remember details from a particular event.[33]

I assisted in an asylum case involving the sexual assault of a woman in front of her daughter, where the woman's testimony was heard via a teleconferencing line because she was being detained at a center three hundred miles away from the immigration court. The government's attorney was critical of the halting manner in

---

[33] Carol M. Suzuki, Unpacking Pandora's box: Innovative techniques for effectively counseling asylum applicants suffering from post-traumatic stress disorder. *Hastings Race and Poverty Law Journal*, 4, 235 (2007).

which she testified, so we supplemented the record with an assessment of the client by Dr. Annika Sridharan, a specialist in dealing with trauma victims. Dr. Sridharan submitted an affidavit of support, discussing in her expert opinion, how the client's trauma and posttraumatic stress affected her testimony,

> Each individual survivor has a complex array of conscious and unconscious coping strategies and defenses to manage the unspeakable experiences, unbearable memories, and overwhelming emotions that plague them. This broad range of affective and cognitive presentations is normal, well documented in the trauma research literature, and very familiar to clinicians working with this population. Having blunted or incongruent affect does not in any way indicate that a person has not experienced trauma, is not suffering from post-traumatic symptoms, or is being untruthful in their account. To the contrary, these varying and at times incongruent responses are typical reactions to trauma, and characteristic for highly traumatized populations."

Indeed, Dr. Sridharan explained that "it is likely that [the client] was in a post-traumatic state after having experienced a sexual assault in the presence of her daughter, and being forced to flee and leave her young child behind." She went on to explain that, "many survivors have difficulty relaying such details, especially when highly anxious and under pressure, such as during a court hearing."

In short, the BIA and REAL ID Act demand for consistency and the failure to presume credibility is problematic for traumatized UACs and AWCs who have fled the pervasive violence of Central America.

5.2.3.4. Particular Social Group Parameters

The vast majority of Central American women and children who have fled to the United States seeking asylum do not fit easily into asylum categories of persecution based on race, religion, nationality, or political opinion. As a result, their asylum claims are based on an argument that they have a well-founded fear of persecution as a member of a particular social group. Their challenge is establishing that they fall in a particular social group that will be recognized by asylum decision-makers.

The BIA (which sets precedent for immigration courts) set forth its definition of "particular social group" in *Matter of Acosta*,[34] a 1985 decision involving a thirty-six-year-old male from El Salvador who had been a taxi driver. In 1976, he, along with several other taxi drivers, founded COTAXI, a cooperative organization of taxi drivers of about 150 members. COTAXI was designed to enable its members to contribute the money they earned toward the purchase of their taxis. It was one of five taxi cooperatives in the city of San Salvador and one of many taxi cooperatives throughout the country of El Salvador. Between 1978 and 1981, the applicant held

---

[34] 19 I&N Dec. 211 (BIA 1985).

three management positions with COTAXI, the duties of which he described in detail, and his last position with the cooperative was that of general manager. He held that position from 1979 through February or March of 1981. During the time he was the general manager of COTAXI, the respondent continued on the weekends to work as a taxi driver.

Starting around 1978, COTAXI and its drivers began receiving phone calls and notes requesting that they participate in work stoppages to protest against the government. The requests were anonymous but the applicant and the other members of COTAXI believed them to be from anti-government guerrillas who had targeted small businesses in the transportation industry for work stoppages, in hopes of damaging El Salvador's economy. COTAXI's board of directors refused to comply with the requests because its members wished to keep working. As a result, COTAXI received threats of retaliation. Over the course of several years, COTAXI was threatened about fifteen times. The other taxi cooperatives in the city also received similar threats.

Beginning in about 1979, taxis were seized and burned, or used as barricades, and COTAXI drivers were assaulted or killed. Ultimately, five members of COTAXI were killed in their taxis by unknown persons. Three of the COTAXI drivers who were killed were friends of the respondent and, like him, had been founders and officers of COTAXI. Each was killed after receiving an anonymous note threatening his life. One of these drivers, who died from injuries he sustained when he crashed his cab in order to avoid being shot by his passengers, told his friends before he died that three men identifying themselves as guerrillas had jumped into his taxi, demanded possession of his car, and announced they were going to kill him. The applicant received three anonymous threats and then was assaulted. He fled to the United States, fearing for his life. He sought asylum based on this past persecution and fear of future persecution because of his participation in COTAXI.

The BIA interpreted the phrase "persecution on account of membership in a particular social group" to mean persecution that is directed toward an individual who is a member of a group of persons all of whom share a common, "immutable characteristic." The shared characteristic might be an innate one such as sex, color, or kinship ties, or in some circumstances it might be a shared past experience such as former military leadership or land ownership. In the BIA's view, the particular kind of group characteristic that will qualify under this construction should be determined on a case-by-case basis. However, whatever the common characteristic that defines the group, it must be one that the members of the group either cannot change, or should not be required to change because it is fundamental to their individual identities or consciences. Only when this is the case does the mere fact of group membership become something comparable to the other four grounds of persecution under the Act, namely, something that either is beyond the power of an individual to change or that is so fundamental to their identity or conscience that it ought not be required to be changed. By construing "persecution on account of membership in a particular social group" in this manner, the BIA sought to preserve the concept that refuge is restricted to individuals who are either unable by their own actions, or as a matter of conscience should not be required, to avoid persecution.

In Acosta's case, the BIA understood that the guerrillas sought to harm the members of COTAXI, along with members of other taxi cooperatives in the city of San Salvador, because they refused to participate in work stoppages in that city. The characteristics defining the group of which the applicant was a member and subjecting that group to punishment were: (1) being a taxi driver in San Salvador; and (2) refusing to participate in guerrilla-sponsored work stoppages. However, the BIA felt that neither of these characteristics is immutable because the members of the group could avoid the threats of the guerrillas either by changing jobs or by cooperating in work stoppages. To the BIA, it may be unfortunate that the respondent either would have had to change his means of earning a living or cooperate with the guerrillas in order to avoid their threats. But the applicant's membership in the group of taxi drivers was something he had the power to change, so that he was able by his own actions to avoid the persecution of the guerrillas, he had not shown that the conduct he feared was "persecution on account of membership in a particular social group" within the BIA's construction of the asylum law.

That was a pretty harsh result, especially if one tries to imagine being in Acosta's shoes. It was also outrageous that the BIA position essentially required that Acosta change his occupation or his willingness to participate in political protest.

However, federal courts also appear to be reluctant to recognize the "particular social group" category when the size of the group is large. At the height of the civil strife in El Salvador in the 1980s, young males who were not in the military were targeted for recruitment by anti-government guerrillas. Many of these young men fled to the United States to avoid getting caught in the middle. However, the BIA and the federal Ninth Circuit Court of Appeals refused to recognize the particular social group of "young, urban, working class males of military age who had never served in the military or otherwise expressed support for the government of El Salvador." The court concluded:

> [S]uch an all-encompassing grouping as the petitioners identify simply is not that type of cohesive, homogeneous group to which we believe the term "particular social group" was intended to apply. Major segments of the population of an embattled nation, even though undoubtedly at some risk from general political violence, will rarely, if ever, constitute a distinct "social group" for the purposes of establishing refugee status. To hold otherwise would be tantamount to extending refugee status to every alien displaced by general conditions of unrest or violence in his or her home country. Refugee status simply does not extend as far as the petitioners would contend.[35]

---

[35] *Sanchez-Trujillo* v. INS, 801 F.2d 1571 (9th Cir. 1986).

In the context of the violence that has led to the surge of UACs since 2014, the Obama administration refused to recognize "former gang members" fleeing gang activity as a particular social group.[36] The BIA has refused to recognize the proposed particular social group of "Salvadoran youth who have resisted gang recruitment, or family members of such Salvadoran youth."[37] The BIA also found that the proposed group of "former members of the Mara 18 gang in El Salvador who have renounced their gang membership" was too diffuse and broad because "the group could include persons of any age, sex, or background."[38]

On the other hand, in *Henriquez-Rivas v. Holder*,[39] the federal Ninth Circuit Court of Appeals recognized witnesses against gangs as a social group. And in *Hernandez-Avalos v. Lynch*,[40] the Fourth Circuit Court of Appeals held that a mother who got death threats from gang members for refusing to turn her son over to them had viable social group claim based on family.[41] In *Perdomo v. Holder*,[42] the Ninth Circuit went far, ruling that "women in a particular country ... *could* constitute a particular social group."[43] The Ninth Circuit remanded the case to the BIA and clarified that Ninth Circuit precedent does not require a particular social group to be narrowly defined. In that case, Perdomo left Guatemala in 1991, at age fifteen, to join her mother in the United States. She feared returning to Guatemala because of the high murder rates for women there and the systematic violations of human rights women suffer. As pointed out in the Afterword, Attorney General Sessions made asylum claims based on domestic or gang violence much more challenging in June 2018 in the case *Matter of A-B-*.

In spite of the success of some particular social group claims as in the latter examples, Central American asylum applicants face tremendous challenges under the asylum law framework. Asylum and SIJS laws and procedures are simply a slice of the intricacies of immigration laws that "have been termed second only to the Internal Revenue Code in complexity. A lawyer is often the only person who could thread the labyrinth."[44] Thus, if a UAC or AWC is to have a fighting chance at a successful asylum claim, having a competent attorney is critical.

5.3. RIGHT TO AN ATTORNEY

The challenge to UAC and AWC asylum seekers is exacerbated by the fact that most do not have the assistance of an attorney to guide them through the complexities of asylum law and procedure. A person in deportation proceedings has a right to an

---

[36] *See* Joseph E. Langlois, Chief of Asylum Division of USCIS, March 2, 2010, available at: www.uscis .gov/USCIS/Laws/Memoranda/2010/Asylum-Ramos-Div-2-mar-2010.pdf.

[37] *Matter of S-E-G-*, 24 I&N Dec. 579 (BIA 2008).

[38] *Matter of W-G-R-*, 26 I&N Dec. 20 (BIA 2014).

[39] 707 F.3d 1081 (9th Cir. 2013) (en banc).

[40] 784 F.3d 944 (4th Cir. 2015).

[41] *See also Cordova v. Holder*, 759 F.3d 332 (4th Cir. 2014).

[42] 611 F.3d 662 (9th Cir. 2010).

[43] Perdomo, 611 F.3d at 667 (emphasis added).

[44] *Baltazar-Alcazar v. I.N.S.*, 386 F.3d 940, 948 (9th Cir. 2004).

attorney, but not at government expense. So if the asylum applicant cannot afford a private attorney and no legal services attorney is available, he or she is out of luck.

Obviously, given the challenges of the asylum process, having an attorney makes a difference. From July 18, 2014 to October 21, 2014, when 11,392 fast-tracked master calendar hearings were held, 1,542 children were ordered deported, and 94 percent of these UACs had no counsel.[45] From 2012 to 2014, children represented by counsel were allowed to remain in the United States in 73 percent of removal proceedings.[46] In contrast, only 15 percent of children who appeared without representation were permitted to stay in the United States.[47] As of October 2014, attorneys represented children in only about 32 percent of the 63,721 cases pending in Immigration Court.[48] Overall, legal representation correlated with up to a 43 percent increase in success rate for all respondents (adults and children) before the immigration court.[49]

Immigrants' rights groups and advocacy organizations such as the American Civil Liberties Union (ACLU) and Northwest Immigrants Right Project have taken the federal government to task for its failure to ensure that UACs have adequate legal representation in their removal proceedings. In July 2014, the ACLU and several immigrant advocacy groups brought a class action lawsuit against the Department of Homeland Security and the Department of Justice seeking to establish a right for UACs to have government-provided legal counsel in removal proceedings. In an earlier case, the US District Court for the Central District of California ordered the federal government to provide counsel to immigrant detainees with mental disabilities who are facing deportation and who are unable to adequately represent themselves in immigration hearings.[50] So arguing on behalf of UACs, litigators figured that the same principle should apply to minors. The hope was to persuade a federal judge of a UAC's right to government-provided counsel in part due to the sheer volume of Central American youths crossing the southern border and the fact that the fate of children was involved.

In *JEFM v. Lynch*, a lawsuit filed in the Western District of Washington, D.C. a group of UACs asserted that immigration authorities continually violate both the Due Process Clause of the Fifth Amendment as well as various sections of the Immigration and Nationality Act (INA) for its failure to provide all undocumented minors the right to government-provided legal representation.[51] In the most basic terms, the Due Process Clause of the Federal Constitution ensures all persons with

---

45 David Rogers, *Many child migrants lack lawyers*, Politico, November 6, 2014.
46 Transactional Records Access Clearinghouse (TRAC) Immigration Project, *Representation for Unaccompanied Children in Immigration Court* (November 25, 2014).
47 Ibid.
48 Ibid.
49 Ingrid V. Eagly and Steven Shafer, *A national study of access to counsel in immigration court*. University of Pennsylvania Law Review, 164(1), 49–50, 57 (2015).
50 *Franco-Gonzalez v. Holder*, 828 F.Supp. 2d 1133 (C.D. Cal. 2011).
51 Complaint at 2–3, JEFM v. Holder, No. 2:14-cv-01026 (W.D. Wash. July 9, 2014).

legal claims pending before a court of law shall have a fair opportunity to have their cases heard, to be able to present evidence, establish defenses, and in some circumstances, to have a trial by jury. Ironically, the INA provides that all persons in removal proceedings have the privilege of legal representation, but without expense to the government.[52] Unfortunately, an immigrant's right to counsel is far from a judicially established right in which the government has an obligation to provide such representation for those unable to afford it.[53]

Overwhelming evidence suggests that the US government has consistently violated the due process rights of immigrants regardless of their legal status. One might think that the nation's immigration laws are reasonably applied in full and fair proceedings presided over by immigration judges under supervision by the Executive Branch. However, the court filings in *JEFM* v. *Lynch* focus a bright light on systemic violations that run rampant throughout the immigration system. To be clear, *JEFM* v. *Lynch* is merely a snapshot of a troubling narrative that has only worsened with the surge of traumatized Central American youth crossing our southern borders.

The children who were plaintiffs in *JEFM* v. *Lynch*, ranging from age three to seventeen, received NTA before an immigration judge to face removal from the United States. Yet, no lawyer stood with them in their defense from deportation. For some plaintiffs, deportation proceedings had already begun, but others only received a NTA for the first time before the immigration court. Each individual child attempted to find legal representation through pro bono legal aid providers, but was unable to find any community-based legal organization with enough capacity to take their case. Thus, these children, and the class they represented, were faced with the daunting task of not only defending themselves in deportation proceedings, but also confronted with the complicated feat of presenting a viable legal claim for remedy such as asylum, cancellation of removal, or a torture convention claim. No counsel was available even though the scheme of immigration provisions and enforcement policies applied by border officials, administrative officers, and the federal courts has been compared to the tax code in both their intricate nuances and overall complexity.[54]

The group of plaintiffs who were unrepresented in their deportation hearings included:

J.E.F.M. is a ten-year-old boy, and a native and citizen of El Salvador. He was the youngest of four children born to his parents. His father was a former gang member, who then converted to Christianity and later became a pastor. J.E.F.M.'s mother was also a pastor. His parents met at church and together they started a rehabilitation center for people leaving gangs. Gang members retaliated against the center for

---

[52] 8 U.S.C. § 1362.

[53] Eagly, and Shafer, A national study of access.

[54] Joshua Daley Paulin, *Immigration Law 101*, American Bar Association (September 2013), available at: www.americanbar.org/publications/gp_solo/2013/september_october/immigration_law_101.html.

housing young people trying to leave the gangs. First, they warned J.E.F.M.'s parents to stop assisting former gang members. Then they killed J.E.F.M.'s cousin. Two weeks later, gang members murdered J.E.F.M.'s father in the street in front of their house, while J.E.F.M. and his siblings watched. J.E.F.M.'s mother continued to be threatened after this incident, so she fled the country, leaving her children with their grandmother. Approximately seven years later, the children also became targets of gang members in El Salvador. Gang members demanded that the children join and threatened them with harm if they did not. Rather than enter the gang, J.E.F.M. fled with his two older siblings. At the time he was only nine years old. J.E.F.M. and his two siblings entered the United States around July 2013, were apprehended by CBP and then placed in the custody of Office of Refugee Resettlement (ORR). They were released to a family member fifteen days later. His brother and sister also were plaintiffs.

F.L.B. is a fifteen-year-old boy, and a native and citizen of Guatemala. He was the fourth of six children born to his parents. Throughout F.L.B.'s childhood, his father, an alcoholic who abused F.L.B. and his siblings, resided in a different city and only visited occasionally. F.L.B.'s father did not make any financial contributions to the home. When he was ten years old, F.L.B. dropped out of school to work with his father in order to provide for himself, his mother, and his two younger siblings. After two years of living and working with his father, F.L.B. returned to his mother's home because he was no longer able to bear his father's abuse and excessive drinking. However, after six months at home he had to leave again due to the family's poor financial situation. F.L.B. moved back to the town where he had worked with his father, but this time lived with acquaintances. After more than a year of working and living outside the family's home, F.L.B. set out for the United States hoping to be able to support himself and have the opportunity to enroll in school. He spent approximately one month traveling through Mexico and crossed the United States border in August 2013, at the age of fourteen.

G.M.G.C. is a fourteen-year-old girl, and a native and citizen of El Salvador. Her parents left El Salvador when she was a young girl and she grew up living with her grandparents, sisters, and aunts. Although her parents were living in the United States, they called frequently and sent money to support the family. Around 2001, her father received temporary protected status (TPS) in the United States. G.M.G.C. was forced to leave her home of El Salvador after gang members began threatening the young women in her family. Her uncle in El Salvador, who is a police officer, refused to provide supplies to gang members in their town. In retaliation, the gang members made threats to the young women in the family, surveilled the family home, and harassed the young women. On one occasion, gang members attacked G.M.G.C. and her older sister while they were out buying dinner. After these incidents, the young girls were too scared to leave the family home. Fearing for their lives, G.M.G.C., her two sisters, and her young aunt, fled El Salvador and came to the United States. Border Patrol agents apprehended G.M.G.C., her sisters, and her aunt. After spending approximately one day at holding facilities near the border, G.M.G.C. was transferred to ORR custody. She remained in ORR custody before she was taken to Los Angeles, California, to reunite with her father.

G.D.S. is a fifteen-year-old boy and a native and citizen of Mexico who has lived in the United States since he was approximately one year old. He is the second youngest in a family of five children, all of whom reside in this country. G.D.S., his mother, and an older brother all possess U nonimmigrant visa status and are now seeking to adjust their status to become lawful permanent residents. G.D.S. was in the ninth grade when he was placed in a juvenile rehabilitation facility after pleading guilty to charges in juvenile court. ICE then filed a detainer against him, which advised that he faces removal proceedings where the government will seek to take away his lawful status and deport him from his home. He thus faces the threat of permanent separation from his mother and siblings.

M.A.M. is a sixteen-year-old boy, and a native and citizen of Honduras. M.A.M. has limited communication skills and special education issues, as a result of which he has limited ability to recount the suffering that he and his family endured in Honduras. M.A.M. spent his first eight years in Honduras, raised primarily by his maternal grandmother. During that time, M.A.M.'s mother left him and came to the United States, where she received TPS. Although M.A.M.'s grandmother cared for him, she could not shield him from life's brutality there. At some point prior to his eighth birthday, someone attacked M.A.M.'s father with a machete, leaving him profoundly disabled. M.A.M.'s half-brothers' father was kidnapped and murdered during those years as well. Eventually, M.A.M.'s grandmother grew elderly and ill. His father was not involved in his life, and no one else could care for him. As a result, M.A.M. came to the United States at the age of eight. Since 2006, he has resided with his mother in California. Despite the lack of an adult conviction, M.A.M. was swept into the net of interior immigration enforcement. ICE arrested M.A.M. and took him into custody in September 2011, when he was only thirteen years old and placed him into removal proceedings. Rather than transfer M.A.M. to ORR custody, however, ICE retained custody over him until his mother came forward, after which ICE released him into her care. He and his mother are indigent. They cannot afford to hire private counsel.

S.R.I.C. is a seventeen-year-old boy, and a native and citizen of Guatemala. His father left Guatemala for the United States when S.R.I.C. was a young boy. S.R.I.C. lived in Guatemala with his mother and three siblings. Although the father was in the United States during S.R.I.C.'s childhood, he called the family frequently and sent money to support S.R.I.C. and the rest of the family. The father became a lawful permanent resident of the United States in 2009. S.R.I.C. was forced to flee Guatemala when gang members began attempting to recruit him. The gang members would wait outside of his school and threaten S.R.I.C. During one such confrontation, one of the gang members cut S.R.I.C.'s leg with a knife. He still has the scars from that confrontation. When S.R.I.C. continued to resist their recruitment efforts, the gang threatened to kill S.R.I.C. and his family unless S.R.I.C. agreed to join the gang. Fearing for his life and for the well-being of his family, S.R.I.C. came to the United States to reunite with his father. In February 2014, CBP apprehended S.R.I.C. and held him in custody near the United States–Mexico border. The government thereafter initiated removal proceedings against him. After several days in detention at the border, S.R.I.C. was sent to a shelter in Houston, TX, where he remained until he was sent to Los Angeles, CA to reunite with his father in March. S.R.I.C. now resides in Los Angeles, where he is currently enrolled in school.

None of the plaintiffs could afford to pay private attorneys, no pro bono attorney was available, and legal services programs were at capacity and turned them away. So the question the plaintiffs wanted answered was whether it was fair to force them to go through deportation proceedings without representation. The plaintiff children claimed a due process and statutory right to appointed counsel at government expense in immigration proceedings. They claimed that, as minors, they "lack the intellectual and emotional capacity of adults," yet are "force[d] … to appear unrepresented in complex, adversarial court proceedings against trained [government] attorneys." According to the complaint, this lack of representation "ensure[s] that [they and] thousands of children [are] deprived of a full and fair opportunity to identify defenses or seek relief for which they qualify" in immigration court.

In defending its position that the court should not mandate the appointment of counsel, the Obama administration offered as a potential witness Jack H. Weil, a long-time immigration judge who is responsible for training other judges. Judge Weil was deposed in the case, and made an utterly unbelievable statement during questioning. He testified that children can learn immigration law well enough to represent themselves in court. "I've taught immigration law literally to 3-year-olds and 4-year-olds. It takes a lot of time. It takes a lot of patience. They get it. It's not the most efficient, but it can be done."[55]

However, most critically, the government moved to dismiss the complaint on multiple technical grounds, including "ripeness" – not ready for litigation. In some cases the removal proceedings had not commenced and in others they had not concluded at the time the complaint was filed. The government also asserted that the court did not have jurisdiction or power to make a decision at this point, because the INA channels judicial review of claims arising out of removal proceedings through the a particular petition for review process for each case individually. In other words, rather than entertain a case with a group of plaintiffs, the government argued that

---

[55] Molly Hennessy-Fiske, *This judge says toddlers can defend themselves in immigration court*, LA Times, March 6, 2016.

each individual plaintiff needed to go through the deportation hearing process and raise the right to counsel issue in the individual case one at a time.

In response to the government's request to throw out the case, on April 13, 2015, the district court ruled that the plaintiffs in *JEFM* v. *Lynch* had sufficiently stated facts to maintain their lawsuit to claim a constitutional right to counsel. As such, the district court asserted jurisdiction to entertain the children's Fifth Amendment due process rights as a group.[56] On the other hand, the court also held that federal appellate courts, not the district courts, have the jurisdiction to hear certain legal claims based on the INA. Under our immigration laws, each child would need to exhaust all administrative procedures starting with the deportation hearing before an immigration judge. As such, the district court ordered the immigration law claims dismissed because an initial individually based determination before the immigration courts was the proper starting point for such relief.[57]

The district court's ruling on the constitutional argument was, however, a small victory for the unaccompanied minors. The court felt that "the due process question plaintiffs ... raised ... [was] far too important to consign it, as defendants propose[d], to the perhaps perpetual loop of the administrative and judicial review process."[58] The court went even further to indicate that without legal representation there was a distinct possibility that the children would be deprived of their guaranteed rights afforded to them under the Federal Constitution. It has been well established that "[a] fundamental precept of due process is that individuals have a right to be heard,"[59] the court said. For UACs, any derogation by the government of their absolute constitutional right to be heard could result in a loss of life if they were ordered removed to the violence they worked so hard to flee.

On a broader level, the district court reaffirmed decades of Supreme Court jurisprudence on which advocates had tirelessly worked to gain. The Supreme Court on numerous occasions has recognized that once an undocumented individual enters US territory, that individual is vested with the full complement of due process rights guarantee by the federal Constitution, regardless of whether that presence is lawful, unlawful, temporary, or permanent.[60] The attorneys in *JEFM* v. *Lynch* were attempting to materialize these due process rights under the Fifth Amendment into an absolute right to legal representation for UACs in deportation proceedings at the government's own expense. If granted, this absolute right in civil immigration proceedings would be analogous to the right to government-provided counsel that criminal defendants have under the Sixth Amendment. However, before a determination

---

[56] *JEFM* v. *Holder*, 107 F.Supp.3d 1119, 1131–2 (W.D. Wash. 2015).
[57] Ibid., at 1143–4.
[58] Ibid., at 1126.
[59] Ibid.
[60] *See, e.g., Zadvydas* v. *Davis*, 533 U.S. 678, 693 (2001); *Plyler* v. *Doe*, 457 U.S. 202, 210 (1982); *Mathews* v. *Diaz*, 426 U.S. 67, 77 (1976); *Kwong Hai Chew* v. *Colding*, 344 U.S. 590, 596–598 (1953).

could be made on this point, both sides appealed to the Ninth Circuit Court of Appeals.

After extensive briefs were filed, the Ninth Circuit heard oral argument from the parties on July 7, 2016, and issued its opinion a few months later.[61] The panel of judges reviewed the applicable laws and cases under the INA and reached a conclusion that differed from that of the district court. The panel ruled that because all of the named and class-wide plaintiffs were children either already in deportation proceedings or soon to be in such proceedings, the law mandates that statutory and constitutional due process concerns must be raised exclusively through an individual case mechanism known as a petition for review before the courts of appeals.[62] Essentially, since the law does not afford the district court with the power to hear these particular claims from persons in immigration proceedings, the lawsuit was asking the district court to grant relief it had no power to implement. Congress has clearly provided that all claims – whether statutory or constitutional – that "aris[e] from" immigration removal proceedings can only be brought through the petition for review process in the federal courts of appeals. A class action challenging the process affirmatively rather than as a review of individual deportation cases, therefore, was inappropriate.[63]

In its disappointing decision, the court also pointed out that unrepresented minors already receive additional special protections in removal proceedings. Unless the child is accompanied by "an attorney or legal representative, a near relative, legal guardian, or friend," the immigration judge cannot accept the child's admission of removability. Immigration judges also must ensure that any waiver of the right to counsel is knowing and voluntary; otherwise, on review, the reviewing court can "indulge every reasonable presumption against waiver,"[64] and when the petitioner is a minor, the court factors "the minor's age, intelligence, education, information, understanding, and ability to comprehend" into its analysis.[65] Further, recognizing "a growing need for support systems the courts can use to effectively and efficiently manage the cases of unaccompanied minors," in 2014, the Office of the Chief Immigration Judge provided guidelines for "The Friend of the Court Model for Unaccompanied Minors in Immigration Proceedings." Although the friend of the court does not act as a representative, the friend's assistance role can be critical in monitoring the proceedings.

Although the appellate panel felt bound by the prior application of the law in right-to-counsel immigration cases, it was not shy about voicing its opinion about the moral disparity and legal inequities these children face in deportation proceedings: "Jurisdictional rulings have an anodyne character that may suggest insensitivity

---

[61] *JEFM v. Lynch*, 837 F.3d 1026 (9th Cir. 2016).
[62] Ibid.; *see also* 8 U.S.C. §§ 1252(a)(5) and 1252(b)(9).
[63] *J.E.F.M. v. Lynch*, 837 F.3d 1026 (9th Cir. 2016).
[64] *United States v. Cisneros–Rodriguez*, 813 F.3d 748, 756 (9th Cir. 2015).
[65] *Jie Lin v. Ashcroft*, 377 F.3d 1014, 1033 (9th Cir. 2004).

to the plight of the parties, particularly in a case involving immigrant children whose treatment, according to former Attorney General Eric Holder, raises serious policy and moral questions."[66] The panel went further and issued a challenge: "[T]he Executive and Congress have the power to address this crisis without judicial intervention. What is missing here? Money and resolve – political solutions that fall outside the purview of the courts."[67]

The court of appeals acknowledged:

> Given the onslaught of cases involving unaccompanied minors, there is only so much even the most dedicated and judicious immigration judges ... can do. Immigration judges are constrained by "extremely limited time and resources." Indeed, those judges may sometimes hear as many as 50 to 70 petitions in a three-to-four-hour period ... leaving scant time to delve deeply into the particular circumstances of a child's case.
>
> In light of all this, it is no surprise that then-Attorney General Holder took the position in 2014 that "[t]hough these children may not have a Constitutional right to a lawyer, we have policy reasons and a moral obligation to ensure the presence of counsel." But Congress has clearly – and repeatedly – indicated that these policy and moral concerns may not be addressed in the district court. Rather, these issues come initially within the Executive's purview as part of the administrative removal process, with review available in the Courts of Appeals through the petition for review process.
>
> To its credit, the Executive has taken some steps within this process to address the difficulties confronting unaccompanied and unrepresented minors. Through the Justice AmeriCorps program, the government awarded $1.8 million to support living allowances for 100 legal fellows who will represent children in removal proceedings. The government has also partnered with the United States Conference of Catholic Bishops and the United States Committee for Refugees and Immigrants to provide legal representation to unaccompanied children. The Executive Office for Immigration Review offers legal orientations for custodians of unaccompanied children in removal proceedings and it launched a pilot program to provide legal services to unaccompanied minors.
>
> Yet these programs, while laudable, are a drop in the bucket in relation to the magnitude of the problem – tens of thousands of children will remain unrepresented. A meritorious application for asylum, refuge, withholding of removal or other relief may fall through the cracks, despite the best efforts of immigration agencies and the best interests of the child. Additional policy and funding initiatives aimed at securing representation for minors are important to ensure the smooth functioning of our immigration system and the fair and proper application of our immigration laws.
>
> Congress and the Executive should not simply wait for a judicial determination before taking up the "policy reasons and ... moral obligation" to respond to the

---

[66] Ibid.
[67] Ibid.

dilemma of the thousands of children left to serve as their own advocates in the immigration courts in the meantime. The stakes are too high. To give meaning to "Equal Justice Under Law," the tag line engraved on the US Supreme Court building, to ensure the fair and effective administration of our immigration system, and to protect the interests of children who must struggle through that system, the problem demands action now.

However, the bottom line is that the court refused to require the government to provide counsel to minors facing the complexities of the deportation process.

The Ninth Circuit Court of Appeals subsequently did rule in a relevant case ripe for decision, but disappointed unrepresented children and immigrant rights advocates again. In an incredibly insensitive decision, on January 29, 2018, the court ruled in *C.J.L.G.* v. *Sessions* that minors are not entitled to court-appointed counsel at government expense in removal proceedings. The three-judge panel denied C.J.L.G.'s petition for review of a BIA decision, holding that neither the Due Process Clause nor the INA creates a categorical right to court-appointed counsel at government expense for alien minors, and concluding that the Board's denial of asylum, withholding of removal, and relief under the Convention against Torture was supported by substantial evidence. When C.J. entered the United States he was thirteen years old and was accompanied by his mother. So arguably, the decision could be different for unaccompanied minors.

The panel held that it is not established law that alien minors are categorically entitled to government-funded, court-appointed counsel and held that the minor had not shown a necessity for such counsel to safeguard his due process right to a full and fair hearing. The panel determined that the minor was not prejudiced by any procedural deficiencies in his proceeding. The panel concluded that the record compelled a finding that C.J. had a well-founded fear of persecution based on threats he received from the Mara gang when he resisted their recruitment efforts, but rejected C.J.'s asylum claim because he had not established that the threats had a nexus to a protected ground, or that the government was unable or unwilling to control the Maras. The panel deemed waived any argument that he was denied due process on his withholding and Convention Against Torture (CAT) claims, but noted that his withholding claim would also fail.

The panel also rejected C.J.'s argument that the INA's fair hearing provision implicitly requires court-appointed counsel at government expense for all alien minors. The panel further held that the IJ was not required to inform C.J. that he might be eligible for SIJS, concluding that the IJ's duty to inform aliens of "apparent eligibility" for relief was not triggered because, at the time of his removal proceeding, C.J. did not have a state court order that could have made him apparently eligible for SIJ status.

Finally, the panel concluded that the agency's denial of CAT relief was supported by substantial evidence. The panel concluded that: (1) the Board did not error in concluding that C.J.'s experience of having a member of the Maras put a gun to his head did not amount to "severe pain or suffering"; (2) there was no showing that the Honduran government acquiesced in the act; and (3) the record did not compel the conclusion that the government either turned a blind eye to the Maras' threats or that it would be unable or unwilling to control the Maras in the future. One of the judges in the case went out of his way to state that this ruling does not technically apply to UACs, because the juvenile in this case was accompanied by his mother. But the ruling is definitely not a good sign.

Dignity matters. Fairness matters. Justice matters. But, once again, the courts were restrained from drafting a broad, class-based, appropriate judicial remedy so badly warranted. The outdated and ill-equipped immigration laws sometimes cannot be reasonably applied in light of Congress' somewhat opaque and antiquated intentions. Unfortunately, a UAC's right to government-paid counsel is nonetheless an undeniably political headache relegated to the lawmakers in Washington, D.C.

So for now, UACs and AWCs without the resources to hire an attorney nor the luck of living or being detained in a place where pro bono or free legal services is available, must go through the complicated asylum and/or SIJS process alone.

5.4. STIPULATED REMOVALS AND DETENTION-BASED DUE PROCESS VIOLATIONS

In addition to the right-to-counsel issues, there have been reports of systemic due process abuses committed by both enforcement officers in the field and those tasked with ensuring the legality of immigrant detention conditions throughout the country. Media outlets have reported on these problems for quite some time, which suggests that widespread and systemic violations are in fact more abhorrent than the government would suggest. For at least the past ten years, the government has employed a program called "stipulated removal" where the government has expeditiously deported more than 160,000 non-US citizens.[68] Stipulated removal takes advantage of immigrants seized by border patrol or ICE agents. The affected immigrants agree to have a formal removal order entered against them without a hearing. This method of rapid deportation presents serious due process concerns because it effectively results in a government-initiated waiver of a non-citizen's right to appear before an immigration judge.

The due process violations involving stipulated removal are inherent in the deportation process that begins with an immigrant's contact with ICE officers or border patrol agents. The government's own records suggest that many ICE officers are providing detainees with poorly translated, misleading, and false information about

---

[68] Jennifer Lee Koh, et al., *Deportation Without Due Process*. National Immigration Law Center (September 2011), available at: www.nilc.org/wp-content/uploads/2016/02/Deportation-Without-Due-Process-2011-09.pdf.

their cases and the consequences of signing a stipulated removal order.[69] This data highlight a failure of the government's duty to fully and fairly inform immigrants about their substantive and procedural rights under US immigration laws and the Federal Constitution.

How can immigrants make rational, informed decisions about available legal relief when they are misled about the rights and procedures they are entitled to access? Federal regulation mandates the immigration judge to find that an immigrant's waiver of legal rights is "voluntary, knowing, and intelligent" before a stipulated removal order can be approved.[70] However, immigrants at the border confronted by enforcement authorities are in a daze. Suffering from the horrors of their journey, PTSD, and other physical illnesses, it is wholly unreasonable to conclude that adults or children can appreciate the serious implications of the documents that border agents ask them to sign.

Once newly arrived immigrants are detained by enforcement authorities, widespread evidence suggests that due process violations occur at short-term border patrol detention facilities along the southern border. The detainees are men, women, and children that have spent days if not weeks in the deserts of Mexico and the United States. Many are severely dehydrated, suffering from nutritional deficiencies, exhaustion, heatstroke, and viral infections. Some have been physically abused or sexually exploited by "coyotes" (human smugglers) on their journey across the border.

In June 2015, the ACLU brought a class action lawsuit, *Doe v. Johnson*, against the Department of Homeland Security and the Border Patrol alleging that immigrants who were subject to detention along the southern border at sites in the Tucson Sector were subject to severe due process violations. The violations included sleep deprivation, deprivation of hygienic and sanitary conditions, deprivation of adequate medical screening and medical care, deprivation of adequate food and water, and deprivation of warmth. The claims were based in part on the border patrol's failure to follow its own protocols and procedures to ensure that immigrant detainees were treated humanely and fairly during detention before being transferred to more permanent ICE centers.[71]

The Tucson Sector is the second biggest border patrol zone with over 60,000 people detained there during 2015. Many of the immigrants detained in this sector are often held in what are supposed to be short-term holding cells for no more than twelve hours. However, immigration officials developed a practice of holding some immigrants for as long as seventy-two hours, in conditions described as horrific and deplorable. Accounts from many detainees detail officials instructing detainees to strip down to single layer of clothing and being kept in extremely cold cells with

---

[69] Ibid.

[70] 8 C.F.R. § 1003.25(b).

[71] *See Complaint, Doe v. Johnson*, CV 15-00250-TUC-DCB (D. Ariz. June 8, 2015).

only thin aluminum sheets provided for warmth. Moreover, the individual holding cells are severely overcrowded with only concrete benches to sit on.[72] Further, the detainees are prevented from showering and are not provided with the most basic hygiene products. Lights are kept on at the facilities twenty-four hours a day, which makes sleep very uncomfortable, if not almost impossible, for many of the detainees.

Several anecdotes illustrate this troubling pattern across all border patrol facilities within the Tucson Sector of the Arizona–Mexico border. One immigrant detainee, Odilla Velasquez Vasquez was apprehended by the Border Patrol and placed in a holding cell at the Douglas, AZ border station for eighteen hours. Upon arrival at the holding facility neither she nor her daughter were screened for any medical issues. Vasquez inquired about the availability of medicine or healthcare services to help treat her daughter's ear infection and border agents responded that, "there is no medicine here."[73] Another detainee, Anselma Angela Ambrosio Diaz and her seven-year-old son were detained at the Douglas facility one night and then transferred to a main border patrol facility in Tucson. The two were held for nearly twenty-four hours and received little food or water; they were provided only two tiny juice boxes apiece. Jesus Alfredo Mesa Barbosa was detained at a Nogales border site for sixteen hours where he received no food or water. He was then transferred to the main Tucson facility where he was held for three days. He was not provided food or water until the last day of his detention at the Tucson facility.[74] Maria Lorena López arrived at the Naco border station and received no medical screening even though she was "experiencing heavy, sustained vaginal bleeding." After asking for medical attention, the guards simply concluded it was just her "period and gave [her] some tampons." She received no medical screening or treatment until five days later when she was officially placed in ICE custody, when it was discovered that she was suffering from injuries.[75]

As the stories illustrate, much of the mistreatment of immigrant detainees can be classified as grossly negligent, reckless indifference, and possible human rights violations. The deplorable conditions and inhumane treatment have become the accepted norm for many immigrant detainees in border patrol facilities. Apparently, officials expect the migrants to be physically and mentally able to cope with their legal situations even when mistreated.

The litigation over the mistreatment of detainees at the southern border has been met with some success. Soon after the *Doe v. Johnson* litigation started, the government asked the court to throw out the case. However, the district court felt that

---

[72] *Doe v. Johnson: Challenge to Deplorable Detention Conditions in U.S. Customs & Border Protection Facilities*, National Immigration Law Center (September 2016), available at: www.nilc.org/issues/immigration-enforcement/doe-v-johnson-issue-brief/.

[73] Declaration of Joe Goldenson, M.D. in Support of Plaintiffs' Motion for Preliminary Injunction, *Doe v. Johnson*, CV 15-00250-TUC-DCB (D. Ariz. Dec. 4, 2015).

[74] Ibid.

[75] Ibid.

allegations in the lawsuit raised valid and serious concerns about due process violations happening across the Tucson Sector. On January 11, 2016, the district court granted plaintiffs' motion for class certification to open up the possibility of relief to all those immigrants currently subject to, or those that could become subject to, border patrol detention within the Tucson Sector. The district court's order included a mandate that any current or future immigrant detainees subject to "one or more nights" of detention in Tucson Sector are eligible for relief.[76] Thus, the breadth of the January 11, 2016, order indicates the high level of concern that members of the federal judiciary have with regard to systemic due process violations committed against immigrant detainees. In late summer, 2016, the court denied the government's attempt to seal all the evidence filed with the plaintiffs' motion for a preliminary injunction asking the court to halt the unconstitutional conditions of detention while the case proceeds. The court's ruling allowed for the public release of evidence, including photographs showing deplorable conditions in the detention cells, which gained significant media coverage.

Eleni Wolfe-Roubatis, Immigration Program Director at Centro Legal de La Raza in Oakland, CA has worked extensively to address detention conditions through advocacy, education, and litigation. She has been on the front lines to help address due process violations like the ones seen along the Arizona–Mexico border. According to her first-hand experiences "the majority of people in detention have had their due process rights violated."[77] In over a decade of work, Wolfe-Roubatis has represented almost 1,000 immigrants subject to detention and indicates that such inhumane treatment and deplorable conditions are not "uncommon." As to who should be held accountable, she submits, "The executive branch of the government is ultimately responsible for this because they train these folks out in the field."[78] However, systemic due process violations largely continue unaddressed because the majority of detainees do not know their rights, they often lack access to legal representation, and in some places they are subject to prejudicial deportation proceedings once they find their way to an immigration courtroom.

The pattern of serious due process violations highlighted in *Doe v. Johnson* does not stop with border patrol apprehensions. In fact, these violations permeate throughout ICE detention facilities and affect the immigration hearings held at these sites. Civil rights organizations have been able to conduct investigations and fact-finding missions at various ICE facilities. Immigrant detainees, lawyers, and advocates present at these facilities report widespread due process concerns, including ethical violations committed by immigration judges.

---

[76] Order Granting Plaintiffs' Motion for Class Certification, *Doe v. Johnson*, CV 15-00250-TUC-DCB (D. Ariz. January 11, 2016).

[77] Interview with Eleni Wolfe-Roubatis, Esq., September 28, 2016.

[78] Ibid.

In August 2016, the Southern Poverty Law Center and Human Rights First lodged a formal complaint with the director of the Executive Office of Immigration Review (EOIR) with respect to ongoing concerns at the Stewart Detention Center located in Lumpkin, GA. Data shows that the rate of available legal representation at Stewart is shockingly low. Only 6 percent of detainees at Stewart were able to obtain representation between 2007 and 2012.[79] The EOIR complaint lodged by SPLC and HRF alleges widespread and systemic due process violations suffered by unrepresented immigrant detainees while their deportation cases are heard at the Stewart facility.

The allegations voiced by those detained at the Stewart Center are quite disturbing. Detainees report that immigration judges frequently show bias against unrepresented Central Americans that are seeking asylum claims. One immigration judge, Sandra Arrington, was reported to make off-the-record admonitions to Central American detainees that indicated that, "they will not receive relief."[80] Before the start of the master hearing calendar, Judge Arrington separated unrepresented respondents from those with lawyers, by asking one group to sit on one side of the courtroom, while those with lawyers were asked to sit on the other side. She also informed Central American respondents through an interpreter that they would not receive asylum, withholding of removal, or Convention Against Torture relief.[81] Another judge, Dan Trimble, denied bond for a detainee without looking at the bond motion. He also rarely refers detainees to the detention center's "Legal Orientation Program," which provides information about court proceedings and offers assistance.

Such prejudicial conduct exhibited in the immigration courts at the Stewart Detention Center is not only patently unfair and biased, but also operates in express contradiction to the 2011 Immigration Judge Guide on Professionalism and Ethics. This guide published by the EOIR directs all immigration judges to be: "patient, dignified, and courteous, and should act in a professional manner towards all litigants, witnesses, lawyers, and others with whom the Immigration Judge deals in his or her official capacity, and should not, in the performance of official duties, by words or conduct, manifest improper bias or prejudice."[82] Prejudicial comments toward unrepresented Central American migrants violates the professional standards of conduct expected of all immigration judges and evinces character not indicative of the principles of fairness and equality that the immigration system should aspire to.

[79] *See* Eagly and Shafer, A national study of access, at 1, 7, 38.
[80] Southern Poverty Law Center and Human Rights First, Complaint Letter re: Reports raising due process concerns for detained pro se Respondents, Stewart Immigration Court, Lumpkin, Georgia (August 25, 2016).
[81] Ibid., at 2.
[82] See Ethics and Professionalism Guide for Immigration Judges at p. 3 (2011).

In addition, detained immigrants being held at the Stewart Detention Center have also reported being discouraged from filing appeals by immigration judges in a widespread fashion. Not only is this conduct prejudicial to the chances of an unrepresented detainee to be able to have their case reviewed for errors, the action is unlawful under the INA. The law requires that when an immigration judge orders an individual to be removed, the judge must "inform the alien of the right to appeal that decision."[83] Further, officials at the Stewart Detention Center have failed to provide the required forms to allow unrepresented detainees the ability to appeal their cases to the BIAs.[84]

These accounts demonstrate how unfair, unequal, prejudicial, and biased the immigration enforcement regime is for many immigrants, starting from first contact with border patrol agents and ICE officials, and continues through the adjudication of removal proceedings before immigration judges. For many immigrants, as soon as they step across the border, they are destined for deportation. Without being apprised of asylum rights and a guaranteed right-to-counsel, the chances of obtaining legal relief will continue to be out of reach for most UACs and adults fleeing violence.

5.5. MENTAL HEALTH EVALUATIONS AND INTERFERENCE WITH LEGAL REPRESENTATION FOR DETAINEES

In August 2017, the parties in another case, *Dilley Pro Bono Project v. ICE*, reached a settlement that ensures access to mental health evaluations for certain detained mothers and children seeking asylum. The case was filed after ICE officials barred Caroline Perris, a full-time legal assistant with the Dilley Pro Bono Project (DPBP), from entering the South Texas Family Residential Center (STFRC) in Dilley, TX. The DPBP is a consortium of the American Immigration Council, the American Immigration Lawyers Association, the Catholic Legal Immigration Network, Inc. (CLINIC), and Texas Rio Grande Legal Aid (TRLA).

ICE claimed that Perris inappropriately facilitated a mental health evaluation by telephone in March 2017. She had, in fact, facilitated an evaluation with a mental health professional to avert the imminent deportation of a DPBP client and her child back to the terrible danger from which they fled. The evaluation proved critical to establish their eligibility for protection under asylum law. In May 2017, ICE formulated a policy requiring pre-approval for telephonic mental health evaluations. The agency tried to retroactively rely on the policy to justify revoking Perris' access to STFRC.

---

[83] 8 U.S.C. § 1229a(c)(5); see also, Complaint Letter, at 3.
[84] See Complaint Letter, at 3.

Because the mothers and children held in Dilley have fled countries with some of the highest levels of femicide and gender-based violence in the world, a mental health evaluation is often a crucial piece of evidence to obtain protection in the United States. For many families, such an evaluation makes a life-or-death difference: safety in the United States versus deportation to targeted violence in their home countries. A mental health evaluation can corroborate past persecution in the home country – a big step toward asylum relieve. Of course, such an evaluation also is relevant to an individual's current psychological well-being as well. Evaluations by mental health providers, which are typically conducted on a pro bono basis and telephonically at the STFRC, also assist attorneys in determining whether clients are competent to consent to representation and participating meaningfully in their cases without safeguards.

ICE's new policy raised serious challenges to the ability to engage in competent representation. DPBP legal staff was placed in an untenable position. The new policy provided no timetable or standards for obtaining approval for mental health evaluations. Staff would have to choose between potentially compromising the needs of their clients while awaiting ICE's approval or putting themselves at risk of losing access to the facility by providing the legal services they considered to be in their clients' best interests.

Perris was reinstated shortly after the lawsuit was filed. The settlement, which applies at both the Dilley and Karnes immigration detention facilities, sets forth a timetable for the approval process and limits the grounds on which ICE can deny a request for telephonic mental health evaluation. Specifically:

1. Between 7 am and 6 pm, Monday to Friday, ICE must respond to a request for approval of a new health provider within four business hours. If ICE fails to do so, the request is deemed approved.
2. ICE may deny the request only if: the provider's relevant professional license/credential is currently revoked or suspended; the provider has a relevant criminal history that indicates a risk of harm or abuse to a detainee; the provider's access to Dilley or Karnes is currently revoked for misconduct that indicates a risk of harm or abuse to the detainee. If ICE denies a request, it must provide sufficient information to permit the requester to independently verify the basis.
3. For previously approved providers, Dilley or Karnes Pro Bono Project staff must give two hours' notice that a mental health evaluation will take place.
4. If there is disagreement with ICE's assessment, the request can be elevated to the Assistant Field Office Director and/or Deputy Field Office Director.
5. The US District Court for the District of Columbia will retain authority for thirty months to adjudicate disputes concerning interpretation and enforcement of the settlement agreement and over the propriety of ICE's denial of a request for a telephonic mental health evaluation.

5.6. MENTAL HEALTH CONCERNS OF
CLIENTS AND SERVICE PROVIDERS

Another significant challenge to legal representation is maintaining the mental health of clients and service providers themselves. Chapter 3 reviewed some of the mental health challenges of the migrants themselves caused by their experiences back home, on their treacherous journey to the United States, and exacerbated by ICE detention. Relatedly, since UACs and AWCs are not provided legal services by the federal government, all too often, the provision of services, where available, falls on the shoulders of legal service attorneys who are strapped for resources and over-burdened by a pressing caseload. Consider the experiences at the USF deportation clinic that I started in response to the UAC and AWC influx in 2014.

At the beginning of each semester, Jacqueline Brown Scott, the supervising attorney, and I conduct an intensive training session for the law school clinic students on law, procedure, client counseling and interviewing, and case preparation. Those lessons are reinforced throughout the semester during weekly group case review sessions, as well as one-on-one meetings with each student. My basic immigration law course is a prerequisite for enrollment into the clinic, although the courses can be taken simultaneously. In the 2016 spring semester, four clinic students had already taken the basic immigration law course. Applying the law to practice is another matter, of course. However, all four students were relatively advanced. Kaitlin Talley and Ned Juri-Martinez had worked in immigration law prior to law school, and both were in the clinic the prior semester. Nuha Abusamra had done asylum work already at the Arab Resource and Organizing Center, and Brooke Longuevan had worked on UAC cases at Catholic Charities as part of a Rebellious Lawyering seminar.

Describing some of the basic work of the clinic provides a sense of the clients and their trauma, but also provides some idea of the pressure and responsibility the students face in their work. No doubt as they do their work, they also face the basic stress or pressures of daily life as fulltime law students. But honestly, Jacqueline and I make it very clear during our interviews of clinic applicants and at orientation that the clinic work must be their highest priority, and we have received little push-back on that position.

5.6.1. *Hearing Preparation*

Laura is a twenty-one-year-old female client who fled Honduras because she was targeted by MS-13 gang members who had a vendetta against her brother. Ned has been working with her for several weeks now, and her hearing is scheduled in a couple weeks, on April 2016. When Ned was assigned the case in the Fall semester, only the basic framework of the case had been developed. Laura was a client that Jacqueline accepted after volunteering and meeting Laura at a "rocket docket" master calendar. They met at the law school a few days later, and Jacqueline conducted a lengthy interview, prepared the asylum application, and submitted the application at a subsequent follow up appearance at the immigration court. Part of Jacqueline's work up to that point was to develop a preliminary case theory for asylum eligibility. In the Fall, Ned was assigned the responsibility of working with Laura to develop a lengthy supporting declaration, gather supporting statements from witnesses if possible, and researching relevant country conditions – evidence to be submitted to the court. As with so many of our clients, Ned learned of Laura's survival skills in fleeing violence in Honduras and her amazing ability to cope, first in ICE detention, then finally making her way to northern California. This semester, Ned must work with Laura and prepare her for direct examination.

Laura's mother and father separated when Laura was only eight days old. Her mother had to work in the fields and do domestic work for other families to make ends meet. Later, Laura stayed home to care for younger siblings. Although she did not have much of a relationship with her father, when Laura was thirteen, he invited her to the town where he lived to visit him for Christmas for about five days. However, during a holiday party at her father's house, she was drugged by one of his friends and raped. The people at the party were using drugs, and Laura was given a drink. Shortly after drinking what she thought was a soft drink, she started feeling drowsy and disoriented. She woke up the next day in another home. She had been stripped of her clothes and was in great pain; she realized she had been raped.

When Laura told her father about what happened, he did not believe her. On the contrary, her father beat her with a belt, blaming her for whatever happened. After she went home to her mother, her mother also did not believe Laura. So, on her own, Laura went to a doctor who confirmed that she had been raped. Laura was traumatized and became very depressed and suicidal. She attempted suicide on two occasions. The doctor referred her to a psychologist for counseling, which proved helpful.

Meanwhile, as her brother Daniel got older he started to get into a lot of trouble and became involved with the MS-13 gang. Initially, he just hung out with members socially, often meeting up just to drink and take drugs like marijuana and cocaine. However, as Daniel became more deeply involved in drug use, he became addicted and more aggressive. He started selling drugs for the gang. Daniel attacked Laura three times, and the police arrested and detained him for over two months.

When Laura was sixteen, she started dating Agustin, who was about six years older. She eventually moved in with Agustin and his mother, and they had a daughter, Ana. Agustin, who had previously lived in the United States, soon returned to the United States to find work, in order to help support the family. His mother was ill and unable to work, so Laura and Ana continued to live with her.

Meanwhile, MS-13 started to get more aggressive with Laura's brother Daniel. He owed them drug money, so they recruited him to rape and kill in addition to selling drugs. He was told that if he refused, they would target his family. Instead, he fled into hiding, and he continues to move around only in disguise. Gang members went to Laura's mother demanding to know where Daniel was. She felt so threatened, that she moved into hiding herself in a very poor barrio. She lives in constant fear and is afraid to leave home by herself. She was distraught as that a week or so before Laura's deportation hearing, Laura learned that her mother had attempted suicide.

One day in October 2014, while Laura was living with Agustin's mother, Laura was home with her daughter Ana and two nieces. She heard a knock on the door and answered. Three men were at the door whom she immediately recognized as MS-13 because of how they were dressed and the tattoos on their arms and necks. One asked: "Are you Laura, the sister of Daniel?" She responded yes, and the inquisitor said they were there for Ana. She asked why, and he yelled: "Give us the girl or you die!" He pulled out a knife, and Laura slammed the door shut and locked it. She grabbed the three children and ran out the back door. She saw a neighbor and shouted to her to call the police. She saw the men running away, but Laura proceeded to the police station which was five or six minutes away. When she got to the station, no one was there and the door was locked.

Laura went back to the house and later called Agustin. She was upset. Three days later, she packed some belongings into a backpack and left with Ana. She felt that she could never be safe in Honduras. Getting through Mexico was especially harrowing for Laura, as it has been for countless others. It took her weeks, but she made it to the United States where she was taken into ICE custody upon attempting to enter.

Ned's job is to prepare Laura for direct examination at her upcoming deportation hearing. We have trained the clinic students on direct examination, and they have read the BIA decisions on how immigration judges and the BIA assess credibility. As with any courtroom testimony, the demeanor of the client witness is critical, but students have learned that credibility will turn quite heavily on consistency of the testimony – internally, but also when compared with the client's detailed declaration that was previously submitted and any other supporting documents or evidence.

Laura has suffered from severe trauma, and that affects her life, including how her preparation proceeds. Jacqueline told me that at an early meeting, she gave Laura a coloring book to doodle on during their interview. More relaxed, Laura was able to open up quite a bit with Jacqueline. Last semester after the second or third meeting, Laura opened up to Ned, who has a very kind and gentle demeanor; she told him about the rape – the first time she had mentioned it to anyone in the clinic. Since arriving in San Francisco, Laura has been able to receive more counseling at a community mental health center.

Ned begins the direct examination prep by meeting again with Laura for two hours about two weeks before the hearing date. He is very familiar with the facts of the case and has prepared some draft questions. Jacqueline sits in to observe and takes notes. Ned explains the process that will take place at the hearing, and shares with Laura the concepts of credibility and testimony consistency. She asks questions about who will be at the hearing; Ned explains. Ned then goes through his preliminary draft of questions with Laura. With feedback from Jacqueline after the meeting, Ned redrafts the direct examination questions and emails them to Jacqueline and me. Ned has learned for the first time that Laura's mother attempted suicide because of all the stress and anxiety from which she is suffering. From his experience and hours of clinic case review discussions, Ned knows that learning new facts from asylum clients is not uncommon, even after many meetings. Ned knows that he has to work all that in and to explain to Laura why that information is useful to the case. Ned knows that we will be going over and over the testimony with Laura. He explains to Laura the clinic's obsession with consistency and details, because of the scrutiny that the immigration judge, the government attorney, and potentially the BIA will have concerning her testimony.

Another prep meeting is scheduled a week before the hearing. Now we get more formal. For the first time, Ned does not speak with Laura in Spanish. We bring in Michael, one of our undergraduate interpreters, to serve as the court interpreter for this practice. I sit in to serve as the government attorney to raise objections during cross questioning. Most of the objections are to leading questions or assuming facts not in evidence. We explain to Laura the objections that have been raised to Ned's questions. Ned, like most students and neophyte trial attorneys, is a bit frustrated at how to ask certain questions in a non-leading manner to elicit the desired answer. The session lasts about two hours. Laura is tired, but she has done well. Having observed Laura for the first time in this setting, I tell her that her demeanor appears forthright and her mannerisms are natural. Of course, she is nervous, but nothing that indicates a lack of trustworthiness. I think she comes across very credibly. I tell her that; she is thankful.

We all meet again two days before the hearing. Ned has reworked the direct exam questions again. Michael is present again. This time Laura had to bring four-year-old Ana with her, because no one was available to babysit. Ana is chatty – wanting everyone's attention – not only her mother's. Michael, the undergrad, gives her colored markers for the erasable white board in the room. Jacqueline comes in a little late because another client had popped in unexpectedly. When Jacqueline sees Ana at the white board, Jacqueline she runs back up to her office and returns with coloring books and crayons for Ana. Ned only goes over certain sections of the direct examination with Laura. Jacqueline and I explain to Laura that the government will cross examine her. We ask relatively straightforward cross-examination questions to give Laura a feel for what might happen. We stop after an hour and a half. Laura is exhausted; Ana has been distracting to all of us (more to us clinic folks than to her mother). Laura did not do well during the examination; she was tired, and she comes across that way. We fear that we have overworked her, and hope that she recovers by hearing time, otherwise her lethargy may reflect poorly on her credibility. At every prep session, some new fact or nuance comes up. Some new items might affect consistency and credibility if not presented in the right context.

We explain that to Laura. She always understands and helps to clarify and to restate. Ned revises the direct examination questions again; Jacqueline and I review the questions with Ned over the next day and a half.

The day of the hearing, Ned, Jacqueline, and I meet Laura at 8 am, 30 minutes before the hearing is to begin. Jacqueline and I have both explained to Laura that the immigration judge – Cynthia Alvarez (not her real name) – is someone we both know. Someone who is fair. The judge is an old friend of mine, as are five of the other immigration judges in San Francisco. Cynthia had worked for Catholic Charities once upon a time, and I came close to hiring her years ago at the Immigrant Legal Resource Center. Jacqueline knows most of the immigration judges because she clerked at the court right out of law school. Jacqueline also knows the government attorney, who likely will be rigorous in cross-examination.

Laura is nervous. That's to be expected. Ned is nervous, and that's to be expected as well. Jacqueline and I reassure both Laura and Ned that they are well prepared. Jacqueline focuses on Laura, and I can see the trust that Laura has in Jacqueline her.

After we enter the courtroom, we acknowledge the court interpreter who already is present. We encourage a little conversation between the interpreter and Laura, just so that Laura can hear her voice. The interpreter is new to us. She's good – clear, calm, concise throughout; careful to clarify with the court's permission whenever necessary.

The judge enters and begins the case. She's on the record, pointing out that Ned, a second-year law student, is appearing on behalf of the respondents – Laura and her daughter Ana, who does not need to be present due to her age. After some preliminaries, direct examination begins. Ned and Laura are close to perfection. The government attorney raises few objections – those that are raised are off base. In fact, with responses from Ned and the judge's understanding of what's going on, the examination goes off without any hiccups. The direct examination runs for over an hour, including a handful of clarifying questions from the immigration judge.

A short recess is called, and during that time we assure Ned and Laura that they did great. Laura is relieved, but still nervous. There are some clarifications that will need to be made, and we warn Laura that the government attorney may ask about certain things that were stated in the declaration differently than in her testimony. Laura understands quickly.

During the direct examination, the government attorney was typing away, as if creating a transcript of her own even though a recording was being made. She often asked the interpreter to repeat a translation, just so that she could type it down correctly. I was wondering whether, as transcriptionist, she was actually paying close enough attention to what was actually being said to conduct an effective cross-examination.

As the cross-examination begins, I am impressed that the government attorney seems not only to have listened, but also has thought through some tough questions: Why is Laura's sister seemingly safe in Honduras if Laura is worried that MS-13 is targeting the family? Why doesn't Laura have a letter of support from a different relative who had been attacked? Why didn't Laura ask her mother for medical verification that her mother had attempted suicide?

The cross-examination goes on much longer than we had anticipated. However, nothing too damaging has been done to Laura's credibility. A courtroom discussion ensues about whether the government attorney needs to hear from a psychologist that we have standing by a phone to testify about Laura's PTSD and how that might affect her credibility. The government attorney waivers, then says she does not think the psychologist's testimony is necessary.

At that point, the immigration judge announces that she finds that Laura's testimony is credible and consistent. Laura, Ned, Jacqueline, and I breathe a collective, but silent, sigh of relief. The judge declares that she grants asylum. She turns to the government attorney and asks her whether the government will appeal. If yes, then the judge says she will issue a much lengthier decision with detailed credibility findings. At that point, the government attorney says that no appeal will be filed. Asylum granted. Case closed!

In the hallway outside the courtroom, we all embrace. Laura is crying tears of joy. She's grateful. We complement her. We will be in touch for final paperwork. In the meantime, Jacqueline explains to Laura the process of going upstairs to a different office to immediately have her ankle monitor removed.

In the course of the semester, both Nuha and Brooke do their own client preparations, using student interpreters, in preparation for the Asylum Office and/or for SIJS. With assistance from Mary, an undergrad interpreter, Nuha helps two sisters from El Salvador, Lizett (age eighteen) and Susana (age thirteen). It took a while for the younger sister to understand the importance of what was going on in their situation and to open up to Nuha. Over time, Nuha develops a good relationship with the sisters – one wants to be a nurse, the other a lawyer. Their mother initially came to the United States without them. They lived with an aunt who was abusive. A grandmother was harsher toward Susana. Susana had to cook and clean. After the grandmother found that Lizett was not really her grandchild (she has a different father from Susana), the grandmother made Lizett do more housework. They lived in the middle of the gang turfs. One gang member from MS-13 flirted with Lizett. This caught the attention of 18th Street gang members, who then threatened her. She got a threatening text as well. People knew that their mother was in the United States and they wanted money. The sisters fled to the United States shortly after that and ended up in an ORR shelter in Texas for a couple of months. Nuha completes the multitude of forms necessary for SIJS on Lizett's behalf in Santa Clara County. The petition is granted two weeks before Lizett turned eighteen. Susana's Asylum Office interview takes place on May 16; it too is granted. Nuha had been an Arabic interpreter herself in asylum matters. In reflecting on needing and using a Spanish interpreter, she has this reflection: "When working with an interpreter, I had to remember that a lot gets lost in translation, including but not limited to the tone of the speaker. I had to speak in sentences that were concise and clear, to not confuse the interpreter or complicate the translation process. I made an effort to ensure my client that while a language barrier existed, I was aware of and sensitive to the cultural differences at hand."

Brooke spends a lot of time during the semester also working with two UAC sisters: Aida and Amagda from El Salvador. Their stories – liked the stories of many clients – have many complicated facts. Brooke's basic task for the sisters is working with them through a student interpreter – Miriam – to prepare their written declarations to support their asylum applications. Their mother, Lorena, also needs to submit a supporting declaration because she knows so much of the back story. She fled El Salvador first. Because of a debt that her husband owed, Lorena was approached by gang members who sliced her hand and threatened to kill her and her daughters. They moved to live with grandparents (Lorena's husband was already in United States). Lorena continued selling *empanadas* in the market place, but then her friend also got harassed, and later that friend was killed; MS-13 carved initials on the body. So Lorena fled without Amagda and Aida in 2013 because she did not have enough money to bring them with her at that time. Amagda and Aida stayed with grandparents, but then an uncle gets murdered by gang members; his body was unrecognizable. This uncle had been their surrogate dad. Another neighbor got murdered, and gang members told Aida she had to join the gang or get killed. At one point they stopped Aida on the bus and threatened her. So Aida fled with the aid of a cousin Oscar; after she fled, the gang members continued to ask about her. Oscar fled because he had been attacked by the MS-13. When they got to the US border, Aida and Oscar were separated, and he got deported. When Oscar was deported, he got assaulted again by MS-13. After Aida fled, Amagda ended up at her boyfriend's home and got pregnant. Amagda was approached by the gangs as well, and they threatened her and her newborn daughter, so she fled. When we met her, Amagda, was fifteen years old with a baby she was breastfeeding. Miriam has translated documents for Brooke. Also, during the semester, Brooke interviewed Lorena the mother, after Brooke represented her at a master calendar hearing to set a final hearing date. Brooke learns that Lorena was a child during the civil war in the 1980s. As a child, she had to hide from guerrillas. Her parents dug a hole in the backyard, where the family hid when soldiers came to the neighborhood. At times, Lorena stayed down in the hole for days. When Lorena fled to the United States, she did try to raise money to bring Amagda and Aida, but could not raise enough. Lorena's crossing into the United States was bad; at the end, she had to stand overnight in the river. The smuggler had left the group she was with. One of Lorena's cousins, Francisco, is an MS-13 member. He threatened to kill the grandmother who was trying to get him to quit the gang. Lorena says that Francisco ordered the killing of another cousin, Rufino, who was beaten to death. Francisco was imprisoned. Brooke learns from Lorena that when she got attacked in the market place, the gang wanted the key and deed to her house in order to use it as a gang execution site.

5.6.2. *Stockton's Marvin and Marvin*

Stockton, California, is a Central Valley town – the seat of San Joaquin County. Stockton has a long, rich history that includes a role during California's gold rush era, as a river port development linking agriculture with the railroad lines. Stockton is also home to Marvin and Marvin. Marvin, the seventeen-year-old, is a UAC who fled to the United States from Guatemala because of gang violence. Marvin, the thirty-year-old, used to live in Guatemala a few houses away from Marvin, the teen. Marvin, the adult, fled Guatemala ten or twelve years ago and settled in Stockton, where he now works for a painting contractor.

When Marvin the teen made it to the US border, he was immediately apprehended by the border patrol, then spent a couple days in the cold, refrigerator-box-like holding facilities which detainees call *hieleras*. After ICE officials determined that Marvin the teen was from Guatemala (and not Mexico), he was transported to an ORR facility in upper state New York, where he eventually was able to reach Marvin the adult with the aid of Catholic Charities staff.

Marvin the adult had a vague recollection of Marvin the teen, because Marvin the teen was only a small kid when the older Marvin fled to the United States. Adult Marvin is a kind gentleman. He has opened his heart and limited resources to teen Marvin, because he understands the life that teen Marvin has fled.

Because of the huge caseload, the clinic has recruited pro bono attorneys to assist with a handful of the cases. One, Karen, is a former student of mine who has retired. She prepared the paperwork for a state court guardianship order on the Marvin and Marvin case. The case involved obtaining a predicate order for a SIJS application for permanent residence, based on abuse, neglect, or abandonment by a parent. Clinic students from the previous semester helped Karen with preparation of the seemingly countless state court forms that are necessary for the guardianship petition in, of all places, the probate department of the state superior court. In support of the petition, Karen and the students worked with Marvin the teen to prepare his declaration, which reads:

1. Until I fled Guatemala last June 2014, I lived at home with my parents in Aldea Los Planes, Acatenango, Chimaltenango, Guatemala. My five siblings also lived with us: two older brothers, Eddie, Daniel, two older sisters, Reina, and Noe, and one younger sister, Heidi.

2. A lot of fierce, violent gang activity took place in Aldea Los Planes. The main gang was the 18th Street Gang. The violence often involving killings and kidnappings. Sometimes [the corpses] of killing victims would just appear on the streets and neighborhoods. The gangs also assaulted the buses and people just walking at night.

3. These gang assaults were constantly happening in my town. Towns people, including my family, could readily see what had happened. The aftermath

of the violence was all around us. For example, when a bus was assaulted the word would spread and someone would tell us and we would go look.

4. I recall this type of violence my entire life in Guatemala. Gangs were not always local, but their members often came and stayed in the area where I lived.

5. Gang members would threaten me and tell me to join them. This began happening intensively when I was fifteen and sixteen years old. They would tell me that they would give me money, that I would have a better life, and that I would get protection. I refused.

6. I was physically assaulted by gang members; they hit me several times. They left scars and they did it with a pocket knife. One time they hit me with a gun on my face, and this left a scar on my lip. I lost two front teeth because of the attacks. These assaults took place mostly in my neighborhood. This would happen on my way to the store or to work. Usually this happened when I was by myself and four or five gang members would attack me.

7. This happened to other people in my family. The gang members told me not to tell the police or even my parents. I did not tell my parents, because I was warned that things would be worse for everyone if I complained. When my parents saw my bruising and bleeding, I would tell them that I fell or just got into a fight. I was worried that if I told them about the 18th Street Gang attacks on me, my parents would get attacked.

8. The gangs were everywhere. My family could not help me; the gangs would tell me that they could kill me if I told my family something or also if I told the police. I had no other relatives or friends in Guatemala who could protect me.

9. The police were not helpful. They never arrived in time to do anything. If we called them, they would arrive when everything was already over, and they would arrive late, I think because they were also afraid.

10. The assaults on me continued for a long time. I decided to flee because the last time I was attacked, right before I left, the gang members warned me that if I did not join them, they would kill me or someone in my family. My family was also threatened when they were walking in town. I believe the gang targeted me because I was the youngest boy in the family. I know other friends were also scared, and I know that others in my situation had been killed or kidnapped by the gang.

11. I left Guatemala last June, when I was sixteen years old. I was afraid that the gangs would do something to me or something to my family. The threats and assaults reached a point that I could not take. I had to leave.

12. I left in secret, without telling my parents. I heard about others who fled to the United States. I knew that it would be dangerous to cross Guatemala and Mexico. I was not sure if I would make it to the United States or if I would be able to stay if I reached the United States. But I had to do it because of the threats and assaults on me and my family. I finally told my parents when I was arrested crossing into Arizona.

13. I left Guatemala around June 25, 2014, with the little money I had from cutting wood and field work. I took a bus to the capital of Guatemala and from there I went to Chiapas, Mexico, and from Chiapas I left somewhere else, I don't remember the name. I had enough money to pay for the buses at first but the trains I did not pay. Others that I met and I would get up on top of trains and ride; that was scary. However, it was on top of the trains that I traveled most of the way here. I did not pay a smuggler.

14. I crossed the US border with some friends, the ones I met on the way, somewhere around Sonora. But, that was where we were caught. This was around July 15, 2014.

15. I was taken into custody and after a few days, I was transferred to a juvenile facility in New York. From there, I contacted Marvin, a family friend, who lived in Stockton, CA.

16. I did not remember Marvin well, but I knew that he was my parents' neighbor. My parents are close to his parents. I contacted him for the first time when the detention officials gave me a chance to make one call and they told me I had 5 minutes to talk to someone. I called my parents and my parents told me that they were going to look for someone who could help me. Immigration officials gave me a second call and my dad told me he got the number of Marvin, and that is how we connected with each other. He completed all the federal paperwork to become my custodian and went through a background check. Officials released me to Marvin on August 14, 2014.

17. I talk to my parents perhaps two or three times per month. They support the idea of Marvin being my guardian.

18. If I were to return to Guatemala, my parents would be unable to protect me from the gangs and the gang violence. The police also would not be able to adequately protect me.

19. I like my life in Stockton. I feel better because no one hits me, and I am not threatened anymore. Marvin is very good to me. We talk, go to the park, shop and go out to eat. I am happy. He enrolled me in school and encourages me to study and to be a good person. He does not want me to lose educational opportunities. He treats me well. He gives me food and he pays the rent. He buys me clothes and everything.

20. I did okay in school this last year, I did sort of good. It is difficult to learn English when one is already older. But I worked hard. I have made new friends who are good and well behaved.

21. There are some computers at school where one can stay after school after classes are over to learn English. You put on headphones to listen and you learn by repeating back what the headphones say. I use these computers often.

22. I want to stay in the United States. I want to stay because I do not want to go back and suffer through the same things again. I am afraid that if I go back the same thing will happen again.

23. I need the support of Marvin so that I am cared for and so that I am able to navigate the educational and legal systems to make sure that my basic needs are met. He is making sure that I am healthy and happy. I want to create a productive life for myself, but I cannot do it on my own.

24. Thus, I request that the Court allow me to continue to reside in the United States with Marvin as my guardian.

A special request has been made to schedule the guardianship hearing immediately, because Marvin the teen is about to turn eighteen in two weeks. At the time, California state law requires that the child be under age eighteen in order to obtain the SIJS predicate order. We are warned by the folks behind the counter at the County Clerk's Office that the probate court judge does not like these last-minute requests. However, we decide to proceed because, if we are successful, SIJS will serve as a basis for terminating deportation proceedings, and if we fail, at least we have asylum to fall back on. In other words, Marvin and Marvin understand that in a sense we have two bites at the apple, although a successful SIJS process avoids an asylum route that can be much more challenging. The students use their conventional research and writing skills to fully brief the propriety of issuing such orders at the eleventh hour. They explain the arguments to Marvin and Marvin.

The students from the previous semester, Alexandra and Lorena, and I arrive at the San Joaquin courthouse. We meet Marvin and Marvin and review their respective declarations, in case they are asked to testify. We don't know for sure, because the procedures for probate court guardianship vary from county to county in California. In fact, in some counties, the parties wait in the hallway, while a court investigator goes into the courtroom to present the case. In San Joaquin County, we know the judge wants us in the courtroom. The students and I have reviewed the arguments that have to be made to the probate court judge about jurisdiction, the federal law, the state law, the policies behind SIJS, and the necessity and propriety of signing the SIJS order that day.

We expect pushback from the judge, but get none. Apparently, he has read the pleadings. He peers over his bench and acknowledges Marvin and Marvin. He states that everything appears to be in order and signs the paperwork. The appearance is thankfully uneventful.

The judge did not provide translation to Marvin and Marvin during the five-minute proceeding, so after we are dismissed, we all retire to an attorneys' conference room in the building. We explain what just happened and the final formalities that lie ahead for terminating deportation proceedings against teen Marvin and the application for lawful permanent resident status.

At that point, adult Marvin whispers to me that he wants to speak with us privately – outside of teen Marvin's presence. We huddle off into a corner as we ask teen Marvin to step outside. Adult Marvin thanks us again and says he's been getting some pushback about going to school from teen Marvin. Teen Marvin just wants to quit school and find a job. Adult Marvin wants us to encourage the younger Marvin to stay in school.

At that point, a former clinic student Lorena takes over. Prior to coming to USF, coincidentally, she worked for the school district in Stockton. She knows of possible resources. She goes over that information with both Marvins and promises to provide them with more information in a few days.

As the students and I debrief on the drive back to San Francisco, we are reminded once again about how the clinic's job (and the job of most immigration lawyers) seems to end once we obtain relief for the client. But the client's life ahead provides many more challenges that we do little to touch upon. We resolve to have a longer conversation with both Marvins about what lies ahead, although we are arguably clueless about what they in fact may encounter in their day-to-day lives. We resolve to find more resources to share with them. We resolve to find more information to share about San Joaquin County. We resolve to find more allies to work on these challenges for all of our clients.

5.6.3. *Concern with Secondary Trauma*

At our weekly case review the day before Spring Break is about to begin, we begin the session with a discussion with our undergraduate interpreter students about the UAC and AWC process. As much as we try to demystify the asylum and/or SIJS process for our clients, we missed doing this general overview for the student interpreters, which is an oversight on our part. Understandably, the student interpreters have asked for the overview, so that they can do their jobs better. All three also are interested in attending law school someday.

I give the overview. I go over what happens at the border: how everyone who presents themselves at the border without documents or who gets caught is placed in frigid holding facilities for up to seventy-two hours; how UACs from Mexico essentially are turned back immediately, while UACs from Guatemala, El Salvador, and Honduras are sent off to ORR detention facilities scattered around the country; how men are sent off to ICE detention centers such as the one in Berks, PA; how women with children are sent to the family detention centers in Dilley or Karnes, TX, that are run by private prison companies GEO Group and Corrections Corporation of America. I explain how everyone is placed in removal proceedings initially, but that UACs seeking asylum get a chance at the Asylum Office first; adults on the other hand file their asylum applications in removal proceedings before immigration judges. UACs who are eligible for SIJS can also seek that route initially in state court after informing the immigration court. The undergrads have plenty of questions, and the clinic law students help to answer and have questions of their own. For example, the undergrads want to know what it takes to win asylum and about the conditions at the Texas detention centers. I talk a bit about well-founded fear, knowing that in the weeks ahead, the students will be exposed to the nuances of credibility findings and the need for intensive preparation for a hearing testimony. Ned and Kaitlin provide rich descriptions about what they saw and experienced at the Dilley detention center.

The clinic students then go through the weekly routine of updating everyone on their cases, including client conferences, preparation for Asylum Office interviews, client preparation for immigration court proceedings, preparation of witness declarations, and further information on the overall cases. As we get to Kaitlin, she talks about a Mexican client, Andrea, whose case is being wrapped up because asylum has been granted. Kaitlin has just spoken with Andrea's mother Nayeli. Nayeli's sister, Andrea's aunt, has been kidnapped by drug cartel members. The cartel gave her one day to leave her ranch and family, and if she didn't, they said they would kill her in front of her family and children. She left to meet the cartel and they took her to Tijuana, and Nayeli's family hasn't been able to reach her and they haven't heard anything from her since then. Nayeli and Andrea, understandably, are frightened and very worried.

This kind of trauma is not a new experience for Kaitlin (and recall Ned's client Laura, whose mother attempted suicide). Besides the fact that Kaitlin had volunteered at the Dilley detention center with Brown Scott in October, where almost everyone they encountered was deeply affected by fresh trauma, something similar happened to one of Kaitlin's other clients, Luz, from El Salvador. A month before her deportation hearing in February, one of Luz's female cousins, about twenty years old, who lived in the same neighborhood was kidnapped by the MS-13 gang. Her family saw the gang put her in a car and take her away. They didn't hear anything from her after that. Then two days before Luz's hearing, a male cousin in the same neighborhood was killed by gang members. The immigration judge focused a lot on questioning Luz about the recent events. It was devastating for Luz, but she was still able to testify well, and she was so happy to find out she wouldn't have to go back to El Salvador when the judge granted asylum.

At this point in the case review, Kaitlin is speaking in a matter-of-fact manner. She never strikes me as being super emotional, but I worry about the toll on Kaitlin – and the other students – when hearing about traumatic client experiences so often. I am concerned about Kaitlin's needs as well as the client's. I ask Kaitlin about her conversation with the client's mother Nayeli. "I spoke to Nayeli over the phone when she told me that her sister had been kidnapped by the cartel. It was very hard for her to talk about the kidnapping and tell me what had happened because it had happened only weeks before. Her family was still hoping that they might hear from her, yet they hadn't heard anything for over two weeks by then. She started crying when she told me about what had happened. She said her family was struggling to keep hoping for good news and were worrying about all the things that her sister might have suffered at the hands of the cartel."

I ask, "And how were you feeling, Kaitlin?" She says, "I was heartbroken to hear the news from Nayeli. I couldn't fathom the grief of not knowing what had happened to your sister, especially when she was last seen being smuggled into a car by a cartel. I tried to comfort her as much as I could and told her I hoped her family would hear good news soon. We talked about what she knew about the kidnapping and the last time she had heard from her sister. She was grateful for the support, but I could tell she was grappling with the reality of all the things the cartel could have done to her sister in the weeks they had not heard from her." Kaitlin adds,

> I spoke to Nayeli in person when she told me that her cousin had been kidnapped and another cousin had been killed. She is such a strong woman and we had already talked about very difficult events in her life, including witnessing her partner being killed by gang members and dealing with the rape of her three-year-old son. She started to cry when she told me the news of her cousin's kidnapping. Nayeli described how she had watched her cousin grow up in the same neighborhood where she grew up. She was devastated by the news and the gangs' continued cruelty. I told her I hoped that her family would hear good news soon and that her family would be safe from the gangs' violence.

Kaitlin's response is emblematic of maturity and humanistic qualities – qualities that are apparent in every responsibility she has taken on as my research assistant and in the clinic. These qualities may have been groomed in her legal services work prior to law school, but I want to believe that the calm, measured approach that Jacqueline, Vanessa, and I try to model for our students has helped. Other students that I have had in other clinics certainly fall short of Kaitlin's maturity, so we are blessed to have her in our clinic. Nonetheless, I reminded Kaitlin about the psychologist whom I had invited in the Fall to talk with all of us about secondary traumatization. Dr. Yvette Flores told us about how attorneys, first responders, health and mental health professionals can experience trauma symptoms upon hearing client accounts of their traumatic experiences. Common reactions include anxiety, sadness, disbelief, and any of the trauma symptoms reported by the client. Dr. Flores's recommendations to us included:

- Frequent debriefings.
- Balance the workload – do not take only asylum cases, for example.
- Get support and/or mental health consultation.
- Be aware of how you cope with stress.
- If you have personal history of trauma most likely you will be triggered.
- If you have history of trauma – go to therapy or consult with your religious leader.
- Work out/exercise/dance.
- Do yoga.
- Avoid alcohol or anything that disrupts your sleep.
- Obtain support and consultation at work.
- Do whatever helps you maintain or regain your faith in humanity.

- Remember that there are good people out there and you are one of them.
- Remember that your work is important.

I remind Kaitlin that USF also provides on-campus psychological counselors available for students. Kaitlin responds:

> Sure, it's definitely a good idea generally for anyone working with clients who have gone through so much trauma as this. This kind of support is especially important for those who work fulltime with these clients. At least as students, we're only doing it part-time, so the rest of our schedules breaks up any intense sessions with clients. That being said, I'm pretty sure we all had nightmares after Dilley. I think personally, since I've worked with other immigrant clients before the clinic, I've become more used to hearing the terrible events, figuring out their legal effect, and trying not to really think about them emotionally while I'm not with the client. My work before was usually talking with clients over the phone though, so meeting with clients in person makes things even more memorable and vivid.
>
> When I heard the news from Luz, it was also hard for me to try to comfort her. It was really hard for me to hear how the gangs had targeted yet another member of her family. I immediately thought of my own cousins and how terrible it would be to hear similar news.
>
> Also, as we don't have backgrounds in counseling or therapy, at some point I'd love to learn more about different approaches to sensitive ways of asking clients to start talking about their really traumatic events, asking them about the precise factual and emotional details we need, and supporting them as we talk through the events.

Kaitlin's advice on bringing someone in to teach us how to bring out and discuss traumatic events with our clients is something we need to do. While Jacqueline, Vanessa, and I have worked with trauma victims for years, our approach and advice on discussing traumatic events with our clients – to be calm, to be sensitive, to consider mindfulness exercises, to take your time – need supplementing. We must keep an eye out for allies who can collaborate with us for our own mental health and that of our clinic students. To that end, we are taking advantage of relevant trainings and resources provided by allies when we can. For example, for the Fall 2016 semester, we required our clinic students to enroll in a one-day training on "Cultivating Resilience" sponsored by the Center for Gender and Refugee Studies, featuring an expert from Survivors International. Through discussion and interactive exercises, the training will focus on best practices for working with survivors of trauma. The objectives of the training include increasing the ability to recognize signs of vicarious traumatization, increasing the ability to cope with these signs and symptoms, and enhancing overall professional health and longevity.

As Jacqueline and I discuss our clinic clients who have counseling needs, we also regularly make referrals to places that provide mental health services. While some resources are available in San Francisco, Oakland, and San Jose, our clients in more outlying communities – especially those in the Central Valley – do not have such services readily available. Those are definitely allies that we need to find.

5.7. CONCERNS, DOUBTS, REFLECTIONS, AND RESPONSES

Over the course of my career as an immigration attorney, advocate, and law professor, I have had the distinct honor to work with many talented legal aid lawyers and community-based advocates. The disappointing outcomes in the *JEFM* v. *Lynch* and *C.J.L.G.* v. *Sessions* cases, as well as the systemic due process violations noted above, have triggered serious concerns from many stakeholders worried about the fate of asylum seekers and especially UACs. For example, according to immigration attorneys Alison Kamhi and Rachel Prandini, the Ninth Circuit's ruling on the *JEFM* lawsuit discloses a burdensome path that unrealistically "requires an unrepresented child to make sophisticated arguments in immigration and federal court, as well as avoid deportation despite having a final order of removal."[85]

The capacity that legal aid organizations have to provide legal representation to UACs remains inadequate. Without a dramatic increase in the amount of funding provided to these groups and absent of an absolute right-to-counsel at government expense, the *JEFM* decision will continue to cause a category of unaccompanied youth to be deported back to deplorable and violent conditions in Central America. The deportation orders are, in effect, death sentences. News reports confirm that many UAC are killed after arriving back in their home countries after being deported by US immigration authorities.[86]

Abigail Trillin, the executive director of Legal Services for Children in San Francisco has worked tirelessly with vulnerable youth and immigrant children for over twenty years. She has a keen insight about the range of challenges legal aid attorneys face when representing UACs in deportation proceedings. According to Trillin, the overall scope of the border crisis, as well as the effects of violence on each immigrant child are extremely overwhelming and quite sobering. When asked what hurdles her organization faces on a daily basis with unaccompanied minor cases, she indicates that the majority of CBOs "are constantly struggling to find the right balance between the hours of work an individual UAC case requires while also balancing the needs of other children that need a representative." She went on to explain that, "without a doubt, it's a fine line to walk, especially since the nature of these cases is inherently labor intensive from the perspective of both the advocate and the child."[87]

Notwithstanding the commitment of hundreds of CBOs, there remain tens of thousands of UACs that are unable to obtain legal representation every year. For those youngsters, the prospect of remaining in the United States is slim. A 2014

---

[85] Alison Kamhi and Rachel Prandini, *Unrepresented immigrant youth, Esq.*, SF Daily Journal, 122(194), at 7 (2016).

[86] *See, e.g.*, Sibylla Brodzinsky and Ed Pilkington, *US Government Deporting Central American Migrants to their Deaths*, The Guardian (October 12, 2015), available at: www.theguardian.com/us-news/2015/oct/12/obama-immigration-deportations-central-america.

[87] Interview with Abigail Trillin, Esq., October 24, 2016.

report published by the Transactional Records Access Clearing House found that only about one-third (32 percent) of UAC out of 63,721 cases pending before the immigration courts as of October 31, 2014, were able to find a legal representative.[88] Additionally, the report noted that the presence of legal counsel was the single biggest determinative factor in determining whether a UAC could obtain a positive outcome in their deportation proceedings.[89] The data confound both newly minted immigration attorneys and seasoned advocates alike. In the face of such startling statistics, I wonder why the federal government continues to treat the arrival of UACs as an enforcement threat, rather than as a humanitarian crisis requiring all the trappings of fairness and due process.

In 2016, a report authored by immigration law experts Ingrid Eagly and Steven Shafer and published by the American Immigration Council presented data for the first national study of access to counsel in US immigration courts. This study based its findings on approximately 1.2 million deportation cases decided between 2007 and 2012. Of the cases examined, only 37 percent of immigrants nationwide in deportation proceedings were lucky enough to secure legal representation.[90] Moreover, detained immigrants had drastically lower legal representation numbers, with only 14 percent of them able to obtain counsel.

Not surprisingly, legal representation rates vary widely depending on the geographic location of the immigrant. For example, non-detained immigrants in New York City and San Francisco, had representation rates of 87 percent and 78 percent respectively, compared to a representation rate of only 47 percent for those subject to removal proceedings in Kansas City, Missouri. Strikingly, over the six-year period studied, immigrants with their cases heard in small cities were four times less likely to obtain representation.[91] Therefore, it is very doubtful that immigrants living in smaller population centers and adjacent rural areas will be lucky enough to find an immigration attorney. I have seen that in California there are few immigration legal representatives available and willing take clients who reside in the agricultural Central Valley; in fact, the staff at my law school clinic are of the few willing to regularly accept clients in this vast rural region.

Representation rates also varied greatly between nationalities, with immigrants from China able to obtain counsel 92 percent of the time, while less than one in four Hondurans could do so. While UACs were not presented separately in the AIC study, it is reasonable to conclude that their legal representation rates suffer from, and are subject to, the same rates of ethnic, incarceration, and geographic disparities as those cases reported in the AIC study. UACs are a severely vulnerable subset of the undocumented immigrant population and generally have less ability to cope with

[88] Transactional Records Access Clearing House, *New Data on Unaccompanied Children in Immigration Court* (November 25, 2014), available at: http://trac.syr.edu/immigration/reports/359/.
[89] Ibid.
[90] Eagly and Shafer *Access to Counsel in Immigration Court*.
[91] Ibid., at 10.

loss and trauma in the way that adults do. As reported by the ACLU, 44 percent of the 23,000 unaccompanied minors that were required to appear before an immigration judge in 2016 had no lawyer, and 86 percent of those children were deported back to their home countries.[92]

As Abigail Trillin reminds us,

> We have to remember that we're dealing with a very discrete population of minors here that have sustained a fair amount of trauma and it usually takes several sessions with their lawyer to build that trust element that is so critical to successful outcomes. [The public] needs to understand that the crisis is still happening, it's still unfolding, there's a misconception that the crisis has disappeared. They're fleeing insurmountable odds and circumstances just to cross the border. It's out of necessity and I think it's important for the public to understand the plight that's going on.[93]

Reports by advocates and the data make clear that fashioning a solution to the crisis in legal representation is imperative. The fact that courts are reluctant to order a remedy means that the government needs to step up to recognize its ethical responsibility.

Of course, lack of due process and right-to-counsel issues are not the only barriers that UACs face after crossing our borders. Children age seven to eleven experience special challenges to understanding the processes that are involved in what lies ahead in seeking asylum or permission to stay.[94] The ability of teenagers aged fourteen to sixteen to understand legal reasoning varies widely.[95] In addition, when violence or other forms of trauma are part of the youngster's history, cognitive abilities for decision-making and reasoning are substantially diminished. Thus, it is critically important to consider a UAC's mental and emotional ability to make complex, informed decisions in a legal environment. Our immigration system does not have built-in safeguards and preventative measures to deal with any of the physiological barriers faced by UACs.

During a speaking engagement in 2016, US Supreme Court Associate Justice Sonia Sotomayor indicated that: "as a society, we need to be thinking more clearly … about the principles that are important to us as a nation. To speak the words 'justice' means that with it comes responsibilities, responsibilities as citizens and as participants in our society to ensure that people accessing the courts are given a fair and equal opportunity to do that … the lack of legal representation in some critical areas

[92] Tina Vasquez, From Protected Class to High-Priority Target: How the 'System is Rigged' Against Unaccompanied Migrant Children, Rewire. News, Aug. 24, 2016, https://rewire.news/article/2016/08/24/protected-class-high-priority-target-system-rigged-unaccompanied-children/.

[93] Interview of Abigail Trillin, Director of Legal Services for Children, San Francisco, CA, Oct. 24, 2014.

[94] Monica K. Miller, et al., *Psychology, Law, and the Wellbeing of Children*, 20 (Oxford Press, 2014).

[95] Ibid., at 21.

is one of the things we don't do well."[96] Now more than ever, as Central American youth continue to flee unfathomable violence and poverty, the government needs to ensure that it does the right thing as the key player in our immigration system. Without increased funding for services, a guaranteed right-to-counsel, and implementation of other due process safeguards, UACs will continue to be deported to their deaths. Major changes must be made to ensure a fair process for children and women fleeing for their lives.

---

[96] U.S. Supreme Court Associate Justice Sonia Sotomayor, Robert W. Kastenmeier Lecture, University of Wisconsin – Madison (September 8, 2016).

PART III

Entering the Trump ICE Age

6

Contextualizing the Trump Immigration
Enforcement Regime

6.1. INTRODUCTION

A week before the November general election in 2016, I'm on a conference call
with the policy team of the Immigrant Legal Resource Center (ILRC). We are planning on how to push having ILRC staff attorney Angie Junck to be named to Hillary
Clinton's transition team. Angie will be key to the immigration team, because we
need someone to advocate hard to urge Clinton to not throw so-called criminal
immigrants under the bus when it comes to comprehensive immigration reform
or expansion of prosecutorial discretion. We also are talking about who Clinton
might name to be the new Deputy Attorney General to head the Department of
Justice's (DOJ) civil division – the key person who will be leading the charge on
defending the constitutionality of the president's power to issue the Deferred Action
for Parents of American citizens (DAPA) prosecutorial discretion directive that
Clinton has pledged to stand behind.

A few days before the election, in typical activist academic fashion, I'm assessing
how to best strategize my approach and allocate my time, while on a partial sabba-
tical, to do my writing and to help supervise the Immigration Clinic students. My
writing projects include this book critical of the Obama administration's handling
of the surge of unaccompanied children fleeing Central America and an immigration law textbook with Jennifer Chacón and Kevin Johnson. The clinic students are
working on asylum cases involving unaccompanied children and women and children who have fled various forms of violence in Central America. At the time, I also
am looking forward to the pledge that Clinton has made that she will shut down the
ICE family detention centers and not deport unaccompanied children.[1]

---

[1] David Nakamura, *Clinton's Stance on Immigration Is a Major Break from Obama*, Washington Post,
March 10, 2016.

The day before the general election, Monday, November 7, 2016, I'm at a conference at University of California, Los Angeles (UCLA) – The Network for Justice Planning Summit. The convening involves a nationwide, interdisciplinary research initiative of the American Bar Foundation. This project is devoted to producing innovative scholarship on the Latino population in the United States and locating the sites of intervention that promise to be the most impactful in promoting opportunity and mobility through law and policy. The aim is to generate findings that can be utilized by organizations and individuals who work to advance justice for the Latino community. We spend much of the day planning progressive work with the Latino community, partnering with academia and community-based organizations (CBOs) over the next few years of the Clinton administration.

Less than forty-eight hours later, Donald Trump has been elected President of the United States. I get a late morning call from Afra Afsharipour, a former colleague at University of California, Davis, who lives in San Francisco. She reports that when she dropped off her children at Alvarado Elementary School that morning, immigrant parents arrived scared and in tears. They were concerned that they would be deported. They weren't sure if they should bring their kids to school anymore. They weren't sure whether it's safe to leave their homes.

That call marked the start of the Trump age of Immigration and Customs Enforcement (ICE) – the Trump ICE age – for me.[2] As we witness the unfolding of President Trump's ICE enforcement, embodied by Executive Orders, unleashed ICE agents, Border Wall construction proposals, targeting of sanctuary cities, and the president's funding wish list, fear is spreading throughout immigrant communities. Immigrants and their allies are watching and reporting every perceived ICE action, perhaps contributing to a state of hysteria through social media and listservs.

During the early stages of the Trump ICE age, we seem to be witnessing and experiencing an unparalleled era of immigration enforcement. But is it unparalleled? Didn't we label Barack Obama the "Deporter-in-Chief?"[3] Wasn't it George W. Bush who used the authority of the Patriot Act to round up nonimmigrants from Muslim and Arab countries, and didn't his ICE commonly engage in armed raids at factories and other worksites?[4] Aren't there strong parallels that can be drawn between Trump enforcement plans and actions and those of other eras?

---

[2] Since that first call, I have received dozens and dozens of requests for immigration and know your
     rights presentations from countless individuals and organizations in response to Trump's immigration
     enforcement threats. They include calls from individuals at K-12 schools, junior colleges, colleges,
     churches, health care clinics, apartment complexes, libraries, community-based organizations,
     restaurants, and other businesses.
[3] Amanda Sakuma, *Obama Leaves Behind a Mixed Legacy on Immigration*, NBC News, January 15,
     2017.
[4] *See generally*, Bill Ong Hing, Institutional Racism, ICE Raids, and Immigration Reform, 44 *USF L.
     Rev.* 307 (2009).

What about the fear and hysteria in immigrant communities? Is the fear unparalleled? Why is there so much fear? Is the fear justified? Why do things seem different, in spite of rigorous immigration enforcement in the past, and even in recent years?

Chapter 6 begins with a comparison of what the Trump administration has done in terms of immigration enforcement with the enforcement efforts of other administrations. For example, I compare: (1) the attempted Muslim travel bans with post-9/11 efforts by George W. Bush and Iranian student roundups by Jimmy Carter; (2) the Border Wall proposal with the Fence Act of 2006 and Operation Gatekeeper in 1994; (3) restarting Secure Communities (fingerprint sharing program) with Obama's enforcement program of the same name; (4) expanding INA § 287(g) agreements with Bush efforts under the same statute; (5) the threat of raids by an ICE deportation army with Bush gun-toting raids; (6) extreme vetting of immigrants and refugees with what already existed under Bush and Obama; (7) threatening to cut off federal funds to sanctuary cities with the prosecution of sanctuary workers in the 1980s; (8) prioritizing "criminal" immigrants with Obama's similar prioritization; and (9) expedited removal in the interior with Bush and Obama expedited removals along the border. Then I turn to the fear and hysteria in immigrant communities that has spread throughout the country. I ask why that fear has occurred and whether this fear has a reasonable basis.

6.2. COMPARING TRUMP POLICIES WITH PAST ENFORCEMENT

Some pundits credit Trump's successful bid for the White House, at least in part, to his tough stance on immigration enforcement. His venomous attack on Mexican immigrants, his pledge to build a "great, great wall" along the southern border that would be paid for by Mexico, and his call for a "total and complete shutdown of Muslims entering the United States" were among his most publicized campaign pledges.[5] Combined with actual immigration enforcement actions that have occurred after Trump took office, his pre election rhetoric undoubtedly contributed to the fear that has flooded across the country in immigrant communities. Truth is, when Trump administration actions and proposals are juxtaposed with those of other eras, many similarities surface – and in some cases are more harsh than what Trump has offered.

---

[5] TIME, Trump's election speech, available at: http://time.com/3923128/donald-trump-announcement-speech/. From Trump's presidential announcement speech. Also, Jenna Johnson, Trump calls for 'total and complete shutdown of Muslims entering the United States', Washington Post, December 7, 2015, available at: www.washingtonpost.com/news/post-politics/wp/2015/12/07/donald-trump-calls-for-total-and-complete-shutdown-of-muslims-entering-the-united-states/?utm_term=.8beb99a424e1.

6.2.1. *The Muslim Ban*

On January 27, 2017, Trump issued Executive Order 13,769, "Protecting the Nation from Foreign Terrorist Entry into the United States" (EO-1).[6] The stated purpose was to "protect the American people from terrorist attacks by foreign nationals admitted to the United States."[7] Two courses of action were attempted. The first was, under 8 U.S.C. §1182(f), to suspend for ninety days "the immigrant and nonimmigrant entry ... of aliens" from Iraq, Libya, Sudan, Somalia, Syria, and Yemen as "detrimental to the interests of the United States."[8] The second ordered the suspension of the Refugee Admissions Program for 120 days and imposed an indefinite ban on Syria refugees; no more than 50,000 refugees were to be admitted in 2017, and a preference would be given to refugee claims based on "religious-based persecution, provided that the religion of the individual is a minority religion" in the country.[9] Within hours, several federal courts enjoined EO-1 on a range of grounds, including due process, equal protection, and the Establishment Clause.[10]

Before the restraining orders on EO-1 were issued, the damage had been done. January 27, 2017, was a Friday, and that weekend chaos ensued at a variety of airports across the country.[11] Volunteer attorneys staked out arrival areas at international terminals in New York, Chicago, Newark, Washington Dulles, Los Angeles, and San Francisco.[12] They quizzed relatives and friends awaiting the arrival of individuals from the seven countries.[13] Access to US Customs and Border Protection (CBP) agents by attorneys on behalf of anticipated arriving passengers was limited

---

[6] White House, Office of the Press Secretary, January 27, 2017. Exec. Order No. 13,769 of January 27, 2017, Protecting the Nation From Foreign Terrorist Entry Into the United States, 82 Fed. Reg. 8,977 (February 1, 2017), available at: www.federalregister.gov/documents/2017/02/01/2017-02281/protecting-the-nation-from-foreign-terrorist-entry-into-the-united-states and www.whitehouse.gov/the-press-office/2017/01/27/executive-order-protecting-nation-foreign-terrorist-entry-united-states.

[7] Ibid., § 1.

[8] Ibid., § 2. *Id.* § 3(c)

[9] Ibid., § 5(d). *Id.* § 5(b).

[10] *See, e.g., State of Washington v. Trump,* No. C17-0141JLR (W.D. Wash. February 3, 2017); *Mohammed v. United States,* No. CV 17-00786 AB (PLAx), 2017 WL 438750 (C.D. Cal. January 31, 2017); *Doe v. Trump,* No.: C17-126, 2017 WL 388532 (W.D. Wash. January 28, 2017); *Aziz v. Trump,* No. 1:17-cv-116, 2017 WL 386549 (E.D. Va. January 28, 2017).

[11] Michael D. Shear et al., *Judge Blocks Trump Order on Refugees Amid Chaos and Outcry Worldwide,* N.Y. Times, January 28, 2017, available at: www.nytimes.com/2017/01/28/us/refugees-detained-at-us-airports-prompting-legal-challenges-to-trumps-immigration-order.html?_r=0.

[12] Gene Johnson, *What Will the New Trump Travel Ban Look Like?,* U.S. News, February 28, 2017, available at: www.usnews.com/news/politics/articles/2017-02-28/airports-legal-volunteers-prepare-for-new-trump-travel-ban; The World Staff, *Volunteer lawyers come forward to assist travelers detained under Trump travel ban,* PRI, January 30, 2017, available at: www.pri.org/stories/2017-01-30/volunteer-lawyers-come-forward-assist-travelers-detained-under-trump-travel-ban; Ted Phillips, *JFK airport volunteer attorneys continue to help travel ban cases,* Newsday, February 5, 2017, available at: www.newsday.com/news/new-york/jfk-airport-volunteer-attorneys-continue-to-help-travel-ban-cases-1.13066591.

[13] *See* Victoria Macchi, *Preparing for New Travel Ban, Layers Step Up to Help Immigrants,* VOA NEWS, March 4, 2017, available at: www.voanews.com/a/immigrant-lawyers-prepare-for-travel-ban/3749414.html.

and hampered.[14] According to one list provided by the government, 746 people were detained or processed under the executive order in the "turbulent 27 hours after a judge partially blocked enforcement" of the order.[15]

Given his bad luck with the courts on EO-1, Trump segued to version 2.0. So on March 6, 2017, Trump issued a revised Executive Order (EO-2) and revoked EO-1.[16] EO-2 reinstated the ninety-day ban on travel for six of the original seven countries, removing Iraq from the list.[17] The ban was narrowed to respond to "judicial concerns" by applying only to individuals outside the United States who did not have valid visas, expressly exempting lawful permanent residents (LPRs) and refugees already admitted to the United States.[18] The refugee suspension for 120 days continued, but the minority religion preferences in refugee applications and the complete ban on Syrian refugees were removed.[19] This time around, one federal court – the Eastern District of Virginia – refused to enjoin the new ban. Judge Anthony J. Trenga, a George W. Bush appointee, was the first federal judge to uphold the Trump travel ban.[20] Interestingly, the same Eastern District of Virginia struck down EO-1, but the EO-1 case enjoining portions of EO-1 was before a different judge, Judge Leonie Milhomme Brinkema, a Bill Clinton appointee.[21] This time, Judge Trenga understood that 1965 immigration laws prohibited nationality discrimination in the

[14] Edward Helmore and Alan Yuhas, *Border Agents Defy Courts on Trump Travel Ban, Congressmen and Lawyers Say*, The Guardian, January 30, 2017, available at: www.theguardian.com/us-news/2017/jan/29/customs-border-protection-agents-trump-muslim-country-travel-ban.

[15] Larry Neumeister, *746 People Subjected to Travel Ban, January 28–29*, Associated Press, February 24, 2017. The supervising attorney of the University of San Francisco immigration law clinic, Jacqueline Brown Scott, and our law students, assisted with half a dozen cases at San Francisco International Airport, over a five-day period.

[16] White House, Office of the Press Secretary, March 6, 2017. Exec. Order of March 6, 2017, available at: www.whitehouse.gov/the-press-office/2017/03/06/executive-order-protecting-nation-foreign-terrorist-entry-united-states.

[17] Ariane de Vogue et al., *US President Donald Trump Signs New Travel Ban, exempts Iraq*, CNN, March 7, 2017, available at: www.cnn.com/2017/03/06/politics/trump-travel-ban-iraq/index.html.

[18] EO2, at § 1(b)(i).

[19] Ibid., § 1(b)(iv); *See generally* Order, *see above* note 17.

[20] Laura Jarrett, *Federal Judge Sides with Trump Administration in Travel Ban Case*, CNN Politics, March 24, 2017, available at: www.cnn.com/2017/03/24/politics/virginia-federal-judge-revised-travel-ban/index.html. (But Virginia-based US District Judge Anthony Trenga was not persuaded that Trump's past statements automatically mean the revised executive order is unlawful, especially given the changes it made from the first version. "This court is no longer faced with a facially discriminatory order coupled with contemporaneous statements suggesting discriminatory intent," Trenga explained. "And while the President and his advisers have continued to make statements following the issuance of EO-1 (the first executive order) that have characterized or anticipated the nature of EO-2 (the revised ban) the court cannot conclude for the purposes of the motion that these statements, together with the President's past statements, have effectively disqualified him from exercising his lawful presidential authority.") *Sarsour v. Trump*, 2017 WL 1113305, (E.D. Va. Mar. 24, 2017).

[21] *Aziz v. Trump*, No. 1:17–cv–116, 2017 WL 386549 (E.D. Va. January 28, 2017) (granting temporary restraining order forbidding federal government agencies from removing, pursuant to EO 13769, individuals from Dulles International Airport in Virginia and ordering respondents to "permit lawyers access to all legal permanent residents being detained at Dulles International Airport.")

issuance of visas, however, he construed EO-2 as relying on the authority to deny entry even after the issuance of a visa.[22] Also, because EO-2 was "facially neutral," Judge Trenga rejected plaintiffs' arguments that the ban violated the Establishment Clause because it disfavored the religion of Islam.[23] He focused on what he regarded as EO-2's secular purpose of protecting US citizens from terrorist attacks and rejected plaintiffs' references to the stream of anti-Muslim statements made by Trump and his close advisors before and after the election.[24] Instead, Judge Trenga relied on Supreme Court doctrine related to Congressional plenary power over immigration, and the Executive's authority to deny visas given the government's facially legitimate and non discriminatory stated purposes, citing *Kleindienst v. Mandel*, 408 U.S. 753 (1972).[25]

The US Court of Appeals for the Fourth Circuit had a conflict on its hands over EO-2. Several days before Judge Trenga's decision in Virginia, on March 15, 2017, US District Judge Theodore D. Chuang, of the District of Maryland, enjoined a major portion of the Trump order.[26] In the Maryland District Court case, Judge Chuang, an Obama appointee, saw things quite differently. He cited statement after statement by Trump and his advisors that revealed great animus toward Muslims.[27] Those statements were "highly relevant" to the intent behind EO-2, especially when Stephen Miller, the Senior Policy Advisor to the President, described EO-2 changes as "mostly minor technical differences," and stated that the "basic policies are still going to be in effect."[28] White House Press Secretary, at the time, Sean Spicer stated that the "principles of [EO-2] remain the same."[29] To Judge Chuang, the fact that EO-2 was facially neutral in terms of religion was not dispositive. The core outcome of a blanket ban on entry of nationals from the designated countries remained. Judge Chuang noted: "When President Trump discussed his planned Muslim ban, he described not the preference for religious minorities, but the plan to ban the entry of nationals from certain dangerous countries as a means to carry out the Muslim ban. These statements thus continue to explain the religious purpose behind the travel ban."[30]

Judge Chuang was not impressed by the government's attempt to adorn EO-2 with more national security window dressing. The question was not simply

---

[22] Rachel Weiner, *Virginia Judge Sides with Trump Administration on New Travel Ban*, Washington Post, March 24, 2017, available at: www.washingtonpost.com/local/public-safety/virginia-judge-gives-okay-to-new-trump-travel-ban/2017/03/24/a304be4c-0e60-11e7-ab07-07d9f521f6b5_story .html?utm_term=.838dbc6088fc.

[23] Ibid.

[24] *Sarsour v. Trump*, 2017 WL 1113305, (E.D. Va. Mar. 24, 2017).

[25] Ibid.

[26] *International Refugee Assistance Project v. Trump*, 2017 WL 1315538 (D. Maryland, April 10, 2017)

[27] Ibid.

[28] Ibid.

[29] Ibid.

[30] Ibid.

"whether the Government has identified a secular purpose for the travel ban."[31] If the secular purpose is "secondary to the religious purpose, the Establishment Clause would be violated."[32] There was no interagency consultation process. To Chuang, the "fact that the White House took the highly irregular step of first introducing the travel ban without receiving the input and judgment of the relevant national security agencies strongly suggests that the religious purpose was primary, and the national security purpose, even if legitimate, is a secondary *post hoc* rationale."[33] On the *Kleindienst* v. *Mandel* issue, the deference due to the Executive on matters of an officer's decision to deny a visa was not appropriate. That approach does not apply to the promulgation of sweeping immigration policy at the highest levels of government.[34]

The Supreme Court's intervention in the travel ban challenges has served to support the Trump administration. The Court was willing to allow the ban to go forward pending its review, given the administration's claim that national security was at stake. Then by the time the Court was going to hear oral argument in the case, the timing of the EO-2 ban had lapsed, making the case moot. By then, a new ban, EO-3, was in place, and challenges to that version were rejected by the Supreme Court as described in the Afterword.

Trump's travel bans on Muslims could draw immediate historical comparisons with Chinese and other Asian exclusion laws.[35] However, perhaps the most obvious comparisons are with post-9/11 targeting of Muslims and Arabs and the round-up of Iranian students during the Carter administration.

---

[31] Ibid.

[32] Ibid.

[33] Ibid.

[34] In my view, Judge Chuang had it right, as did US District Judge Derrick K. Watson of the Hawaii District, who enjoined EO-2 as well (noting that the populations of the six banned countries were over 90 percent Muslim and rejecting the government's argument that one can demonstrate animus toward any group of people only by targeting all of them). While they focused on the Establishment Clause violation, I think more could have been said about Trump's reliance on 8 U.S.C. § 1182(f) as statutory authority for the ban. That provision provides: "Whenever the President finds that the entry of any aliens or of any class of aliens into the United States would be detrimental to the interests of the United States, he may by proclamation, and for such period as he shall deem necessary, suspend the entry of all aliens or any class of aliens as immigrants or nonimmigrants, or impose on the entry of aliens any restrictions he may deem to be appropriate." How can the president actually assert that he has found "that the entry of" all nationals from the six countries "would be detrimental to the interests" of the country? He cannot. This provision should be reserved for an actual "class of aliens," such as a terrorist group or entity that would be coming to do us harm. He does not have the factual basis to support his ban. He cannot even come close to providing that factual basis for the assertion that entry of any random person from the six countries would be detrimental to the United States.

[35] *See generally*, Bill Ong Hing, Making and Remaking Asian America Through Immigration Policy (1993).

6.2.1.1. Post-9/11

On September 11, 2001, the United States suffered one of its most severe tragedies in modern history. Two passenger airplanes were commandeered by terrorists who crashed into the twin towers of Manhattan's Word Trade Center, causing their total destruction.[36] A third hijacked plane crashed into the Pentagon.[37] In all, almost 3,000 lives were lost that fateful day.[38]

Quick and early suspicion of the attackers focused on Muslim and Arab terrorists.[39] Although the swift Islamophobic impulse to blame Muslims was completely erroneous a few years earlier when the Mira Federal Building in Oklahoma City was bombed,[40] subsequent evidence demonstrated that this time the culprits were trained by the Muslim-extremist Osama Bin Laden.[41] The stage was set for the country's "War on Terrorism" that consumes us to this day.

In truth, one of President Bush's first public actions suggested that he actually would work hard to not foment anti-Muslim sentiment in his search for justice and to apprehend those behind the attacks. Six days after the attack, Bush visited a Washington mosque,[42] where he referred to Arab and Muslim Americans as "patriots" underserving of intimidation and harassment.[43] He boldly proclaimed, "The face of terror is not the true faith of Islam."[44] In the televised visit, he reminded the nation that American Muslims are "friends" and "taxpaying citizens."[45]

Unfortunately, it did not take long for that feel-good, multicultural moment to be overcome by one that fomented hate.[46] In its investigation of the attacks, the Bush administration detained more than 1,200 individuals, mostly of Arab and Muslim descent.[47] In February 2002, the Immigration and Naturalization Service (INS)

---

[36] N.R. Kleinfield, *U.S. Attacked, Hijacked Jets Destroy Twin Towers and Hit Pentagon in Day of Terror*, New York Times, September 12, 2011.

[37] Ibid.

[38] Joanna Walters, *9/11 Health Crisis: Death Toll from Illness Nears Number Killed on Day of Attacks*, The Guardian, September 11, 2016.

[39] Jake Tapper, *Setback for Arab-Americans*, Salon.com, September 17, 2001, available at: www.salon .com/2001/09/17/muslims/

[40] Melinda Henneberger, *Terror in Oklahoma: Bias Attacks; Muslims Continue to Feel Apprehensive*, New York Times, April 24, 1995.

[41] Brian Ross, *While America Slept: The True Story of 9/11*, ABC News, August 11, 2011, available at: http://abcnews.go.com/Blotter/ten-years-ago-today-countdown-911/story?id=14191671

[42] Samuel G. Freedman, *Six Days After 9/11, Another Anniversary Worth Honoring*, New York Times, September 7, 2012.

[43] David E. Sanger, *A Nation Challenged: The President; Bin Laden Is Wanted in Attacks, 'Dead or Alive,'* *President Says*, New York Times, September 18, 2001.

[44] Ibid.

[45] Freedman, *Six Days After 9/11*.

[46] Eric Lichtblau, *Hate Crimes Against American Muslims Most Since Post-9/11 Era*, New York Times, September 17, 2016 (a record 481 documented hate crimes against Muslims were committed in 2001).

[47] Office of Inspector General, US Dept. of Justice, The September 11 Detainees: A Review of the Treatment of Aliens Held on Immigration Charges in Connection with the Investigation of the September 11 Attacks 1–14 (April 2003), available at: https://oig.justice.gov/special/0306/full.pdf

announced that it would soon begin apprehending and interrogating thousands of undocumented Middle Eastern immigrants who apparently ignored deportation orders, seeking ways to prosecute anyone who had ties to terrorism. The results of these interviews would be compiled in a new computer database to facilitate future monitoring of these individuals.

Soon the strategy evolved into the National Security-Entry-Exist Registration System (NSEERS) targeting males from twenty-five Arab or Muslim majority countries, plus North Korea, that was maintained through the end of the Obama administration.[48] NSEERS netted not one terrorist conviction.[49]

Perhaps the best-known piece of legislation that resulted from the 9/11 attacks is the USA PATRIOT Act. Without much opposition, the act included a range of provisions authorizing the detention and exclusion of noncitizens based on speech or support of certain suspicious groups.[50] President Bush used the PATRIOT Act to close down Muslim charities with little notice or opportunity for the organizations to object.[51]

6.2.1.2. Iranian Student Roundup of 1979

Trump's targeting of nationals of particular countries also is reminiscent of the Carter administration's roundup of Iranian students in the United States in 1979. President Carter and the nation were shocked by the takeover of the US embassy in Tehran by a band of militant students in November 1979.[52] The militants supported the Iranian Revolution and opposed the United States because of its support for the Shah of Iran, whose regime had been toppled in January 1979.[53] Carter had allowed the Shah into the United States for cancer treatment, and the Iranian militants demanded the return of the Shah.[54] Dozens of US citizen embassy workers were held hostage in a crisis that lasted more than a year.[55] To many pundits, the embassy

---

[48] Kevin Liptak and Shachar Peled, *Obama Administration Ending Program Once Used to Track Mostly Arab and Muslim Men*, CNN, December 22, 2016.

[49] Ibid.

[50] Claudia, *What Does the Patriot Act Allow the Government to Do?*, The Ultra Violet, October 20, 2013, available at: www.theultraviolet.com/wordpress/2013/10/what-does-the-patriot-act-allow-the-government-to-do-2/; American Civil Liberties Union, *Surveillance Under the Patriot Act*, available at: www.aclu.org/infographic/surveillance-under-patriot-act; Department of Justice, The USA Patriot Act: Preserving Life and Liberty, available at: www.justice.gov/archive/ll/highlights.htm

[51] Neil MacFarquhar, *As Muslim Group Goes on Trial, Other Charities Watch Warily*, New York Times, July 17, 2007; Eli Lake, *U.S. Stopped Blacklisting Domestic Terror Charities Under Obama*, Bloomberg, May 12, 2016, available at: www.bloomberg.com/view/articles/2016-05-12/u-s-stopped-blacklisting-domestic-terror-charities-under-obama

[52] Stephen Kinzer, *Thirty-Five Years After Iranian Hostage Crisis, Aftershocks Remain*, Boston Globe, November 4, 2014.

[53] Raymond H. Anderson, *Ayatollah Ruhollah Khomeini, 89, Relentless Founder of Iran's Islamic Republic*, New York Times, June 5, 1989.

[54] Ibid.

[55] Ibid.

takeover and the ensuing attention that Carter paid to the crisis cost him reelection to a second term.[56]

The Carter administration implemented a range of strategies in an attempt to resolve the hostage crisis.[57] Billions of dollars in Iranian assets in the United States were frozen.[58] Diplomatic ties were cut off with Iran.[59] A rescue by an elite paramilitary group was attempted, but failed.[60] Mediation with the aid of Algeria was initiated.[61]

In actions that parallel Trump's executive actions, within days of the embassy takeover, Carter also asked his Attorney General Benjamin Civiletti to identify all Iranian students in the United States who were not in compliance with their visas.[62] Iranian students were the largest group of foreign students in the United States at the time, and many of them had spoken out in opposition to the Shah's regime.[63] Within a year, more than 54,000 students reported to local offices of the INS and thousands were found to be deportable. The basis for deportation often was simply for "small technical violations, such as changing from one college to another" without permission or failing to maintain a full course load.[64]

In the process, the Carter administration also ended a humanitarian program that had been extended to Iranian students in the United States prior to the embassy takeover. In the spring of 1979, the INS commissioner announced that no enforcement actions should be taken against Iranians in the country who "indicate an unwillingness to return to Iran because of the instability of the conditions."[65] But days after the hostage crisis began, the deferred departure order was rescinded, and previously protected students fell within the general order to report to INS.[66] Those actions also parallel Trump's end of Deferred Action for Childhood Arrivals (DACA) and Temporary Protected Status (TPS) for El Salvadorans and Haitians.

---

[56] Harold Jackson, *How Jimmy Carter Squandered His Electoral Assets*, The Guardian, November 5, 1980; Martin Meenagh, *Why Did Jimmy Carter Fail to Gain Re-Election in 1980*, Martin Meenagh Blog, June 26, 2014, available at: martinmeenagh.blogspot.com/2014/06/why-did-jimmy-carter-fail-to-gain-re.html

[57] *Iran Hostage Crisis Fast Facts*, CNN, October 29, 2016, available at: www.cnn.com/2013/09/15/world/meast/iran-hostage-crisis-fast-facts/index.html

[58] Ibid.

[59] Ibid.

[60] Ibid.

[61] Ibid.

[62] Joseph D. Whitaker, Art Harris and Phil McCombs, *U.S. Appeals Court Approves Iranian Student Deportation*, Wash. Post, December 28, 1979.

[63] Andrea Nasrine Shahmohammadi, Masked resistance: The Iranian student movement in the United States, 1977–1979, University of Maryland, Baltimore County, 2008, 160; 1457199, dissertation abstract, available at: http://pqdtopen.proquest.com/doc/304415205.html?FMT=ABS

[64] Whitaker, *U.S. Appeals Court Approves*.

[65] *Yassini v. Crosland*, 618 F.2d 1356, 1358-59 (9th Cir. 1980).

[66] Ibid.

6.2.2. *Trump's Extreme Vetting*

Many immigration experts were left a little puzzled when Trump's January 27 travel ban also called for "extreme vetting" of immigrants.[67] The "screening process is already rigorous [and] multi-layered."[68] In April 2017, Trump officials explained that extreme vetting might now include forcing visitors "to provide cellphone contacts and social-media passwords and answer questions about their ideology."[69] However, consider what was already in place for refugee and visa processing:

> An individual from Iraq who wants to visit the [United States] as a tourist, for example, first fills out an online application for a visa. Before the interview, information in the application is run against US terrorism watch lists and databases. Any derogatory information would be flagged for a specially-trained State Department consular officer in a US embassy or consulate in or near that person's home country who conducts the interview. For high-risk countries, the Department of Homeland Security (DHS) is involved ...
>
> During the interview, the officer tries to determine whether the person poses a terrorist or criminal threat, and also whether the person is a potential illegal immigrant. The visa applicant needs to show proof that a return ticket has been purchased, a defined place to stay in the United States and ties to his or her home country. Applicants are asked basic biographic questions, but also queried about their demeanor.
>
> [According to Stephen W. Yale-Loehr, an immigration law professor at Cornell University's law school:] "We have a terrorist watch database. We have a known immigration violators database. We have a criminal background check database that they have to go through. They don't just take the visa applicant's word ... They do go through all of these computer databases to verify for themselves that it's appropriate to issue the visa to a particular individual."
>
> If and when the person is approved for a visa, photos and fingerprints are taken. Before departing for the United States, all air passengers coming into the United States are subject to information analysis by officials on the ground overseas and at the National Targeting Center in Virginia.
>
> Once the traveler arrives at a United States airport, an officer with CBP will have access to all of the information collected through the targeting center, will ask the person for his or her fingerprints again to match with the original set, and will ask questions again about the trip to the United States.
>
> Seth Stodder, a former senior DHS official on border and immigration issues in the administrations of both Presidents Obama and George W. Bush, said both presidents used "the correct approach" to stop terrorists from entering the United States ... "The system that we have constructed since 9/11 to identify potential

[67] Ibid.; Rebecca Shabad, *Inside the U.S. Vetting System Trump Wants to Replace*, CBS News, February 27, 2017.

[68] Ibid.

[69] Laura Meckler, *Trump Administration Considers Far-Reaching Steps for 'Extreme Vetting'*, Wall Street Journal, April 4, 2017.

threats coming into the country – is it foolproof? No ... You're never going to have a foolproof system. You're only going to have a foolproof system if we decide to become North Korea and shut our borders."

The United States has built an international regime, Stodder explained, so that officials can detect people who pose a risk before they board a United States-bound flight overseas. CBP, for example, runs the Immigration Advisory Program, which posts personnel at various airports where they assist airline and security employees with reviewing traveler information for United States-bound flights. It also operates Preclearance, a program in which more than 600 US law enforcement officers are stationed at fifteen airports in six countries. In 2015, those officers stopped more than 22,000 high-risk travelers and determined that 10,648 of the 16 million air travelers hoping to enter the United States were inadmissible ...

The process to vet refugees, meanwhile, is the toughest for anyone coming into the country.

"They're the most carefully screened people that we allow into our borders," said Benjamin Webb, who just left DHS after serving as executive director of [CBP's] office of planning, analysis and requirements. "That's a very stringent process."
Refugees must first apply for refugee status and resettlement with the UN High Commission on Refugees, which collects initial documentation and biographic information, which is then transferred to a State Department-funded Resettlement Support Center. Afterwards, the center conducts an in-depth interview with the applicant, enters the documentation into a State Department system, and then cross-references and verifies data, and sends the information needed for a background check to other US agencies.

From there, five entities – the National Counterterrorism Center, FBI, DHS, Defense Department, and the State Department – screen the applicant using data from the centers. The screening process includes checks for security threats such as connections to bad actors and any past criminal or immigration violations.

Syrian refugees receive even more scrutiny with an additional enhanced review. The results from the screening process are then returned to DHS and State and trained DHS officers review them, conduct an in-person interview in the host country and collect biometric data ... Before the refugee arrives in the United States, CBP and TSA conduct additional screening.

"I don't know what extreme vetting's supposed to be. I mean, are you going to waterboard them or something?" said Webb. "They have to follow a strict protocol. They're monitored for two years. That would be the least efficient way for a terrorist to get into the United States."

Toward the end of the Obama administration, the United States also began asking refugee applicants for their social media handles as part of the screening process. While some think sifting through that information could be another tool to vet people, others suggest it could be a waste of time and difficult to decipher.

"I think it would be very difficult to find anyone who would be willing to disclose a bad social media account to the United States. Therefore, it's unlikely that they would help sort of collect much information on the bad guys," said Betsy Cooper, who served as attorney adviser to the deputy general counsel at DHS and a policy counselor in the office of policy.

"There's a balancing act that the United States has to have in terms of making sure that we do have adequate screening," said Yale-Loehr. "But at not such high a cost that either nobody comes to the United States or it's too astronomically expensive to go through all of the vetting possible."[70]

Not surprisingly, the reaction of many US government employees who had been involved in this vetting process to the Trump "extreme vetting" proposal was upsetting. In their view, extreme vetting was always in place, and their work had not been valued or recognized.[71]

6.2.3. *Expanding Expedited Removals*

In his border enforcement memo of February 20, 2017, then DHS Secretary John Kelly expanded the use of expedited removal under INA §235(b)(1)(A)(iii)(I) to anyone caught anywhere in the country who has resided in the United States for less than two years.[72] This action is part of a long-standing enforcement trend of trying to deport undocumented immigrants more efficiently – in my view a euphemism for providing fewer rights for immigrants. Administration after administration has sought ways to remove deportable aliens as soon as possible.

"Expedited removal" is the term the government uses to describe the swift deportation of undocumented immigrants without an appearance before an immigration judge – and, as pro-immigrant advocates point out, without due process protections.[73] During the Obama administration, the use of expedited removal was limited to undocumented immigrants apprehended within 100 miles of the border who had been in the United States for less than two weeks.[74] But under the Kelly memo, expedited removal could now be applied nationwide to those who cannot produce documentation that they have been in the country continuously for at least two years.[75] In 2014, the most recent year for which relevant statistics are available, 176,752 people were given expedited removal orders.[76]

---

[70] Shabad, *Inside the U.S. Vetting System.*

[71] *This American Life*, May 13, 2017, episode.

[72] John Kelly, DHS Secretary, Enforcement of the Immigration Laws to Serve the National Interest, February 20, 2017, available at: www.dhs.gov/sites/default/files/publications/17_0220_S1_Enforcement-of-the-Immigration-Laws-to-Serve-the-National-Interest.pdf.

[73] Amr. Immigration Council, *A Primer on Expedited Removal*, February 3, 2017, available at: www.americanimmigrationcouncil.org/research/primer-expedited-removal.

[74] Ibid.

[75] From Laura Smith, *Donald Trump Can Deport People Without Even Giving Them a Hearing*, Mother Jones, February 27, 2017.

[76] Ibid.

For some time, many advocates have been concerned about how the impulse to close off full hearing rights affects asylum seekers in particular. A 2013 study by the ACLU found that some asylum seekers were quickly deported because CBP agents failed to adequately screen them in credible-fear interviews, discussed in Chapter 2, which immigrants must pass before getting a full hearing before an immigration judge.[77]

The proposed use of the expedited removal power far into the interior of the country essentially is an expansion of the authority that immigration authorities have at the border. An early example of border expansion is the establishment and validation of fixed border patrol checkpoints far away from the border that began appearing in the 1970s.[78] Although DHS does not release information on the exact number of fixed checkpoints (some pop up and disappear on short notice), the number of interior checkpoints today likely exceeds 100.[79]

In condoning fixed checkpoints, in 1976, the Supreme Court carved out a major exception to the Fourth Amendment's protection against search and seizure to accommodate the Border Patrol. The case, *United States* v. *Martinez-Fuerte*, involved the legality of a fixed checkpoint located on Interstate 5 near San Clemente, California.[80] The checkpoint is sixty-six road miles north of the Mexican border.[81] The "point" agent, standing between the two lanes of traffic, visually screens all northbound vehicles, that the checkpoint brings to a virtual, if not a complete, halt.[82] In a small number of cases, the agent will direct cars to a secondary inspection area for further inquiry.[83] In the three situations that were challenged in *Martinez-Fuerte*, the Government conceded that none of the three stops was based on "articulable" suspicion that the cars were carrying noncitizens.[84] The defendants argued that the routine stopping of their vehicles at a checkpoint was invalid because such stops should be prohibited in the absence of reasonable suspicion that undocumented immigrants were present.[85] However, the Court deferred to the government's position and held that maintaining a traffic-checking program in the interior is necessary because "the flow of illegal aliens cannot be controlled effectively at the border." In the words of the Court,

---

[77] Ibid.

[78] *See generally* Deborah Waller Meyers, From Horseback to High-Tech: U.S. Border Enforcement, MPI Migration Information Source, February 1, 2006, available at: www.migrationpolicy.org/article/horseback-high-tech-us-border-enforcement

[79] Amy Lieberman, *Arizona's Checkpoint Rebellion*, Slate, July 24, 2014, available at: www.slate.com/articles/news_and_politics/politics/2014/07/arizona_immigration_checkpoint_criticism_border_patrol_harasses_people_and.html

[80] 428 U.S. 543 (1976).

[81] Ibid., at 546.

[82] Ibid.

[83] Ibid.

[84] Ibid., at 547.

[85] Ibid., at 550.

A requirement that stops on major routes inland always be based on reasonable suspicion would be impractical because the flow of traffic tends to be too heavy to allow the particularized study of a given car that would enable it to be identified as a possible carrier of illegal aliens.[86]

Fixed checkpoints, even miles and miles away from the border, now were constitutional, even in the absence of articulable facts. The importance of supporting the Border Patrol's efforts in enforcing immigration laws was overriding to the Court.[87]

The Supreme Court majority was not concerned with racial overtones even though the Border Patrol based secondary inspections on those who looked Mexican.[88] This was very troubling to Justice William Brennan who warned in a dissenting opinion: "Every American citizen of Mexican ancestry and every Mexican alien lawfully in this country must know after today's decision that he travels the fixed checkpoint highways at [his or her] risk."[89]

The tendency to expand the use of expedited removal was, however, outdone by the Reagan administration in its effort to stem the flow of Haitian refugees to our shores. At the time, poverty and infant mortality rates in Haiti ranked the highest in the Western hemisphere. The flow of refugees to the United States was steady, in spite of procedures implemented attempting to thwart asylum applicants. The administration's opposition to Haitian asylum claims was consistent with that of the predecessor Carter administration.

Large-scale Haitian immigration to the United States began during the 1970s when Haitians, attempting to escape Jean-Claude "Baby Doc" Duvalier's dictatorship, sailed for the United States. Before 1977, about 7,000 people had arrived in the United States by boat; by 1979, 8,300 more had arrived. The Carter administration treated Haitians as economic migrants, not political refugees, who were seeking jobs and better living conditions, making them ineligible for asylum. Thus, no Haitians were given refugee status, and every Haitian landing in the United States was subject to immediate deportation. The 1980 Mariel boatlift, in which 125,000 Cubans and 60,000–80,000 Haitians tried to immigrate to the United States, caused Carter to reevaluate United States–Haitian policies. He created a class of immigrant, the "Cuban/Haitian entrant (status pending)," allowing Haitians who had entered up to October 10, 1980, to apply for asylum. However, any Haitian entering after that date was faced with detention and deportation. In one week alone in April 1980, over 900 Haitian people arriving by boat were taken into custody and more than 2,400 in the six weeks prior.[90] Refugee rights advocates observed that Cubans and Nicaraguans

[86] Ibid., at 556–7.
[87] Ibid., at 562.
[88] Ibid., at 563.
[89] Ibid., at 573 (Brennan, J. dissenting).
[90] Ward Sinclair, *Haitian Boat People: Flotsam in an American Sea of Plenty*, Washington Post, April 19, 1980.

automatically receive political asylum, while Haitians did not – a suggestion of government racism. Furthermore, a former Duvalier presidential guard, himself a boat person, left no doubt about the immigrants' status once they were shipped back to Haiti. He said that between 1972 and 1979, when he was in the elite guard unit, his orders were to treat all returnees as traitors.[91]

Yet, the Reagan administration simply doubled-down on the Carter approach toward Haitians. Rather than recognizing the crisis and assisting the refugees, President Ronald Reagan sought strategies for denying asylum. The government's sinister new idea was that if the Haitians could be turned away on the high seas before they reached US shores, they could be barred from seeking asylum.[92]

On September 29, 1981, Reagan authorized the interdiction of vessels containing undocumented aliens from Haiti on the high seas.[93] The president based this action on the argument that undocumented aliens posed a "serious national problem detrimental to the interests of the United States," and that international cooperation to intercept vessels trafficking in such migrants was a necessary and proper means of ensuring the effective enforcement of US immigration laws.[94] By executive order, the Coast Guard was directed "to return the vessel and its passengers to the country from which it came, when there is reason to believe that an offense is being committed against the United States immigration laws."[95] The Coast Guard's interdiction took place outside the territorial waters of the United States.[96]

In *Haitian Refugee Center* v. *Gracey*, a federal court upheld the actions of the president, holding that the president has inherent authority to act to protect the United States from harmful undocumented immigration.[97] The program was purportedly carried out pursuant to an agreement with Haiti. The court used that information to conclude that the action came within matters of foreign relations – a topic that should not be disturbed by the court.[98] Disappointingly, the court ruled that the action did not violate the United States' obligations under the Refugee Act of 1980 or the country's obligations under the United Nations Protocol Relating to the Status of Refugees.[99]

---

[91] Ibid.
[92] *See* Reagan Orders Alien Stopped on the High Seas, New York Times, September 29, 1981, available at: www.nytimes.com/1981/09/30/us/reagan-orders-aliens-stopped-on-the-high-sea.html.
[93] 46 Fed.Reg. 48109 (pub. October 1, 1981), reprinted in 8 U.S.C. § 1182 (supp. note).
[94] Haitian Refugee Center v. Gracey, 600 F. Supp. 1396 (D.D.C. 1985); 46 Fed. Reg. 48107 (pub. October 1, 1981), reprinted in 8 U.S.C. § 1182 (supp. note).
[95] Ibid.; 46 Fed. Reg. 48109, 48110 (published October 1, 1981), reprinted in 8 U.S.C. § 1182 (supp. note).
[96] Ibid.
[97] 600 F. Supp. 1396 (D.D.C. 1985).
[98] Ibid.
[99] Ibid., at 1405–6.

6.2.4. *Criminal Immigrants: Obama's Priorities*

In early April 2017, a reporter called me somewhat incredulous about this story. How could this person be deported? Is this a new thing under Trump?

> He is a Christian and a former soldier who fought for America and supported Donald Trump. But Nahidh Shaou is also an Iraqi immigrant who was jailed for 35 years in 1983 for injuring a cop during an armed robbery. Now after completing his sentence he is facing deportation to Iraq in one of the most complicated such cases since Trump became President. Shaou, 55, fears that if he will tracked down and beheaded by ISIS because they are persecuting Christians in Iraq. He does not even speak Arabic and argues that his serving in the military including patrolling the demilitarized zone in Korea should allow him to stay here with his family.
> Shaou's case is particularly striking because of his religion and the President's promises to protect Christians and to favor them over Muslim refugees. The father-of-one had thought he was going to be finally freed from prison last September after serving 33 years for shooting the cop in an incident he says was caused by PTSD. Instead Shaou was transferred into the custody of ICE. He was told he would be put on the [a] charter flight ... carrying deported Iraqis back to Baghdad.
>
> Shaou's niece Tiara Shaya, [said]: "My uncle joined the military at 17 because felt that he had a duty to serve his country because he did move here from Iraq and felt that it was his way of giving back." During his 33 years in jail he was a model inmate and earned several degrees – and supported Trump in his run for the presidency. "He's absolutely a patriot. America is the only country he knows." Tina Ramirez, president of Hardwired, a group which campaigns for religious freedom, added: "As we all know too well, our veterans do not receive enough support for PTSD, and this man committed a crime in the 1980s when even less support was available. He's served his time honorably and should be granted a second chance for serving our country."[100]

I assured the reporter that this type of deportation – the removal of longtime LPRs (lawful permanent residents) with strong equities and ties to the United States – happens every day. As for deportations to Iraq, it wasn't until 2017, that the United States persuaded Iraq to agree to start accepting deportees – especially aggravated felons.[101] From time to time, ICE officials during the Obama administration would exercise discretion and place aggravated felons under orders of supervision.[102] But Obama officials definitely deported longtime LPRs with aggravated felony

---

[100] Daniel Bates, *Iraqi Immigrant Who Fought for America but Was Jailed for 35 Years in 1983 for Injuring a Cop During an Armed Robbery Now Faces Deportation and Beheading by ISIS in Iraq – Even Though He is a Christian,* Daily Mail, April 17, 2017.

[101] Abigail Hauslohner, *A Charter Flight Left the U.S. Carrying 8 Iraqis. A Community Wonders Who Will Be Next,* The Washington Post, April 28, 2017.

[102] Ala Amoachi, *A Glimmer of Hope for Immigrants on an Order of Supervision,* October 29, 2011, available at: https://amjolaw.com/2011/10/29/a-glimmer-of-hope-for-immigrants-on-an-order-of-supervision/

convictions – even those who likely were rehabilitated, remorseful, and in the eyes of many, deserving of a second chance.[103]

The enforcement memos of DHS Secretary Kelly and his predecessor Jeh Johnson emphasize criminal immigrants.[104] In his November 2014 enforcement memo, Obama's DHS Secretary Johnson spoke of convictions for gang-related activities, felonies under state or federal laws, aggravated felonies under the Immigration and Nationality Act (INA), "significant" misdemeanors, or more than two misdemeanors.[105] However, the Trump enforcement executive order sweeps up more than those convicted of crimes and includes any undocumented immigrant who simply has been charged with any criminal offense, along with those who have committed acts that "constitute a chargeable criminal offense."[106] That means anyone the authorities believe has broken any type of law – regardless of whether that person has been charged with a crime – is in trouble.[107]

Although the Obama criminal immigration priorities presumably focused on those with convictions, Obama's ICE often swept up non criminal immigrants along the way. Consider Obama's Criminal Alien Removal Initiative (CARI).[108]

Under the CARI program, ICE officials presumably would target for arrest noncitizens who had been convicted of crimes that rendered them deportable.[109] However, when the target was approached at home or at work, other individuals in the vicinity would be questioned about their immigration status.[110] Many of those individuals also got detained or arrested. A sharp increase in those types of "collateral" arrests related to criminal enforcement were reported across the United States under the Obama administration.[111] And CARI's collateral impact made life unpleasant for any noncitizen who was at the wrong place at the wrong time.

---

[103] *See generally*, Bill Ong Hing, *Re-Examining the Zero-Tolerance Approach to Deporting Aggravated Felons: Restoring Discretionary Waivers and Developing New Tools*, 8 Harv. L .& Pol. Rev. 141 (2014).

[104] See, Camila Domonoske, *What's New In Those DHS Memos on Immigration Enforcement?*, NPR, February 22, 2017, available at: www.npr.org/sections/thetwo-way/2017/02/22/516649344/whats-new-in-those-dhs-memos-on-immigration-enforcement.

[105] Secretary Jeh Charles Johnson, *Policies for the Apprehension, Detention and Removal of Undocumented Immigrants*, Department of Homeland Security Memorandum, November 20, 2014, available at: www.dhs.gov/sites/default/files/publications/14_1120_memo_prosecutorial_discretion.pdf.

[106] January 25, 2017, Trump's Interior Enforcement memo.

[107] Jennifer Medina, *Trump's Immigration Order Expands the Definition of 'Criminal,'* New York Times, January 26, 2017.

[108] Bill Ong Hing, Civil Rights Abuse: Evil Nature of Obama Deportation Machine in New Orleans, ImmigrationProf Blog (August 7, 2014), available at: www.lawprofessors.typepad.com/immigration/2014/08/civil-rights-abuse-evil-nature-of-obama-deportation-machine-in-new-orleans.html

[109] Ibid.

[110] Ibid.

[111] Bill Ong Hing, Civil Rights Abuse: Evil Nature of Obama Deportation Machine in New Orleans, ImmigrationProf Blog (August 7, 2014), available at: www.lawprofessors.typepad.com/immigration/2014/08/civil-rights-abuse-evil-nature-of-obama-deportation-machine-in-new-orleans.html

Under CARI, ICE squads – sometimes accompanied by local police – raided apartment complexes, grocery stores, laundromats, Bible study groups, parks, and anywhere else Latinos might gather. The officers made stop-and-frisk type arrests based on racial profiling and indiscriminate mobile fingerprinting. The raids made daily routines such as going to buy groceries or bringing the car to get repaired a terrifying task that could lead to deportation.[112]

So far, the criminal enforcement efforts under the Trump administration – and its collateral consequences – strongly simulate that of the Obama administration.[113]

Prioritizing criminal immigrants by Trump or Obama is an easy sell to the American public. However, the public may not know that the crazy thing is that noncitizen crime rates, even among undocumented immigrants, is not any worse (and some data show better) than that of the general population.[114] For well over a century, immigrants have faced hostility in the United States going back to Italians, Irish, and Chinese.[115] Social science research dating back nearly as long consistently has found there is no link between immigrants and criminality.[116] Although the research is limited, apparently undocumented immigrants do not commit crimes at rates that are any different from those of the general population.[117]

During the presidential primaries, candidate Trump often talked about the shooting of Kate Steinle in San Francisco by undocumented immigrant Juan Francisco Lopez-Sanchez.[118] Trump's focus on criminal immigrants, and for that matter, Obama's similar focus, sends a message of hysteria about the link between immigration and crime. However, time and again, studies demonstrate that immigrants are less crime prone than natives or have no effect on crime rates.[119] Relatedly,

---

[112] Ibid.

[113] Camila Domonoske, *75 Percent of Immigration Raid Arrests Were for Criminal Convictions, DHS Says*, NPR, February 13, 2017 ("[L]ast week's ICE arrests included 'collateral damage,' or people who were picked up despite not being targeted in the operations – because, for example, they were in the same place as a person who *was* targeted, and did not have documentation."

[114] Richard Perez-Pena, *Contrary to Trump's Claims, Immigrants Are Less Likely to Commit Crimes*, New York Times (January 26, 2017), available at: www.nytimes.com/2017/01/26/us/trump-illegal-immigrants-crime.html?_r=0; Rafael Bernal, *Reports Find that Immigrants Commit Less Crimes Than US-Based Citizens*, The Hill (March 19, 2017 8:00 a.m.), available at: http://thehill.com/latino/324607-reports-find-that-immigrants-commit-less-crime-than-us-born-citizens.

[115] Brian Resnick, *Racist Anti-Immigrant Cartoons from the Turn of the 20th Century*, The Atlantic (November 21, 2011), available at: www.theatlantic.com/national/archive/2011/11/racist-anti-immigrant-cartoons-from-the-turn-of-the-20th-century/383248/.

[116] Robert Adelman, Lesley Reid, Gail Markel, Saskia Weiss, and Charles Jaret. (2016). Urban crime rates and the changing face of immigration: Evidence across four decades. Journal of Ethnicity in Criminal Justice, 15, 52–77, available at: http://dx.doi.org/10.1080/15377938.2016.1261057.

[117] John Burnett, *Spotlight on Migrant Crimes Drums Up Support for Trump's Immigration Dragnet*, NPR (April 3, 2017, 4:55 PM), available at: www.npr.org/2017/04/03/522424593/immigration-dragnet-gains-support-are-migrants-are-arrested-for-crimes.

[118] *See, e.g.,* Allison Weeks, *Donald Trump Says He Would Pass Law After Kate Steinle*, KRON, August 31, 2016, available at: http://kron4.com/2016/08/31/donald-trump-says-he-will-pass-law-after-bay-area-native/

[119] Alex Nowrasteh, *Immigration and Crime – What the Research Says*, Cato Institute, July 14, 2015, available at: www.cato.org/blog/immigration-crime-what-research-says

macro level analysis show that increased immigration does not increase crime and sometimes even causes crime rates to fall.[120] Also, immigrants convicted of crimes serve their sentences before facing deportation.[121]

6.2.5. *Raids and Mass Deportation*

The public has anticipated large-scale immigration enforcement and ICE raids by the Trump administration.[122] Among his campaign promises, Trump pledged to deport "millions and millions of undocumented immigrants."[123] Early in his administration, his advisors pledged "more vigorous immigration enforcement activities," and the arrests of hundreds of immigrants in the first week of February 2017 "marked the first large-scale raid under the Trump administration – and a crackdown was, by all indications, just the start of much more to come."[124] In early January 2018, Trump's ICE hit the front pages with reports of a massive raid of nearly one hundred 7-Eleven stores across the country! Only twenty-one workers were arrested, but the startling message was delivered nonetheless.

If Trump's ICE engages in regular, mass ICE raids, such operations will not be the first.[125]

6.2.5.1. The Bush Raids

In Chapter 1, Bush's ICE age was reviewed beginning with when DHS was established in 2003.[126] The new DHS took over the old INS from the DOJ (Department of Justice).[127] Repackaged, interior enforcement functions were channeled into the ICE agency.[128] Border enforcement remained in the hands of the Border Patrol.[129]

Immigration raids, including worksite operations, have been part of immigration enforcement for decades.[130] However, the courts had placed constraints on INS and

---

[120] Ibid.

[121] Ibid.

[122] Ray Sanchez, *After ICE Arrests, Fear Spreads Among Undocumented Immigrants*, CNN (February 12, 2017, 7:10 AM), available at: www.cnn.com/2017/02/11/politics/immigration-roundups-community-fear/index.html.

[123] Amy B. Wang, *Donald Trump Plans to Immediately Deport 2 Million to 3 Million Undocumented Immigrants*, Washington Post, November 14, 2016.

[124] Seung Min Kim and Ted Hesson, *Trump Just Getting Started with Immigration Raids*, Politico, February 13, 2017.

[125] Amy Choznick, *Raids of Illegal Immigrants Bring Harsh Memories, and Strong Fears*, New York Times (January 2, 2017), available at: www.nytimes.com/2017/01/02/us/illegal-immigrants-raids-deportation.html.

[126] Our History, U.S. Citizen and Immigration Services, available at: www.uscis.gov/about-us/our-history.

[127] Ibid.

[128] Ibid.

[129] Ibid.

[130] David Bacon, *Fire and ICE: The Return of Workplace Immigration Raids*, Prospect (April 27, 2017), available at: http://prospect.org/article/fire-and-ice-return-workplace-immigration-raids.

Border Patrol agent activities during raids. For example, in *INS* v. *Delgado*, 466 U.S. 210 (1994), although the US Supreme Court did not find the particular worksite operation in question unconstitutional, the Court held that INS agents cannot seize an entire worksite, must allow workers to remain silent, and must depart if agents have no reasonable suspicion that the workers are unauthorized to be in the United States.[131] In *Illinois Migrant Council* v. *Pilliod*, 548 F.2d 715 (7th Cir. 1977), a federal court of appeals upheld a trial court opinion in Chicago that INS agents could not stop and question individuals simply because of Latin appearance.[132] And, in *International Molders' and Allied Workers' Local Union No. 164* v. *Nelson*, 799 F.2d 547 (9th Cir. 1986), another federal court of appeals required INS warrants to be very specific in naming suspected undocumented workers.[133]

In spite of these restrictions, the Bush administration engaged in aggressive, gun-wielding immigration raids that often resulted in large numbers of arrests.[134] For example, on the morning of December 12, 2006, six Swift & Company meatpacking plants in Colorado, Texas, Nebraska, Utah, Iowa, and Minnesota were raided by hundreds of ICE agents in riot gear.[135] In all, 13,000 workers were detained.[136] A midnight ICE raid in Stillmore, Georgia earlier that Fall resulted in the arrest and deportation of 125 workers, causing family members to flee into hiding in nearby woods.[137] A 2008 raid in Postville, Iowa, that included helicopters circling above, resulted in the arrest of 389 immigrants, many held at a cattle exhibit hall.[138] Children were absent from school the next day, "because their parents were arrested or in hiding."[139]

ICE activity and Trump rhetoric suggest that we will witness many more of these types of raids under the Trump administration.

6.2.5.2. The Palmer Raids

A history of mass raids in the United States must include the Palmer Raids during the height of the Red Scare and fear of anarchists. In 1919, millions of workers went on strike as part of organizing efforts in industries such as steel work, meatpacking, and coal mining.[140] Immigrants dominated much of these workforces, and the

---

[131] *INS* v. *Delgado*, 466 U.S. 210, 218 (1984).
[132] *Illinois Migrant Council* v. *Pilliod*, 548 F.2d 715 (7th Cir. 1977).
[133] *International Molders' and Allied Workers' Local Union No. 164* v. *Nelson*, 799 F.2d 547 (9th Cir. 1986).
[134] Hing, Institutional Racism, ICE Raids.
[135] Ibid.
[136] Ibid.
[137] Ibid.
[138] Spencer, S. Hsu, *Immigration Raid Jars a Small Town*, Washington Post, May 18, 2008.
[139] Ibid.
[140] Bill Ong Hing, *Defining America Through Immigration Policy*, at 130 (2012).

threat of deportation was viewed as a method of combating union organizing.[141] Immigration enforcement supporters gained new strength following the mailing of bombs to prominent Americans, including the Attorney General A. Mitchell Palmer.[142] Palmer responded by establishing a special DOJ division devoted to exposing "aliens" and "Communists," and vowing to roundup "radicals."[143] He began with eighteen violent raids on November 7, 1919, focused on union meeting rooms, with many of the arrestees being sent to the Ellis Island immigration center.[144]

The major raids took place on January 2, 1920, in fifty-six cities that resulted in the arrests of 3,000 individuals. No warrants were issued, the detentions were arbitrary, and the detentions that followed included severe questioning.[145]

Eventually, a federal court criticized the basis and methods that were used for deportation during the Palmer Raids.[146] However, the damage had been done to many noncitizens. Officials at Ellis Island had already deported 249 individuals, including noted activists Emma Goldman and Alexander Berkman.[147]

In a similar vein, the Trump ICE targeted immigrant activists. In early January 2018, reports surfaced that ICE had detained or deported several prominent immigrant activists across the country, prompting accusations that the Trump administration was improperly targeting political opponents. Detention Watch Network, a nonprofit organization that tracks immigration enforcement, said that several activists were targeted, including Maru Mora Villalpando in Washington state, Eliseo Jurado in Colorado, and New York immigrant leaders Jean Montrevil and Ravi Ragbir. New York Congressman Jerry Nadler (D-N.Y.) agreed: "They're trying to intimidate people … These are well-known activists who've been here for decades, and they're saying to them: Don't raise your head."[148]

6.2.5.3. Mexican "Repatriation" in the 1930s

Trump's anti-Mexican immigrant rhetoric throughout his campaign and his continued call to build a wall along the United States–Mexico border is a stark reminder of the forced repatriation of about a million individuals of Mexican descent across the southern border in the 1930s.[149]

[141] Ibid.
[142] Ibid.
[143] Ibid.
[144] Ibid. *See also Attorney General A. Mitchell Palmer on Charges Made Against the Dept. of Justice by Louis F. Post and Others*, 66th Cong., 2d sess., 156–7 (1920) (statement of Attorney General A. Mitchell Palmer regarding action by the Radical Division in the Naugatuck valley in Connecticut).
[145] Hing, *Defining America*, at 130.
[146] *See Colyer v. Skeffington*, 265 F. 17, 43-44 (Ma. 1920).
[147] Hing, *Defining America*, at 130.
[148] Maria Sacchetti and David Weigel, ICE has detained or deported prominent immigration activists, Wash. Post, January 19, 2018.
[149] Francisco E. Balderrama and Raymond Rodríguez, Decade of Betrayal: Mexican Repatriation in the 1930s (1995).

Scapegoating and the Depression set the stage for what happened.[150] There was no federal law mandating what happened, simply the targeting of Mexicans in part because they were the most recent immigrant group.[151] In familiar-sounding rhetoric, deportations were announced to "provide jobs for Americans." Big industries like US Steel, Ford Motor Company, and Southern Pacific Railroad told their Mexican workers that they might be better off in Mexico because of the crisis.[152] Local officials also hoped to save welfare dollars by cutting off Mexican families.[153] Some officials even encouraged US citizens of Mexican descent to leave by offering free train tickets.[154]

As Professor Kevin Johnson wrote:

> The forced "repatriation" of an estimated one million persons of Mexican ancestry from the United States included the removal of hundreds of thousands of people from California, Michigan, Colorado, Texas, Illinois, Ohio, and New York during the Great Depression. From today's vantage point, the conduct of federal, state, and local officials in the campaign clearly violated the legal rights of the persons repatriated, as well as persons of Mexican ancestry stopped, interrogated, and detained but not removed from the country. The repatriation campaign also terrorized and traumatized the greater Mexican-American community.

> To assist in the round-up, police conducted raids of public places, including the church La Placita on Olvera Street in downtown Los Angeles, where persons of Mexican ancestry were known to frequent. Olvera Street was not a tourist spot in the 1930s like it is today; then it was simply a meeting place for working class Mexicans near a church serving the Mexican immigrant and Mexican-American community. The people rounded up were often herded onto trains and buses or driven by social workers to the border. This was true for citizens by birth and those who had lawfully naturalized to become citizens.[155]

The repatriation program is a sad example of anti-Mexican rhetoric that evolved into the actual targeting of Mexicans for removal.

6.2.5.4. Operation Wetback

Operation Wetback is another infamous chapter in the deportation of Mexicans from the United States. This time it was 1954 and President Dwight D. Eisenhower's turn,

---

[150] Terry Gross, *America's Forgotten History of Mexican-American 'Repatriation'*, Fresh Air NPR, September 10, 2015.
[151] Ibid.
[152] Ibid.
[153] Ibid.
[154] Ibid.
[155] Kevin R. Johnson, *The Forgotten "Repatriation" of Persons of Mexican Ancestry and Lessons for the "War on Terror,"* 26 Pace L. Rev. 1 (2005).

and an estimated 1.1 million undocumented Mexican migrants were removed.[156] The deportations were directly related to the formal establishment of the Bracero program, a bilateral agreement with Mexico that presumably would help United States growers maintain a stable, lawful workforce for their harvests.[157] However, to make the program work, undocumented farm workers had to be expelled, especially after the Attorney General Herbert Brownell visited the border in 1953 and concluded that the border was too open.[158]

Operation Wetback was implemented by command teams of Border Patrol agents, buses, planes, and temporary processing stations implemented with the purpose of locating and deporting Mexicans who had surreptitiously entered the United States.[159] With little due process, teams focused on quick processing, and airplanes for some removals into the interior of Mexico were even used.[160] Although about 1.1 million arrests were made in the first year of Operation Wetback, many other undocumented immigrants fled to Mexico to avoid apprehension – about half a million from Texas alone.[161]

6.3. TRUMP'S BORDER WALL

Trump's signature campaign promise on immigration was the border wall. In his candidacy announcement speech in June 2015, Trump first proposed the idea of building a wall along the southern border, adding that, due to his real estate experience, he was uniquely qualified for the job.[162] "I will build a great wall – and nobody builds walls better than me, believe me – and I'll build them very inexpensively. I will build a great, great wall on our southern border, and I will make Mexico pay for that wall. Mark my words."[163]

Everything about Trump's "build a border wall" rhetoric and efforts is offensive. From the premise – i.e., "Mexico is not our friend" – and calling some Mexican immigrants "rapists and criminals," to the request for proposals for the wall construction that reads: "The north side of wall (i.e., the United States facing side) shall be aesthetically pleasing in color, anti-climb texture, etc., to be consistent with general surrounding environment."[164]

---

[156] Louis Hyman and Natasha Iskander, *What the Mass Deportation of Immigrants Might Look Like*, Slate, November 16, 2016.
[157] Hing, *Defining America*, at 130.
[158] Ibid.
[159] Mae M. Ngai, *Impossible Subjects: Illegal Aliens and the Making of Modern America*, at 155 (2004).
[160] Ibid., at 156.
[161] Ibid., at 156–7.
[162] CBS News, 30 of Donald Trump's wildest quotes, available at: www.cbsnews.com/pictures/wild-donald-trump-quotes/14/ (last accessed June 18, 2017).
[163] Dan Gunderman, *President-Elect Donald Trump's 'Big, Beautiful Wall' May End Up Just Being a Modest, Double-Layered Fence*, New York Daily News, November 10, 2016.
[164] Ron Nixon, *Trump Seeks Proposals for 'Physically Imposing' Wall with Mexico*, New York Times, March 18, 2017.

6.3.1. *The Fence Act*

As offensive as Trump's wall proposal may be, we have seen equivalent grandstanding before in the form of the Fence Act of 2006. The bill was introduced on September 13, 2006, by Peter T. King (R-NY).[165] In the House of Representatives, the Fence Act passed 283–138.[166] On September 29, 2006 – the Fence Act passed in the Senate 80–1,[167] with the backing of Barack Obama and Hillary Clinton, both senators at the time.[168] On October 26, 2006, President Bush signed the Secure Fence Act of 2006 (Pub. L. 109–367) into law proclaiming, "This bill will help protect the American people. This bill will make our borders more secure. It is an important step toward immigration reform."[169]

Although more than 600 miles of fencing and vehicle barriers along the border from California to Texas was constructed by April 2009, Congress has never provided more than the initial $1.2 billion to complete the fence.[170] A follow-up proposal in 2008 (H.R. 5124) that would add 700 miles of two-layered fencing died in committee.[171] A proposal by Senator Jim DeMint (R-SC) to finish the fence suffered a similar fate.[172] The failure to complete the fence can largely be attributed to the high estimated cost of $4.1 billion – an amount higher than the Border Patrol's annual budget of $3.55 billion.[173]

6.3.2. *Operation Gatekeeper*

In my view, Trump's Wall and the Fence Act pale in comparison to the death trap of Operation Gatekeeper, instated by President Clinton's regime that continues to this day. This militarization of the United States–Mexico border region has been the centerpiece of the immigration enforcement policies of past three decades. Reliance on border policing spiked in the mid-1990s with a series of military-style operations along the United States–Mexico border that ultimately resulted in a much bigger and better-funded presence along that border.[174]

Operation Gatekeeper was implemented by the Clinton Administration's in 1994 as a method of stopping the flow of undocumented migration across the southern

---

[165] *H.R. 6061 (109th): Secure Fence Act of 2006*, Govtrack, available at: www.govtrack.us/congress/votes/109-2006/s262 (last accessed June 18, 2017).
[166] Ibid.
[167] Ibid.
[168] Ibid.
[169] *See* Secure Fence Act of 2006, H.R. Res. 6061, 109th Cong. (2006).
[170] Jerome R. Corsi, Law to Build U.S. Border Wall Already Passed, Word Net Daily, November 15, 2016, available at: www.wnd.com/2016/11/1-main-reason-u-s-border-wall-hasnt-been-built/
[171] Ibid.
[172] Ibid.
[173] Tyler Russo, *Problems with the U.S.–Mexico Border*, Prezi.com, November 5, 2014, available at: https://prezi.com/uxj3iwjospwc/problems-with-the-us-mexico-border/
[174] Ibid.

border.[175] The idea seemed simple enough – if the parts of the border that are most easy to cross are cut off, then folks will stop coming.[176] Thus, the policy of "control through deterrence" was implemented by first building a fence along the heavily used, fourteen-mile stretch from the Pacific Ocean eastward.[177] Eventually, other parts of the border that were the most easily traversed were fenced off or monitored more heavily with electronic equipment and Border Patrol units.[178]

Unfortunately, the strategy failed. Driven by social and economic pressures, migrants continued to come.[179] But now that the easy paths had been cut off, the migrants were pushed to navigate treacherous terrain in their travels north.[180] They faced the searing heat of the Sonoran desert of southern Arizona in the summer and the freezing cold of the rugged Tecate Mountains in the winter.[181] Not surprisingly given the conditions, hundreds of migrants began to die each year trying to reach the United States as Operation Gatekeeper unfolded.[182] Deaths along the border due to Operation Gatekeeper continue to this day.

6.4. 287(G) AGREEMENT EXPANSION

Trump's interior enforcement executive order and Secretary Kelly's enforcement memo emphasize the intent to rely heavily on increasing "287(g)" agreements with local law enforcement officials.[183] The name comes from Section 287(g) of the INA which can be found in Title 8 of the United States Code, § 1357(g). These agreements essentially deputize local law enforcement officers to double as federal immigration agents.[184] Once trained, local officers are authorized to interview, arrest, and detain any person who may be in violation of immigration laws depending on the terms of the agreement.[185] Within six months of taking office, Obama's DHS also

---

[175] Bill Ong Hing, The Dark Side of Operation Gatekeeper, 7 *U.C. Davis J. of Int'l L. & Pol'y* 121, 126–27 (2001).

[176] Ibid., at 128.

[177] Ibid., at 124, 129.

[178] Ibid., at 129–30.

[179] Ibid., at 146–51.

[180] Ibid., at 158, 165.

[181] Ibid., at 130, 135–7.

[182] Ibid., at 135–7.

[183] Amanda Sakuma, *Donald Trump's Plan to Outsource Immigration Enforcement to Local Cops*, The Atlantic, February 18, 2017, available at: www.theatlantic.com/politics/archive/2017/02/trump-immigration-enforcement/517071/.

[184] *Trump Asks Congress for $3 Billion in Supplemental Funding for FY 2017*, CRImmigration (March 16, 2017, 4:25 PM), http://crimmigration.com/2017/03/16/trump-asks-congress-for-3-billion-in-supplemental-funding-for-fy-2017/.

[185] Amanda Sakuma, Donald Trump's Plan to Outsource Immigration Enforcement to Local Cops, The Atlantic (February 18, 2017). www.theatlantic.com/politics/archive/2017/02/trump-immigration-enforcement/517071/

expanded 287(g) agreements.[186] Although the Obama administration eventually reduced the number of such agreements to less than forty, at one time, total 287(g) agreements exceeded seventy under the Obama and Bush eras. By July 31, 2017, the Trump administration increased the number of agreements to sixty, including eighteen new agreements in Texas alone.[187]

The terms of these agreements can vary. Deputized officers can be authorized to engage in a huge range of federal immigration enforcement functions, such as interviewing individuals to determine immigration status, accessing DHS databases, issuing ICE detainers to hold individuals for potential deportation, bringing charges to initiate deportation proceedings, and making recommendations on detention and bond amounts.[188] In essence, the state or local officer becomes a federal employee.[189]

Unfortunately, local enforcement under 287(g) agreements has resulted in a dark side of abuse – most notably racial profiling. Perhaps the most infamous example is the 287(g) escapades of Sheriff Joe Arpaio of Maricopa County, Arizona, who touted himself as "America's toughest sheriff."[190] A 2011 DOJ investigation found that his deputies menaced Latino neighborhoods; Latinos driving cars were much more likely to be stopped than other drivers.[191] In May 2013, a federal judge agreed that Arpaio's law-enforcement practices illegally targeted Latinos.[192]

Similarly, in 2011, the American Civil Liberties Union discovered that 287(g) agreements in two Georgia counties led to a "pattern of police inventing pretexts to stop and search immigrants."[193] Then in 2012, a DOJ investigation of Alamance County, North Carolina, found that sheriff's deputies focused on Latino neighborhoods to set up checkpoints.[194]

During the Bush administration, the Los Angeles County Sheriff's Office was party to a 287(g) agreement that resulted in the deportation of a US citizen. Pedro Guzman, who was born in Lancaster, CA, is developmentally disabled and cannot read or write. Guzman was arrested on charges of trespassing and spraying graffiti at an airplane junkyard and spent forty days in jail for the offense. Even though he produced a California driver's license (at the time, only lawful immigrants and US citizens could obtain such licenses), sheriff's deputies thought he was undocumented and they convinced him to sign papers waiving his hearing rights. He was

---

[186] Amy Goodman, *Obama Admin Expands Law Enforcement Program 287(g), Criticized for Targeting Immigrants and Increasing Racial Profiling,* Democracy Now, July 29, 2009, available at: www .democracynow.org/2009/7/29/obama_admin_expands_law_enforcement_program

[187] Dianne Solis and Ray Leszcynski, *18 Texas Sheriffs Sign Up to Join Forces with Federal Immigration Officers,* Dallas Morning News, July 31, 2017.

[188] The 287(g) Program: An Overview, American Immigration Council, available at: www .americanimmigrationcouncil.org/sites/default/files/research/the_287g_program_an_overview_0.pdf.

[189] 8 U.S.C. § 1357(g)(7).

[190] Joe Sterling, *Joe Arpaio, Once America's Toughest Sheriff, to Go on Trial,* CNN, June 26, 2017.

[191] Mat Coleman and Sarah Horton, *Driving While Latino,* Huffington Post, September 30, 2016.

[192] Megan Cassidy, *Justice Dept. to charge Arpaio with Contempt of Court,* USA Today, October 11, 2016.

[193] Coleman and Horton, *Driving While Latino.*

[194] Ibid.

deported to Mexico. After almost three months of foraging for food in garbage cans and bathing in rivers, Guzman was found by his relatives and was brought back to the United States. After the ordeal, his mother sobbed: "They didn't return me back my whole son. They returned half my son to me. He isn't normal."[195] His family filed a civil suit against ICE and the Los Angeles Sheriff seeking damages. The case was settled for an undisclosed amount.

For that and other reasons, the Obama administration severely reduced the number of 287(g) agreements.[196] There was serious concern over the proper training of local officers and the lack of oversight to prevent racial profiling.[197] Furthermore, immigrant communities tended to "fear and mistrust [local] authorities when they realized that local police could act as immigration agents."[198]

6.5. DISCOURAGING ASYLUM APPLICANTS THROUGH CREDIBLE FEAR REVISIONS

Without a great deal of fanfare, the Trump administration quietly made it more difficult for incoming asylum seekers to pass the credible fear screening standard that enables would-be applicants to seek asylum in the United States.[199] As the surge in unaccompanied alien children began in early 2014, US Citizenship and Immigration Services (USCIS), whose asylum office handles asylum cases, revised its lesson plan to officers on how to determine whether asylum applicants who make it to the border meet the credible fear screening standard.[200] Those credible fear standards were criticized as being misleadingly and inappropriate.[201] They language and tone instructed asylum officers to impose a burden on applicants that surpassed the well-founded fear standard for asylum established by the Supreme Court in *INS v. Cardoza-Fonseca*,[202] when in fact the actual standard should be more deferential than the asylum standard. In spite of that critique, in 2016, nearly 80 percent of

---

[195] Sam Quinones, *Disabled Man Found After 89-Day Ordeal; Pedro Guzman, a U.S. Citizen, Wandered in Mexico After Being Wrongly Deported. Family, ACLU Criticize Immigration Officials*, LA Times, August 8, 2007.

[196] The 287(g) Program, American Immigration Council.

[197] Toby Talbot, *The Obama Administration is Starting to Shut Down a Program that Deputized Local Police Officers to Act as Immigration Agents*, USA Today, February 17, 2012.

[198] Ibid.

[199] Tal Kopan, *Trump Admin Quietly Made Asylum More Difficult in the US*, CNN, March 8, 2017.

[200] *Credible Fear: Lesson Plan Overview*, February 28, 2014, available at: http://cmsny.org/wp-content/uploads/credible-fear-of-persecution-and-torture.pdf; Catholic Legal Immigration Network, *USCIS Amends Credible Fear Lesson Plans*, available at: https://cliniclegal.org/resources/uscis-amends-credible-fear-lesson-plans

[201] Bill Ong Hing, *Ethics, Morality and Disruption of U.S. Immigration Laws*, 73 *Kansas L. Rev.* 981 (2015).

[202] 480 U.S. 421 (1987).

credible fear cases nationwide were granted, so that more than 73,000 migrants flee-ing persecution were allowed to apply for asylum.[203]

That figure is expected to drop under the Trump administration's revisions to the credible fear lesson plan. For example, the new guidance removes a passage from the previous version that said if an asylum officer has reasonable doubt about a person's credibility, they should likely find credible fear and allow an immigration judge to hear the question at a full hearing.[204] In another change, a passage has been altered on individuals' "demeanor, candor, and responsiveness" as a factor in their credibility.[205] Both the 2017 and 2014 versions note that migrants' demeanor is often affected by cultural factors, including being detained in a foreign land and perhaps not speaking the language, as well as by trauma sustained at home or on the journey to the United States.[206] But the new version removes guidance that said these factors should not be "significant factors" in determining someone's credibility – essentially allowing asylum officers to consider signs of stress as a reason to doubt someone's credibility.[207]

6.5.1. *Discouraging Haitians*

As a candidate, Trump criticized Obama for "letting in too many refugees," calling it "stupid."[208] As President, of course, his travel bans and reductions in refugee quo-tas are meant to discourage refugees. Sadly, discouraging legitimate asylum seekers is not new to the United States. Think only of President Franklin D. Roosevelt's turning away of the SS *St. Louis* carrying European Jewish refugees fleeing the Nazis in 1939. Another glaring example of unthinkable refugee rejection involves thousands of Haitians who were fleeing the social, economic, and violent repression of the Duvalier regime of the 1970s and 1980s.[209] They faced an accelerated pro-cessing program dubbed the "Haitian program" that became the subject of federal litigation.[210]

The Haitian program was the INS's response to the massive influx of Haitian asylum seekers in south Florida in the late 1970s. By the summer of 1978, 6,000

---

[203] Kopan, *Trump Admin Quietly.*

[204] Ibid.

[205] Ibid.

[206] Ibid.

[207] Ibid.

[208] Ahmad Khan Rahami, *Trump: Our Leaders Are "Stupid" for Letting in Too Many Refugees,* New York CBSlocal.com, September 19, 2016, available at: http://newyork.cbslocal.com/2016/09/19/trump-refugees-chelsea-bombing/

[209] Jim Wyss and Jacqueline Charles, *After Death of Jean-Claude 'Baby Doc' Duvalier, Calls for Justice Remain in Haiti,* Miami Herald, October 4, 2014; Jeff Hardy, Haitian Refugees Celebrate Duvalier's fall, UPI, February 7, 1986, available at: www.upi.com/Archives/1986/02/07/Haitian-refugees-celebrate-Duvaliers-fall/2584508136400/.

[210] *Haitian Refugee Center* v. *Smith,* 676 F.2d 1023, 1029 (5th Cir. 1982).

to 7,000 Haitian cases were pending in Miami.[211] Operating under the assumption that the asylum seekers were "economic" migrants rather than political refugees, officials decided to implement an accelerated program that would discourage a further influx.[212]

The features of the Haitian program constituted stark violations of due process.[213] Immigration judges were instructed to increase productivity, so at its peak, immigration judges were each holding more than eighteen deportation a day.[214] Asylum officers were forced to increase their efficiency as well, having to handle forty asylum interviews each day, severely reducing the time that could be spent with each applicant.[215] Although authorities knew that only about a dozen attorneys were available to represent Haitians, hearings were scheduled with little regard to attorneys' availability; an attorney might have "three hearings at the same hour in different locations."[216] More than 4,000 Haitians were processed under the program, and none received asylum.[217]

Ultimately, the federal courts ended the Haitian program, concluding, "the government created conditions which negated the possibility that a Haitian's asylum hearing would be meaningful in either its timing or nature. Under such circumstances, the right to petition for political asylum was effectively denied."[218] The Trump administration also is threatening due process by ordering immigration judges to complete seven hundred cases a year, and 95 percent of all cases must be completed on the initial scheduled hearing date. Never before have immigration judges been subjected to a performance matrix.

6.5.2. *Discouraging Guatemalans and El Salvadorans*

The surge in migrants fleeing violence from Central America since 2014 was preceded by a related influx a generation earlier. Thousands of El Salvadorans and Guatemalans fled to the United States in the late 1970s and 1980s due to the repression and violence caused by civil war. Although thousands applied for asylum, only about 2 percent of their applications were granted due to discriminatory treatment.[219] That discrimination is highlighted in two federal court cases.

In *Orantes-Hernandez* v. *Smith*,[220] a class action case was brought challenging the way El Salvadorans were processed when they were apprehended by INS officers. The

---

[211] Ibid.

[212] Ibid., at 1030.

[213] Ibid., at 1041.

[214] Ibid., at 1031.

[215] Ibid.

[216] Ibid.

[217] Ibid., at 1032.

[218] Ibid., at 1039–40.

[219] Sarah Gammage, El Salvador: Despite End to Civil War, Emigration Continues, MPI Migration Information Source, July 26, 2007, available at: www.migrationpolicy.org/article/el-salvador-despite-end-civil-war-emigration-continues. According to some, the asylum approval rate for El Salvadorans was "fewer than 3%," and "1% or less" for Guatemalans. *See* Carolyn Patty Blum, *The Settlement of American Baptist Churches v. Thornburgh: Landmark Victory for Central American Asylum-Seekers*, 3 *Int'l J. Refugee L.* 347 (1991), available at: http://scholarship.law.berkeley.edu/facpubs/1967

[220] 541 F.Supp. 351 (C.D. Cal 1982).

federal court recognized that El Salvadorans were fleeing their country due to "perva-sive and arbitrary violence" and were eligible to seek asylum and request a deportation hearing.[221] However, most of those apprehended signed voluntary departure forms forgoing their right to ask for asylum. After taking evidence of what was happening, the court concluded "that the widespread acceptance of voluntary departure is due in large part to the coercive effect of the practices and procedures employed by the INS and the unfamiliarity of most Salvadorans with their rights under the immigration laws."[222] Government agents essentially used coercion and intimidation to get those apprehended to sign the voluntary departure forms.[223] Given the abuse, the court ordered authorities affirmatively to notify all apprehended El Salvadorans of their right to apply for asylum and to provide them with a list of free legal services providers.[224]

American Baptist Churches, et al v. Thornburgh,[225] another class action, was an unusual case brought by more than eighty religious and refugee rights programs.[226] In spite of the government's motion to dismiss, the court allowed the case to proceed on the issue of discriminatory treatment of the asylum seekers, citing the low approval rates for applicants from El Salvador and Guatemala.[227] During the discovery phase of the case, the government announced the establishment of a new asylum officer corps that would began handling affirmative asylum applications beginning in April 1991.[228] Furthermore, in new legislation that was passed by Congress in 1990, a new category of protection – TPS – was created that eventually proved beneficial to many asylum seekers.[229] Of course, we now know that Trump has acted to end TPS for Haitians, El Salvadorans, and others.

The parties in the *American Baptist Churches* case thereafter reached a settle-ment, providing that all Guatemalans and El Salvadorans who had been denied asylum, withholding or extended voluntary departure would have the right to a new asylum application before an asylum officer.[230] They would be provided with a list of free legal services providers.[231] Limitations on whether class members could be detained were established, and employment authorization would be afforded to the class members.[232] The Trump administration's 2018 family separation policy (discussed in the Afterword) also was intended to send a questionable message to Central Americans that asylum is not available.

---

[221] Ibid., at 358–9.
[222] Ibid., at 359.
[223] Ibid., at 359, 372–3.
[224] Ibid., at 386.
[225] 760 F.Supp. 796 (N.D. Cal 1991).
[226] Carolyn Patty Blum, *The Settlement of American Baptist Churches v. Thornburgh: Landmark Victory for Central American Asylum-Seekers,* 3 *Int'l J. Refugee L.* 347 (1991), available at: http://scholarship .law.berkeley.edu/facpubs/1967
[227] Ibid.
[228] Ibid.
[229] Ibid.
[230] 760 F.Supp. at 799.
[231] Ibid., at 803.
[232] Ibid., at 804–5.

6.6. SANCTUARY CITIES FUNDING AND SHAMING THREATS

Throughout his campaign, Trump promised that he would block federal funding for sanctuary cities: "Block funding for sanctuary cities. We block the funding. No more funds ... Cities that refuse to cooperate with federal authorities will not receive tax-payer dollars."[233] Then within the first week of his administration, Trump's January 25, 2017, executive order announced that the Attorney General would "ensure that ... sanctuary jurisdictions [would not be] eligible to receive Federal grants."[234] On top of that, Trump's administration announced that it would "shame sanctuary cities" in a weekly report by listing localities that do not cooperate with immigration detainer requests.[235] In January 2018, Attorney General Jeff Sessions escalated the attempt to crack down on "sanctuary" jurisdictions, threatening to subpoena twenty-three states, cities and other localities that have policies that DOJ suspects might be unlawfully interfering with immigration enforcement. Local leaders criticized the move. New Orleans Mayor Mitch Landrieu, A Democrat and president of the US Conference of Mayors, complained, "An attack on one of our cities' mayors who are following the constitution is an attack on all of us." New York Mayor Bill de Blasio, a Democrat, similarly wrote on Twitter that Trump's Justice Department has "decided to renew their racist assault on our immigrant communities. It doesn't make us safer and it violates America's core values."[236]

Like Trump's Muslim bans, the sanctuary funding threat and the shaming strategy have run into legal and/or technical problems. Seattle, San Francisco, Santa Clara County (California), and Richmond (California) all filed lawsuits challenging the funding threat. After hearing arguments on the matter, a federal judge in San Francisco imposed a nationwide injunction on the threat to withhold federal funding.[237] And it turned out that even the shaming reports were halted after local police agencies complained the reports were "filled with errors." For example, the first report, issued March 20, confused three different Franklin counties in Iowa, New York, and Pennsylvania.[238] It incorrectly blamed Williamson and Bastrop counties in Texas for refusing ICE detainers even though the suspects in question had been transferred to other jurisdictions.[239] And Chester County, Pennsylvania, and Richmond County, North Carolina, were falsely accused of not complying

[233] Tom LoBianco, *'Sanctuary cities' Gird for Trump White House*, CNN, November 15, 2016.

[234] David Post, *The 'Sanctuary Cities' Executive Order: Putting the Bully Back into 'Bully Pulpit,'* Washington Post, May 11, 2017.

[235] Olivia Beavers, *Trump Administration Seeks to Shame Sanctuary Cities*, The Hill, March 20, 2017.

[236] Matt Zapotosky, *Sessions Threatens to Subpoena 'Sanctuary' Jurisdictions in Immigration Fight*, Washington Post, January 24, 2018.

[237] David Post and Maria Sacchetti, *Trump Blasts Federal Court Ruling that Blocks His 'Sanctuary City' Order*, Washington Post, April 26, 2017.

[238] Alan Gomez, *Errors Prompt Trump to Halt Reports Shaming 'Sanctuary Cities,'* USA Today, April 10, 2017.

[239] Ibid.

with detainer requests even though neither county had custody of the suspects in question.[240]

Of course, one thing that the Trump ICE machine could probably do without is to waste more time and effort on enforcement in self-declared sanctuary jurisdictions. For example, ICE apparently deliberately targeted Austin, TX after talks between the agency's officials and local authorities went awry.[241] Austin is typically described as a sanctuary city for its welcoming stance on immigration.[242] Officials reported at least fifty people were arrested there in February.[243] Twenty-eight of them had no criminal record whatsoever.[244] Texas-based federal magistrate, Judge Andrew Austin, recalled how ICE officials had told him to "expect a big operation" and that it was "a result of the [Travis County] sheriff's new policy."[245] In January 2018, news reports claimed that ICE officials were planning widespread raids with the goal of arresting more than 1,500 people in San Francisco and other Northern California cities.[246]

Trump's efforts to shame and defund sanctuary jurisdictions are unique. But the idea of sanctuary has not been popular with other enforcement-minded administrations. In the 1980s, when the sanctuary movement over Central American refugees of that era was in full swing, individual supporters of the sanctuary movement were targeted.[247] In many respects, the sanctuary cities phenomenon grew out of the sanctuary movement led by many religious leaders.[248] And some of those leaders were targeted by the Reagan administration.[249]

6.6.1. *Criminal Prosecution of Sanctuary Workers*

I had been practicing immigration law for about a decade and by then running a law school immigration clinic when I first heard of Jack Elder and Stacey Lynn Merkt. Back in 1982, Catholic Bishop John Joseph Fitzpatrick opened Casa Oscar Romero

---

[240] Ibid.

[241] Chris Riotta, *ICE Raids Target Austin, Texas,* Yahoo News, March 29, 2017, available at: www.yahoo .com/news/ice-raids-target-austin-texas-163840314.html

[242] Ibid.

[243] Ibid.

[244] Tony Plohetski, Austin No. 1 in U.S. – for non-criminals arrested in ICE raids, KVUE News, February 22, 2017, available at: www.statesman.com/news/austin-for-non-criminals-arrested-ice-raids/ R8suKsN9kUIjnpz10S2DII/

[245] Sam Knight, *Pattern of Deportation As Retaliation Emerging in Trump Era,* District Sentinel, March 21, 2017, www.districtsentinel.com/pattern-deportation-retaliation-emerging-trump-era/

[246] Sarah Ruiz-Grossman, *California Leaders Slam Trump Administration Over Report of Planned ICE Raids,* Huffington Post, January 17, 2018.

[247] Susan Gzesh, Central Americans and Asylum Policy in the Reagan Era, MPI Migration Information Source, April 1, 2006, available at: www.migrationpolicy.org/article/central-americans-and-asylum-policy-reagan-era

[248] Ibid.

[249] Ibid.

in San Benito, TX, as a shelter for increasing numbers of Central Americans crossing the Rio Grande into Texas.[250] Jack Elder became the director of the Casa Romero, named in honor of the assassinated Roman Catholic Archbishop of El Salvador.[251] Stacey Lynn Merkt was a volunteer there.[252] They often knowingly drove migrants to bus stops where the migrants would continue their migration.[253] This chronology provides some context for what led to their actual criminal convictions.

In February 1984, near remote Guerra, Texas, Border Patrol Officers stopped and arrested Catholic Nun Dianne Muhlenkamp of the Poor Hand Maids of Jesus Christ, Fort Wayne, Indiana, Merkt, then-affiliated with the Bijou House Religious Community in Colorado Springs, Colorado, and Dallas Times Herald reporter Jack Fischer on federal alien transportation charges.[254] An undocumented man, woman, and baby from El Salvador were inside the car owned by the Diocese of Brownsville.[255] By May 4, 1984, Merkt was convicted of the felony offense, but the government declined to prosecute the newspaper reporter and the nun agreed to deferred adjudication.[256] The two adult Salvadorans testified they fled El Salvador after seeing the murders of associates and being threatened.[257] On June 27, 1984, Merkt was sentenced to ninety days in jail, but the sentence was suspended and she was placed on two years' probation.[258]

In March 1984, Elder was spotted by the Border Patrol dropping three Salvadoran men off at a bus station five miles from the Casa Romero shelter.[259] Then the next month, federal agents entered Casa Romero, church-owned property, and arrested Elder on three felony charges punishable by up to fifteen years in prison.[260] In December 1984, Elder and Merkt, who by then was working with Elder, were indicted by a federal grand jury on charges they conspired and transported two Salvadoran adults and three children from Brownsville to a bus station in McAllen during November.[261] On February 21, 1985, Elder was convicted of conspiracy and illegal transportation.[262] Merkt, indicted on one conspiracy count of transportation

---

[250] *Chronology of Sanctuary Movement members Stacey Lynn Merkt and Jack Elder*, UPI, March 27, 1985, www.upi.com/Archives/1985/03/27/Chronology-of-Sanctuary-Movement-members-Stacey-Lynn-Merkt-and-Jack-Elder/9771480747600/
[251] Ibid.
[252] Ibid.
[253] Ibid.
[254] Ibid.
[255] Ibid.
[256] Ibid.
[257] Ibid.
[258] Ibid.
[259] Ibid.
[260] Ibid.
[261] Ibid.
[262] Ibid.; *See United States v. Elder*, 601 F. Supp. 1574 (S.D. Tex. 1985).

of undocumented immigrants and two substantive transportation counts, was found guilty only of the conspiracy count.[263]

Both Elder and Merkt spent time in jail. Initially, Elder was offered two years' probation, on the condition that he would move out of Casa Romero, no longer aid Central American refugees, and stop discussing publicly the refugees' problems.[264] Elder refused those conditions, and was sentenced to a year in prison.[265] Merkt was sentenced to 179 days in prison and put on similar restrictions.[266] Elder could have been fined $28,000 and sentenced to thirty years in prison; Merkt faced a potential fine up to $10,000 and a five-year prison sentence.[267]

The experiences of Elder and Merkt were only two examples of the Reagan administration's attack on sanctuary workers. On January 14, 1985, more than sixty arrests were made in a crackdown on church groups.[268] Indictments were based in part on evidence gathered by four undercover agents who, wearing concealed tape recorders, attended church meetings in Tucson, AZ.[269] While the workers argued that they were helping to provide sanctuary to refugees fleeing persecution and death squads in El Salvador and Guatemala, the Reagan administration contended that most asylum applicants from Central America were fleeing poverty, not persecution.[270] Sixteen individuals were named in a seventy-one-count indictment that included: Reverend John M. Fife of the Tucson Southside United Presbyterian Church, the first clergymen in the United States to declare his church a sanctuary for refugees from Central America; James A. Corbett, a retired rancher in Tucson, and Philip M. Conger, director of the Tucson Ecumenical Council Task Force on Central American Activity; Antonio Clark, a Catholic priest at the Sacred Heart Church in Nogales, AZ; Ramon Dagoberto Quinones, a Catholic priest and Mexican citizen from Nogales, Sonora, Mexico; Darlene Nicgorski of Phoenix, a member of the School Sisters of St. Francis in Milwaukee; Ana Priester and Mary Waddell of Phoenix, members of the Sisters of Charity of the Blessed Virgin Mary; and Mary Kay Espinosa of Nogales, AZ, secretary of the Association of Educational Reform of Sacred Heart Church.[271]

---

[263] *Chronology of Sanctuary Movement Members Stacey Lynn Merkt and Jack Elder*, UPI, March 27, 1985, available at: www.upi.com/Archives/1985/03/27/Chronology-of-Sanctuary-Movement-members-Stacey-Lynn-Merkt-and-Jack-Elder/9771480747600/; *See also United States. v. Merkt*, 794 F.2d 950 (5th Circ. 1986).

[264] Storer Rowley, *2 Sentenced in Sanctuary Case*, Chicago Tribune, March 28, 1985.

[265] Ibid.

[266] Ibid.

[267] Storer Rowley, *2 Sentenced in Sanctuary Case*, Chicago Tribune, March 28, 1985.

[268] Stuart Taylor, *16 Indicted by U.S. in Bid to End Church Smuggling of Latin Aliens*, New York Times, January 15, 1985.

[269] Ibid.

[270] Ibid.

[271] Stuart Taylor, *16 Indicted by U.S. in Bid to End Church Smuggling of Latin Aliens*, New York Times, January 15, 1985.

6.7. REINSTITUTING SECURE COMMUNITIES PROGRAM

Trump's interior executive order of January 25, 2017 revives the controversial "Secure Communities" program that first expanded and then ended during the Obama administration (see Chapter 1). The program requires local authorities to share fingerprints and other arrest data to help track down removable immigrants.[272]

The initiative referred fingerprint information to DHS via the FBI for all participating jurisdictions and was intended to focus on serious criminals.[273] Yet, the vast majority of individuals removed as a result of Secure Communities referrals were noncriminal or low-level offenders.[274] And DHS took the strict position on Secure Communities that it could access all fingerprints submitted to the FBI by local law enforcement officials even without the permission of state and local officials.[275] In fact, Secure Communities casts a wide net and scoops up the fingerprints of everyone not born in the United States, whether or not they pose a criminal risk.[276] For example, after an abused woman in San Francisco worked up the courage to call police to report her abuser, she was arrested because the police saw a "red mark" on the alleged abuser's cheek.[277] The charges against the victim were dropped, but her fingerprints were already forwarded to ICE under the Secure Communities program, and she faced deportation.[278] This case was an exact replica of one that occurred in Maryland.[279]

Under Secure Communities, the FBI automatically sends the fingerprints to DHS to check against its immigration databases.[280] During the Obama administration, if these checks revealed that an individual was unlawfully present in the United States or otherwise removable due to a criminal conviction, ICE would take enforcement action-prioritizing the removal of individuals who presented the most significant threats to public safety as determined by the severity of their crime, their criminal history, and other factors, including prioritizing those who had repeatedly violated immigration laws.[281]

---

[272] Tal Kopan and Catherine E. Shoichet, *Key Points in Trump's Immigration Executive Orders*, CNN, January 26, 2017.

[273] Aarti Kohli et al., Secure Communities by the Numbers: An Analysis of Demographics and Due Process 1. The Chief Just. Earl Warren Inst. on L. & Soc. Pol'y 3 (2011), available at: www.law.berkeley.edu/files/Secure_ Communities_by_the_Numbers.pdf.

[274] Ibid., at 3, 9.

[275] Immigration Policy Center, *Secure Communities: A Fact Sheet*, American Immigration Council (November. 29, 2011), available at: www.immigrationpolicy.org/just-facts/secure-communities-factsheet.

[276] Ibid.

[277] Lee Romney and Paloma Esquivel, Noncriminals Swept Up in Federal Deportation Program, LA Times (April 25, 2011).

[278] Ibid.

[279] Shankar Vedantam, Call for Help Leads to Possible Deportation for Hyattsville Mother, Washington Post (November 1, 2010).

[280] Immigration Policy Center, *Secure Communities*

[281] Ibid.

The Secure Communities program dwarfs all other prior efforts to involve states and localities in immigration enforcement.[282] From a federal perspective, the advantage of Secure Communities is that it expands federal enforcement capacity by processing information about local arrests without bestowing the increased enforcement powers on sub-federal agents required by the 287(g) program.[283] The first appropriations for the program were authorized in December 2007 during the Bush presidency.[284] In its heyday during the Obama administration, the program operated in more than 3,000 jurisdictions across the country, including all jurisdictions along the United States–Mexico border.

Thus, the Secure Communities program represents a super-sized immigration enforcement effort by roping in state and local law enforcement without their consent.[285] As Professor Jennifer Chacón pointed out during the Obama administration's operation of the program:

> From a federal perspective, the advantage of Secure Communities is that it expands federal enforcement capacity by processing information about local arrest without bestowing the increased enforcement powers on sub-federal agents required by the 287(g) program. At least in theory, if not in practice, discriminatory power concerning enforcement is shifted back to the federal government. The first appropriations for the program were authorized in December 2007 [during the Bush administration]. Currently, the program is operating in more than 3,000 jurisdictions across the country, including all jurisdictions along the United States–Mexico border.[286]

After being reactivated by Trump, the ICE website boasts that through the second quarter of fiscal year 2017, "more than 43,300 convicted criminal aliens have been removed as a result of Secure Communities."[287] The site is silent with respect to how many noncriminal aliens have been removed under the revival of Secure Communities.

6.8. REPORTS OF WIDESPREAD FEAR

Since the election of Trump, reports of widespread fear in immigrant communities have been common. On February 12, 2017, CNN headlined: "Fear Spreads Among Undocumented Immigrants" and reported:

---

[282] Sasha Bagley and Delphine Nakache, *Immigration Regulation in Federal States: Challenges and Responses in Comparative Perspective* (2014).

[283] Ibid.

[284] Ibid.

[285] Jennifer M. Chacón, *The Transformation of Immigration Federalism*, 21 Wm. & Mary Bill Rts. J. 577, 603 (2012).

[286] Ibid.

[287] U.S. Immigration and Customs Enforcement, *Secure Communities*, available at: www.ice.gov/secure-communities

Across the United States, some unauthorized immigrants are keeping their children home from school. Others have suspended after-school visits to the public library. They have given up coffee shop trips and weekend restaurant dinners with family.

Some don't answer knocks on their doors. They're taping bedsheets over windows and staying off social media. Nervous parents and their children constantly exchange text messages and phone calls.

From New York to Los Angeles, a series of immigration arrests this week have unleashed waves of fear and uncertainty across immigrant communities.[288]

A few days later, The Guardian warned: "'Psychological warfare': immigrants in America held hostage by fear of raids" and wrote:

[An] 11-page [draft enforcement] memo has compounded fears among immigrant communities that Trump's campaign promise of a hardline clampdown on immigration, dismissed by some at the time as little more than heated rhetoric, is about to be realized.

"It's almost like it's psychological warfare that's being waged against people of color to create a constant feeling of fear and uncertainty," said Juanita Molina, the executive director of Border Action Network, a human rights organization in Tucson, Arizona ...

"I've had border patrol ask me for my documents just going for a jog by my house. I'd go to get a gallon of milk at the store and have officers stop me and say 'Well, what are you doing?'" ...

"We don't have just basic freedom of movement."[289]

Then the New York Times chimed in: "Immigrants Hide, Fearing Capture on 'Any Corner'"

No going to church, no going to the store. No doctor's appointments for some, no school for others. No driving, period – not when a broken taillight could deliver the driver to Immigration and Customs Enforcement.

It is happening on Staten Island, where fewer day laborers haunt street corners in search of work; in West Phoenix's Isaac School District, where 13 Latino students have dropped out in the past two weeks; and in the horse country of northern New Jersey, where one of the many undocumented grooms who muck out the stables is thinking of moving back to Honduras.

If deportation has always been a threat on paper for the 11 million people living in the country illegally, it rarely imperiled those who did not commit serious crimes. But with the Trump administration intent on curbing illegal immigration – two memos outlining the federal government's plans to accelerate deportations were released Tuesday, another step toward making good on one of President Trump's

[288] Sanchez, *After ICE Arrests.*
[289] Julia Carrie Wong, *'Psychological Warfare': Immigrants in America Held Hostage by Fear of Raids*, The Guardian, February 18, 2017.

signature campaign pledges – that threat, for many people, has now begun to distort every movement.[290]

As the reports disclose, fear is manifested in a variety of disturbing ways. According to one attorney in New York, "There are people that I work with who essentially want to go dark ... They don't want to be public in any way whatsoever. They spend less time on the street. They go to work and go straight back home. They don't go on Facebook. They put curfews on themselves."[291] One family no longer goes to the local park where they used to play baseball in the evenings; young men avoid a soccer field where pickup games were once common.[292] One woman, Meli, who arrived in Los Angeles from El Salvador more than twelve years ago, lives "in a state of self-imposed house arrest, refusing to drive, fearing to leave her home, wondering how she will take her younger son, who is autistic, to doctor's appointments.[293] [She says,] 'I don't want to go to the store, to church – they are looking everywhere, and they know where to find us ... They could be waiting for us anywhere. Any corner, any block.'"[294] From North Carolina, Maryland, New York, and California demonstrate that immigrants are forgoing medical care and not picking up medication out of fear of immigration enforcement.[295] According to Mary Clark, the executive director of Esperanza Immigrant Legal Services in Philadelphia.: "There's a real fear that their kids will get put into the foster care system ... People are asking us because they don't know where to turn."[296] Stories abound of immigrants who qualify and already participate in social support programs – such as to feed themselves and their families or to provide health insurance for their qualified children – withdrawing from the programs out of fear of deportation or of hurting their chances of citizenship. Groups that help low-income families get food assistance are alarmed by a recent drop in the number of immigrants seeking help. Some families are even canceling their food stamps and other government benefits, for fear that receiving them will affect their immigration status or lead to deportation. Many of the concerns appear to be unfounded but have been fueled by the Trump administration's tough stance on immigration. Officials at Manna Food Center in Montgomery County, Maryland, report that about 20 percent of the 561 families they have helped apply for food stamps, or Supplemental Nutrition Assistance Program (SNAP) benefits, in the past few months have asked that their cases be closed.[297] Even in San Francisco, an outspoken sanctuary city, fewer eligible residents are using food stamps because

---

[290] Vivian Yee, *Immigrants Hide, Fearing Capture on 'Any Corner,'* New York Times, February 22, 2017.
[291] Ray Sanchez (quoting Cesar Vargas).
[292] Vivian Yee, *Immigrants Hide.*
[293] Ibid.
[294] Ibid.
[295] Jan Hoffman, *Sick and Afraid, Some Immigrants Forgo Medical Care,* New York Times, June 26, 2017.
[296] Vivian Yee, *Immigrants Hide.*
[297] Pam Fessler, *Deportation Fears Prompt Immigrants to Cancel Food Stamps,* NPR, March 28, 2017.

of fears about immigration crackdowns under the Trump administration.[298] Police departments across the country report a decrease in crime reporting in predominantly Latino neighborhoods, which some officials believe are related to the fear of immigration enforcement; the Houston police chief reports a 13 percent decrease in violent crime reporting by Latinos during the first three months of 2017.[299] Teachers in the Austin area say parents who once drove their children to school are now sending them on the bus instead, to avoid running into immigration authorities.[300]

One minister in Columbus, GA, has a similar observation. The Reverend Ivelisse Quiñones, director of Hispanic ministries at St. Luke United Methodist Church, said the angst is evident at church on Sunday mornings. "Yes, people are very concerned," said the associate pastor at St. Luke and lead pastor of the Hispanic ministry, which has about fifty congregants.[301] "We are transporting many of our members because they're afraid of driving ... And every Sunday, I make sure I'm abreast of the news that happens during the week. Before I start preaching, I give them 15 minutes of training, teaching, and counseling, because there are a lot of worries here."[302]

Graciela, a fifty-one-year-old mother-of-four, made a plan to leave her two teenagers, ages thirteen and fourteen, with her twenty-four-year-old daughter, if she's forced to return to Mexico after living in Phoenix since 2004.[303] "I want them to be able to finish their studies, but she won't be able to handle them for very long," says Graciela.[304] "She has two kids of her own, and it's a lot to ask her. I've got to be prepared to take them back with me."[305] Graciela is also devastated by the idea of leaving her older children behind. "I can't imagine not seeing my grandkids grow up," she says.[306] "Since Trump became president, I'm so depressed. I'm eating out of control, and I wake up in the middle of the night and can't go back to sleep. I have bags under my eyes. It's really starting to wear on me."[307]

In the auditorium of the Benjamin Franklin Health Science Academy in Brooklyn, a parent coordinator, Christian Rodriguez, noted: "I have children crying in the classroom, crying in my office ... When I ask them, 'Why are you crying?' They have expressed to me that they don't want their moms to be apprehended and

[298] Tara Duggan, *Immigrants' Fear Cited in Declining Food Stamp Use in SF*, SF Chronicle, May 17, 2017.

[299] Lindsey Bever, *Hispanics 'Are Going Further into the Shadows' Amid Chilling Immigration Debate, Police Say*, Washington Post, May 12, 2017.

[300] Elise Foley, Roque Planas, *Immigration Officers Test Boundaries of Rules Discouraging Arrests At Schools, Churches*, Huffington Post, March 22, 2017.

[301] Ibid.

[302] Alva James-Johnson, *Columbus Undocumented Immigrants Fear Raids, Deportations*, Ledger-Enquirer, March 12, 2017.

[303] Sarah Elizabeth Richards, *How Fear of Deportation Puts Stress on Families*, The Atlantic, March 22, 2017.

[304] Ibid.

[305] Ibid.

[306] Ibid.

[307] Ibid.

taken away from them."[308] The effect on some high students is tragic in a different way, as noted in this email request:

> Dear Professor Hing,
>
> We are wondering if one of you (or the University of San Francisco (USF) students) could do a KYR [know-your-rights] talk in Spanish at [ ] School in the [... neighborhood] on 4/25 at 6 pm.
>
> The teachers and principal there are worried because the high school students and families have expressed a lot of anxiety. In addition, many of the undocumented students are now feeling discouraged and don't want to keep studying hard or apply for college. We are having a talk for the students on 4/19 at 10.30 am with a DACAmented lawyer to give some encouragement and perspective.
>
> But we need to do a KYR on how to defend and prepare families for the parents on 4/25 at 6 pm ...
>
> Let me know either way.
>
> Thank you so much
>
> Lorena[309]

Tragically, even domestic abuse victims are afraid to come forward. Undocumented immigrants suffering from domestic violence are worried they will get deported if they seek help in dealing with their abuse.[310] The concern spiked following executive actions by the Trump administration.[311] Staff at clinics and domestic violence shelters in cities with high populations of undocumented immigrants said they have seen a large drop in the number of women coming in for services. "Even people who work with these issues are saying they have not seen this level of fear," said Sandra Henriquez, executive director of the California Coalition Against Sexual Assault.[312] The Travis County, TX, district attorney's office had to grapple with how to move forward in at least one (felony domestic violence) case in which a victim stopped cooperating with investigators out of fear that ICE will deport her.[313] "Our office has worked for a long time over many years to try to build up our credibility with the immigrant community," said Mack Martinez, chief of the domestic violence division at the Travis County attorney's office.[314] "When someone is arrested

---

[308] Ana Kamenetz, '*I Have Children Crying in The Classroom*', NPR, March 9, 2017.
[309] Email to Bill Hing from Lorena Melgarejo (SF Archdiocese Office) April 15, 2017.
[310] Tyler Kingkade, Domestic Abuse Victims Aren't Coming Forward Because They're Scared of Being Deported, BuzzFeed News, March 16, 2017.
[311] Ibid.
[312] Ibid.
[313] Philip Jankowski, *Travis DA: Witness' Deportation Fears Stall Domestic Violence Case*, My Statesman, March 8, 2017, available at: www.mystatesman.com/news/crime-law/travis-witness-deportation-fears-stall-domestic-violence-case/rmFeprwRlWKYJFUjAUz5oN/.
[314] Ibid.

in the courthouse, it makes it very difficult for these people to trust that they will be safe if they make an outcry of abuse."[315]

Even LPRs are afraid. According to a veteran private immigration lawyer, "The problem is that Trump and his policies have sown real fear and panic into the hearts and souls of our clients, whether they are undocumented or documented … We have long-term LPRs who are afraid to leave the United States, fearing detention upon their return."[316] In a twist, the fear engendered by Trump among LPRs has resulted in an uptick in naturalization applications as well.[317]

The increased level of fear is measurable. A UCLA social science poll in Los Angeles found that 37 percent of respondents said they were afraid that they, a family member, or a friend would be deported because of their immigration status.[318] Of those, 80 percent said the risks of deportation increased if a friend or family member enrolled in any kind of governmental health, education or housing program.[319] Latinos were more likely to express fear of a friend or family member being deported: 56 percent, followed by 31 percent of Asians.[320] But many whites expressed concern as well. Nineteen percent of the Anglos were worried, perhaps concerned about a maid, gardener, or office co-worker.[321] Fear of deportation was higher among younger Angelinos: 56 percent of respondents between the ages of eighteen and twenty-nine said they were concerned.[322] And 83 percent of younger Latinos who were worried about deportation were wary of signing up for government programs.[323]

The fear appears pervasive even in the states and localities that have done the most to allay fear through sanctuary or other protective policies. California Dream Act scholarship applications for undocumented college students are down significantly despite repeated assurances from the state that it will do everything within its power to protect the privacy of student information.[324] Reports by Latinos of sexual assault have dropped 25 percent in Los Angeles, the city with the longest standing police policy (special order 40, 1979) prohibiting the reporting of immigrant victims

---

[315] Philip Jankowski, *Deportation Fears Keep Victim from Cooperating in Domestic Violence Case, Travis DA Says*, Austin American-Statesman, March 8, 2017.

[316] Email to Bill Hing, from Paula Solorio, March 30, 2017.

[317] Steven Riznyk, *Citizenship Applications Are on the Rise, and the Reasons Are Interesting*, Waiver-Strategy.com, May 14, 2017. [email announcement May 10]

[318] George Foulsham, *Deportation, Loss of Health Care Raise Concerns in L.A. County, According to UCLA Survey*, UCLA Newsroom (April 4, 2017), available at: http://newsroom.ucla.edu/releases/deportation-loss-of-health-care-raise-concerns-in-l-a-county-according-to-ucla-survey.

[319] Ibid.

[320] Ibid.

[321] Ibid.

[322] Ibid.

[323] Mike McPhate, *California Today: Worries Over Immigration*, New York Times, April 5, 2017

[324] Cynthia Moreno, *DREAMers Urged to Apply for California Dream Act*, Vida en el valle, March 6, 2017, available at: www.vidaenelvalle.com/news/state/california/sacramento/article136795893.html

to ICE, and the city whose current police chief and mayor have clearly expressed support and protection for undocumented immigrants since the election.[325]

Whatever one might say about comparative ICE enforcement efforts from administration to administration or Trump's specific strategies, fear is up in immigrant communities since he assumed the presidency.

6.8.1. *Why the Fear?*

As noted in the introduction, fear in the immigrant community started the moment that Trump was elected. His round-them-up-and-deport-them rhetoric was ubiquitous in the media throughout the primary and general elections, along with his build-a-wall-make-Mexico-pay and anti-Syrian refugee corollaries.[326] The rhetoric was difficult to ignore – for everyone, including immigrants – because the coverage reached ethnic and social media, as well as mainstream outlets.[327] As one writer reported from Brownsville, TX, the "news here on the border with Mexico travels fast. Most of it is, in fact, 'fake news' – conjecture and unverifiable gossip exchanged over 'el Feisbuk,' which is what people here in the Rio Grande Valley call the social network. Instead of snapshots and emojis, it now disseminates warnings. People are frightened, and frightened people repeat things that frighten them more."[328]

> Stay at home tomorrow. Immigration and Customs Enforcement is conducting raids in the kitchens.
> Don't send your kids to school on Wednesday. The border patrol is looking for kids with no papers.
> Don't drive down 802 on Fridays anymore.
> There's a checkpoint at the grocery store. They arrested 100 people last night at 10.[329]

Some of the stock images on the "news are from long before the last election, or instances in which warrants are being served after months of investigation."[330] But the damage has been done.

If you are a noncitizen or care about the well-being of a noncitizen, then being on edge about ICE enforcement is easy to understand. Reports of apprehensions and removals of individuals – some of whom had been allowed to stay by the Obama

[325] James Queally, *Latinos are Reporting Fewer Sexual Assaults Amid a Climate of Fear in Immigrant Communities, LAPD says*, LA Times, March 21, 2017. *See also*, Bill Ong Hing, Immigration Sanctuary Policies: Constitutional and Representative of Good Policing and Good Public Policy, 2 *UC Irvine L. Rev.* 247 (2012).
[326] BBC, *Trump's Promises Before and After the Election* (June 16, 2017), available at: www.bbc.com/news/world-us-canada-37982000.
[327] Ibid.
[328] Domingo Martinez, *How Scared Should People on the Border Be?*, New York Times, March 31, 2017.
[329] Ibid.
[330] Ibid.

administration – have become common. Consider this range of examples, form across the country, of arrests and/or removals that received media attention in the first few months of the Trump administration.

1. **Restaurant owner, husband of US citizen, resident for seventeen years deported – Indiana.** Helen Beristain voted for Donald Trump even though she is married to an undocumented immigrant. In November, she thought Trump would deport only people with criminal records – people he called "bad hombres" – and that he would leave families intact. "I don't think ICE is out there to detain anyone and break families, no," Beristain told CNN in March, shortly after her husband, Roberto Beristain was detained by ICE. On Wednesday, Beristain was proven wrong as ICE split her family across two countries. Roberto Beristain, forty-four, was deported back to Mexico despite having no criminal record, family attorney Adam Ansari said. Beristain, was the owner of the popular Granger restaurant Eddie's Steak Shed.[331]

2. **Grandfather with no criminal record – California.** Nineteen-year-old Estefany Ortiz says ICE agents came to her house in Pasadena, CA, last month looking for someone who did not live there. They arrested her father, Carlos Ortiz, instead. He was in the country illegally, but had no criminal record. "Why did we open the door," Estefany said. "Nobody is going to want to open the door. Everyone is scared." Ortiz also is a grandfather.[332]

3. **Twenty-six-year-old with no criminal record – North Carolina.** Edwin Guillen has lived in Durham for four years and works as a painter. The twenty-ix-year-old has no criminal record. His attorney, Becky Moriello, questions why he was detained by immigration officers in the first place. "The fact that he is brown or the fact that he does not speak English does not mean that he is necessarily an immigrant," Moriello said ... Thursday, Moriello, argued in court filings that Guillen was a victim of being in the wrong place at the wrong time – since he was not initially accused of any crime, nor does he have a past criminal record. When they approached the home, ICE says two people ran and one of them was Guillen.[333]

4. **US resident for seventeen years and father of three US citizens – New York.** Perez is a dairy farm employee and an advocate for migrant workers ... Born in Mexico, he has lived in Livingston County, NY, for seventeen years and has four children, three of whom are US citizens. Perez had a deportation case

[331] Joseph Dits, *Granger Restaurant Owner Roberto Beristain Deported*, South Bend Tribune, April 6, 2017.

[332] *Activists Call for Release of Grandfather Detained by ICE*, CBS Los Angeles, March 16, 2017, available at: http://losangeles.cbslocal.com/2017/03/16/activists-call-for-release-of-grandfather-detained-by-ice/

[333] *ICE Agents Arrest Man in Durham*, ABC11.com, March 30, 2017, available at: http://abc11.com/news/ice-agents-arrest-man-in-durham/1826686/

against him that was administratively closed in September 2016. He had no criminal record, and possessed a social security number, and a work permit. When ICE officials asked him to come into a local office for a routine check-in this year, he was subsequently detained.[334]

5. **Parents of two citizens, one battling cancer – Arkansas.** Amanda and Juan Aristondos most recent stay of removal request was denied after the executive order was put into place, leaving the family eligible for deportation. With one of their daughters battling cancer, leaving her to fight alone is not an option the parents want to consider. "When I hugged them this morning I felt I would hug them again," Amanda Aristondos said. The mother-of-two fled Guatemala with her husband back in 2008. They filed an asylum request that was denied, so for the past nine years they've been filing stay of removals to remain legal.[335]

6. **Married to citizen, resident for twenty-five years – New Mexico.** Emma Membreno-Sorto, who is about fifty-nine years old, has only one traffic ticket in New Mexico and no criminal history. Her attorney, Roderick DeAguero, said he doesn't believe she uses any public assistance programs. "She's not a drain on the American public," he said, referencing the common argument from anti-immigration activists who worry about immigrants using tax-funded programs. "We need to support our government in many ways, but I think we could do this better. There has to be a better way." Membreno-Sorto, speaking in Spanish, said on Tuesday that she arrived from Honduras in the 1990s, applied for political asylum but never received notice of a court date and went about her life, moving from Atlanta to Colorado to New Mexico.[336]

7. **Married to citizen, father of two – Iowa.** Marielda Moreno, thirty-two, is a US citizen living in Des Moines and the father of her children is undocumented. He was picked up by immigration officials on March 2, 2017, on his way to work. "He said that it's very hard to be locked up in there and more difficult when he can hear his daughters crying and when they're asking when he can come home," Moreno said. Moreno admits that she worries about her family's future in her new home under a new administration that has taken a harder approach to illegal immigration. "I want to believe that something good will come of this. I don't want to believe that things will get worse," Moreno said. "I want to believe that we are going to be OK and that we won't have to go back to a country that my children don't know."[337]

---

[334] Meaghan M. McDermott, *Activists Rally in Batavia for Detained Farmworker*, USA Today, March 30, 2017.

[335] Beraiah Baker, *Family Faces Possible Deportation Due to New Executive Orders*, KFSM 5 News, March 14, 2017.

[336] Maggie Shepard, *Quaker Meeting House Provides Sanctuary for Immigrants*, Albuquerque Journal, March 14, 2017.

[337] Grant Rodgers and MacKenzie Elmer, *Family "Hoping We Are Going to be OK" Amid Dad's Deportation*, Des Moines Register, March 10, 2017.

8. **Mother of eighteen-year-old with cerebral palsy and epilepsy deported – Utah**. An undocumented Draper mother being deported to Colombia missed her flight to South America on Thursday, providing a brief "glimmer of hope" that she would receive legal permission to stay in the United States, her friends said. Her attorneys rushed to the airport. They overnighted legal paperwork to federal immigration officers. Senator Orrin Hatch's office tried to snag her more time. The Colombian Consulate in San Francisco also flexed its muscle. It wasn't enough. Her lawyers ran out of time to revive years-old proceedings that would allow her to stay and care for her eighteen-year-old son with cerebral palsy and epilepsy, as well as her eighty-six-year-old mother. "There is a glimmer of hope she might stay," said Sharlee Mullins Glenn, a friend of the woman and leader of the recently formed Mormon Women for Ethical Government.[338]

9. **Ten-year resident, father of two US citizens – Pennsylvania.** He was in a car, on his way to work at a Harrisburg pizzeria on Thursday when he was apprehended by ICE agents, she (his wife) said. He was one of four undocumented immigrants that were apprehended during the same stop. She said her husband, who now sits in immigration detention in York County Prison, is the sole breadwinner for a family that includes two daughters, ages eight and a year-and-a-half. Like her husband, the woman, who is from Jalisco, Mexico, is undocumented. She has been in the United States for nine years; her husband ten. He's worked all those ten years, most recently in a pizza shop. She said neither have ever committed a crime. Fearing she could also be detained, she asked that her name not be used.[339]

10. **Fifty-year-old mother-of-six ordered deported – Illinois.** Her (Francisca Lino's) check-in Tuesday couldn't have been more excruciating. It marked the first time the fifty-year-old mother-of-six, who lives outside Chicago, had to report to ICE since Donald Trump became President. At the federal building in Chicago, about an hour passed before Lino reemerged through the glass doors. She clapped her hands together, then quickened her step and ran, arms outstretched in joy. "Thank God!" she yelled. "Thanks to all of you!" "They gave me a year until I have to come back," Lino told CNN. "So we're going to try to fight for my visa." Relief reigned for five minutes. Then Lino's lawyer came back. "They called," Bergin said, "and they said the officer we talked to was filling in, and the main officer in charge of her case wants to talk to her about it, he's got some information on her case. I don't know what that means." The family disappeared back into the building. Less than a half-hour

[338] Annie Knox, *Draper Mother Deported Despite Last-Minute Push*, KSL.com, April 6, 2017, available at: www.ksl.com/?sid=43773540&nid=148

[339] Ivey DeJesus, *ICE Raids Causing Fear and Anxiety Among Harrisburg's Latino Community*, Advocate Says, March 11, 2017, available at: www.pennlive.com/news/2017/03/ice_raids_illegal_immigrants_u.html

later, Lino was back. "There were changes," she said. Immigration officers told Lino to return July 11, suitcases packed and plane ticket in hand. In other words, her deportation date is set.[340]

11. **Small business owner, father of two US citizens – Maryland.** Segundo Paucar was a pillar of Highlandtown's tight-knit, Ecuadorian–American community: a thirty-one-year-old married father-of-two who employed eight people in a small business that rehabbed about fifty properties in the city each year. The next day, he was gone, picked up by federal agents on charges related to his allegedly entering the country illegally when he was fifteen. His sudden disappearance from his family and community ... has sent shock waves through East Baltimore ... the whole family is worried particularly the children. "They've been asking 'Where is dad? When is dad going to come back?' We've been trying to help them. There's a fear and mistrust about what is happening."[341]

12. **Father of two-year-old citizen facing deportation after stopped for vehicle violation – Texas.** State troopers pulled over Jesus Vazquez for having dark window tint on his vehicle in the Montana Vista area, where he had been raised since he was brought illegally from Mexico to the United States as a child ... Family and friends say they consider Vasquez a good man, hard worker and a devoted father of a four-year-old girl, a US citizen. They said he planned to save up money to marry his girlfriend, also a US citizen.[342]

13. **Married to US citizen with two children – West Virginia.** Two employees at El Mariachi in Beaver were detained by ICE last week, according to El Mariachi owner Jose Rizo. Rizo said one of the men has been in the United States for twenty years. At least one of the workers is married to an American woman and is the sole provider for his wife and two children, according to workers' statements. American Civil Liberties Union-West Virginia attorneys reported Monday that the number of ICE raids of Hispanic-owned businesses in the state have increased dramatically over the past three weeks. "Until recently, I'd never heard of raids on any work place here in West Virginia," said Jaime Crofts, ACLU attorney. "Over the last three to four weeks, I have heard of several raids being conducted at Mexican restaurants in the state ... A raid is only legal if ICE already has some sort of evidence that people who are here are undocumented, and they know who those people are," she said.[343]

[340] Katie Mettler, *Francisca Lino, mom of 6, Is About to be Deported. Her Congressman Protested and Was Handcuffed.*, Washington Post, March 14, 2017.
[341] Luke Broadwater, et al., *Arrests of Immigrants in Baltimore Leave Many Fearful*, Baltimore Sun, March 8, 2017.
[342] Lorena Figueroa, *US Citizen's Dad Stopped by DPS Faces Deportation*, El Paso Times, March 6, 2017.
[343] Jessica Farrish, *ICE Detains Two Local Men*, Register-Herald, March 7, 2017.

14. **Father-to-be LPR with no violent criminal record – New York.** Joel Guerrero, a thirty-seven-year-old green card holder from the Dominican Republic, has been going in for a routine check-in with the ICE agency in New York City every six months for the past seven years. But when Guerrero went in for a check-in on Tuesday morning with his wife Jessica, who is six-months pregnant, he was detained and arrested. The reason that ICE detained him? He missed a court date on January 6, 2011 and has a misdemeanor charge for marijuana possession from a decade ago. Guerrero says the charge stemmed from having a marijuana plant when he lived in North Carolina ... "How can you possibly do this to a family and tear a family apart?" she said. "The officer literally ripped me from my husband's arms as I was saying goodbye to him." An ICE spokesperson was unable to comment on Guerrero's case at the time of publication.[344]

15. **Father of three citizens with no violent criminal record – Arizona.** Juan Carlos Fomperosa Garcia, a forty-four-year-old construction worker from Mexico who lives in Arizona, went in for a routine check-in at the ICE office in Phoenix on Thursday morning ... At a press conference held on Thursday, Fomperosa Garcia's daughter explained through tears that he had gone into the agency's office to check in, thinking he would be home by dinner to celebrate his son's birthday that night. But the single father of three kids was never left the building.[345]

16. **Father of two citizens with no violent criminal record – Texas.** The call came in about 2.30 pm yesterday afternoon, and Jose Escobar asked his wife, Rose, if she was sitting down. "I'm in El Salvador," he said. Rose was shocked. Just last week, ICE had taken Escobar, an undocumented immigrant, into custody at one of his regular annual check-ins. He never saw a judge ... He is the father of two American children and the husband to a naturalized US citizen. He worked 7 am to 7 pm Monday through Friday as a supervisor at a company that repaints and repairs apartment units when tenants move out. He was the dad who drove all the neighborhood kids to school in the morning.[346]

17. **Father of two citizens with no violent criminal record – Ohio.** Immigration enforcement agents in Cleveland pulled Leonardo Valbuena aside that Monday morning in late January. They told him he would be jailed then deported – maybe tomorrow, maybe next week. "I almost lose my balance," he said in his video testimony in admittedly poor English. "I say, 'Sir, I have my

[344] Nancy Dillon, *Upstate Newlywed with Pregnant Wife Suddenly Detained During Routine ICE Meeting After Years Without Incident*, Daily News, March 3, 2017.

[345] Esther Yu His Lee, *Meet 3 Dads Detained by ICE This Week*, Think Progress, March 3, 2017, available at: thinkprogress.org/meet-3-dads-whose-ice-detentions-you-havent-heard-about-this-week-9bc6c92f226a/

[346] Lomi Kriel, *Deported Immigrant Trying to Adjust to Life Alone in the Foreign Land of His Birth*, Houston Chronical, March 11, 2017.

children in school. My daughter. My son. And my wife, she doesn't drive'" ... Valbuena left with his family Tuesday minutes after US ICE removed a tracking monitor from his ankle at the Delta Airlines luggage counter in Cleveland.[347]

18. **Grandmother of military vet – California.** The grandmother of a Mira Mesa military veteran's family was sent back to Mexico on Friday, more than two weeks after she was picked up by immigration agents outside her house in unmarked SUVs on Valentine's Day. Clarissa Arredondo, forty-three, is an unauthorized immigrant, as is her daughter, Adriana Aparicio. Aparicio's husband is a Navy veteran working as a contractor in Afghanistan. The couple has two daughters, two and three, and Arredondo helped take care of them ... Aparicio, twenty-seven, said officials told her family that her mom was an enforcement priority. "They consider my mom as a criminal for lying on paperwork to get welfare," Aparicio said, adding that officials said that happened more than a decade ago.[348]

19. **Father of five American citizens, lived in the United States for sixteen years, no criminal record – Oregon.** It (the arrest) happened so quickly, Roman Zaragoza-Sanches left his Honda on the shoulder of Highway 26, with the lights on. Rosalina didn't have the keys and doesn't know how to drive. In shock, she asked a neighbor to help her hire a tow truck to retrieve it. "They are reporting in the news that they are going to get only people who are criminals, but it is not the truth because my husband is not that person," Rosalina said. "And they took him."[349]

20. **Mother of two, with no violent criminal record – Arizona.** Guadalupe García de Rayos – entered the United States at age fourteen, mother of two US citizens, no violent criminal record. Guadalupe García de Rayos, a thirty-six-year-old mother of two US citizens, was a non violent felon who had for years complied with ICE orders after being convicted of using a fake social security number to work. But on Wednesday, when she went for her usual check-in, ICE agents took her into custody instead, separating her from her husband and children, who were waiting outside. Jacqueline García de Rayos, fourteen, described having to pack her mother's luggage so she could send it to Mexico. "I don't think it's fair that she was taken away from us," Jacqueline said. "Her only crime was to work here so she could support us. She is a very

[347] Doug Livingston, *Akron Immigrant Shackled by ICE 'Self-Deports' to Avoid Prosecution*, Akron Beacon Journal, March 5, 2017.
[348] Kate Morrissey, *San Diego Union Tribune: Clarissa Arredondo – Grandmother, 'Backbone' of Veteran's Family, Sent Back to Mexico*, March 4, 2017.
[349] Amelia Templeton and Roxy De La Torre, *ICE Plans to Deport Oregon Immigrant With 5 Children, No Criminal Background*, Oregon Public Broadcasting, March 2, 2017, available at: www.opb.org/news/article/oregon-immigrant-deport-criminal-background-children/

kind person," Jacqueline said. "She treats everyone like family. She hasn't done anything to harm anyone."[350]

21. **Father of a US citizen, lived in the United States for twelve years, no criminal record – Tennessee.** In September 2014, Gilberto Velasquez, a thirty-eight-year-old house painter from El Salvador, received life-changing news: The US government had decided to shelve its deportation action against him. The move was part of a policy change initiated by then-President Barack Obama in 2011 to pull back from deporting immigrants who had formed deep ties in the United States and whom the government considered no threat to public safety. Instead, the administration would prioritize illegal immigrants who had committed serious crimes. But in May, things changed again for the painter, who has lived in the United States illegally since 2005 and has a US-born child. He received news that the government wanted to put his deportation case back on the court calendar, citing another shift in priorities, this time by President Donald Trump. The Trump administration has moved to reopen the cases of hundreds of illegal immigrants who, like Velasquez, had been given a reprieve from deportation, according to government data and court documents reviewed by Reuters and interviews with immigration lawyers. It represents one of the first concrete examples of the crackdown promised by Trump and is likely to stir fears among tens of thousands of illegal immigrants who thought they were safe from deportation. Between March 1 and May 31, prosecutors moved to reopen 1,329 cases, according to a Reuters' analysis of data from the Executive Office of Immigration Review, or Executive Office for Immigration Review (EOIR).[351]

22. **Deportation of DACA recipient – California.** The deportation of an actual DACA recipient with no criminal problems was a particular surprise. Federal agents ignored President Trump's pledge to protect from deportation undocumented immigrants brought to the United States as children by sending a young man back to his native Mexico...

After spending an evening with his girlfriend in Calexico, CA, on February 17, Juan Manuel Montes, twenty-three, who has lived in the United States since age nine, grabbed a bite and was waiting for a ride when a US CBP officer approached and started asking questions.

Montes was twice granted deportation protections under the DACA program created by President Barack Obama and left intact by President Trump.

Montes had left his wallet in a friend's car, so he couldn't produce his ID or proof of his DACA status and was told by agents he couldn't retrieve them.

[350] Samantha, Schmidt, *'I Can't Take that Place.' An Arizona Family Struggles with a Mother's Deportation*, Washington Post, February 27, 2017.

[351] Mica Rosenberg and Reade Levinson, *Exclusive: Trump Targets Illegal Immigrants Who Were Given Reprieves from Deportation by Obama*, Reuters, June 9, 2017.

Within three hours, he was back in Mexico, becoming the first undocumented immigrant with active DACA status deported by the Trump administration's stepped-up deportation policy.

"Some people told me that they were going to deport me; others said nothing would happen," Montes told USA TODAY in his aunt and uncle's home in western Mexico where he's been staying. "I thought that if I kept my nose clean nothing would happen." He asked that the exact location of their home be withheld.

Since taking office, Trump has followed through on his campaign pledge to crack down on illegal immigration by signing executive orders to step up enforcement against the estimated 11 million undocumented immigrants living in the United States. The new policy calls for expanding the criteria for detaining and deporting undocumented immigrants and hiring thousands of new agents.

Yet Trump declined to revoke the DACA protections Obama had granted to more than 750,000 undocumented immigrants, repeatedly saying he had a soft spot for these young people who are leading productive lives and have few, if any, ties to the countries of their birth.

"They shouldn't be very worried," he told ABC News in January. "I do have a big heart."[352]

23. **Arrest of Michigan Doctor, Resident for forty years.** A respected doctor who has been in the United States for nearly forty years has been picked up by American immigration agents after the Trump administration denied his attempt to renew his green card. Lukas Niec, an internal medicine doctor known for long hours at the hospital in Kalamazoo, Michigan, was picked up by ICE agents over the weekend. He's now reportedly sitting in a jail cell waiting for word on when he'll be allowed to return to his normal life – or if he'll allowed to do so at all.

Niec, an internal medicine doctor at Kalamazoo's Bronson Methodist Hospital, moved to the United States nearly forty years ago when he was five years old. His parents brought him from Poland in 1979, alongside his sister, who said that they had packed just two suitcases before making the journey. But now Niec is facing potential deportation after living here for the vast majority of his life.[353]

24. **Sensitive locations violated.** A 2011 agency memo instructs ICE agents not to conduct enforcement activities at "sensitive locations" like churches and

[352] Alan Gomez and David Agren, *First Protected DREAMer is Deported under Trump*, USA Today, April 18, 2017.
[353] Clark Mindock, *US Immigration Officers Arrest Michigan Doctor Who Has Lived in US for 40 Years*, The Independent, January 22, 2018.

schools, but it's not clear whether ICE is following that memo under Trump. So far, it remains ICE policy to direct agents to avoid conducting enforcement activities at schools, hospitals, places of worship, and public ceremonies or demonstrations.[354] But in May, a US immigration agent reportedly was turned away from an elementary school in Maspeth, Queens, NY, where he was reportedly looking for a fourth-grader.[355] In February, a group of Latino men were apprehended and some of them arrested by ICE agents as they were leaving a church shelter in Alexandria, VA; the men left the hypothermia shelter at Rising Hope Mission Church at about 6.45 am.[356] In late January, ICE agents looking for an undocumented immigrant in San Francisco's Mission District went to the man's home, but not before first stopping at a building housing a preschool next door purportedly by mistake.[357] In June, Border Patrol agents raided the desert camp of the humanitarian organization No More Deaths and arrested four migrants. The camp provides medical aid to migrants crossing the desert, and the organization had a separate 2013 agreement that its operations would not be interfered with by border officials.[358] In October 2017, ICE agents stalked a ten-year-old girl with cerebral palsy who had gallbladder surgery at a hospital in Corpus Christi, TX.[359] While courthouses are not on the sensitive locations list, in March 2017, the Chief Justice of the California Supreme Court wrote to Trump administration officials to stop immigration agents from "stalking" California's courthouses to make arrests. Judges and lawyers in Southern California have complained of seeing immigration agents posted near courts.[360] However, DHS officials have refused to back down and warn that ICE agents may arrest crime victims and witnesses at courthouses: "Just because they're a victim in a certain case does not mean there's not something in their background that could cause them to be a removable alien … Just because they're a witness doesn't mean they might not pose a security threat for other reasons."[361]

[354] Jason McGahan, *L.A. Health Clinic Protects Immigrants Against Illness – and Deportation*, LA Weekly, March 15, 2017.

[355] Alex Eriksen, *ICE Agent Tried to Apprehend a 4th-Grader but Was Turned Away by the School*, Yahoo News, May 14, 2017, available at: www.yahoo.com/beauty/ice-agent-tried-apprehend-4th-grader-turned-away-school-224058706.html

[356] Julie Carey, *ICE Agents Arrest Men Leaving Fairfax County Church Shelter*, NBC Washington, February 15, 2017.

[357] Joe Fitzgerald Rodriguez, *ICE Agents Appear at Family Center in SF's Mission District*, SF Examiner, January 26, 2017.

[358] Paul Ingram, *Border Patrol raids No More Deaths Camp, Arrest Migrants Seeking Medical Care*, Tucson Sentinel, June 15, 2017.

[359] Jenn Gidman, ICE Agents Swoop In, Take Child From Hospital Post-Surgery, Newser.com, October 26, 2017.

[360] Maura Dolan, *California to Trump: Keep ICE Out of Our Courthouses*, LA Times, March 16, 2017.

[361] Devlin Barrett, *DHS: Immigration Agents May Arrest Crime Victims, Witnesses at Courthouses*, Washington Post, April 4, 2017 (quoting DHS spokesman David Lapan).

Trump's antics and belligerence toward immigrants encourages and emboldens vigilantes to step forward, exacerbating the fear. For example, given Congress's initial hesitance to fund the border wall construction, two US military veterans stepped forward to create the American First Foundation to raise money for "Great Southern Wall."[362] Excerpts from their press release were clear:

Citizens Unite to Raise Funds & Build That Wall!
Founded by Military Vets, America First Foundation Raises Money to Supplement Wall Construction, Protect Government Programs from Budget Cuts

New York, NY; March, 22, 2017 – If the 2016 Election taught us anything, it's that Voters are concerned about illegal immigration from our southern border. The reality, however is that any effort to further crack down on illegal immigration – and build a Great Southern Wall – will cost money that the Trump administration will have to draw from existing national security programs.

A recent proposal issued by the Office of Management and Budget illustrated that funds for increased border security and wall construction would be at the expense of the Federal Emergency Management Agency, The United States Coast Guard and the Department of Homeland Security. Simply put, construction of the Great Southern Wall would *"rob Peter to pay Paul"* unless concerned patriotic citizens step in to help.

And to the rescue, a group of patriotic Americans have banded together to address the urgent need for increased border security while seeking to save FEMA, the Coast Guard and DHS from deep budget cuts. The America First Foundation (AFF) was created to raise money from ordinary Americans to build a Great Southern Wall as a symbol of American strength and unity.

"This is a golden opportunity for concerned citizens to vote with their wallets and cast a second ballot for border security," said Steven Vulich, co-founder of AFF. "By raising private funds for a public wall, we can accelerate construction and hold our leaders accountable for their promise to secure our borders."

AFF was founded by Vulich, US Army Veteran and Wounded Warrior who served a tour in the Iraq War (OIF) and John McCormack, a Veteran of the United States Air Force. The idea for AFF came about once it became apparent that Mexico has no intention to pay for the Great Southern Wall as the President had promised.

"We're realists," added Vulich. "President Trump and Mexican President Enrique Peña Nieto are going to bicker and grandstand over this matter. It's up to regular citizens like us to take the first step and carry this idea into implementation."

AFF will seek to support the construction of a Great Southern Wall through a public–private partnership. The use of public–private partnerships (otherwise known as P3's) to defray the cost of government projects is steadily gaining popularity as government agencies seek new sources of funding in light of budget constraints.

[362] Thomas Phippen, *Group Wants to Crowd-Source Money For Trump's Border Wall*, Daily Caller (March 22, 2017), available at: http://dailycaller.com/2017/03/22/this-group-wants-to-crowd-source-money-for-trumps-border-wall/.

Contributors to AFF will be kept apprised of the campaign's progress. In addition, AFF supporters gain emotional equity on the broader campaign to build the wall and place their country first once again.[363]

About America First Foundation
The America First Foundation is a 501(c)(3) nonprofit organization dedicated toward unifying all citizens under the belief that America's interests must be placed first in order for it to effectively lead. The organization seeks to raise funds to bolster American efforts toward immigration enforcement, disaster recovery and other areas where government efforts fall short of acceptable standards ...

Trump supporters also were emboldened to disrupt meetings designed to provide immigration information and know your rights lessons to immigrants.

A group of protesters, some sporting "Make America Great Again" (MAGA) hats and other clothing in support of President Donald Trump, interrupted a "Know Your Rights" information forum for undocumented immigrants hosted by Congresswoman Grace Napolitano, D-El Monte ...

The event, held at the city's Grace T. Black Auditorium, was meant to provide residents with information about legal protections and resources for immigrants, as well as about the naturalization process ...

One of the protesters wearing a MAGA hat and a Trump flag as a cape had his cellphone knocked out of his hand, then was pushed by another man. Quintero and police separated the two. A pair of officers then escorted the protester from the building ...

The congresswoman said the event, which included representatives from Coalition for Humane Immigrant Rights of Los Angeles and Catholic Charities Los Angeles, still provided all the information the hosts intended to, despite the interruptions and early end ...

"Someone said they had called (Immigration and Customs Enforcement)," Napolitano said. "They were trying to intimidate our residents."

One of those people who said he called ICE and US Attorney General Jeff Sessions to report the event was Torrance resident Arthur Schaper, the protester who was later pushed.

"It was offensive," Schaper said ... "(Napolitano) took an oath to uphold [the] Constitution, and now she's sponsoring a town hall that teaches illegal aliens about rights they don't have."

Schaper [is] president of the Beach Cities Republicans and member of pro-immigration-enforcement group We the People Rising ...[364]

Then there are threats of arrests by scam artists, preying on immigrant fears. This email was sent out by an immigrant rights attorney in Oakland, CA:

---

[363] Ibid.
[364] Christopher Yee, *Illegal Immigration Protesters Interrupt 'Know Your Rights' Forum in El Monte*, San Gabriel Valley Tribune, April 16, 2017.

Hello all,

I met a man last week at a clinic in Livermore who received threatening phone calls from people claiming to be from US immigration. The callers told him he needed to pay them several thousand dollars in order to avoid deportation.[365]

This is not an isolated incident. USCIS has put out information for reporting these types of scams.[366]

Disturbingly, although ICE is known to lie about who they are when conducting enforcement operations, federal officials apparently are not always truthful with local law enforcement departments either. In Santa Cruz, CA, police were misled by ICE and talked into helping make immigration arrests during a raid on suspected gang members.[367] The local police chief said that federal officials "lied" about a joint operation involving a raid of an El Salvador-based gang.[368] The police were told that the operation would not include immigration-related arrests.[369] But in fact, immigration arrests were made.[370]

As a result of the Trump threats and reports of arrests, know your rights presentations for immigrants provided by immigrant rights organizations have become very common.[371] Although the presentations principally are focused on how undocumented immigrants can exercise their right to remain silent when confronted with an ICE agent, family emergency plans have become part of many curricula.[372] The trainings now include preparing documents in case a parent is deported.[373]

Brothers Miguel, fourteen, and Angel, fifteen, know exactly what to do if they come home from school one day and their mom isn't there.

"I would immediately just grab the binder and just call my family here," Angel says. He's talking about a black, three-ring binder they keep in a closet. Their mother,

---

[365] Email to San Francisco Immigration Legal Defense Collaborative (SFILDC) from Alisa Whitfield, March 23, 2017.

[366] U.S. Citizenship and Immigration Services, *Avoid Payment Scams: USCIS Does Not Accept Fees By Phone or Email*, available at: www.uscis.gov/news/alerts/avoid-payment-scams-uscis-does-not-accept-fees-phone-or-email

[367] David Marks, *Santa Cruz Police: ICE Lied to Us About Immigration Arrests*, KQED News (February 24, 2017), available at: https://ww2.kqed.org/news/2017/02/24/santa-cruz-police-ice-lied-to-us-about-immigration-arrests/.

[368] Ibid.

[369] Ibid.

[370] Michael Todd, *Santa Cruz Police: Homeland Security Misled City with 'Gang' Raids that Were Immigration Related*, Mercury News, February 23, 2017. Police say they were misled by the Department of Homeland Security into helping make immigration arrests during a raid on suspected gang members. Because of that experience, the Santa Cruz department will no longer work with the federal agency because they cannot be trusted. Ibid.

[371] *See generally* Catholic Legal Immigration Network Inc., *Know Your Rights: A Guide to Your Rights When Interacting with Law Enforcement*, available at: https://cliniclegal.org/resources/know-your-rights-law-enforcement.

[372] Ibid.

[373] Ibid.

whose name is not used because of her fear of being deported, put it together a few months ago. Her six children are all US citizens, but she came here illegally from Mexico 18 years ago. And while she prays every day that she won't be picked up and deported, Angel says she's prepared them all for the worst.[374]

Similarly,

When Natividad Gonzalez packs her daughters' homework and lunches for school each morning, she slips a freshly charged cellphone into her eldest child's bag. The 11-year-old knows the plan: If she and her younger sister, age 8, walk home from the bus to find an empty house, she's supposed to call Gonzalez's friend who will come get them. Her daughter also knows the combination to the family safe, inside which is an ATM card and a quickly drafted power-of-attorney letter granting custody to the family friend in case Natividad and her husband are arrested and sent back to Mexico. "These are things that an 11-year-old shouldn't have to be thinking about," says Gonzalez, age 32, who came to Clanton, Alabama with her husband nearly 13 years ago, and is still undocumented.[375]

So, given the loud and constant noise of Trump's enforcement plans and activities that began even before his election, the resulting widespread fear is not surprising. As the examples demonstrate, much of the enforcement is real. He has taken off the gloves in attacking immigrants and does so in a very public way that receives much attention. But even the efforts that have been curtailed, such as the Muslim bans and sanctuary funding threats, have created confusion and chaos that can contribute to the fear. One could argue that Trump and his people are intentionally reckless with how they rolled out the enforcement efforts – to create an even scarier scene.

In a sense, immigrants and their allies also may be contributing to the hysteria. They have built up a great network of CBOs, activists, experts, and service providers that each little thing by Trump or ICE gets noticed, called out, and responded to right away.[376] That means Trump is less likely to get away with something illegal (for long), but of course that also plays into the fear in the community as each incident is misunderstood as perhaps carrying more import than it should.

In the end, Trump's unwillingness to clarify that he is not trying to be anti-Muslim or anti-Mexican in any meaningful way speaks the loudest. Perhaps the obvious hypocrisy of the whole thing makes things stand out. Early on it was clear Trump was essentially faking or incompetently feeling his way around. Yet he holds so much power, it makes a mockery of the institution many immigrant rights groups were just getting to think – after eight years – might be trustworthy. Now, however,

---

[374] Jennifer Guerra, *Fearing Deportation, Families Plan For The Worst*, NPR, March 13, 2017.

[375] Richards, *How Fear of Deportation*.

[376] *See generally Community-Based Organizations*, U.S. Citizen and Immigration Services, available at: www.uscis.gov/avoid-scams/community-organizations/community-based-organizations.

the actual widening enforcement actions of Trump's ICE provide a solid foundation for the fear.

6.8.2. *Is the Fear Justified Objectively?*

During the presidential campaign, candidate Trump promised a "deportation force" to round up the more than eleven million immigrants in the country illegally.[377] Logistically and resource-wise, the realistic deportation of eleven million immigrants is hard to imagine. Even Republican leaders in Congress have made clear that the prospect of massive deportations is not high.[378] So one might reasonably conclude that the chances are small that a typical undocumented person who avoids criminal problems will get deported.

Yet, an objective basis for greater fear among immigrants is undeniable. As noted above, individuals previously not likely to be deported under the Obama administration – like Juan Manuel Montes, Guadalupe Garcia de Rayos, and Roberto Beristain – have been removed. These are not necessarily random acts by rogue ICE agents, but enforcement decisions made under the interior enforcement framework that has been installed.

The Obama administration created a list of detailed enforcement priorities with strict hierarchy, and removable immigrants who did not fall within the narrow priorities had a chance of being protected from any enforcement.[379] For example, under enforcement memos issued in 2011 and 2014, the top priorities were individuals who posed threats to national security, border security, and public safety (e.g., terrorists, gang members, and persons apprehended at the border attempted to enter unlawfully).[380] The second priority included those who committed misdemeanors and immigration violators (including convictions for domestic violence, gun use, or driving under the influences (DUIs)), as well as those who entered unlawfully recently – i.e., after January 1, 2014. The final priority group included persons with a final order of removal after January 1, 2014.[381] The memos also laid out factors that should be considered in exercising prosecutorial discretion to deprioritize or

---

[377] Tom LoBianco, *Donald Trump Promises 'Deportation Force' to Remove 11 Million*, CNN, November 12, 2015.

[378] Paulina Firozi, *Ryan on Trump's Mass Deportation Plan: 'It's Not Happening,'* The Hill, January 13, 2017.

[379] Bill Ong Hing, *The Failure of Prosecutorial Discretion and the Deportation of Oscar Martinez*, 15 *Scholar: St. Mary's L. Rev. & Soc. Just.* 437 (2013).

[380] John Morton, ICE Director, *Exercising Prosecutorial Discretion Consistent with the Civil Immigration Enforcement Priorities of the Agency for the Apprehension, Detention, and Removal of Aliens*, June 17, 2011, available at: www.ice.gov/doclib/secure-communities/pdf/prosecutorial-discretion-memo.pdf; and Johnson, *Policies for the Apprehension*.

[381] Ibid.

not take action against otherwise removable persons, including things like family or community ties and length of time in the country.[382]

Most undocumented immigrants were not considered enforcement priorities under the Obama enforcement memos. Researchers estimated that under Obama's 2011 enforcement memo, about 27 percent of the undocumented population were priorities for enforcement, while only 13 percent were prioritized under the 2014 memo.[383] The effect of the Obama priorities on the profile of those deported was clear – they were mostly people convicted of crimes:

> The 2014 priorities had a significant impact on both the number and criminal make up of ICE removals form the interior of the country ... In FY2016, 98 percent of all interior removals met one of the priorities ... and 92 percent (or about 60,000 out of 65,000 total interior removals) were convicted of a crime. Strict adherence to the priorities by ICE agents and the use of prosecutorial discretion significantly reduced overall interior removals, from 224,000 in FY2011 to 65,000 in FY2016.[384]

Trump's interior enforcement order and the subsequent DHS memo by Kelly rescind all previous policy related to the priorities for removal (except for DACA and the DAPA orders, at least initially).[385] The new priorities target a much broader set of unauthorized persons for removal and empowers individual enforcement officers with broad discretionary authority to apprehend and detain any immigrant believed to be in violation of immigration law. They can start removal proceedings for any immigrant who is subject to removal under any provision of the INA – this essentially includes any and all unauthorized immigrants in the country.[386]

The executive order calls on DHS to prioritize individuals for removal based on criminal, security, and fraud grounds that make foreign nationals inadmissible or deportable under the INA.[387] The order also references persons described in INA §§235(b) and (c), which addresses the inspection and removal of all persons in the country who have not been lawfully admitted or paroled, to be subject to expedited removal – deportation without the right to a deportation hearing.[388] In addition, the executive order specifically targets unauthorized immigrants who:

---

[382] Ibid.

[383] Marc R. Rosenblum, *Understanding the Potential Impact of Executive Action on Immigration Enforcement*, Migration Policy Institute, July 2015, available at: www.migrationpolicy.org/research/understanding-potential-impact-executive-action-immigration-enforcement.

[384] Lazaro Zamora, *Comparing Trump and Obama's Deportation Priorities*, Bipartisan Policy Center, February 27, 2017, available at: https://bipartisanpolicy.org/blog/comparing-trump-and-obamas-deportation-priorities/

[385] *See DHS Released a Memo Implementing President Trump's Executive Order on Interior Enforcement*, AILA (February 20, 2017), available at: www.aila.org/infonet/leaked-dhs-memo-implementing-president-trump.

[386] Ibid.

[387] Ibid.

[388] Ibid.

a. have been convicted of any criminal offense;
b. have been charged with any criminal offense;
c. have committed acts that constitute a chargeable criminal offense;
d. have willfully committed fraud in any official matter before a government agency;
e. have abused public benefits programs;
f. have final orders of removal; and
g. are otherwise considered a public safety or national security risk by an immigration officer.[389]

Unlike the priorities put in place in 2014, there is no inherent hierarchy in the list of priorities listed in Trump's order – all are listed as equally important for removal.[390] Additionally, "criminal offenses" is not defined (felonies versus misdemeanors, etc.), and could include minor misdemeanors like traffic offenses or crimes related to immigration status like illegal entry or reentry, that were specifically deprioritized by the Obama policy.[391] The order also moves away from a focus on convictions to people "charged" or believed to have "committed acts that constitute a chargeable" offense – broad categories that presume guilt not proven in court.[392] Combined with the re-broadening of 287(g) agreements that would deputize state and local law enforcement as immigration agents, these changes raise concerns that some jurisdictions will make individuals priorities for deportation by first arresting and charging them with a crime, regardless of the merits of the case.

As Lazaro Zamora of the Bipartisan Policy Center warns:

> The memos also give much wider latitude to ICE agents with little guidance or oversight. Although the 2014 Obama policy also allowed ICE agents to target individuals they considered risks, it required a supervisory review by a Field Office Director. Secondly, while the use of prosecutorial discretion in the Obama policy focused on when removable persons could get a reprieve, prosecutorial discretion in the context of Trump's policy is strictly framed as a disclaimer that the listed priorities do not constrain ICE agents' ability to otherwise apprehend, detain, or remove any unauthorized immigrant. Lastly, the category for immigrants with a previous removal order does not list a date cut off, which will mean that long-time unauthorized residents will be prioritized regardless of when they received their removal order.
>
> The impact of this bottom-up system of prioritization is still unclear, but it will likely mean that who is in line for removal will be determined only by whom ICE can practically and easily apprehend ("low hanging fruit") and the discretion of

---

[389] Ibid.
[390] See 2014 Executive Actions on Immigration, U.S. Citizenship and Immigration Services, available at: www.uscis.gov/immigrationaction.
[391] See *DHS Released a Memo.*
[392] Ibid.

individual ICE officers. It is also likely that adherence to less strict priories will lead to an increase in the number of deportations in the years ahead, especially if the number of enforcement officers increased, as was called for by other provisions in the order. The implementation memo left room for agencies to determine whether further guidance is necessary to prioritize enforcement activities, but for now, the language of both the order and memo are an explicit warning that all unauthorized immigrants are at risk of deportation at any time.[393]

Data released by ICE on May 17, 2017, showed a marked increase in interior enforcement during Trump's first 100 days over the same period in 2016.[394] Within a hundred days of Trump's executive order regarding immigration enforcement priorities, ICE arrested more than 41,000 individuals suspected of being deportable. That was an increase of 37.6 percent over the same period in 2016.[395] Arrests of immigrants with no criminal records more than doubled to 5,441, over the comparable period a year earlier.[396] In the first six months of fiscal year 2018, ICE arrested more than 26,000 "non-criminals," about double the number in the same period for 2017.[397]

In that time period, ICE's immigration enforcement activity resulted in more than 400 arrests per day.[398] However, at the height of Obama ICE enforcement, ICE interior enforcement was even more. In October 2012 about 700 arrests per day were made; the figure declined to about 300 per day after the Johnson memo on enforcement priorities went into effect in late 2014.[399] Importantly, during the Obama years, "only a small portion were direct arrests by ICE itself. Most occurred when ICE simply assumed custody of individuals arrested or detained by local, state, and other federal law enforcement agencies." [400] Given changes under the Trump administration, anticipating greater removals from the interior is quite plausible; consider jurisdictions afraid of losing federal funds that now vow to cooperate fully with ICE,[401] the reinstitution of the Secure Communities fingerprint-sharing

[393] Zamora, *Comparing Trump and Obama's Deportation*

[394] Paul Bedard, *ICE Arrests 41,000 Illegals in Trump's First 100 Days, Up 37 Percent*, Washington Examiner (May 17, 2017), available at: www.washingtonexaminer.com/ice-arrests-41000-illegals-in-trumps-first-100-days-up-37-percent/article/2623357.

[395] U.S. Immigration and Customs Enforcement, *ICE ERO Immigration Arrests Climb Nearly 40 Percent Compared to Last Year*, May 17, 2017, available at: https://content.govdelivery.com/accounts/USDHSICE/bulletins/19b23ab

[396] Maria Sacchetti, *ICE Immigration Arrests of Noncriminals Double Under Trump*, Washington Post, April 16, 2017.

[397] Hamed Aleaziz, ICE arrests of noncriminals in California soar amid Trump crackdown, San Francisco Chronicle, May 17, 2018.

[398] Ibid.

[399] Email to Bill Hing from Lena Graber, May 17, 2017.

[400] ICE Immigration Raids: A Primer, Transactional Records Access Clearinghouse, February 13, 2017, available at: http://trac.syr.edu/immigration/reports/459/

[401] *See, e.g.,* Alan Gomez, *Miami-Dade Commission Votes to End County's 'Sanctuary' Status*, USA Today, February 17, 2017.

program, the re-expansion of 287(g) agreements between ICE and local officials, and the widespread reports of ICE arrests without local assistance.

Furthermore, ICE actually has two components: Homeland Security Investigations (HSI) and Enforcement and Removal Operations (ERO).[402] ERO generally carries out the immigration enforcement responsibilities of ICE, while HSI agents usually focus on human rights violations, human smuggling, trafficking, transnational gangs, counterfeit identity documents, and even child pornography via the internet.[403] However, under the Trump administration, HSI is now mandated to make collateral immigration arrests of non-targeted individuals found at the scene of criminal violations.[404]

While difficult to quantify, the election of Donald Trump has "unleashed" ICE officers bent on greater enforcement who may have felt constrained under the Obama administration.[405] Clearly, many ICE agents did not like the prosecutorial discretion memos issued by the Obama administration[406]; the ICE union unsuccessfully tried to sue the Obama administration over the DACA program, arguing that the deferred action program undermined their duty to enforce the law.[407] Even the border patrol union – an organization that had never before endorsed a presidential candidate – threw its support behind candidate Trump during the primaries, stating that he would "embrace the ideas of rank-and-file Border Patrol agents [representing] a refreshing change that we have not seen before – and may never see again."[408] Thus, the fact that many immigration agents welcome Trump's enforcement regime provides another objective basis for the fear that immigrants are feeling. Consider also the phenomenon of "collateral arrests" of non criminals:

> What distinguished last week's raids [in February 2017] from the Obama era were three things: First, ICE agents broke with years of Obama-administration policy by making "collateral arrests" – arresting unauthorized immigrants who happened to be in the place they were raiding, even if they didn't have a warrant for them. Second, the agency deliberately coordinated a series of nationwide raids, scooping up more people in less time than ICE raids typically do ...
>
> For the most part, the raids appear to have been targeted efforts to catch individual immigrants that ICE had gotten warrants to arrest. DHS's statement claimed that "approximately 75%" of the immigrants arrested were "criminal aliens,"

[402] *Who We Are*, U.S. ICE, available at: www.ice.gov/about.
[403] Ibid.
[404] Hamed Aleaziz, *Police Alliance Strained by Raids*, San Francisco Chronicle, April 30, 2017.
[405] Email to Bill Hing from Mark Silverman, March 30, 2017 ("It's the 'Doberman [dog] effect.' Many ICE Dobermans feel that they are no longer on the leash. There have been very, very few raids, but there have been actions by rogue Doberman ICE agents.")
[406] Jason Howerton, *ICE Union Boss Blasts Obama Admin. for Making U.S. Immigration Law 'Essentially' Unenforceable*, The Blaze, February 5, 2013.
[407] Elizabeth Llorente, *Judge Dismisses ICE Agents' Lawsuit Challenging Obama's Deferred Action*, Fox News, August 1, 2013.
[408] Joe Davidson, *Border Patrol Agents Union Endorses Trump*, Washington Post, March 30, 2016.

implying they had criminal convictions – though many of those convictions were almost certainly for minor crimes (or simply for reentering the country illegally).

But it's also clear that when ICE agents encountered other unauthorized immigrants along with the person they were seeking – or when they didn't find that person, but found other unauthorized immigrants instead – others were arrested too.

To millions of immigrants and their communities, last week's raids represented a potential threat of the type they hadn't seen in years: the threat of becoming a "collateral" victim of an ICE raid simply for being in the wrong place at the wrong time.

The immigrants caught up in "collateral arrests" last week aren't authorized to be in the US, but have never had a criminal record or been deported or ordered deported. In some cases, they happened to be in the same apartment as someone ICE was looking for. In others, ICE had the wrong address but fingerprinted and arrested anyone who was there anyway.

Collateral arrests were known to happen under the Obama administration. But generally, ICE agents were under instructions to arrest people identified in advance, and only those people.

Many rank-and-file ICE agents hated this.

Now, as then, there's nothing concrete that local leaders and advocates can offer immigrants to ensure they won't be deported. Indeed, they have little ability to dismiss the worst rumors – because under Trump, no one knows what is possible.

In most cases, ICE agents weren't sweeping through whole neighborhoods or stopping drivers at random – but there wasn't anything stopping them from doing so, and no indication they won't start in future."[409]

Thus, immigrants in fact do have objective bases for fearing greater ICE enforcement under the Trump administration. Although the likelihood of an ICE encounter may still be small, immigration enforcement since the election of Donald Trump is up.[410] ICE is following the new enforcement priorities and making collateral arrests along the way. And Trump has struck a positive chord with eager, enforcement-minded ICE agents as well.

---

[409] America's Voice, *Cutting Through Confusion Around the Immigration Raids*, February 14, 2017, available at: https://yubanet.com/usa/cutting-through-confusion-around-the-immigration-raids/

[410] Maya Rhodan, *Arrests of Undocumented Immigrants Went Up During President Trump's First 100 Days*, TIME (April 28, 2017), available at: http://time.com/4759713/trump-100-days-arrests-undocumented-immigrants/.

PART IV

And the Winner Is ...

7

Closing

Challenging the New Deportation King

No one is perfect. No president has been perfect. President Barack Obama severely scarred his immigration policy record by failing to address the human rights crisis of migrants forced to flee the Northern Triangle of Central America with a humanistic approach. Despite clear warning signs reviewed in Chapter 4, the administration was caught flat-footed in 2014 when tens of thousands of women and children from those nations surged across the United States southern border, overwhelming Border Patrol stations in the Rio Grande Valley in Texas. The Central American women and children were fleeing escalating violence and persecution perpetrated by gangs, drug cartels, organized crime, and even family members in their home countries. But the Obama administration responded to the mounting humanitarian crisis with a multipronged strategy and treated the crisis as a political embarrassment. The strategy aimed to stem the flow by sending a message that the migrants were not welcome to the United States, using detention, rocket dockets, hurdles to seeking asylum, and deportation to achieve its goals. Obama and Vice President Joe Biden pressured Mexican President Enrique Peña Nieto to tighten his country's borders with its neighbors and intercept those who made the journey north under the guidance of human smugglers.[1] Truly, the Obama administration expanded a humanitarian crisis into a crisis of faith in a fair process for refugees seeking protection.

The White House attempted to justify the policy by citing the dangers of the journey for women and children, some of whom were robbed, assaulted, and raped along the way. But the policy hope of discouraging migrants did not work. How could it? The strategy did not address the violence in the Northern Triangle that has not subsided. As illustrated in Chapters 2 and 3, the numbers who crossed

---

[1] David Nakamura, *Obama Thanks Mexico for 'Absorbing' Central American Refugees. His Own Administration Wants to Turn them Away.* Wash. Post, September 20, 2016.

the border swelled again in 2016 and continue at high levels today. The vast majority of Central American migrants arriving since 2014 have been held in temporary shelters or family detention centers, awaiting court hearings. Those not granted asylum have been deported – highlighted by Obama's Department of Homeland Security (DHS) in January 2016 when raids were initiated in several cities to apprehend dozens of Central Americans with outstanding deportation orders.[2] And now the Trump administration is using the pretext of gang allegations to round up more young Central Americans.[3]

Obama refused to acknowledge that the continued influx from the region demonstrated that his administration's deterrence policy misdiagnosed or ignored the root causes and failed to adequately address the humanitarian needs.[4] In fact, although Congress, with White House support, approved $750 million in development aid for the region, the administration broadcast advertisements imploring would-be migrants to stay put.[5] Additionally, Obama continued to pay millions to Mexico to help turn away Central Americans before they even reach the US border; in 2016, Mexico returned 143,057 Central American migrants to their countries of origin – more than 59,000 Guatemalans, nearly 48,000 Hondurans, and around 31,000 Salvadorans.[6]

Under mounting pressure, the Obama administration did acknowledge the humanitarian challenges in 2014 by establishing a program that would grant Central American minors (CAM program) temporary legal residence in the United States if they had a parent already legally present in the country. The problem is that the vast majority of the tens of thousands of unaccompanied migrant children (UACs) created by violence in Central American do *not* have a parent who is lawfully in the United States. Thus, after three years in operation, only 2,714 children had won conditional approval to enter the country by August 2017.[7]

7.2. WHAT SHOULD HAVE BEEN DONE

Given the circumstances from which UACs and adults with children (AWCs) have fled, the Obama administration should have granted the migrants Temporary Protected Status (TPS) – the ability to reside and work in the United States until the dust has settled. TPS was established as part of the Immigration Act of 1990, giving authority to the Attorney General to provide TPS to immigrants in the United States

2 Ibid.
3 Julianne Hing, *ICE Admits Gang Operations Are Designed to Lock Up Immigrants*, The Nation, November 20, 2017.
4 David Nakamura, *Flow of Central Americans to U.S. Surging, Expected to Exceed 2014 Numbers*, Wash. Post, September 20, 2016.
5 Nakamura, *Obama Thanks Mexico for 'Absorbing'*.
6 Eduardo Porter, *President Trump Wants a Wall? Mexico Is It*, NY Times, February 21, 2017.
7 David Nakamura, *Trump Administration Ends Obama-era Protection Program for Central American Minors*, Wash. Post, August 16, 2017.

TABLE 7.1. Countries Designated for TPS as of May 2018

Designated Country	Most Recent Designation Date	Current Expiration Date	Current Re-Registration Period	Current Initial Registration Period	Employment Authorization Document (EAD) Automatically Extended Through
El Salvador	March 9, 2001	September 9, 2019	July 8, 2016–September 6, 2016	N/A	September 9, 2019
Haiti	July 23, 2011	July 22, 2019	May 24, 2017–July 24, 2017	N/A	July 22, 2019, but only if you reregister and request a new EAD
Honduras	January 5, 1999	January 5, 2020	May 16, 2016–July 15, 2016	N/A	January 5, 2020
Nepal	June 24, 2015	June 24, 2019	October 26, 2016–December 27, 2016	N/A	June 24, 2019
Nicaragua	January 5, 1999	January 5, 2019	May 16, 2016–July 15, 2016	N/A	January 5, 2019
Somalia	September 18, 2012	March 17, 2020	January 17, 2017–March 20, 2017	N/A	March 17, 2020
Sudan	May 3, 2013	November 2, 2018	January 25, 2016–March 25, 2016	N/A	November 2, 2018
South Sudan	May 3, 2016	May 2, 2019	January 25, 2016–March 25, 2016	January 25, 2016–July 25, 2016	May 2, 2019
Syria	October 1, 2016	September 9, 2019	August 1, 2016–September 30, 2016	August 1, 2016–January 30, 2017	September 30, 2019
Yemen	March 4, 2017	March 3, 2020	January 4, 2017–March 6, 2017	January 4, 2017–July 3, 2017	March 3, 2020

who are temporarily unable to safely return to their home country because of ongoing armed conflict, an environmental disaster, or other extraordinary and temporary conditions.[8] This table lists the countries whose refugees were designated for TPS as President Obama left office.

Although El Salvador and Honduras were on this list, in order to qualify for TPS, the applicant must have been continuously physically present in the United States since the effective date of the most recent designation date of that country, which was March 9, 2001, for El Salvador, and January 5, 1999, for Honduras. So, arrivals from those countries in more recent years did not qualify for TPS. Given what we know about the violent conditions in El Salvador, Honduras, and Guatemala (reviewed in Chapter 4), Guatemala should be designated now while El Salvador and Honduras should be given new designation dates. Granting TPS would be one way to relieve the courts of having to adjudicate the majority of these cases and give people the opportunity to support themselves while they remain in the United States.

Unfortunately, the Trump administration has gone in the opposite direction when it comes to TPS. As part of its efforts to rein in both legal and undocumented immigration, in January 2018, the administration announced that TPS for El Salvadorans would end, and more than 200,000 beneficiaries of the humanitarian program would have to leave the United States within eighteen months (by September 9, 2019). Then, the administration decided to terminate TPS for Hondurans. These announcements came on the heels of a November 2017 announcement that Haitians on TPS would have to leave the United States by July 2019.

Other advocates have argued for the creation of legal vehicles including humanitarian visas that would allow imperiled children with family in the United States to travel legally to the United States.[9] The circumstances demand a "paradigm shift," with more of a focus on protection and less on the enforcement side. Policymakers need to treat this as a real refugee crisis.[10]

Professor Shani M. King has called on Congress to adopt a new legal model in UAC cases based upon human rights norms and standards, including the appointment of properly trained attorneys for UACs. Under the Convention of the Rights of the Child, he further argues that children should be allowed to participate in the legal process by including opportunities for children to voice their thoughts and opinions. That would be consistent with the "collaborative model of advocacy" where attorneys work with the children to understand their rights and enhance their ability to contribute to the decision-making process. Moreover, special training regarding

---

[8] 8 U.S.C. § 1254a(b)(1).

[9] Donald Kerwin, *Why the Central American Child Migrants Need full Adjudication of Their Protection Claims*, Huffington Post, July 19, 2014.

[10] Nakamura, *Flow of Central Americans*.

immigration law focused on UACs should be implemented that includes culturally sensitive techniques and information about the development of the child.[11]

Professor King also argues that the failure to appoint government-paid counsel for UACs may, in fact, be unconstitutional:

> While the government's interest in avoiding the administrative costs of appointed counsel is significant, legislation that systematically denies any possibility of government-appointed counsel to [UACs], an entire class of immigrant defendants most of whom would have no chance at being heard at all, or at least in any meaningful way, if not through the voice of an attorney, cannot pass constitutional scrutiny. Certainly, deportation with no right to a hearing would violate the constitutional guarantees of due process, as would affording the right to a hearing, but "at no expense to government." What Congress has opted for, in this case, is nothing but a hollow pretense or a "shell" of a right to a fair hearing for [UACs]. Circumscribing an immigration judge's discretion to appoint government-funded counsel to an entire sub-group of undocumented immigrants like [UACs] who simply cannot get a fair hearing without an attorney was likely unconstitutional when it was enacted in 1952, but the judicial evolution of the appointment doctrine since then leaves little room for any doubt.[12]

Furthermore, today, due process balancing must be refined to accommodate the interests of easily identifiable (at least from the perspective of modern technology standards) subgroups. Technology has changed in monumental ways. What may have been justifiable a few years ago as putting too much of a burden or strain on government to identify subgroups and tailor due process more specifically to accommodate the needs of subgroups is no longer a true assumption today. The government can much more easily collect and share data today, making it easier to identify subgroups in order to more specifically tailor the due process calculus to the needs of that subgroup (as opposed to creating blanket rules that cover the "average litigant" which reflect an outdated concern that tailoring due process calculus to subgroups would burden the government too much). The courts (and Congress) should update both archaic immigration laws with respect to UACs along with updating the due process approach for the modern-day administrative state in order to better accommodate subgroups.[13]

---

[11] Shani M. King, *Alone and Unrepresented: A Call to Congress to Provide Counsel for Unaccompanied Minors*, Harv. J. Leg. 50, 331 (2013).
[12] Shani M. King, *The Right to a Fair Deportation Hearing for Unaccompanied Minors: How a Tale of Two Provisions Can Create a Voice for the Voiceless In Spite of the Limitations of the Modern-Day Appointment Doctrine*, February 5, 2018 (unpublished paper on file with author).
[13] Ibid.

Other sensible approaches to the challenge of UACs include:

1. Incorporating a "best interest of the child" standard into all decision-making, not just custody decisions. Bipartisan immigration reform legislation which passed the Senate in 2013 (S. 744) would have required the Border Patrol, in making decisions, to give "due consideration" to the best interest of a child, "family unity," and "humanitarian concerns." Amendment 1340 to S. 744, which was not voted on as part of a compromise, would have made the best interests of a child the "primary consideration" in all federal decisions involving unaccompanied immigration children.
2. Child welfare screening to replace or augment Border Patrol screening. Border Patrol agents are currently tasked with screening Mexican and Canadian children for trafficking and persecution and preventing their return to persecutors or abusers. The Border Patrol's ability to do so adequately and fairly is questionable, and reform proposals have ranged from improved training for CBP officers (included in S. 744), to pairing CBP screeners with child welfare experts (also in S. 744) or NGO representatives, to replacing CBP screeners with United States Citizenship and Immigration Services (USCIS) asylum officers.
3. Due process protections and resources. NGOs have advocated for a system that provides procedural protections and resources to appropriately protect children and families from violence, under international and US laws, without unduly delaying decision-making. Proposals include appointed counsel, additional resources to legal orientation programs, and additional resources to backlogged immigration courts (all included in S. 744). Related proposals include additional post-release caseworker services to protect children, assist families, and ensure attendance at proceedings.
4. Aid to sending countries. Massive financial aid should be provided to Northern Triangle countries and Mexico, to invest in systems that protect and care for children, help youth live productive lives, and ultimately reduce violence and address root causes of flight. Right now, the DHS annual budget is about $40 billion, Trump's wall would cost about $3 billion, and we spend close to $2 billion maintaining immigration detention beds.[14] Taking a chunk of that money and using it for investment in the region would be much wiser and much more effective because the root causes of migration would be addressed.
5. Detention reforms. There should be a presumption against detention. Children should be detained as little as possible, released to families or other sponsors whenever appropriate, and if detained, supervised in a community-based setting because of detention's severe impact on children. Detention of asylum-seeking families should be ceased if no family member poses a threat

---

[14] Dan Lamothe, et al., *To Fund Border Wall, Trump Administration Weighs Cuts to Coast Guard, Airport Security*, Wash. Post, March 7, 2017.

to the public or a flight risk. Detention funding should be re-allocated to cheaper alternatives to detention.

One alternative to outright detention already exists. ICE operates two alternatives to detention (ATD) programs for adult detainees – a "full service" program with case management, supervision, and monitoring (either by GPS or telephone check-in), and a "technology-only" program with monitoring only. According to US government data, 95 percent of participants in ICE's full service program appeared at scheduled court hearings from fiscal years 2011 to 2013. Further, in FY 2012 only 4 percent were arrested by another law enforcement agency. In addition to being more humane, the alternative programs are also less expensive than detention – $10.55/day as opposed to $158/day. In fact, a prior US government-commissioned study found that "asylum seekers do not need to be detained to appear," and "they also do not seem to need intensive supervision."[15] In early 2015, ICE issued requests for proposals for "family case management services" for immigrant families in Baltimore/Washington, NYC/Newark, Miami, Chicago, and Los Angeles.[16] That type of program needs further consideration.[17]

Detention raises serious due process and fundamental fairness concerns. Experienced attorneys can attest to how difficult it is to prepare for an asylum case when the applicant is in custody. A study conducted in the New York immigration courts found that 74 percent of immigrants who are represented and not detained have successful outcomes. However, only 3 percent of those who are unrepresented and remain in detention have successful outcomes. Data collected at the Karnes facility clearly shows that detained mothers are more likely to pass their credible fear interviews when first given the opportunity to consult with legal counsel. From August through December 2014, prior to the expansion of pro bono attorney programs focused on preparing families for credible fear interviews, the average rate at which asylum-seekers at Karnes were found to have a credible fear was 71 percent. In contrast, from January through March 2015, after access to counsel became more widely available for these early interviews through pro bono programs, the average rate increased dramatically to 91 percent. A comparable, notable increase in passage rates for the screening interviews occurred at Artesia as pro bono attorneys arrived at the facility in greater numbers.[18]

Beyond the violations of the *Flores* agreement discussed in Chapters 2 and 3, the United States has signed, but failed to ratify, the United Nations Convention

[15] American Immigration Council, *A Guide to Children Arriving at the Border: Laws, Policies and Responses*, June 26, 2015.
[16] Ibid.
[17] Vera Institute of Justice, "Testing Community Supervision for the INS: An Evaluation of the Appearance Assistance Program," New York: Vera Institute of Justice, 2000, www.vera.org/sites/default/files/resources/downloads/INS_finalreport.pdf, at 31.
[18] July 31, 2015 ABA report.

on the Rights of the Child (CRC).[19] That agreement requires certain standards in facilities caring for children which are not met by US family detention centers, such as forbidding the forced separation of parents and children, except in cases in which it is in the best interest of the child. There is a terrible irony in the fact that families fleeing trauma in their home country and seeking refuge in the United States are detained, separated, and subjected to conditions that induce trauma. Clearly the efforts to deter asylum-seeking migrants by increasing detention have not worked, and clearly, incarcerating these people in former prisons is not the most cost-effective option. Instead, our privatized detention system exploits these vulnerable women and children by "treating [them] as commodities, building profits for private prison companies."[20]

Although never passed, there was one piece of legislation introduced in the summer of 2016 that recognized that the situation is a humanitarian crisis. Senate and House Democrats introduced the Secure the Northern Triangle Act, a bill designed to provide a coordinated plan to effectively manage the continuing humanitarian crisis in El Salvador, Guatemala, and Honduras and protect asylum seekers who come from the region. The bill envisioned the United States working with international partners, including the United Nations High Commissioner for Refugees (UNHCR), to support and provide technical assistance to strengthen the capacity of Mexico and other countries in the region to provide asylum to eligible children and families. Only eighteen children were granted asylum in Mexico in 2014. In 2015, the Mexican Refugee Agency had only fifteen officers who were qualified to make refugee status determinations. The bill also would have expanded the capacity of the CAM program by requiring the hiring of additional refugee officers for in-country processing and adding new processing locations.

The House bill included mandatory training for prosecutors, judges, and police on issues related to sexual and gender-based violence and lesbian, gay, bisexual, transgender, and queer issues as a condition for US assistance. The bill included a requirement that best interest determinations be conducted on children before they are repatriated to ensure that return is in their best interests, and that child appropriate reintegration procedures for kids who are returned be developed.

In addition, this bill provided improvements domestically. It would have enhanced protection for children reunified with sponsors following release from an Office of Refugee Resettlement (ORR) detention facility. Moreover, the bill would have strengthened screening and follow-up mechanisms to ensure the children's safety and access to due process. By including the Fair Day in Court for Kids Act, UACs would have been guaranteed counsel. Finally, this bill would have help to

[19] Amber D. Moulton, *No Safe Haven Here: Children and Families Face Trauma in the Hands of U.S. Immigration*, Unitarian Universalist Service Committee (2015), at 8, www.uusc.org/sites/default/files/no_safe_haven_here_-_children_and_families_face_trauma_in_the_hands_of_u.s._immigration.pdf
[20] Ibid., at 2.

eradicate barriers UACs face in accessing education by providing funding to school districts with fifty or more UACs.

While the bill included important measures like access to counsel and legal orientation programs, it did not include provisions to end family detention or address other very serious due process failures in our current system.

Credible fear evaluations at the border should be done fairly. The entire content of the guidelines on how to screen for credible fear, discussed in Chapters 2 and 3, should be reconsidered so that asylum seekers are treated fairly at the basic screening stage. If they meet the correct, contextualized credible fear standard, they should be allowed to make a case for asylum in front of an immigration judge at a later date, where all the nuances of asylum law can be fairly evaluated on the merits of the claim. Given the likely manifestations of post-traumatic stress disorder, complications in assessing credibility, possible challenges with translation, and other logistical challenges, the screening function of credible fear determinations is most correctly viewed as one of deference to the applicant. The integrity of the asylum system should be protected by suspending USCIS's guidelines and installing instructions to asylum officers that more accurately reflect the statutory framework as well as the purpose and minimal legal requirements that attach to credible fear determinations.

In summary, those who come to our borders seeking asylum deserve fair treatment. Unfortunately, the Obama administration is now associated with the tragic anti-asylum eras of the past. Obama allowed politics to get in the way of the humanistic instincts he may have had. And now Trump has exploited the Obama tools.

7.3. THE CASE FOR TRUMP AS THE NEW DEPORTATION KING

For reasons not that complex, President Donald Trump and his ICE army want to disrupt the lives of undocumented immigrants and their families. They want to create confusion and chaos even when it may not be legally justified, and that's working. The Trump White House has instilled a get-tough attitude among the ICE officers and makes the whole world think that this is normal and permissible. That makes Trump and his troops so much harsher than the "mainstream" Republican approach to immigration which was just strict, but not purposefully spiteful. Combine that with Trump's immigration-savvy advisors' approach of using old dormant immigration law provisions (like expansion of expedited removal), sometimes beyond the constitutionally permitted boundaries, and the nightmare is complete.

Certainly, we can stop the unconstitutional actions like forced separation of children from their parents and racial profiling through litigation, but in the meantime, the anti-immigrant message has been sent and becomes the lead story: Trump is banning Muslims; he's taking bids to build the Wall; random Deferred Action for

Childhood Arrivals (DACA)/Dreamers are getting arrested; Guadalupe García de Rayos, a married mother of two US citizen children gets deported even though the Obama administration suspended her removal after having a clear record for more than twenty years; Trump and Attorney General Sessions threaten to defund sanctuary cities. The array of enforcement headlines seems endless. The resulting fear is real. And although the travel ban was held up in court for a time, the number of refugee arrivals from Syria, Somalia, and Iraq plummeted.[21]

Truth is we have all lived through the anti-Muslim aspect of the Trump rhetoric in the aftermath of 9/11. In fact, it's very possible that Trump's ban/rhetoric/anti-Syrian refugee position is simply a crescendo of the continuing 9/11 aftermath. The same could be said of his anti-Mexican/undocumented rhetoric. Today is starkly reminiscent of the period through which I have lived and practiced – of an anti-Mexican/ undocumented era starting when I practiced as a legal aid attorney in the 1970s, and the Proposition 187 era in California in the 1990s.

We have to remember that Trump's anti-immigrant message struck a populist chord with many voters. Pro-deportation/anti-refugee voters accounted for almost three-quarters of Trump's support during the presidential primaries. And today, almost half of Republican voters favor deporting all undocumented immigrants and barring Syrian refugees from entering the United States.

As we contemplate the subjective as well as objective basis for fear in the immigrant community, we need to keep in mind that things are always worse when something is taken away. Obama's prosecutorial discretion policy and public pronouncements provided non-priority immigrants (e.g., those without criminal records) with a sense of relief and stability; a sense that they could come out of the shadows and go about their lives. That has now been taken away, producing a whiplash feeling that is worse than before there was a prosecutorial discretion policy. The fact that there is no viable possibility of a federal fix, such as a broad legalization plan, on anyone's horizon feeds into a sense of hopelessness and despair, especially when it seemed close or at least a priority to the candidate that most pundits predicted would be in the White House today – Hillary Clinton.

Even amid the worst periods of the 1970s to early 1990s, being undocumented was not a long term, indefinite life circumstance. It was more typically a period of several years. Most people who stayed long enough could find ways to adjust through a variety of means such as registry (for those who entered before 1972), suspension of deportation relief (for those who had resided in the United States for seven years), the old "section 212(c)" waiver for aggravated felons who deserved a second chance, employers, marriage, or other family categories. But changes in immigration law did away with many of these remedies in large part because of the

---

[21] Human Rights First, *Declines in U.S. Resettlement of Muslim Refugees under the Trump Administration*, June 11, 2017, www.humanrightsfirst.org/sites/default/files/hrffactsheet-declines-in-us-resettlement-muslim-refugees.pdf.

death trap of Operation Gatekeeper and the ten-year unlawful presence bar instituted in 1996. Living with undocumented status has become a longer way of life for more people who are now much more rooted. As such, they have much more to lose than ever before. The rhetoric around the border wall, border enforcement, and increased interior arrests signal to migrants that if they are caught and deported, they may never be able to return. In that sense, especially for people with family in the United States who need to return, the consequences of deportation appear higher than before.

Trump's boastfulness and the loud anti-Trump rhetoric by pundits (including by immigrant rights groups) has created a false sense that mass deportation is actually now occurring. Yes, interior arrests are up. But, in fact, Trump's executive orders are only a blueprint for a mass deportation machine. Unleashed current ICE personnel is enough to get things going. But the mass deportation machine has not been built. Congress needs to appropriate the funds to hire all the new CBP and ICE officials. Admittedly, by July 31, 2017, the Trump administration had increased the number of agreements to 287(g) agreements to sixty (up from less than forty for Obama), including eighteen new agreements in Texas alone.[22] With every new 287(g) agreement, state and local law enforcement agencies serve as force multipliers of enforcement. But raids are not occurring at an unprecedented rate, in spite of the sense we get from the news, following listservs and email action alerts, or from *el Feisbuk*.

Trump's shenanigans during his campaign and since he has become president make clear that we are not dealing with someone whom we would call a particularly brilliant strategist who is in total control or who has a long-term, mapped-out, ideological vision. However, as much as he and his confidants appear to be bumbling idiots tripping over themselves, the actions they have taken on immigration enforcement have been effective in scaring the hell out of immigrants and many supporters. And someone in his inner circle knows enough about immigration enforcement to make some ICE actions quite effective.

A few months after Trump took office, I invited a former student, Matt Gonzalez, to have a conversation with my clinic students about a piece he put on his blog only half facetiously supporting the construction of The Wall.[23] His points primarily were about how the resulting impact on food prices would stir up immigration reform because the need for cheap labor would be recognized, social conservatives would be prevented from entering, and that the wall would protect Mexicans from unfair reentry criminal laws. My students and I mostly challenged him on grounds such as how he failed to see the enormous effect on migrants fleeing violence.

[22] Dianne Solis and Ray Leszcynski, *18 Texas Sheriffs Sign up to Join Forces with Federal Immigration Officers*, Dallas Morning News, July 31, 2017.
[23] Matt Gonzalez, *The Wall*, The Matt Gonzalez Reader, November 7, 2017, https://themattgonzalezreader.wordpress.com/2016/11/07/border-wall/

We also challenged him on the symbolism of the wall. To me, the symbolism is significant. Its message of exclusion is clear. Latinos – primarily Mexicans – are not wanted. But the message of exclusion reaches communities on *both* sides of the border – you're not wanted whatever side of the border you are on. This is a message not simply intended for undocumented immigrants. The wall's message is one of de-legitimizing Latinos and Muslims already in the United States.

This message of de-legitimacy is in essence a message of de-Americanization: Latinos and Muslims are not, and cannot be, "true Americans." Haitians, Africans, and El Salvadorans are not welcome, because they come from "shithole" countries.[24] Recall also Trump's message about the federal court judge of Mexican descent who was hearing a lawsuit by former students alleging fraud by Trump University. In repeated statements and interviews, such as with CNN and The Wall Street Journal, Trump referred to Indiana-born Judge Gonzalo Curiel variously as "of Mexican heritage" or just "Mexican." The relatively tame message was always the same, that the judge had what Trump called "a conflict of initerest" because of his ethnicity.

Of course, this is not simply Trump's message. And this is a message not simply from the racists who support Trump. This is a message long-touted by the Republican Party: some members of whom spew the same racist venom, others who want to keep out people whom Republicans believe are attracted to the Democratic Party. This long historical attitude of the Republican Party toward Latinos in particular is part of the foundation for the case that has been made that Trump is in fact an image of the Republican Party's own making – its own Frankenstein's monster. Thus, Trump's handpicked appointments to key immigration enforcement positions have easily and wholeheartedly implemented long-held Republican enforcement strategies. As the DHS Secretary for six months before becoming White House chief of staff, John Kelly pushed ICE arrests numbers up 40 percent, ended prosecutorial discretion for undocumented immigrants, expanded "criminal aliens" to include noncitizens arrested but not convicted, revived 287(g) agreements, and expanded expedited removals.[25] In February 2018, following deportations that ripped apart immigrant families, Trump's acting director and nominee to head ICE, Thomas Homan, said, "This isn't a job I particularly wanted in the beginning, but I'll tell you what, I'm enjoying it."[26] Earlier he warned that undocumented immigrants "should be uncomfortable" and constantly "looking over their shoulder[s]."[27]

As the Republican Party's monster, Trump has wrested the title of Deporter-in-Chief from Obama. Trump's monthly interior enforcement numbers have surpassed

[24] Eli Watkins and Abby Phillip, *Trump Decries Immigrants From 'Shithole Countries' Coming to US*, CNN Politics, January 12, 2018.
[25] Julianne Hing, *John Kelly's Promotion is a Disaster for Immigrants*, The Nation, July 28, 2017.
[26] Jake Johnson, *ICE Director Brags About How Much He's 'Enjoying' Tearing Immigrant Families Apart*, Common Dreams, February 1, 2018, www.commondreams.org/news/2018/02/01/ice-director-brags-about-how-much-hes-enjoying-tearing-immigrant-families-apart
[27] Ibid.

those of Obama already. Trump has the enthusiastic support of the vast majority of ICE agents – not needing a new deportation army, because he already has one.

Even in the realm of Obama's shameful treatment of Central American UACs and AWCs, Trump is the winner. Not only has he continued every single bad Obama policy in that regard, but Trump has gone further – canceling the feeble CAM program and also arresting and threatening criminal prosecution of parents of UACs in the United States who may have paid smugglers to help their children escape violence.[28] As noted above, Obama persuaded Congress to approve $750 million in development aid for Central America – not a large amount given the scale of the problem. However, Trump asked for a reduction in development funding for Central America in his proposed budget to Congress – part of a suggested 30 percent cutback across the State Department.[29] Trump's other migration-related policies also are likely to destabilize the region by leading to much higher levels of deportations of Central Americans from the United States. For example, the termination of TPS for El Salvadorans and Hondurans and the deportation of young migrants with alleged gang affiliations pose serious threats to the region.[30] Mass deportations could be seriously disruptive in the small, poor countries of Central America. As noted earlier, large-scale deportation of MS-13 gang members to El Salvador beginning in the 1990s helped turn the country into one of the most violent in the world.[31]

Not only do family units from Central America – mothers and their children – often get housed for a day or two at the *hielera* freezer containers, but now the mothers and the children are separated often for days in what the migrants now call *la perrera* – the dog pen, near the border in McAllen, TX. My brilliant, warm-hearted colleague at the USF deportation defense clinic, Jacqueline Brown Scott, sent me this sobering text after participating in a site inspection there:

Bright entry
Smiling guards
Happy to see snow, outside taking pictures
Hallway to locked doors
Their warning – no pictures
Through them
Windowless and large
The middle filled with computers and guards
"Processing" "Subjects"
One side, women, in the cage, a few benches

[28] Nakamura, *Trump Administration Ends Obama*; Jenny Jarvie, *Immigrant Rights Groups Denounce New ICE Policy that Targets Parents of Child Migrants*, LA Times, June 30, 2017.
[29] Kate Linthicum, *The U.S. and Mexico Want to Slow Migration from Central America. Will Mass Deportations Help?*, LA Times, October 27, 2017.
[30] Ibid.
[31] Ibid.

The closer side, many more men, in cages, sprawled on the floor
(I believe what they've said about being kicked awake)
Aluminum everywhere, aka space blankets
Looking at them:
I hope they don't think I work here.
Trying to smile
It's not cold, today. We're warm
(They knew we were coming)
Through the next doors
Like Costco,
But the middle is filled with more cages
Boys in one, mats on the floor, more aluminum
Lined up in rows and rows
Girls behind them on benches
Sadness
In an interview room
Mario's 8. "Donde esta mi abuela?"
Sobbing.
Confusion
Separation
They have apples now. And TVs
La perrera.

Twenty-six years ago, every country formally agreed that children have a special place in the world and are more than just passive beneficiaries of care. The CRC became the most-widely ratified treaty that recognizes children as rights' bearers and obliges state parties to protect and promote a distinct set of rights in the "best interests of the child."[32] This standard is increasingly becoming a source of binding customary international law and today every country in the world has ratified the CRC, that is, every country except the United States.

This is especially concerning in the realm of immigration law, particularly the legal standards governing the treatment and processing of UACs who are apprehended at the border. As we have seen, migrant children who flee to the US border for protection are apprehended by Border Patrol agents who are untrained in child welfare and lack expertise in trafficking or abuse indicators. Rather than erring on the side of protection for children, Border Patrol agents seem bent on proving that a child does not warrant protection.

[32] Convention on the Rights of the Child (CRC), G.A. Res. 44/25, U.N. Doc. A/RES/44/25 (November 20, 1989). The standard is provided by Article 3(1), which states, "In all action concerning children, whether undertaken by public or private social welfare institutions, courts of law, administrative authorities or legislative bodies, the best interests of the child shall be a primary consideration."

The Trafficking Victims Protection Reauthorization Act of 2008 (TVPRA) establishes limited legal standards governing the screening and protection of children at the border. These protections are only extended to the children that Border Patrol agents determine fit the criteria. The UNHCR criticized Border Patrol's interview practices after finding that agents are inadequately trained, biased against protection needs, and that "[c]hildren with needs that Congress intended to protect are likely rejected at the border."[33] Despite the systematic flaws in the processing of UACs, Congress at least recognized through the TVPRA that regardless of their immigration status, children are a vulnerable group that necessitate special treatment. This recognition is now threatened by recent administrative and legislative proposals, which will effectively strip UACs of fundamental legal protections in an effort to deter Central American children from seeking refuge and family reunification in the United States.

Unfortunately, at the height of the surge in UACs in 2014 and 2015 during the Obama era, Congress provided little support for UACs and AWCs. Most legislative proposals focused on rolling back the procedural protections that the TVPRA afforded to Central American unaccompanied children. For example, the House's 2014 "Secure the Southwest Border Act" would have amended the TVPRA to: (1) treat children from non contiguous countries similarly to Mexican and Canadian children; but (2) strike the current requirement that the child be able to make an "independent decision to withdraw the child's application for admission" before proceeding with voluntary return; (3) require those children who may have been trafficked or fear return [or require the remaining children] to appear before an immigration judge for a hearing within fourteen days of screening; and (4) impose mandatory detention until that hearing.

Other proposals at the time offered variations on these themes. For example, the "Protection of Children Act of 2015," which the House Judiciary Committee moved forward on March 4, 2015, would enact the above four changes – but additionally, expand from 72 hours to thirty days the time limit for CBP to transfer remaining UACs to Department of Health and Human Services (HHS) custody. The bill, among others, also proposed restricting HHS's ability to provide counsel to unaccompanied children. Or, the "HUMANE Act," sponsored by Senator John Cornyn (R-TX) and Representative Henry Cuellar (D-TX) in 2014, would have gone further to place children with a fear of return into a new seven-day expedited process, during which the child would be required to prove her or his eligibility for immigration relief to an immigration judge while mandatorily detained, before moving on to a standard removal proceeding in immigration court.

---

[33] UNHCR, *Findings and Recommendations Relating to the 2012-2013 Missions to Monitor the Protection Screening of Mexican Unaccompanied Children Along the U.S.-Mexico Border*, 5 (June 2014), www.immigrantjustice.org/sites/immigrantjustice.org/files/UNHCR_UAC_Monitoring_Report_Final_June_2014.pdf.

Enter Trump, and proposals that relate to UACs have been worse. The current administration has waged a war on migrant children by painting them as criminals to justify stripping them of their legal rights and protections. The Trump administration's "Immigration Principles and Policies" targets UACs under the pretext of national security by pressuring Congress to close a "loophole" in the existing law, which has allegedly attracted an influx of children to exploit our immigration system and resources. The problem with this allegation is that there are no "loopholes" in the existing law. "Loopholes" are unintended consequences of a law,[34] but Congress specifically intended for UACs to receive special protections and did so by enacting the existing treatment standards. Thousands of children are not risking their lives to exploit the US immigration system and resources. As we have seen, substantial evidence demonstrates that the principal push factor for children has been the increasing violence in their home countries. The conditions have become so dire that children are willing to risk death along their journey to the United States in hopes of security.[35] Although the existing legal standards are not perfect, UACs are at least recognized as a vulnerable group in need of special protections and treatment. In contrast, Trump has sought to eliminate protections for UACs in his "Immigration Principles and Policies" that were proposed to Congress in exchange for a DACA deal.[36]

Congress has the chance to pursue a humane approach to processing UACs in a way that addresses children's welfare needs and national security concerns. However, the most relevant legislative proposals with Trump's blessings, the "Protection of Children Act of 2017" and "Asylum Reform and Border Protection Act of 2017" and its Amendment in the Nature of a Substitute, will do just the opposite if passed. These proposals disregard the best interests of children and eliminate their existing protections that safeguard their fundamental human and due process rights. Even without ratifying the CSR (Convention Relating to the Status of Refugees), Congress should at least demonstrate greater willingness to value and uphold children's rights and interests by passing legislation that ensures humane treatment of the most vulnerable children. While the United States is a sovereign nation that has the right to control its borders and enforce the law, it should do so in a manner that does not put children back into the hands of traffickers and war-like conditions. These proposals fail to recognize that national security concerns and respecting children's due process and human rights are not mutually exclusive.

The proposed bills undermine their purported objective of suppressing the flow of UACs by failing to consider the actual root causes of the problem: family

---

[34] Miriam Valverde, *Donald Trump Omits Facts in Claim About Loopholes, Unaccompanied Minors*, Politifact (October 11, 2017), www.politifact.com/truth-o-meter/statements/2017/oct/11/donald-trump/donald-trump-omits-facts-claim-loopholes-minors-un/.

[35] UN Children's Fund, *Risking it All to Escape Gang Violence and Poverty*, Report, (August 23, 2016), https://reliefweb.int/report/honduras/broken-dreams-central-american-children-s-dangerous-journey-united-states.

[36] Valverde, *Donald Trump Omits Facts*.

reunification, gang-related violence, and corruption.[37] If adopted, these policies will function to violate our international, regional, and national legal duties to protect children's basic rights and will betray American values by threatening the psychological and physical well-being of children.

On January 12, 2017, Republican Representative John Carter introduced H.R. 495, the "Protection of Children Act of 2017," to amend section 235 of the TVPRA to eliminate procedural protections provided to UACs from non contiguous countries. This bill also amends sections of the Immigration and Nationality Act to narrow eligibility for Special Immigrant Juvenile Status and streamline UAC asylum claims directly to immigration judges. If implemented, these changes to the law would effectively make children more vulnerable to traffickers as it would limit a child's ability to even apply for relief.

First, the bill would subject all UACs, regardless of nationality and age, to expedited screening by CBP rather than child welfare experts in ORR. This move goes against the child's best interests in obtaining protection as the UNHCR and Government Accountability Office (GAO) have reported that CBP has been inadequately screening and wrongly sending Mexican UACs back to Mexico.[38] Language barriers aside, this provides an unrealistic expectation for children. Without any assistance, children must clearly articulate painful details of a harrowing journey to an armed, uniformed guard who is untrained and unskilled in interviewing for asylum and trafficking claims.[39] Since children are unlikely to be traveling with documents and evidence of persecution, it is even more unlikely that they will be able to provide a plausible claim within the proposed 48 hours. If the CBP official determines that the child did not identify their reasons why they fled to the United States to the satisfaction of that official, they will automatically be sent back to their country regardless of whether that country has a repatriation agreement with the United States.[40] The TVPRA mandates the US government to take the appropriate measures to ensure that children denied relief would be humanely and safely repatriated to their origin country. These agreements were intended to ensure that a child had access to all processes in the United States to obtain protection from trafficking, abuse, and violence before being repatriated. Congress should be improving the safety standards by requiring initial screening to be conducted by officials trained in

[37] Center for Gender and Refugee Studies, *Childhood and Migration in Central and North America: Causes, Policies, Practices and Challenges* (February 2015), https://cgrs.uchastings.edu/sites/default/files/Childhood_Migration_HumanRights_FullBook_English.pdf.

[38] U.S. Government Accountability Office, GAO-15-521, *Unaccompanied Alien Children: Actions Needed to Ensure Children Receive Required Care in DHS Custody* (2015) (hereinafter "GAO-15-521").

[39] More than half of CBP officials reported that they did not believe that it was their job to determine whether a child had a credible fear of returning home. *See:* UNHCR *supra* note 11, at 29.

[40] The TVPRA requires the Department of State ("DOS") to negotiate Local Repatriation Agreements with contiguous countries to provide for safe repatriation and integration of returning UAC. H.R. 495 authorizes DOS to negotiate agreements with any country and remove UAC to countries that refuse to negotiate agreements. *See:* Protection of Children Act, H.R. 495, 115th Cong. §2 (2017).

child welfare and to establish clear policies and procedures that govern repatriation without undermining children's safety. Instead, this law would likely result in sending countless children back into the hands of traffickers, gang violence, and even death.

International law, US policy, and the UNHCR explicitly prohibit detaining children, especially in the migration context; detention is never in the best interest of the child.[41] If children are somehow able to overcome the initial obstacles, this bill provides for prolonged detention. It requires CBP to hold UACs in detention for thirty days instead of the current 72-hour limit before transferring the child to ORR custody.[42] The purpose of the 72-hour holding limit is to ensure children are quickly placed in appropriate placements rather than detained in facilities that are ill-equipped to handle children. As we have seen, CBP's detention facilities are known for conditions that violate their own standards where children are subject to freezing temperatures and stripped of their clothes, subject to psychological and physical abuse, overcrowding and intolerable sleeping and sanitary conditions, and no access to mental health or other services. Prolonged detention would violate the *Flores* Agreement and many international and regional laws and norms.[43] Further, longer detention would subject children to re-traumatization and criminalize them in prison-like settings simply because they chose to flee death and violence in order to survive.

The TVPRA recognizes that children need special protections and assistance in navigating the complex immigration system. Therefore, it mandates that HHS ensures "to the greatest extent practicable," legal representation for all children in legal proceedings and decisions to protect them against trafficking and mistreatment.[44] The TVPRA also protects UACs from expedited removal proceedings by first having a specially trained asylum officer adjudicate their initial requests for asylum. This bill not only prohibits the government from providing or facilitating access to an attorney, it also accelerates removal proceedings by mandating a hearing before an immigration judge within fourteen days of their initial screening by CBP. Together, these provisions would require children, regardless of age or mental capacity, to find an attorney and build a case with sufficient evidence – all while being detained. However, we now know that the children will be suffering the consequences of trafficking, violence, and other forms of persecution, so it is highly

---

[41] For more about the psychological consequences of detaining children seeking refuge, See: UNHCR, *Detention Guidelines: Guidelines on the Applicable Criteria and Standards Relating to the Detention of Asylum- Seekers and Alternatives to Detention*, 33–36 (2012), www.unhcr.org/505b10ee9 html.

[42] H.R. 495.

[43] The Flores Agreement requires that each minor be placed in the least restrictive setting appropriate to the minor's age and special needs, provided that such setting is consistent with its interests to ensure the minor's timely appearance before immigration courts and to protect the minor's well-being and that of others. Stipulated Settlement Agreement, ¶11, *Flores v. Reno*, No. 85-4544 (C.D. Cal. Jan 17, 1997).

[44] TVPRA §235(c)(5).

unlikely that they will be able to access legal representation or adequate information about how and what to prepare for a case. To require children to effectively advocate for themselves without legal knowledge and against government-trained attorneys and judges is not only cruel, but it violates their right to fundamental fairness, a touchstone of due process.[45] The failure to provide or even facilitate access to adequate counsel for children creates a high risk of life-or-death situations. Forcing children to navigate a foreign legal system without counsel is unconscionable where the order of removal can, in effect, be a death sentence. These proposed changes will not, by any means, "protect" children; rather, they threaten the well-being and safety of children.

Currently, the TVPRA requires ORR to release children to approved family members to act as sponsors that can provide for the child's physical and mental wellbeing. This was intended to balance the child's best interests and ORR capacity while the child's removal case proceeds. H.R. 495 asserts that it will prevent children from being released to human traffickers and abusers, which had occurred in 2014.[46] To do so, a provision mandates that HHS checks and shares the immigration status of UAC family members with DHS, and to initiate removal proceedings against any undocumented members. This requirement does not protect children from traffickers, rather it will prolong the detention of UACs by deterring family members from coming forward in fear of adverse immigration consequences. Sponsors' immigration status has no bearing on whether a UAC would be in danger if placed with them. The ORR policy specifically states that it does not disqualify potential sponsors based on their immigration status.[47] The reason for that is that the child's safety and well-being is the principle concern, so reunification with a qualified sponsor is prioritized. Under the proposed change, the best interests of the child are completely neglected by preventing children from being with their families and does not address how children would be prevented from being released to traffickers. The proposal will punish family members who are trying to legally reunite rather than improve ORR's sponsor screening process.

The TVPRA established, with bipartisan support, additional measures to protect and prevent children from falling prey to human traffickers and abusive conditions.[48] H.R. 495 completely guts these safeguards by narrowing the eligibility for UACs

---

[45] The Sixth Circuit Court stated that "fundamental fairness," a touchstone of due process, may be violated by failure to provide an unrepresented alien with counsel at the government's expense. *See: Aguilera-Enriquez v. I.N.S.*, 516 F.2d 565 n.3 (6th Cir. 1975).

[46] Abbie VanSickle, *Overwhelmed Federal Officials Released Immigrant Teens to Traffickers in 2014*, The Washington Post (January 26, 2016), www.washingtonpost.com/national/failures-in-handling-unaccompanied-migrant-minors-have-led-to-trafficking/2016/01/26/c47de164-c138-11e5-9443-7074c3645405_story.html?utm_term=.odda312eab4f.

[47] ORR Policy Guide, *Children Entering the United States Unaccompanied* (April 11, 2016), www.acf.hhs.gov/orr/resource/children-entering-the-united-states-unaccompanied-section-2#2.2.1.

[48] The TVPRA provided additional protections for "children who are at risk of being repatriated into the hands of traffickers or abusers." *See:* Summary, H.R. Rep. No. 101-430 (2007).

to claim relief under the Special Immigrant Juvenile Status rules. The TVPRA amended the INA to expand the eligibility for relief so that a UAC in the United States can petition for special immigrant juvenile status (SIJS) after a state court finds that it is not in the child's best interest to reunite with one or both parents "due to abuse, neglect, abandonment, or a similar basis found under state law."[49] H.R. 495 backtracks on these developments by eliminating protection for a child who has been abused, abandoned, or neglected by only one parent. This proposal will force vulnerable children back to the very danger they fled and to fend for themselves. In contrast to Representative Carter's assertion that H.R. 495 would fix loopholes in the current law, these changes would eliminate the minimal protections that were specifically provided for UACs.[50] Further, this bill would result in serious human rights and due process violations of vulnerable children at the border.

The House Judiciary Committee has also added a dangerous provision to H.R. 391, the "Asylum Reform and Protection Act of 2017," sponsored by Representative Mike Johnson. The proposal would drastically change the humanitarian nature of US asylum law in a manner that would prevent children fleeing horrific violence and persecution from even presenting their claims in court.[51] The Trump administration embraced H.R. 391 by incorporating many of its proposals in the administration's immigration principles and priorities that were released in October 2017 in exchange for a DACA deal.[52] H.R. 391 contains similar inhumane provisions as H.R. 495, including: limiting SIJS to children who can prove abuse or neglect by both parents; repatriating UACs to countries that the United States does not have a repatriation agreement with; extending DHS detention, and prohibiting the government from providing or facilitating access to legal aid. Additionally, the bill would undermine the ability for UACs with legitimate claims to even apply for asylum and send them back to the dangers they fled.

The current law appropriately exempts UACs from the one-year asylum filing deadline. Congress recognized that it is unrealistic for such vulnerable children to be able to navigate their way through the legal system without legal aid under a time

[49] USCIS Memorandum HQOPS 70/8.5, *Trafficking Victims Protection Reauthorization Act of 2008: Special Immigrant Juvenile Status Provisions* (March 24, 2009).
[50] Rep. Carter proposed the same Act in 2014 and 2015 on which he purported that the Act would protect children from human trafficking abuses and that it "fixes a loophole in the current law regarding unaccompanied minors entering the U.S. illegally and proposes common sense solutions." *See: Rep. Carter's Bill Protects Children from Human Traffickers* (2015), https://carter.house.gov/press-releases/rep-carters-bill-protects-children-from-human-traffickers/.
[51] Rep. Jason Chaffetz originally introduced H.R. 391 in January 2017 and Rep. Johnson's amendment was approved by Republicans on the House Judiciary Committee but it is unclear whether it will make it to the House floor. *See:* Andrew Arthur, *Asylum Reform Bill Passes Out of Committee,* Center for Immigration Studies (July 27, 2017), https://cis.org/Arthur/Asylum-Reform-Bill-Passes-out-Committee.
[52] Presidential Memorandum, *President Donald J. Trump's Letter to House and Senate Leaders & Immigration Principles and Policies* (October 8, 2017). Available at: www.whitehouse.gov/the-press-office/2017/10/08/president-donald-j-trumps-letter-house-and-senate-leaders-immigration.

deadline they may not know about, all while dealing with psychological trauma.[53] Despite this common-sense protection, H.R. 391 would eliminate this by subjecting all UACs to the one-year deadline. As a result, victims' legitimate claims for protection would be denied and children would be sent back into harm's way.

Section 8 of H.R. 391 goes further by denying many children the right to UAC treatment and processing. The provision would amend the Homeland Security Act of 2002 (HSA) to narrow the definition of UACs by excluding any child who has a relative over the age of eighteen in the United States. This change would subject children to the mistreatment that the HSA intended to prevent by expanding DHS's authority to keep children in prison-like settings rather than transfer them to child welfare professionals in ORR.

As we have seen, current law subjects asylum seekers at the border to a preliminary credible fear screening by an asylum officer to determine the credibility of the claim.[54] The current standard requires individuals to prove that they have a "significant possibility of establishing eligibility for asylum," without access to legal aid or evidence, which is problematic already. H.R. 391 imposes an additional, increased burden, which would require asylum seekers, including UACs, to demonstrate that "it is more likely than not" that their statements are true. The current standard is already criticized for sending children back into harm's way as a result of CBP's inadequate interview practices and training.[55] Therefore, it is unconscionable to impose an additional obstacle to even accessing the asylum process.

Further, this is an unnecessary requirement that Congress had intentionally waived when it created the credibility determination process in 1996. This standard was incorporated in the initial draft of the bill, however, concerns that it would wrongfully prevent legitimate refugees from applying for asylum were addressed by the bill's author by replacing it with the current standard.[56] The heightened standard would not only betray Congress' original intent, but it would ultimately result in systematic violations of the principle of non refoulement by forcibly removing many legitimate refugees back into abusive, violent, and even lethal situations.

To establish an asylum claim, individuals must show either past persecution or a well-founded fear of future persecution on account of one of the five protected grounds: race, religion, nationality, political opinion, or membership in a particular social group.[57] The majority of UACs from Central America's Northern Triangle are seeking asylum protection from gang-related violence based on a membership in a

---

[53] INA § 208(a)(2)(E); TVPRA, P.L. 110-457, § 235(d)(7)(A).

[54] 8 U.S.C. § 1225(b)(1)(B)(v).

[55] GAO-15-521.

[56] 142 Cong. Rec. S4492 (1996), www.congress.gov/crec/1996/05/01/CREC-1996-05-01-pt1-PgS4457.pdf.

[57] INA § 101(a)(42)(A).

particular social group claim.[58] Although courts are split on recognizing individuals fleeing gang-related persecution as constituting a particular social group, there has been success with these claims where children have shown that those fleeing share a common, immutable characteristic, such as family.[59] H.R. 391 will disproportionately impact UACs from Central America because it will categorically deny asylum or withholding of removal to anyone who has been, or fears becoming, a victim of gang violence or other crimes in their original country by virtue of their status in society.[60]

This change goes against the principle purpose of asylum law and ignores the changing nature of refugee crises. US asylum law is derived from international agreements, most notably the 1951 Convention relating to the Status of Refugees (CSR), which oblige international governments to provide protection to people fearing or fleeing from persecution. The primary purpose of this obligation is to provide protection for people unable to receive protection from their own governments. The United States helped to draft the CSR to prevent governments from turning their backs on the world's most vulnerable groups. However, the proposed change would betray this objective and send the wrong message to all countries. The United States would be evading its duties by sending thousands of children, who survived horrifying violence and torture, back into life-threatening conditions.

If either or both bills supported by the Trump administration are enacted, the US asylum system will be set up to systematically violate children's rights to due process and humanitarian protection. The Protection of Children Act and the Asylum Reform and Border Protection Act in conjunction with Trump's immigration principles prioritize enforcement and deterrence measures without taking adequate steps to protect vulnerable children. If a child flees to the United States seeking refuge, the government's first response should be protection. National security interests and immigration control can be maintained without violating a child's fundamental liberties and human rights. Congress, instead, should be developing legislative reforms that are compatible with the best interests of the child standard and ensure access to a humane process to review their eligibility for legal status.

The Trump administration came into office promoting a hard stance on immigration and a goal to "stop illegal immigration, deport criminal aliens, and save American lives."[61] However, the so-called "criminals," at the border that the

---

[58] UNHCR, *Children on the Run: Unaccompanied Children Leaving Central America and Mexico and the Need for International Protection*, 6 (2017), www.unhcr.org/56fc266f4.html.

[59] To succeed with a gang-based claim, a child must show that they belong to a social group that has a common immutable characteristic which the child is unable or should not be required to change because it is fundamental to the child's identity or conscience. *Matter of Acosta*, 19 I&N Dec. 211 (BIA 1985).

[60] Amendment in the Nature of A Substitute to H.R. 391, 15-17 (2017), https://judiciary.house.gov/wp-content/uploads/2017/07/HR-391-ANS.pdf.

[61] Donald Trump, *Remarks at the Bayfront Park Amphitheater in Miami, Florida,* (November 2, 2016). Available at: www.presidency.ucsb.edu/ws/index.php?pid=123514.

administration so often points to include thousands of children who have survived the grueling and harrowing journey in search of safety and protection. Congress has taken an unprecedented turn against the best interests of children by proposing H.R. 495 and H.R. 391, which fail to address the underlying causes of increased UAC migration. The proposals would deny children access to apply for protection. Trump has endorsed the legislation and included these proposals in his "Immigration Principles and Policies." Together, these proposals would eliminate the legal safeguards and procedures specifically developed for children seeking protection.

History has proven that aggressive immigration enforcement at the border does not deter migrants. Instead, as we have seen in the discussion of Operation Gatekeeper (see Chapter 6), it forces migrants to take dangerous routes that have empowered trafficking rings and increased deaths along the border. Responding to the current situation with tougher enforcement and rigid requirements overlooks the humanitarian factors forcing children from their homes. Doctors Without Borders labeled the Northern Triangle a "neglected humanitarian crisis," reporting that half of the surveyed refugees had a relative killed due to violence, with many suffering from post-traumatic stress disorder symptoms.[62] Children are not making the conscious decision to migrate out of a need to work, they are literally running for their lives and the US immigration system is failing them. The United States cannot ignore this crisis any longer and preventing children from applying for asylum will not stop them from trying unauthorized and dangerous routes.

Despite the United States resistance to ratifying the CRC, it has, as a signatory, a legal obligation to respect the best interests of the child in any action, including its enforcement of immigration laws. The United States has codified the standard in the TVPRA by requiring HHS to consider the unaccompanied child's best interests in placement decisions. The standard also is codified in every state through statutes which require "that the child's best interests be considered whenever specified types of decisions are made regarding a child's custody, placement, or other critical life issues."[63] CBP officials are the gatekeepers for children to access the asylum process, yet CBP is not required by statute to consider the child's best interests, such as children's physical and psychological well-being. Further, immigration judges and ICE attorneys are not required to consider whether their decision would place a child in danger. As a result, our immigration system has been forcing children back into harm's way. The current laws dealing with UACs were an effort to address the vexing

---

[62] Doctors Without Borders, *Report: Forced to Flee Central America's Northern Triangle: A Neglected Humanitarian Crisis* (May 11, 2017), www.doctorswithoutborders.org/article/report-forced-flee-central-americas-northern-triangle-neglected-humanitarian-crisis.

[63] Child Welfare Information Gateway, *Determining the Best Interests of the Child*, 1 (November 2012), www.childwelfare.gov/pubPDFs/best_interest.pdf.

reality that too many children deported by the US government have been killed on return to the countries they fled.[64]

Rather than rolling back on the minimum procedural protections in place, Congress should be improving and developing legal protections in compliance with the best interests of the child standard. Does Congress really believe that it is in our national security interests to rip apart families, detain children in inhumane conditions, and prohibit these children from even having their claims for protection heard? Not every child may have a viable claim under asylum or SIJS requirements to obtain legal status in the United States, but that does not justify infringing on their due process rights to have a fair shot at applying. Incorporating and implementing the best interests of the child standard into immigration laws and procedures would not take away decision makers' discretion to weigh the evidence and facts. Instead, it would ensure information regarding a child's safety is given proper weight and that each child is guaranteed protection against denial of life without due process of law. Congress has the power to improve the treatment and protections of children fleeing to our borders. Its failure thus far has exacerbated the problem, violating the United States' legal obligations to protect and prevent harm to children, and betraying our nation's fundamental values of liberty, equality, and justice.

The United States is more diverse than ever. Of course, increasing diversity is a trend that has been emblematic of the United States since the founding of the nation. But increased diversity of any significance in the first 150 years of the country was primarily European in nature, except of course for the millions of Africans who were transported to the nation as slaves. Thus, until Mexicans (in the 1950s) and Asian immigrants (after 1965) began arriving in significant numbers, the phrase "we are a nation of immigrants" and *e pluribus unum* (from many, one) captured the essence of a largely Eurocentric society.

The domination of the Eurocentric culture and race – in no small part the result of immigration policies – has resulted in a Eurocentric sense of who is an American in the minds of many. When Trump calls for more immigrants from Norway, instead of from El Salvador, Haiti, or Africa,[65] he exhibits that Eurocentrism. Many of that mindset have developed a sense of privilege to enforce their view of who is an American in vigilante, racist style. The de-Americanization of Americans of Muslim, Arab, and South Asian descent in the wake of September 11 is a manifestation of this sense of privilege and the perpetual foreigner image that Eurocentric vigilantes maintain of people of color in the United States – definitely blacks and those whom the vigilantes identify with immigrant groups. The privileged

---

[64] Despite raising fear of gang violence and death in his removal proceedings, Edgar Chocóy Guzman was killed by gangs just seventeen days after being deported to Guatemala. In 2014, up to ten Honduran children were killed after being deported to Honduras. *See* Center for Gender and Refugee Studies, *Childhood and Migration in Central and North America: Causes, Policies, Practices and Challenges* (February 2015).

[65] Watkins and Phillip, *Trump Decries Immigrants*.

perpetrators view themselves as "valid" members of the club of Americans, telling the victims that some aspect of their being – usually their skin color, accent, or garb – disqualifies them from membership.

Sadly, the de-Americanization process is capable of reinventing itself generation after generation. We have seen this exclusionary process aimed at those of African, Jewish, Asian, Mexican, Haitian, and other descent throughout the nation's history. Trump's "shithole" comment is clearly an attempt at de-Americanizing people from certain lands. De-Americanization is not simply xenophobia, because more than fear of foreigners is at work. This is a brand of nativism cloaked in a Eurocentric sense of America that combines hate and racial profiling. This is about "othering" these groups. Whenever we go through a period of de-Americanization like what is currently happening to South Asians, Arabs, Muslim Americans, black migrants, and Latinos – a whole new generation of Americans sees that exclusion and hate is acceptable; that the definition of who is an American can be narrow; that they too have license to profile. That license is issued when others around them engage in hate and the government chimes in with its own profiling. This is part of the sad process of implicit bias and institutionalized racism that haunts our country.

There are two Americas when it comes to race, ethnic background, and who is an American. One is an all-embracing America on the matter of who is an American. This vision recognizes that the United States is a land that includes immigrants, and that in spite of exclusionary policies aimed at different groups throughout its history, the country is comprised of members of all different shades and ethnic backgrounds. The other America is narrow in its view of who is an American. This second vision is Eurocentric, excluding those of African, Latin, and Asian descent, and as we have seen since 9/11, excluding those of Muslim and Arab background.

The nation's public relations position is that we are a proud nation of immigrants and multiculturally inclusive of all. Yes, we take steps in the direction of inclusiveness. But we take steps backwards in that regard as well. We learn and unlearn, and in the process, the bad behavior of vigilante racism is reinforced by the likes of Trump, that was rejected by Obama. In the process, we de-Americanize many communities of color, perpetuating their image as immigrant or partial Americans rather than full Americans, deserving of their place in our communities. Trump clearly is the new king of deportation.

Epilogue

Disrupting the Deportation Royalty

In this project, I have reviewed many of the enforcement tools used by Bill Clinton, George W. Bush, Barack Obama, and Donald Trump, plus others before them, and the unnecessary havoc they have wreaked on immigrant communities. However, there has been resistance to these policies by immigrants and their supporters who have attempted to disrupt the enforcement tools. Even today, immigrants and their supporters are attempting to raise awareness of better strategies to resolve whatever problems they perceive. Disruptive tactics by immigrants and their supporters actually helped to push the Obama administration into engaging in disruptive innovation of its own with respect to how to approach certain classes of removable immigrants.

Administrations and officials who engage in these enforcement approaches need to be held accountable to fair-minded, humanistic-thinking Americans. These actions have occurred on our watch, and we should not stand by idly. We should devise methods of holding officials accountable, perhaps by creating a public oversight group along the lines of citizen oversight panels of police departments that would focus on the anti-humanitarian effects of US immigration enforcement. I offer these highlights of resistance and disruption as examples we should keep in mind.

I.1. IMPACT LITIGATION

When enforcement of immigration laws results in outcomes that we regard as unfair, inappropriate, or unjust, immigrants and their allies rely on a range of strategies or tools to challenge the results or the processes that lead to those results. Conventionally, those strategies include impact litigation and legislative advocacy. Many examples of those strategies demonstrate disruption of immigration enforcement, or unreasonable immigration policies.

Impact litigation examples in the immigrant rights area abound. We have seen those efforts during the Trump administration already in challenging his Muslim bans. Another good example is the Ninth Circuit opinion in *Orantes-Hernandez* v. *Thornburgh* that unveiled immigration officials engaged in a strategy that foreclosed the opportunity to apply for asylum for Salvadorans during the 1980s.[1]

Generally, after aliens were apprehended, either border patrol agents or Immigration and Naturalization Services (INS) officers processed them.[2] INS processing of detained aliens consisted of an interrogation combined with the completion of various forms, including form I-213, Record of Deportable Alien, and the presentation of form I-274, Request for Voluntary Departure.[3] Although the arrested Salvadorans were eligible to apply for political asylum and to request a deportation hearing prior to their departure from the United States, the vast majority of Salvadorans apprehended signed voluntary departure agreements that commenced a summary removal process.[4] Once a person signed for voluntary departure in the course of INS processing, he or she was subject to removal from the United States as soon as transportation could be arranged.[5] A person given administrative voluntary departure in this manner never had a deportation hearing, the only forum before which the detained person could seek political asylum and mandatory withholding of deportation at the time.[6]

The *Orantes-Hernandez* court found that the widespread acceptance of voluntary departure was due, in large part, to the coercive effects of the practices and procedures employed by INS and the unfamiliarity of most Salvadorans with their rights under US immigration laws.[7] INS agents directed, intimidated, or coerced Salvadorans in custody, who had no expressed desire to return to El Salvador, to sign form I-274 for voluntary departure.[8] INS agents used a variety of techniques to procure voluntary departure, ranging from subtle persuasion to outright threats

[1] 919 F.2d 549, 559 (9th Cir. 1990) (explaining finding of facts which "revealed a pattern and practice of interference and coercion on the part of INS agents which prevented Salvadoran aliens who feared return to their country from exercising their right to apply for asylum").
[2] *See* ibid., at 560 (reviewing the record containing evidence of aliens apprehended by INS agents).
[3] *See* ibid., at 559 (discussing the impacts of the I-274 form including voluntary departure) and ibid., at 560 (describing how one alien was given a voluntary departure form and told to sign it).
[4] *See* ibid., at 559 ("Numerous class members testified of being forced or tricked into signing for voluntary departure.").
[5] *See* ibid. ("For example, Freddy Antonio Cartagena signed the voluntary departure form without being given a chance to read it and was just told to 'sign here.' Marta Ester Paniagua Vides was given a form. She asked the agents if the form was for voluntary departure and they assured her it was not. She signed the paper and it in fact turned out to be Form I–274A.").
[6] *See* ibid., at 554 ("There are disadvantages to voluntary departure as well. Aliens who voluntarily depart this country lose the right to apply for asylum before deportation proceedings are initiated. They also give up their right to a deportation hearing at which they may also apply for and have their asylum claim considered before an Immigration Judge.").
[7] *See* ibid., at 567–8 (affirming the decision of the district court).
[8] *See* ibid., at 559.

and misrepresentations.[9] Many Salvadorans were intimidated or coerced to accept voluntary departure even when they had unequivocally expressed a fear of returning to El Salvador.[10] Even when an individual refused to sign form I-274, "Waiver of Rights," INS officers felt that they could present the person with the voluntary departure form.[11]

The court also found that INS processing officers engaged in a pattern and practice of misrepresenting the meaning of political asylum and of giving improper and incomplete legal advice, which denied arrested Salvadorans meaningful understanding of the options presented and discouraged them from exercising available rights.[12] INS officers and agents routinely advised Salvadorans of the negative aspects of choosing a deportation hearing without informing them of the positive options that were available.[13] Without informing them that voluntary departure could be requested at a deportation hearing, INS officers advised detainees that if they did not sign for voluntary departure they could be formally deported from the United States, and that such a deportation would preclude their legal reentry without the permission of the Attorney General.[14]

INS officers and agents routinely told Salvadoran detainees that if they applied for asylum they would remain in detention for a long time, without mentioning the possibility of release on bond.[15] Similarly, without advising that an immigration judge could lower the bond amount and that there were bond agencies that could provide assistance, INS agents regularly told detainees that if they did not sign for voluntary departure they would remain detained until bond was posted.[16] Some agents told individuals the monetary bond amount they could expect or the bond amount given to other Salvadorans, without telling them that the bond amount ultimately depended upon the circumstances of the individual.[17]

INS officers commonly told detainees that if they applied for asylum, the application would be denied, or that Salvadorans did not get asylum.[18] INS officers and agents represented that Salvadorans ultimately would be deported regardless of the asylum application.[19] INS officers and agents misrepresented the eligibility for asylum by saying that it was only given to guerillas or to soldiers.[20] INS processing

---

[9] *See* ibid., at 559–60.
[10] *See* ibid.
[11] *See* ibid., at 559.
[12] *See* ibid., at 559–60.
[13] *See* ibid.
[14] *See* ibid., at 554 ("because an alien who leaves under a grant of voluntary departure, unlike a deported alien, does not need special permission to reenter the United States and does not face criminal penalties for failure to obtain that permission").
[15] Ibid., at 560.
[16] Ibid.
[17] Ibid.
[18] Ibid.
[19] Ibid.
[20] Ibid., at 562.

agents or officers further discouraged Salvadorans from applying for asylum by telling them that the information on the application would be sent to El Salvador.[21] INS processing officers also used the threat of transfer to remote locations as a means of discouraging detained Salvadorans from exercising their rights to a hearing and to pursuing asylum claims.[22]

Furthermore, INS agents often did not allow Salvadorans to consult with counsel prior to signing the voluntary departure forms, although they acknowledged that aliens had this right.[23] Even those Salvadorans fortunate enough to secure legal representation were often unable to avoid voluntary departure, as INS' practice was to refuse to recognize the authority of counsel until a formal notice of representation (Form G-28) was filed.[24] Due to the rapid processing of Salvadoran detainees, it was often physically impossible for counsel to locate their clients and file Form G-28 before the client was removed from the country.[25]

The *Orantes-Hernandez* court noted:

> The record before this Court establishes that INS engages in a pattern and practice of pressuring or intimidating Salvadorans who remain detained after the issuance of an OSC [Order to Show Cause] to request voluntary departure or voluntary deportation to El Salvador. There is substantial evidence of INS detention officers urging, cajoling, and using friendly persuasion to pressure Salvadorans to recant their requests for a hearing and to return voluntarily to El Salvador.
>
> That this conduct is officially condoned, even in the face of complaints, demonstrates that it is a de facto policy. The existence of a policy of making daily announcements about the availability of voluntary departure, coupled with the acknowledgement that the policy is designed to free-up scarce detention space, supports the conclusion that INS detention officers make a practice of pressuring detained Salvadorans to return to El Salvador. This conduct is not the result of isolated transgressions by a few overzealous officers, but, in fact, is a widespread and pervasive practice akin to a policy.
>
> This pattern of misconduct flows directly from the attitudes and misconceptions of INS officers and their superiors as to the merits of Salvadoran asylum claims and the motives of class members who flee El Salvador and enter this country.[26]

---

[21] Ibid., at 560, 562.
[22] Ibid., at 562.
[23] Ibid.
[24] Ibid., at 566.
[25] Ibid.
[26] *Orantes-Hernandez v. Meese*, 685 F.Supp. 1488, 1505 (C.D. Cal 1988), *aff'd sub nom. Orantes-Hernandez v. Thornburgh*, 919 F.2d 549 (9th Cir. 1990).

Thus, the district court order was affirmed:

1. [INS and border patrol agents] shall not employ threats, misrepresentation, subterfuge or other forms of coercion, or in any other way attempt to persuade or dissuade class members when informing them of the availability of voluntary departure pursuant to 8 U.S.C. §1252(b). The prohibited acts include, but are not limited to:

    a. Misrepresenting the meaning of political asylum and giving improper and incomplete legal advice to detained class members;

    b. Telling class members that if they apply for asylum they will remain in detention for a long period of time, without mentioning the possibility of release on bond or indicating that bond can be lowered by an immigration judge and that there are bond agencies which can provide assistance;

    c. Telling Salvadoran detainees the amount of bond given to other class members, without indicating that the bond amount ultimately depends upon the circumstances of the individual class member;

    d. Telling class members that their asylum applications will be denied, that Salvadorans do not get asylum, or that asylum is only available to guerillas or soldiers;

    e. Representing to class members that the information on the asylum application will be sent to El Salvador;

    f. Representing to class members that asylum applicants will never be able to return to El Salvador;

    g. Indicating that Salvadoran detainees will be transferred to remote locations if they do not elect voluntary departure;

    h. Advising Salvadorans of the negative aspects of choosing a deportation hearing without informing them of the positive options that are available;

    i. Refusing to allow class members to contact an attorney; and

    j. Making daily announcements at detention facilities of the availability of voluntary departure.[27]

The bias that INS officials and asylum corps officers exhibited toward both Guatemalan and Salvadoran asylum applicants was further exposed in *American Baptist Churches* v. *Thornburgh*.[28] As the *New York Times* reported on the case:

Such applications have long presented the US Government with an embarrassing choice. The United States supports the Governments of El Salvador and Guatemala, and at the same time it is asked by asylum applicants to find that they have a "well-founded fear of persecution" if they are returned home. Every approval of an application for political asylum thus amounts to an admission that the United States is aiding governments that violate the civil rights of their own citizens.

[27] Ibid., at 1511.
[28] 760 F.Supp. 796 (N.D. Cal. 1991).

Since 1980 the Government has denied 97 percent of applications for political asylum by El Salvadorans and 99 percent of those by Guatemalans. During the same time, applications for political asylum by Eastern Europeans, Nicaraguans, and residents of other countries have a high percentage of approval. For example, 76 percent of applications by residents of the Soviet Union were approved, as were 64 percent of those by residents of China.[29]

A settlement was reached requiring the INS to readjudicate the asylum claims of certain Salvadorans and Guatemalans who were present in the United States as of 1990, and who had sought immigration benefits.[30] The case, known as the "ABC litigation" began in 1985 as a nationwide class action on behalf of Salvadorans and Guatemalans.[31] The plaintiffs alleged that the INS and the Executive Office of Immigration Review were biased in their asylum adjudication process for those two nationalities.[32] Under the settlement, these Central Americans were eligible for new asylum interviews.[33]

In *Haitian Refugee Center* v. *Smith*,[34] the Fifth Circuit chastised the federal government for unfair processes that were imposed on Haitian asylum applicants.[35] In response to the repressive Duvalier regime that caused political and economic havoc in Haiti in the 1970s, many Haitians fled to the United States seeking refuge.[36] Large numbers sought asylum once they reached the shores of Florida.[37] A backlog developed, so INS officials implemented an accelerated program to deal with the situation.[38]

The program of accelerated processing to which the [Haitians were] subjected by the INS-termed the "Haitian Program" embodied the government's response to the tremendous backlog of Haitian deportation cases that had accumulated in the INS Miami district office by the summer of 1978. By June of that year between six and seven thousand unprocessed Haitian deportation cases were pending in the Miami office. These staggering numbers were not the result of a massive influx of Haitians to south Florida over a short period. Although significant numbers of Haitians had entered the United States from Haiti and the Bahamas in the spring of

---

[29] Katherine Bishop, U.S. *Adopts New Policy for Hearings on Political Asylum for Some Aliens*, New York Times (December 20, 1990), available at: www.nytimes.com/1990/12/20/us/us-adopts-new-policy-for-hearings-on-political-asylum-for-some-aliens.html.

[30] 760 F. Supp. at 810.

[31] *See ibid.*, at 799.

[32] *See ibid.*

[33] *See ibid.*

[34] 676 F.2d 1023 (5th Cir. 1982).

[35] Ibid., at 1031–2.

[36] Ibid., at 1042 ("It is beyond dispute that some Haitians will be subjected to the brutal treatment and bloody prisons of Francois Duvalier upon their deportation") (internal citations omitted).

[37] Ibid. at 1026 ("... filed a class action in federal district court on behalf of over 4,000 Haitians in the south Florida area who had sought political asylum in the United States.").

[38] Ibid., at 1029.

1978, the backlog was primarily attributable to a slow trickle of Haitians over a ten-year period and to the confessed inaction of the INS in dealing with these aliens ...

Many officials provided input in the planning process of the Haitian project. Assigned by [the Deputy Commissioner of the INS] with the task of assessing the Haitian situation in Miami, INS Regional Commissioner Armand J. Salturelli submitted the recommendation, among others, that processing could be expedited by ceasing the practice of suspending deportation hearings upon the making of an asylum claim. Salturelli acknowledged that this would contravene internal operations procedures, but suggested that those procedures should be cancelled or "at least be suspended insofar as Haitians are concerned." One July 1978 report from the Intelligence Division of INS to the Associate Director of Enforcement advised in absolute terms that the Haitians were 'economic' and not political refugees and, in belated recognition of the obvious, warned the Enforcement Division that favorable treatment of these Haitians would encourage further immigration. Associate Director of Enforcement, Charles Sava, later visited Miami to find space for holding an increased number of deportation hearings and to discuss with Miami personnel the processing of Haitians. Out of those discussions arose recommended deterrence measures, which Sava outlined in a letter to Deputy Commissioner Noto. These included "detention of arriving Haitians likely to abscond, blanket denials of work permits for Haitians, swift expulsion of Haitians from the United States, and enforcement actions against smugglers.

Planning of the Haitian program culminated in a memorandum sent on August 20, 1978 by Deputy Commissioner Noto to INS Commissioner Leonel J. Castillo. The memo explained the basic mechanics of the accelerated processing already being implemented in the Miami district office. Among the specifics set forth were the assignment of additional immigration judges to Miami, the instructions to immigration judges to effect a three-fold increase in productivity, and orders for the blanket issuance of show cause orders in all pending Haitian deportation cases ...

In accordance with the goal of high productivity demanded of the Miami office, [Acting District Director] Gullage issued a memorandum to all personnel in the office, stating 'processing of these cases cannot be delayed in any manner or in any way. All supervisory personnel are hereby ordered to take whatever action they deem necessary to keep these cases moving through the system.' The Haitian cases were processed at an unprecedented rate." Prior to the Haitian program only between one and ten deportation hearings were conducted each day. During the program, immigration judges held fifty-five hearings per day, or approximately eighteen per judge; at the program's peak the schedule of deportation hearings increased to as many as eighty per day.

At the show cause or deportation hearing, the immigration judges refused to suspend the hearing when an asylum claim was advanced, requiring the Haitians instead to respond to the pleadings in the show cause order and proceed to a finding of deportability. The order entered by the judge allowed the Haitian ten days for filing an asylum claim with the district director, then ten days to request withholding of deportation from the immigration judge if the asylum deadline was not met. Failure to seek withholding in a timely manner effected automatic entry of a deportation order.

Deportation hearings were not the only matter handled during the Haitian program. Asylum interviews also were scheduled at the rate of forty per day. Immigration officers who formerly had worked at the airport were enlisted as hearing officers for these interviews. Prior to the program such interviews had lasted an hour and a half; during the program the officer devoted approximately one-half hour to each Haitian. In light of the time-consuming process of communication through interpreters, the court concluded that only fifteen minutes of substantive dialogue took place. Consistent with the result-oriented program designed to achieve numerical goals in processing, the Travel Control section in the Miami office recorded the daily totals of asylum applications processed. The tally sheet contained space only for the total number of denials; there was no column for recording grants of asylum.

Hearings on requests for withholding deportation also were being conducted simultaneously with asylum and deportation hearings, at several different locations. It was not unusual for an attorney representing Haitians to have three hearings at the same hour in different buildings; this kind of scheduling conflict was a daily occurrence for attorneys throughout the Haitian program. The INS was fully aware that only approximately twelve attorneys were available to represent the thousands of Haitians being processed, and that scheduling made it impossible for counsel to attend the hearings. It anticipated the scheduling conflicts that in fact occurred. Nevertheless the INS decided that resolving the conflicts was 'too cumbersome for us to handle' and adopted the attitude that everything would simply work out.

Under these circumstances, the court concluded that the INS had knowingly made it impossible for Haitians and their attorneys to prepare and file asylum applications in a timely manner. The court found that adequate preparation of an asylum application required between ten and forty hours of an attorney's time. The court further estimated that if each of the attorneys available to represent the Haitians "did nothing during a 40-hour week except prepare [asylum applications], they would have been able to devote only about 2 hours to each client."

The results of the accelerated program adopted by INS are revealing. None of the over 4,000 Haitians processed during this program were granted asylum.[39]

In the end, the federal court of appeals struck down the accelerated program as a violation of procedural due process.[40] The government was forced to submit a procedurally fair plan for the orderly reprocessing of the asylum applications of the Haitian applicants who had not been deported.[41]

As noted in Chapter 3, more recently, litigation challenging the conditions at the Artesia facility contributed to its closure. Of course, pro bono work at the Artesia

[39] Ibid., at 1029–32.
[40] Ibid., at 1040.
[41] Ibid., at 1041.

facility by volunteer attorneys contributed pressure to close the facility as well.[42] They filed affidavits in support of the lawsuit that highlighted both the harsh conditions as well as the fact that through competent representation, the majority of unaccompanied children (UACs) are eligible for relief.[43] Ongoing litigation in the *Flores* case and new litigation challenging Trump's family separation policy also have significantly disrupted unfair enforcement efforts.

I.2. NON-LITIGATION DISRUPTIONS

I.2.1. *Legal Services and Pro Bono Advocates*

The critical role that legal services programs play in representing immigrants in day-to-day cases is well known. A program such as Dolores Street Community Services in San Francisco takes on difficult asylum cases and criminal immigration deportation defense matters.[44] The Florence Immigrant and Refugee Rights Project provides much-needed representation to thousands of immigrants each year held in detention centers in a rural part of Arizona.[45] The Immigration Project in Chicago provides a range of visa and deportation defense services to immigrants from around the world.[46] The same is true for well-established organizations across the country. And their services make a huge difference, serving as a constant disruption to the over-zealous Immigration and Customs Enforcement (ICE) machine.[47]

This important legal services disruption in the immigration area is also epitomized by tremendous pro bono efforts by the private bar. Consider one pro bono effort responding to the unaccompanied alien children border crisis.

For its feature article "Adult Asylum-Seekers Need Lawyers, Too," *The National Law Journal* profiled the work of Akin Gump first-year associate Lauren Connell, whom the firm seconded to its San Antonio office to work full time with undocumented Central American women and children seeking asylum and being held at the Department of Homeland Security's Karnes City, Texas, detention center.

In late August [2014, the national law firm,] Akin Gump[,] formed the Karnes City Immigrant Family Pro Bono Project with representatives from the University

---

[42] Esther Yu-Hsi Lee, *Lawyers Say Detention Center Designed to Quash Legitimate Asylum Claims*, Think Progress (August 27, 2014, 9:00 AM), available at: http://thinkprogress.org/immigration/2014/08/27/3475472/lawsuit-artesia-detention-center/.

[43] Ibid.

[44] *See Dolores Street Community Services*, available at: www.dscs.org/.

[45] *See The Florence Immigrant and Refugee Rights Project*, available at: www.firrp.org/.

[46] *See The Immigration Project*, available at: www.immigrationproject.org/.

[47] "A study by Syracuse University's Transactional Records Access Clearinghouse Immigration Project found that roughly 90 percent of children facing deportation proceedings without a lawyer got deported, compared with about 50 percent for those who had legal representation." Roque Planas, *New York To Pay for Legal Aid For Kids Facing Deportation*, Huffington Post (September 23, 2014, 6:02 PM), available at: www.huffingtonpost.com/2014/09/23/new-york-to-pay-for-lawye_n_5870492.html.

of Texas Law School Immigration Clinic, the Tahirih Justice Center in Houston, the American Immigration Lawyers Association in Austin and Human Rights First in Houston.[48]

The project was a critical response to the Obama administration's incarceration of UAC and children coming with mothers from Central America seeking asylum and being held at the Department of Homeland Security's Karnes City, Texas, detention center.[49] "[T]he Karnes City Residential Center ... holds 170 to 200 female detainees in various early stages of the asylum process who face deportation ... [M]ore than [twenty] Akin Gump attorneys coordinate legal assistance for these women and their children," and the firm has trained dozens of other pro bono attorneys who travel to Karnes from across the country.[50]

> Steven Schulman, Akin Gump's pro bono partner, is on the project's advisory committee. [He was struck by how] many of the women whom the firm is assisting are victims of abuse and sexual assault seeking asylum as a way to escape from the violence they face in their home countries ... [T]he brevity of the asylum screening interview, done via a translator, means that many women can't express their fears well enough by interview's end, saying, "That's why we were called in, [to] see whether we could get lawyers down there to throw sand into the gears. We weren't trying to break a system, but we were trying to slow it down."[51]

I.2.2. *Immigrant Disruptions*

During his campaign for the presidency in 2008, Barack Obama pledged to push for comprehensive immigration reform within the first year of his administration.[52] However, as the president spent most of his first year dealing with the financial crisis, his primary legislative efforts were focused on health-care reform, and the Affordable Care Act was not signed until March 23, 2010.[53] At that point, the president and

[48] *NLJ Features Akin Gump Lawyers, Pro Bono Program for Asylum Seekers in Texas*, Akin Gump (October 13, 2014), available at: www.akingump.com/en/news-publications/nlj-features-akin-gump-lawyers-pro-bono-program-for-asylum.html.

[49] *See* ibid.

[50] Ibid.

[51] Ibid.

[52] Lucia Graves and Elise Foley, *Immigration Advocates Push Obama To Make Good On Campaign Promises*, Huffington Post (March 31, 2011, 5:26 PM), available at: www.huffingtonpost.com/2011/03/31/immigration-obama-campaign-promises_n_843285.html.

[53] Patient Protection and Affordable Care Act of 2010, 42 U.S.C.A. § 18001 (Supp. 2014).

democratic congressional leaders, who controlled both houses at the time tried unsuccessfully to pass a comprehensive immigration bill.[54]

With the chance of comprehensive reform fading in 2010, DREAMers urged congressional leaders at the very least to pass the DREAM Act.[55] The House of Representatives passed the bill on December 8, 2010 by a vote of 216 to 198.[56] However, a few days later, the Senate only came up with fifty-five votes to bypass a filibuster of the DREAM Act – five votes short of the sixty needed to bring the legislation to an actual up or down vote.[57]

Disappointed, DREAMers and immigrant rights advocates continued their well-documented campaign of protests. For example, on June 27, 2011, six DREAMers were arrested in Atlanta, GA, for blocking an intersection in front of the state capitol.[58] Nataly Ibarra, a sixteen-year-old high school student, stated: "It's time to stand up and let the world know that we need to fight for what we believe in."[59] A month later, about twenty DREAMers interrupted a speech by President Obama at a conference in Washington, D.C. One DREAMer from Florida, Felipe Matos, explained: "We stood up while President Obama gave another of his predictable speeches on immigration because we are outraged at his trying to promote his election among Latinos while continuing to deport us at a time when there is no legislative solution to the immigration crisis."

The protestors wore shirts that read: "Obama Deports DREAMers."[60] During the 2012 presidential campaign, two dozen DREAMers staged a sit-in at Obama campaign headquarters in Denver in early June.[61] They demanded an executive order ending the deportation of DREAMers.[62] That spring, their presence was so strong, that even Republican Senator Marco Rubio requested a meeting with Gaby

54 Rachel Weiner, *How Immigration Reform Failed, Over and Over*, Washington Post (January 30, 2013), available at: www.washingtonpost.com/blogs/the-fix/wp/2013/01/30/how-immigration-reform-failed-over-and-over/.

55 The DREAM Act (short for Development, Relief and Education for Alien Minors Act), is legislation for introduced first introduced in Congress in 2001 that would have granted legal status to certain undocumented immigrants who were brought to the United States as children and went to school here. The DREAM Act has been reintroduced many times, but has never passed both houses of Congress.

56 Elise Foley, *DREAM Act Passes The House*, Huffington Post (December 8, 2010, 10:35 PM), available at: www.huffingtonpost.com/2010/12/08/dream-act-passes-house_n_794181.html.

57 Elise Foley, *DREAM Act Vote Fails In Senate*, Huffington Post (December 18, 2010, 11:31 AM), available at: www.huffingtonpost.com/2010/12/18/dream-act-vote-senate_n_798631.html.

58 Kate Brumback, *Georgia Immigration Law: 6 Illegal Immigrants Arrested During Protest*, Huffington Post (June 28, 2011, 11:54 PM), available at: www.huffingtonpost.com/2011/06/28/georgia-immigration-law-illegal-immigrants-arrested_n_886622.html.

59 Ibid.

60 Ibid.

61 John Ingold, *Immigration Activists Stage Sit-in at Denver Obama Office*, Denver Post (June 5, 2012, 9:47 PM), available at: www.denverpost.com/ci_20791243/immigration-activists-stage-sit-at-denver-obama-office.

62 Ibid.

Pacheco, a DREAM leader, to discuss how to get the DREAM Act passed.[63] Rubio considered introducing his own version of the DREAM Act.[64]

The DREAMer disruption yielded results. On June 15, 2012, Obama announced that he would exercise prosecutorial discretion and not deport DREAMers who had entered the United States prior to the age of sixteen.[65] They also would be granted work permits for two years with an opportunity to renew.[66] This was an amazing discretionary act that could benefit 800,000 individuals.[67]

While Obama's action on behalf of DREAMers was consistent with the immigration agency's traditional prosecutorial discretion to grant deferred action to sympathetic, albeit, deportable immigrants,[68] the scope was unprecedented. Republican critics argued that he went beyond the scope of his authority.[69] And the president himself, only a year earlier, denied that he could "just suspend deportations [of DREAMers] through executive order."[70]

As 2010 drew to a close and the DREAM Act failed in the Senate, prospects for comprehensive immigration reform further dimmed as Republicans took control

[63] Julianne Hing, *Marco Rubio Meets with Latino Dems, DREAMers on Alternative Youth Immigration Bill*, Colorlines (April 26, 2012, 2:05 PM), available at: http://colorlines.com/archives/2012/04/marco_rubio_meets_with_latino_dems_dreamers_on_alternative_youth_immigration_bill.html.

[64] Lauren Fox, *Rubio's DREAM Act Gamble; Just in Time for The 2012 Election*, U.S. News (June 12, 2012, 5:31 PM), available at: www.usnews.com/news/articles/2012/06/12/rubios-dream-act-gamble-just-in-time-for-the-2012-election.

[65] Julia Preston and John H. Chushman Jr., *Obama to Permit Young Migrants to Remain in U.S.*, New York Times (June 15, 2012), available at: www.nytimes.com/2012/06/16/us/us-to-stop-deporting-some-illegal-immigrants.html?pagewanted=all. A year earlier, director of ICE John Morton issued a prosecutorial discretion memo that in part was intended to ease up on the deportation of DREAMers. Memorandum from John Morton, Dir., ICE, on Prosecutorial Discretion: Certain Victims, Witnesses and Plaintiffs, to All Field Office Dirs., All Special Agents in Charge, and All Chief Counsel (June 17, 2011), available at: www.ice.gov/doclib/secure-communities/pdf/domestic-violence.pdf. In fact, prosecutorial discretion as outlined by the Morton memo apparently was used on occasion to prevent the deportation of DREAMers. *See, e.g.*, Jessica Coscia, *Arrested DREAMers Won't Be Deported, Authorities Say*, Fox News Latino (September 8, 2011), available at: http://latino.foxnews.com/latino/politics/2011/09/08/dreamers-released-after-arrest-at-immigration-protest-officials-say-wont-face/. But the inconsistent application of the Morton memo across the country prompted the president to be more specific about protecting DREAMers from deportation in the DACA order to ICE employees.

[66] Preston and Chushman, *Obama to Permit Young Migrants*.

[67] Ibid.

[68] *See* Leon Wildes, *The Nonpriority Program of the Immigration and Naturalization Service Goes Public: The Litigative Use of the Freedom of Information Act*, 14 San Diego L. Rev. 42, 44, 55–8 (1976); Bill Ong Hing, *Defining America Through Immigration Policy* 226–8 (2004). *See generally*, Shoba Sivaprasad Wadhia, *The Role of Prosecutorial Discretion in Immigration Law*, 9 CONN. PUB. INT. L.J. 243 (2010); Michael A. Olivas, *Dreams Deferred: Deferred Action, Prosecutorial Discretion, and the Vexing Case(s) of DREAM Act Students*, 21 WM. & MARY BILL OF RTS. J. 463 (2012).

[69] Preston and Chushman, *Obama to Permit Young Migrants*.

[70] Glenn Kessler, *Obama's Royal Flip-Flop on Using Executive Action on Illegal Immigration*, Washington Post (November 18, 2014), available at: www.washingtonpost.com/blogs/fact-checker/wp/2014/11/18/obamas-flip-flop-on-using-executive-action-on-illegal-immigration/.

of the House of Representatives.[71] Serious bipartisan immigration legislation was not considered until after the 2012 presidential elections. With the reelection of Obama, many in the Republican Party sensed that if they were ever to retake the White House, Latino votes would be necessary, and passing comprehensive immigration reform was a prerequisite.[72]

With much fanfare and relative swiftness, on June 27, 2013, the Senate passed a comprehensive bill that was hammered out by four Democrats and four Republicans.[73] The bill was attacked by the right as providing amnesty for lawbreakers and by the left for being too strict on enforcement and providing an unreasonably long path to citizenship.[74] But the Republican-controlled House never permitted an up or down vote on the Senate bill, casting aside any concern over appeasing Latino voters.[75] Thus, efforts at comprehensive immigration reform failed again in 2013 and 2014, as it had in 2010.

While congressional efforts over immigration reform ebbed and flowed in 2013 and 2014, the ICE machine did not ease up. Although the Deferred Action for Childhood Arrivals (DACA) program for DREAMers was in full swing and about 800,000 DREAMers benefited, Obama's ICE deportations continued at record pace.[76] Families continued to be separated as immigrant workers and parents of citizens and DACA recipients were removed.[77] Enforcement was so intense, that Obama was dubbed the "deporter-in-chief" by immigrants, their allies, and even the news media.[78] The image has been exacerbated by the fact that Congress inserted into Homeland Security's 2009 spending bill a requirement that ICE keep a

---

[71] Devin Dwyer, *Republicans Win Control of House with Historic Gains*, ABC News (November 2, 2010), available at: http://abcnews.go.com/Politics/republicans-win-control-house-abc-news-projects-vote-2010-election-results/story?id=12035796.

[72] Julia Preston, *Latino Groups Warn Congress to Fix Immigration, or Else*, New York Times (Dec. 12, 2012, 4:12 PM), available at: http://thecaucus.blogs.nytimes.com/2012/12/12/latino-groups-warn-congress-to-fix-immigration-or-else/.

[73] Alan Silverleib, *Senate Passes Sweeping Immigration Bill*, CNN (June 28, 2013, 6:45 AM), available at: www.cnn.com/2013/06/27/politics/immigration/.

[74] Ibid.

[75] Stoyan Zaimov, *Obama: I Will Fight for Immigration Reform Alone Since House Republicans Refuse to Vote*, CHRISTIAN POST (July 1, 2014, 9:17 AM), available at: www.christianpost.com/news/obama-i-will-fight-for-immigration-reform-alone-since-house-republicans-refuse-to-vote-122524/.

[76] William Selway and Newkirk, *Congress's Illegal-Immigration Detention Quota Costs $2 Billion a Year*, Bloomberg Businessweek (Sept.26, 2013), available at: www.bloomberg.com/bw/articles/2013-09-26/congresss-illegal-immigration-detention-quota-costs-2-billion-a-year.

[77] Michael Alison Chandler, *Deportations of Parents Can Cast the Lives of U.S.-Citizen Kids into Turmoil*, Washington Post (December 29, 2013), available at: www.washingtonpost.com/local/education/deportations-of-parents-can-cast-the-lives-of-us-citizen-kids-into-turmoil/2013/12/29/abdf23aa-6b4c-11e3-b405-7e360f7e9fd2_story.html; Griselda Nevarez, *Dreamers Question How Many Parents of Dreamers Have Been Deported*, VOXXI (December 20, 2012), available at: http://voxxi.com/2012/12/20/dreamers-parents-of-dreamers-deported/.

[78] Rebecca Kaplan, *Obama is "Deporter-in-Chief," Says Prominent Latino Group*, CBS News (March 4, 2014, 12:47 PM), available at: www.cbsnews.com/news/obama-is-deporter-in-chief-says-prominent-latino-group/.

minimum of 33,400 undocumented immigrants locked up at all times (rounded up to 34,000 in 2011).[79] Private prison companies make close to $500 million each year for this ICE "bed mandate."[80]

Thus, in spite of the implementation of DACA for DREAMers, the president came under fierce criticism for record deportations. Congressman Luis Gutierrez and the University of Arizona estimated that as many as 90,000–100,000 undocumented parents were separated from their US citizen children each year.[81] Immigrant rights advocates argued that the Obama administration is only "paying lip service to a different strategy" and that the detention of criminal and noncriminal immigrants under the Bush and Obama administrations are essentially the same.[82]

With no realistic hope for comprehensive immigration legislation, critics of the continuing deportations demanded that the president act administratively to defer the deportation of anyone who would have been granted protection under the Senate bill that had been passed in 2013.[83] In one well-publicized exchange, DACA recipient Ju Hong interrupted the president's speech, exclaiming: "[O]ur families are separated ... Mr. President, please use your executive order to halt deportations for all 11.5 [million] undocumented immigrants in this country right now."[84] The president responded: "[I]f in fact I could solve all these problems without passing laws in Congress, then I would do so. But we're also a nation of laws. That's part of our tradition. And so, the easy way out is to try to yell and pretend like I can do something by violating our laws."[85]

In spite of the president's remarks suggesting that he could not act administratively – just as he had previously denied that he could act specifically on protecting DREAMers,[86] on November 20, 2014, the president took executive action to block the deportation of four to five million more undocumented immigrants, primarily the parents of US citizen children or lawful permanent resident children.[87]

---

[79] Selway and Newkirk, *Congress's Illegal-Immigration Detention.*

[80] Ibid.

[81] Victor Medina, *Aggressive Deportation Tactics Continue to Separate American Families,* Examiner. com (June 3, 2013, 2:04 PM), available at: www.examiner.com/article/aggressive-deportation-tactics-continue-to-separate-american-families; *see also* A. J. Vicens, *The Obama Administration's 2 Million Deportations, Explained,* Mother Jones (April 4, 2014, 6:00 AM), available at: www.motherjones. com/politics/2014/04/obama-administration-record-deportations.

[82] Alfonso Chardy, *Noncriminal, Undocumented Immigrants Aren't Being Left Alone, Activists Complain,* Miami Herald (June 21, 2010), available at: http://articles.sun-sentinel.com/2010-06-21/news/fl-detained-immigrants-enforcement-20100621_1_criminal-deportations-immigrants-in-south-florida-homeland-security.

[83] *See Plea to End Deportations Heard Nationwide as Activist Interrupts Obama Speech on Immigration,* Democracy Now! (November 27, 2013), available at: www.democracynow.org/2013/11/27/my_family_has_been_separated_for (documenting a transcript of the speech).

[84] Ibid.

[85] Ibid.

[86] *See* Wildes, The Nonpriority Program of the Immigration.

[87] Elise Foley, *Obama Moves to Protect Millions From Deportation,* Huffington Post (November 20, 2014, 5:59 PM), available at: www.huffingtonpost.com/2014/11/20/obama-immigration-plan_n_6178774.html.

His announcement even included the intent to end the Secure Communities pro-gram.[88] This was another bold action by the president of unprecedented scope – even broader than the action on behalf of DREAMers. On cue, Republicans claimed that the president acted unconstitutionally,[89] and legal challenges were filed.[90] And the immigrant rights community complained that parents of DREAMers were not included in the order.[91] In the meantime, the White House and community-based organizations were preparing for the implementation of the new program.[92]

I.2.3. *Executive Disruption*

I have been intrigued by the use of the term "disruptive" in the business pages as of late. A disruptive technology is one that displaces an established technology and shakes up the industry or is a ground-breaking product that creates a completely new industry. For example, an October 2014 article in Forbes, *Ten Companies That Are Disrupting Their Industries Through Technology*, noted:

> Looking for a competitive advantage? Try crushing the competition by becoming a leader in your category. How can you do that? By *changing the rules of the game*. By *reinventing the way business is done* in your industry. And by using technology to scale quickly, forcing your competition to play catch-up.
>
> Following are ten companies that have done all of the above. Can you find in their stories best practices that will help you disrupt your industry and become a market leader?[93]

Thus, a disruptive innovation is one that helps create a new market and value net-work, and eventually disrupts an existing market and value network (over a few years

[88] *Obama Was Wise to End Secure Communities Program*, SFGate (November 28, 2014, 3:00 PM), available at: www.sfgate.com/opinion/editorials/article/Obama-was-wise-to-end-Secure-Communities-program-5923254.php.

[89] Julia Preston, *House Republicans and White House Clash on Obama Immigration Plan*, New York Times (December 2, 2014), available at: www.nytimes.com/2014/12/03/us/politics/jeh-johnson-testifies-before-house-homeland-security-committee.html?_r=0.

[90] David Montgomery and Julia Preston, *17 States Suing on Immigration*, New York Times (December 3, 2014), available at: www.nytimes.com/2014/12/04/us/executive-action-on-immigration-prompts-texas-to-sue.html.

[91] Amanda Sakuma, *Obama Explains why DREAMers' Parents Were Left Out of Exec Action*, MSNBC (December 9, 2014, 6:57 PM), available at: www.msnbc.com/jose-diaz-balart/obama-explains-why-dreamers-parents-were-left-out-exec-action.

[92] Winnie Hu, *New York Immigration Groups Prepare to Meet Demands of New Policy*, New York Times (November 28, 2014), available at: www.nytimes.com/2014/11/29/nyregion/new-york-agencies-gear-up-to-meet-demands-of-new-immigration-policy.html.

[93] Larry Myler, *Ten Companies That Are Disrupting Their Industries Through Technology*, Forbes (October 3, 2014, 4:40 PM) (emphasis added), available at: www.forbes.com/sites/larrymyler/2014/10/03/ten-companies-that-are-disrupting-their-industries-through-technology/.

or decades), displacing an earlier technology.[94] The term is used in business and technology literature to describe innovations that improve a product or service in ways that the market does not expect, typically first by designing for a different set of consumers in a new market and later by lowering prices in the existing market.[95] The term "disruptive technology" has been widely used as a synonym of "disruptive innovation," but the latter is now preferred, because market disruption has been found to be a function usually not of technology itself, but rather of its changing application.[96]

Thus, the protests of immigrants, such as DREAMers, and their supporters disrupting and challenging the immigration enforcement regime are important. Their actions – conventional in the sense that sit-ins, protests, and media campaigns are part of the American call for social change – led to changes in immigration enforcement, but are not themselves the disruptive innovation in immigration enforcement. But the results of these actions led to disruptive innovation in immigration enforcement, namely, Obama's executive actions which led to the disruption of the conventional rules of enforcement, thereby forcing ICE officers to defer action against large classes of removable individuals for policy reasons. In other words, the conventional enforcement lens of whether or not the person is removable was forced to give way to a more nuanced lens of giving deference to removable individuals who met certain criteria. That was disruptive innovation that disrupted the way we looked at enforcement – internally and externally.

I.2.4. *Human Rights Disruption*

Viewing immigration enforcement through a comparative lens reveals that disruptive innovation of immigration enforcement already has occurred in the European Union (EU). For example, by adopting a Human Rights Convention with strong commitments to maintaining family ties, the idea of simply deporting someone who is undocumented or who has committed a crime has been disrupted; much more than improper papers or a criminal conviction must be considered before a person is deported. In the EU, someone facing deportation essentially can argue that the punishment of deportation must fit the crime and the effect of deportation on the person and his or her family must be given great weight.[97]

[94] *Disruptive Innovation*, Innovation Zen, available at: http://innovationzen.com/blog/2006/10/04/disruptive-innovation/ (last accessed April 7, 2015).

[95] *Disruptive Innovation*, Clayton Christensen, available at: www.claytonchristensen.com/key-concepts/ (last accessed April 7, 2015).

[96] Ibid.; *see also Disruptive Technology*, WhatIs.com, available at: http://whatis.techtarget.com/definition/disruptive-technology (last accessed April 7, 2015).

[97] *See, e.g., Nasri v. France*, 21 Eur. Ct. H.R. 458 (1996); *AR (Pakistan) v. Secretary of State for the Home Department*, [2010] EWCA (Civ) 816, 2010 WL 2754134 (Eng.).

The idea that the punishment must fit the crime often is stated in legal terms as lacking in "proportionality," related to notions of due process or the prohibition against cruel and unusual punishment when the punishment is too severe.[98] In the deportation context, a strong case has been made that the sanction of removal may very well be impermissibly disproportional to the criminal behavior that makes a person deportable.[99] For example, Professor Angela Banks has reasoned that since deportation can be punitive:

> The [Supreme] Court's conclusion that the Due Process Clause prohibits punishment that is "greater than reasonably necessary to punish and deter" is an important development for deportation. It opens the door for new conversations about the scope of the state's power to deport noncitizens. This jurisprudence suggests that deportation decisions, like punitive damage awards, must be proportional and that excessive or disproportionate deportation orders exceed the authority of the state to regulate immigration.[100]

The use of a proportionality lens in assessing the propriety of deportation is common in European tribunals. For example, in *Nasri v. France*,[101] the European Court of Human Rights blocked the deportation of a thirty-five-year-old Algerian national who had several convictions – including theft, assault, and participation in a gang rape:

> [R]emoving the applicant from his family and sending him to a country with which he has no ties would expose him to suffering of such gravity that to do so might be regarded as inhuman treatment. In a democratic society which adheres to the principle of respect for the dignity of the human person, a measure of such severity *cannot be proportionate* to the legitimate aim of maintaining public order.[102]

The European Commission of Human Rights agreed to review Nasri's case on proportionality grounds and considered several psychological evaluations, the possibility that he would be tortured back in Algeria, and the fact that his "family relationships would be made impossible" if he were deported. After considering these factors, the commission concluded that Nasri's deportation was disproportionate and could not be justified.[103]

---

[98] Angela M. Banks, *Problems, Possibilities and Pragmatic Solutions: Proportional Deportation*, 55 Wayne L. Rev. 1651, 1667–8, 1671 (2009); Michael J. Wishnie, *Proportionality: The Struggle for Balance in U.S. Immigration Policy*, 72 U. Pitt. L. Rev. 431, 447 (2011).

[99] *See* Banks, Problems, Possibilities and Pragmatic Solutions, at 1666–71.

[100] Ibid., at 1669. *See also* Wishnie, Proportionality: The Struggle for Balance, at 457 (arguing that the additional punishments of deportation and exile for lawful permanent residents convicted of aggravated felonies, "may contravene the due process requirement of proportionality.").

[101] *Nasri v. France*, 21 Eur. Ct. H.R. 458 (1996).

[102] Ibid., at 470. (emphasis added).

[103] Ibid., at 466–70.

In *AR (Pakistan)* v. *Secretary of State for the Home Department*,[104] the deportation of an asylum applicant who had been granted indefinite permission to remain in the United Kingdom was upheld, but not until the applicant had been given two warnings following several criminal convictions and unsuccessful participation in drug rehabilitation programs.[105] The question in the words of the Court of Appeal in the United Kingdom in these cases is *"whether deportation is proportionate*, giving due weight to the public interest and to the right to family life."[106] And the "task of deciding whether deportation is or is not proportionate typically involves weighing up conflicting factors."[107]

In deciding that the deportation was not disproportionate, the Court of Appeal considered the criminal record and the warnings that had been issued. But the court also paid close attention to the fact that the applicant had children. The applicant and his wife had divorced, and their three children lived with their maternal grandparents.[108] As in the *Nasri* case, the court was well aware of the fundamental right to family life protected by Article 8 of the European Convention on Human Rights.[109] However, the court was influenced by the fact that the applicant's earlier close contact with his children was no longer the pattern – in part because of his intermittent time in prison – and therefore was insufficient "to outweigh the public interest in his deportation."[110]

In a much broader way, the EU has disrupted the notion of immigration enforcement by the elimination of borders between member states. Under the current structure of the EU, workers who are citizens of different states may freely migrate to other states.[111] Unlike the North American Free Trade Agreement, which provides for the free flow of products – but not workers – between Mexico, Canada, and the United States, the EU includes workers as well as trade goods between its members. That is a wholly disruptive way of looking at immigration – at least between member nations.

1.2.5. *Public Oversight Disruption*

The examples of abusive or morally questionable ICE enforcement strategies outlined in this book demand oversight of the agency through an ethical lens – oversight grounded in a sense of morality, humanistic values, and human rights. While congressional committees may be charged with oversight of DHS, an

[104] [2010] EWCA (Civ) 816, 2010 WL 2754134 (Eng.).
[105] Ibid.
[106] Ibid., at [19] (emphasis added).
[107] Ibid., at [24].
[108] Ibid., at 3.
[109] Ibid., at 7.
[110] Ibid., at 23.
[111] *See* Bill Ong Hing, *NAFTA, Globalization, and Mexican Migrants*, 5 J. L. Econ. & Pol'y 87, 136–7 (2009).

independent public entity is needed that reviews and reports on the enforcement actions of ICE so that the agency's actions are regularly in plain view. The fact of congressional oversight or even an agency internal affairs department clearly is insufficient, given the ICE enforcement efforts that go unchecked except for successful litigation challenges in the most outrageous cases.

The history of civilian review boards of police departments is relevant to understanding why a similar public body is needed to regularly report on questionable immigration enforcement. Civilian review boards are composed of citizen representatives charged with the investigation of complaints by members of the public concerning police misconduct.[112] The general goal of these boards is to enhance police accountability by ensuring that officers treat individuals without bias, use appropriate levels of force, operate free of corruption, and that procedures exist for the fair receipt and investigation of complaints against the police.[113] Citizen involvement in the oversight of police is viewed as a valuable way to prevent misconduct.

The first interest in creating enforceable standards for police behavior emerged in the 1920s.[114] This was an era focused on the police "professional" including the "creation of written policies on the use of force, arrest procedures ... and the advent of Internal Affairs Departments (IADs)."[115] Police reform during this time relied primarily on a strong police chief executive to implement change in a top-down method.[116] One famous example of such a police chief was August Vollmer in Berkeley, CA.[117] His reforms in the police department were heralded as raising personnel standards and modernizing management.[118] However, the problem with reform implemented by police chiefs is that it was a temporary solution; eventually that chief would leave the department and take with them the tools of change.[119] Consequently, another method of regulating police behavior was needed.

In the 1920s and 1930s ideas begin to emerge about how police behavior could be regulated outside of the police department. Volunteer attorneys in the Los Angeles area during the 1920s proposed the idea of having private citizens evaluate complaints against police officers.[120] Later, in 1931 the Wickersham Commission

---

[112] William M. Wells and Joseph A. Schafer, *Civilian Complaint Review Boards, in Encyclopedia of Law Enforcement* 65, 65–68 (Larry E. Sullivan et al., eds., 2004).

[113] Ibid.

[114] Ibid.

[115] John Chasnoff, *A Review of Civilian Review*, Synthesis/Regeneration (2006), available at: www.greens .org/s-r/39/39-10.html.

[116] *See* Samuel Walker, *Institutionalizing Police Accountability Reforms: The Problem of Making Police Reforms Endure*, 32 St. Louis U. Pub. L. Rev. 57, 65 (2012).

[117] Ibid.

[118] Ibid.

[119] Ibid., at 65–6.

[120] Frank V. Ferdik et al., *Citizen Oversight in The United States and Canada: An Overview*, 14 Police Practice and Research 104, 105 (2013).

established by President Herbert Hoover recommended the creation of "some disin-
terested agency" in each city to assist people with their complaints.[121]

By the late 1940s, race riots and civil unrest spurred activists to push for civilian review boards.[122] Continuing racial tensions in cities like New York, Detroit,
Washington, D.C., and Los Angeles finally spearheaded the creation of the first
citizen oversight agency in the United States. Formally instituted in 1948, the citizen review board for the Metropolitan Police in the District of Columbia[123] was
comprised of three citizens who reviewed complaints referred by the police chief
and offered suggestions on the proper disposition of each case.[124] However, as was
the case with many review boards,[125] local politicians and law enforcement representatives worked against the board to hinder its effectiveness. Though the agency
remained in existence until the mid-1990s, lack of adequate funding and a large
backlog of cases eventually led to its demise.[126] Although reformers saw this as a
setback, oversight agencies around the country continued to develop.

The Philadelphia American Civil Liberties Union (ACLU) called for the creation
of a civilian review board in 1957 because of the strained relationship between the
police and the black community.[127] In 1958, Philadelphia would produce the first
significant oversight agency, called the Philadelphia Police Advisory Board.[128] An
executive order issued by Mayor Richardson Dillworth created the agency.[129] The
agency consisted of a board of citizens who would receive complaints, refer the complaints to the police department for investigation, and after reviewing the department's reports, make recommendations for action.[130] Similar to what happened in
Washington, this board suffered from a lack of public and private support.[131] This
lack of support, combined with financial instability and an overwhelming number
of cases collectively led to its closure in 1969.[132]

Unfortunately, the backlash against citizen oversight by police unions, police officials, and police associations, including the International Association of Chiefs of
Police (IACP), continued to limit the viability of citizen review boards. "Arguments
against oversight included the belief that the police could discipline their own, that
corruption was not as rampant as the media led the public to believe, and that
oversight would undermine the police's autonomy and ability to effectively perform

---

[121] Ibid.
[122] Chasnoff, *A Review of Civilian Review*.
[123] Ferdik, Citizen Oversight in The United States.
[124] Chasnoff, *A Review of Civilian Review*.
[125] Ibid.
[126] Ibid.
[127] Sankar Sen, *Enforcing Police Accountability Through Civilian Oversight* (2010).
[128] Ferdik, Citizen Oversight in The United States, at 106.
[129] Ibid.
[130] Ibid.
[131] Ibid.
[132] Ibid.

its job."[133] For example, opponents of citizen oversight, most notably powerful police unions, were successful in their efforts to diminish any momentum on the part of oversight advocates in New York City, leading the New York City Civilian Complaint Review Board (NYCCRB) to suffer the same fate as the Washington and Philadelphia boards.[134] Teamed with the Policeman's Benevolent Association, police unions staged a successful campaign in New York to convince voters to abolish the NYCCRB in 1966.[135]

However, civil rights tensions and progress in major cities in the United States during the late 1960s and early 1970s reversed this trend and reinstated a serious call for citizen accountability of the police.[136] As public confidence and trust in government agencies waned, the desire for increased police accountability was refueled.[137] For example, Kansas City established a citizen review system in 1969 that continues to survive today.[138] Additionally, Chicago established the Office of Professional Standards (OPS) in 1974, a civilian-staffed office that worked to expose police brutality and the misuse of force.[139] This office continues to operate today in Chicago along with a Police Board consisting of nine civilian-appointed members.[140]

The Chicago Police Board functions as an appellate body to which accused officers may seek final review. Police endorsement of these review systems increased public support, leading to a renewed growth in this accountability mechanism across the country.[141] In fact, cities such as Berkeley, Detroit, and San Francisco have developed and maintained citizen oversight agencies since the 1970s and 1980s.[142] In 1993, New York also reconstituted an all-civilian complaint review board (CCRB).[143] The CCRB is now the largest civilian review board in the United States and presides over thousands of complaints annually.[144] Today, 128 citizen oversight agencies operate across the country and have an important impact on the oversight of police misconduct and accountability.[145]

The ICE raids of Swift meatpacking plants in 2006 actually led to the establishment of a short-lived review body, which is a good example of potential public

---

[133] Ibid.
[134] Ibid.
[135] Ibid.
[136] Ferdik, Citizen Oversight in The United States, at 106.
[137] Ibid.
[138] Ibid.
[139] Sen, *Enforcing Police Accountability*.
[140] Ibid.
[141] Ferdik, Citizen Oversight in The United States, at 106.
[142] Ibid.
[143] Ibid.
[144] Larry E. Sullivan, *The SAGE Glossary of the Social and Behavioral Sciences* (2009).
[145] *See* Links to Oversight Agencies U.S., The Nat'l Ass'n for Civilian Oversight of Law Enforcement, available at: http://nacole.org/nacole-resources/oversight-agencies/links-to-oversight-agencies-u-s/ (last accessed April 7, 2015).

review of immigration enforcement.[146] After ICE swept up and detained thousands of workers from six meatpacking plants across the country during one of the nation's largest immigration raids, the United Food and Commercial Workers Union (UFCW) empaneled a group of former elected officials, labor leaders, academics, civil rights leaders, and immigration and legal experts who spent more than a year holding regional hearings, interviewing witnesses and soliciting input from a wide range of workers, elected officials, policy experts, psychologists, and religious and community leaders.[147] The commission, on which I was privileged to serve, then released a comprehensive report documenting the devastation and destruction that immigration raids had on families, workplaces, and communities across the country.[148] After several hearings that took place in places like Georgia, Massachusetts, and Iowa, we issued a report: *Raids on Workers: Destroying Our Rights*. The report offered a critical analysis of one of the central components of the Bush administration's immigration strategy and provided a detailed account of how heavy-handed enforcement tactics led to systemic abuse of workers' rights and a willful disregard for the rule of law.[149]

According to Joseph T. Hansen, founding chairman of the commission and president of the UFCW:

> What we have uncovered is that during the Bush Administration ICE agents repeatedly trampled on innocent workers' constitutional rights. These were not isolated incidents, but systemic problems that occurred in almost every region of the country. No government agency is above the law, and no worker should have to face the mistreatment and misconduct that these hardworking men and women were subjected to under the Bush Administration.[150]

Upon its creation, the commissioners set out to achieve the following objectives: conduct hearings on allegations of ICE abuse and misconduct in locations across the country; hear from workers and their families on the impact of ICE raids; hear testimony from community leaders, academics, constitutional experts, and the business community; inform the public and elected officials; and issue a report on the findings with a plan of action to protect workers' constitutional rights from any future abuse.[151]

---

[146] National Commission Investigating Misconduct by Immigration Enforcement Agents Holds Public Hearing in Des Moines, UFCW (April 30, 2008), available at: www.ufcw.org/2008/04/30/national-commission-investigating-misconduct-by-immigration-enforcement-agents-holds-public-hearing-in-des-moines/.

[147] See *Raids on Workers: Destroying Our Rights: National Commission Condemns Workplace Immigration Raids, Report Finds Raids Were Counterproductive, Unlawful and Ineffective*, Minority News (April 7, 2015), available at: www.blackradionetwork.com/raids_on_workers_destroying_our_rights.

[148] Ibid.

[149] Ibid.

[150] Ibid.

[151] Ibid.

At each hearing, clear patterns began to emerge regarding the tactics used by ICE agents and how the procedures used by these officials were compromising the rights of workers. The testimony the commission received revealed several disturbing patterns: US citizens and legal permanent residents detained for hours unable to leave even after establishing their status; a lack of coordination by ICE with state and local labor and child welfare agencies; violations of the Fourth Amendment; the use of massive amounts of taxpayer resources and personnel to administer civil warrants; repeated incidents of racial profiling and harassment; the human toll of immigration enforcement, including family separation and children left without proper care; and lasting economic and psychological devastation of communities and families in the aftermath of workplace and community raids.[152]

Among its many recommendations, the UFCW report urged vigorous oversight of ICE's activities and the enhancement of legal protections against abuse.[153] At least for a period of time, the report had some impact. As the Obama administration came into office, new DHS secretary Janet Napolitano announced that Bush-style ICE raids were not part of her enforcement strategy.[154] However, as we have seen, several years later, ICE restarted strikingly similar operations under the auspices of its targeted enforcement raids. And other Obama administration enforcement abuses such as Secure Communities were instituted. If the oversight recommended by the UFCW had been in place, those abuses as well as new ones under Trump may have been stopped, or at least minimized.

I.3. CONCLUSION

Speaking before an audience at Washington State University several years ago, I was challenged by a member of the campus Republican student group who was upset at my criticism of the attempted prosecution of Shanti Sellz and David Strauss. Sellz and Strauss were college students who were volunteering with "No More Deaths," a human rights organization at the border that provided water and other sustenance to border crossers facing searing desert heat in the middle of the summer. They were arrested and charged with knowing transportation of undocumented immigrants *within* the United States after they drove two migrants who were dying of exposure to the hospital.[155]

"How can you defend the actions [of Sellz and Strauss]? They knew the crossers were illegal," demanded the young Republican. I asked him, "What would you have

---

[152] Ibid.
[153] Ibid.
[154] *See Secretary Seeks Review of Immigration Raid*, New York Times (February 26, 2009), available at: www.nytimes.com/2009/02/26/washington/26immig.html.
[155] E. J. Montini, *Saving Immigrants from a Horrid Death is Not a Crime – Yet*, azcentral.com, (September 17, 2006, 12:00 AM), available at: www.azcentral.com/news/columns/articles/0917montini0917.html.

them do – allow the individuals they came across to simply die?" His answer was an emphatic "yes." Stunned, my reaction was esoteric – about how the US Attorney should have exercised prosecutorial discretion not to prosecute and how the actions of Sellz and Strauss were acts of civil disobedience.

Back at my hotel later that evening, I thought back on the exchange. In retrospect, what I should have asked the young man was, "Really, let them die? Is that what your parents have taught you?" And since that time, I have realized the question is not simply whether his parents should have done better to help him develop a more humane moral compass. The task belongs to all of us. We have the duty to remind him, and Trump and his supporters, that there is more to life and more to being a member of a global society than enforcing immigration laws that separate families in the name of maintaining borders.

As the work of "No More Deaths" and its volunteers like Sellz and Strauss illustrate, the reaction to migrants fleeing to our borders does not have to be hostile. Indeed, the right response should be a humanitarian one. Right-minded persons would not respond to UACs escaping the violence of Central America the way Presidents Obama and Trump have. Consider the reaction of Julia Tonotti, a high school student, when she learned of the migrants' plight:

> Tognotti, an incoming [high school] senior ... started learning about the thousands of child refugees at the ... border fleeing and trying to escape violence, drug cartels and gangs. In mid-June [2014], she headed down to the border with her dad and two friends to see if they could help with the growing immigration crisis.
> "I watched a documentary on kids traveling up from [Central America] and started realizing how young these kids are ... I begged my dad to go – every week I reminded him ... I collected donations, then started getting some money and ended up having 12 boxes."
> Once at the border, she realized how quickly the children go through all of the items, so she decided to regularly ship boxes of tennis shoes, women's undergarments, sweaters, jeans, toothpaste, and other necessities to the children. While volunteering at a shelter for migrants ... she met a boy who struggled to get up north from Honduras. She just shipped 14 [more] boxes to them the other day. Local neighbors ... have donated more than 3,000 items to the cause ...
> She said she wants to help people in need and suffering, and to raise awareness about their situation. Americans hear about refugees all over the world, but many Americans do not realize that they have their own refugee crisis on the southern border.[156]

Increased ICE raids, stepped-up border enforcement, and employer sanctions have not reduced undocumented immigration to the United States. Any significant reduction is attributable to economy. The failure of harsh enforcement efforts

---

[156] Angela Swartz, *Border Crisis Spurs Action – Belmont Teen Collects Donations for Refugees,* The Daily Journal, August 4, 2014, available at: www.smdailyjournal.com.

is instructive. The enforcement-only approach has resulted in human tragedy, increased poverty, and family separation, while undocumented workers continue to flow into the United States. This is a challenge that requires us to understand why workers come here, and to address the challenge in a more sensible manner.

In the meantime, I encourage those who agree that our nation's methods of enforcing immigration laws are lacking a strong moral base, to engage in disruptive actions until our leaders come up with innovative disruption of that enforcement philosophy. Just as on-the-street disruption has led to disruptive innovation, namely, the monumental administrative relief announcements by Obama, we can push for more – even in the Trump era. Parents of DREAMers and US citizen children have been left out of protections. Lawful permanent residents and refugees who have been labeled "aggravated felons" have been left out – even those who demonstrate clear progress toward rehabilitation. Temporary Protected Status has been terminated for immigrants stranded in the United States. Immigration laws and procedures result in deportation decisions devoid of any sense of human rights values or proportionality.

I was sitting in a very large waiting room of a Redwood City, CA, car wash on a Saturday night, a couple months after the Trump inauguration. It's 7 pm, long after closing time. About fifty car-wash workers from three car wash businesses in the area are gathered in the room. They are there to listen and participate in a "know your rights" presentation that a couple of my students, two volunteers, and I are conducting. The students are in my basic law school immigration law class, whom I've trained. Jazmin Preciado is leading the presentation and discussion. This is the third one she's participated in, so I'm confident that she can lead the talk without a problem. As she, and another student, Lorena Caldera, are doing a role play in Spanish, I gaze around the room. There's laughter at some of the antics that Jazmin and Lorena are employing, but the workers are thoroughly attentive to the seriousness of the lesson. Those who are undocumented realize that exercising the right to remain silent in the contexts presented could mean the difference between deportation or being able to remain in the United States with their loved ones. Their questions are insightful. They press us on a variety of circumstances that they imagine might occur – at work, at home, on the street, and at their child's school. After the three-hour session, we drive back to San Francisco, once again inspired by the lives of everyday workers; here to make a better life for themselves and their families; here to do what they can – in a disruptive manner – to continue a peaceful life.

Constant disruption is needed in all forms – protests, public oversight, immigrant engagement, litigation, and individual representation – if we are to convince public policy leaders to review immigration enforcement policies with a moral foundation. I choose to believe that a majority of Americans can be motivated to at least care – if not demonstrate outrage – over the ICE enforcement strategies that are causing fear in the minds of many immigrants, and turmoil in their families. With that foundation, our leaders can begin to reinvent and disrupt the reigning US approach to immigration enforcement. The rules can be changed and enforcement philosophy reframed. The new Deporter-in-Chief can be restrained.

As I continue to work in the privileged position of a law school clinical program with my colleague Jacqueline Brown Scott, I am constantly reminded of the impact of the work in my interactions with clients, their families, and committed students who continue to inspire. I think back to the Spring 2016 semester described in Chapter 5.

The end of that semester is hard to forget. We call in Karl, a clinic student from the prior semester because one of his clients finally is scheduled for his asylum office interview. Karl meets and works with Andy the client and Michael an undergrad student volunteer interpreter for a few hours. The three are off to the asylum office without Jacqueline or me, because they have formed a team working on the case together. Karl has attended previous asylum office interviews with clients under our supervision; he is ready to do this on his own. Given the caseload and the confidence that we have in our students who have been trained and rehearsed, students appearing without an attorney supervisor at the Asylum Office is common for our Clinic. Kaitlin, another student, will be working at a private immigration law firm that summer – a firm that has donated funds for volunteer trips to the Texas detention center in Dilley. Kaitlin and I schedule several meetings over the summer to work with our client Maria from El Salvador whose asylum hearing in the immigration court is scheduled for August 2. Jacqueline, two law students (Zulma and Gabriela) who will be in the Clinic the coming Fall, and two of the undergrad interpreters are fundraising for another volunteer trip to the Texas detention center scheduled for July 17 to July 22. And Ned? On Friday, April 29, Ned and more than a dozen other USF law students attend a protest rally against Trump who is about to speak at the State Republican Convention in Burlingame, CA, just south of San Francisco. Ned is one of five demonstrators arrested for failing to disperse and resisting arrest. He's held for about twelve hours before being released; his arraignment is scheduled for June 2.

In the middle of May just days before law school graduation, I am reminded that the emotional investment in your clients means that the day-to-day work can make you smile with pride, but also make you cry. Early in the week, I smiled when Jacqueline told me that one of our UAC clients from Guatemala, Jorge, for whom we've applied for asylum, had come by the office to invite Jacqueline to his high school graduation. Plus, he has been accepted to attend college at San Francisco State University! That is so cool, I thought, especially after recalling how he fled the 18th Street gang and narcos in Guatemala who were likely responsible for the disappearance of his brother.

That moment of joy came on Monday, but on Tuesday, I cried over a different client.

The client I cried for was Marvin the teen who lived in Stockton with Marvin the adult guardian.[157] Marvin the teen also had fled Guatemala because the 18th Street gang threatened him and his family for his refusal to join. Neither the police nor his

---

[157] *See* Chapter 5.

parents could protect him; he was so lucky that Marvin the adult, a family friend, took him in. With students and volunteer attorney Karen, we were able to help Marvin the teen get his green card. But I mourned on Tuesday, because we received word that teen Marvin had died in a swimming accident, just weeks after obtaining lawful permanent status – protected from the violence in Central America. Yet, in spite of this tragedy, I will never lose sight of the fact that like so many other UACs, Marvin deserved his fair chance at a peaceful and productive life here.

Afterword

Abuser-in-Chief

"All I hear is my daughter, crying. All I can see is her face when they took her – she was terrified," laments Arnovis Guidos Portillo.[1] Portillo, a single parent, fled El Salvador on May 18, 2018, after two death threats from a local gang. He paid a smuggler to bring him and his six-year-old daughter, Meybelin, to the United States. After a harrowing nine-day trip, they reached the US border near McAllen, Texas, crossed under the international bridge, and approached US border patrol agents to turn themselves in and request asylum. Agents took them into custody, but within a day, the pair was forcibly separated. Portillo was taken to a detention center and criminally charged with misdemeanor illegal entry. He never had a chance to apply for asylum and was deported back to El Salvador five weeks later without knowing Meybelin's whereabouts.

Portillo and Meybelin were not the only child and parent separated on arrival to the US border. While estimates varied, about three thousand migrant children were taken from their parents at the border and detained soon after April 6, 2018. That day, Attorney General Jeff Sessions notified all US Attorney's Offices along the Southwest Border of a new "zero-tolerance policy" for offenses under 8 U.S.C. § 1325(a), which prohibits both attempted illegal entry and illegal entry into the United States by an alien. The administration's rationale for separating families was that children cannot be prosecuted with their parents, so the children must be separated. However, no law or court ruling mandates family separation. In fact, during its first fifteen months, the Trump administration released nearly 100,000 immigrants who were apprehended at the US–Mexico border, a total that included more than

---

[1] Sarah Kinosian, "All I Hear is My Daughter, Crying": A Salvadoran Father's Plight after Separation at Border, *The Guardian*, June 24, 2018.

37,500 unaccompanied minors and more than 61,000 family members.[2] One of the tactics agents at the US–Mexico border reportedly use to separate children from their parents is to tell them they are taking the kids to get a bath. But then they keep them detained away from their families.[3]

Once the policy of taking children away from their parents was revealed, public protest was fast and strong. For example, Congresswoman Pramila Jayapal (D-Wash.) called the family separation policy "pure, unadulterated evil ... cruel and barbaric."[4] Senator Rob Portman (R-Ohio) called the separation practice "counter to our values" and urged the administration to "change course immediately."[5] Catholic Bishops argued that "[s]eparating babies from their mothers is not the answer and is immoral."[6] The Mormon Church denounced the "aggressive and insensitive treatment" of the families.[7] Evangelical leaders "guided by the Bible," asked Donald Trump to reconsider the policy. Jewish leaders based their opposition against the policy "upon the Torah's values." The media published pictures – some of children in chain-link cages – and sounds of young children traumatized by the separation.[8] In opposition to the policy, at least five governors, including two Republicans, refused to send their National Guard troops to the US–Mexico border to aid CBP.[9] CEOs from companies like JPMorgan Chase, Facebook, and Airbnb denounced the practice; for example, Apple's Tim Cook said the "heartbreaking" policy was "inhumane," and the Business Roundtable criticized the action as "cruel" and "contrary to American values."[10] Former first lady Michelle Obama criticized the policy

[2] Salvador Rizzo, The Facts About Trump's Policy of Separating Families at the Border, *Washington Post*, June 19, 2018.

[3] Ellen Cranley, *Border agents telling migrant parents they're taking their kids to get baths illustrates how Trump's 'zero tolerance' policy is being carried out on the ground*, Business Insider, June 18, 2018, http://www.businessinsider.com/border-agents-use-baths-to-separate-kids-from-parents-2018-6

[4] Jake Johnson, After Visiting Immigrant Mothers Detained by Trump, Pramila Jayapal Demands End to 'Cruel and Barbaric' Family Separation Policy, *Common Dreams*, June 10, 2018, available at: www.commondreams.org/news/2018/06/10/after-visiting-immigrant-mothers-detained-trump-pramila-jayapal-demands-end-cruel

[5] Marilyn Icsman, Sen. Portman calls Trump administration's family separation policy counter to our values, *Cincinnati Enquirer*, June 18, 2018.

[6] Patrick T. Fallon, Catholic bishops issue scathing statement on Trump's family separation policy, *Reuters*, June 14, 2018.

[7] Church Statement on Separation of Families at the US-Mexico Border, LDS Newsroom, June 18, 2018, available at: www.mormonnewsroom.org/article/church-statement-separation-of-families-at-us-mexico-border

[8] Richard Gonzales, Trump's Executive Order On Family Separation: What It Does And Doesn't Do, *NPR*, June 20, 2018.

[9] Amita Kelly, Opposing Family Separation, Governors Cancel National Guard Troops On The Border, *NPR*, June 19, 2018.

[10] Gerrit De Vynck, Tech CEOs Voice Opposition to Family Separations at Border, *Bloomberg*, June 19, 2018.

and Laura Bush labelled it "cruel" and "immoral."[11] Physicians for Human Rights charged that the actions violated "fundamental human rights."[12]

Members of the public also expressed their moral outrage over the separation policy. Thousands of individuals protested against the policy across the country.[13] A Silicon Valley couple, intending to raise $1500 on Facebook to cover the bond fees for one detained parent, received a staggering $20 million in donations by more than half a million contributors; the money was turned over to immigrant rights organizations.[14] Therese Patricia Okoumou, a Congolese immigrant, climbed to the base of the Statue of Liberty on the Fourth of July and refused to get down until "all children are released."[15]

International condemnation of the practice also was swift. The United Nations Commissioner for Human Rights denounced the "cruel practice" of separating parents from their children at the border as an "unconscionable ... abuse on children."[16] UK Prime Minister Theresa May criticized the policy as "deeply disturbing [and] wrong."[17] French President Emmanuel Macron noted: "We do not share the same model of civilization; clearly we don't share certain values."[18] Pope Francis called the separation policy "immoral."[19] Although Iran is often viewed as one of the world's worst abusers of human rights, even Iranian Supreme Leader Ayatollah Ali Khamenei said that the images of separation made him "exasperated" and demonstrated "maliciousness."[20]

The backlash to the family separation policy sparked major calls to abolish ICE altogether. Alexandria Ocasio-Cortez, a twenty-eight-year-old Democrat who ousted incumbent Republican Joe Crowley in the New York primary elections,

---

[11] Nomaan Merchant, The Latest: First Ladies Criticize Border Family Separation, *Newser*, June 18, 2018, available at: www.newser.com/article/2cec4810765b4b8090586a4735394754/the-latest-first-ladies-criticize-border-family-separation.html and www.newser.com/article/2cec4810765b4b8090586a4735394754/the-latest-first-ladies-criticize-border-family-separation.html

[12] *Sign the Letter Opposing Separation of Families, Physicians for Human Rights*, June 2018, secure.phr.org/secure/family-separation-sign-letter

[13] See, e.g., Alexandra Yoon-Hendricks and Zoe Greenberg, Protests Across U.S. Call for End to Migrant Family Separations, *New York Times*, June 30, 2018.

[14] Jessica Guynn, Facebook Fundraiser to Help Immigrant Children Tops $20 Million with Global Donations, *USA Today*, June 18, 2018.

[15] Maria Perez, Statue of Liberty Climber Says She Was Inspired By Michelle Obama Quote, *Newsweek*, July 6, 2018.

[16] Noah Lanard, UN Human Rights Chief: Family Separations Forced by Trump Administration Are Child Abuse, *Mother Jones*, June 18, 2018.

[17] Alex Ward, How the World is Reacting to Trump's Family Separation Policy, *Vox*, June 20, 2018, available at: www.vox.com/world/2018/6/20/17483738/trump-family-separation-border-trudeau-may-reaction

[18] Ibid.

[19] Ibid.

[20] Ibid.

garnered great support in part because of her proposal to abolish ICE.[21] Fellow Democratic New Yorkers Senator Kirsten Gillibrand and Mayor Bill de Blasio echoed the progressive demand to abolish ICE.[22] Protesters from Pennsylvania to Oregon also called for the end of ICE.[23] And on July 12, 2018, Congressional Representatives Mark Pocan, D-Wis., Pramila Jayapal, D-Wash., and Adriano Espaillat, D-NY, introduced a bill that would shut down ICE within a year; the legislation would create a commission to determine how best to "transition [ICE] essential functions to other agencies and ensure that these functions comport with our values and are subject to appropriate oversight, accountability, and transparency measures."[24]

In response to the volume and breadth of criticism, on June 20, 2018, Trump signed an executive order ending his administration's policy of separating migrant children from their parents who were detained as they attempted to enter the United States. However, the order potentially replaced family separation with the prospect of indefinite detention of the entire family. The order urged the attorney general to seek an amendment to the *Flores* settlement discussed in Chapters 2 and 3 that governs the conditions of detaining migrant children. The *Flores* agreement requires children to be held in the least restrictive setting possible, but also makes clear that children should not be held longer than twenty days.[25] On July 9, 2018, federal Judge Dolly Gee, who oversees the *Flores* case, refused to modify those conditions to allow long-term detention of migrant families.[26]

In the meantime, other court actions were brought on behalf of parents and children who were separated. In *Ms. L. v. ICE*, filed in February 2018, allegations of family separation were made even before the Sessions April 6 zero-policy directive. When the separation policy expanded, federal Judge Dana Sabraw ordered the reunification of the separated children and parents.[27] In the process, ORR revealed that it was not prepared to handle so many new children into its care, and ICE and ORR did not track the whereabouts of separated children in any

[21] Nicole Goodkind, Who is Alexandria Ocasio-Cortez? Democratic Socialist Who Wants To Abolish ICE Unseats 'Next Speaker' Joe Crowley, *Newsweek*, June 26, 2918.

[22] Ryan W. Miller, New York's Kirsten Gillibrand, Bill de Blasio echo progressive calls to 'abolish ICE', *USA Today*, June 29, 2018.

[23] *See, e.g.*, Neetu Chandak, Protesters March to Portland City Hall, Demand City Disassociate from ICE, *Daily Caller*, June 27, 2018; Courtney DuChene, ICE Protesters in Center City Make Direct Demands to Mayor Kenney, *NBC10*, July 7, 2018, available at: www.nbcphiladelphia.com/news/local/ICE-Protesters-Change-Tactics-as-Demonstrations-Continue-into-the-Weekend-487568651.html

[24] Lee Harris, Progressive Democrats introduce bill to abolish ICE, *ABC News*, July 12, 2018.

[25] Richard Gonzales, *Trump's Executive Order On Family Separation: What It Does And Doesn't Do*.

[26] Miriam Jordan and Manny Fernandez, Judge Rejects Long Detentions of Migrant Families, Dealing Trump Another Setback, *NY Times*, July 9, 2018.

[27] Laura Jarett, Federal Judge Orders Reunification of Parents and Children, End to Most Family Separations at Border, *CNN*, June 27, 2018.

systemic manner.[28] Many children were "languishing for months in foster families or government facilities."[29]

Even after his executive order, Trump appeared to defend the harsh policy. He offered this "solution" to the problem created by his administration's failure to reunite migrant children with their parents in a timely fashion and the matter of family separation generally: "Don't come to our country illegally. Come like other people do. Come legally."[30]

Trump's callous family separation chapter of immigration enforcement has done more than solidify his hold on the "Deporter-in-Chief" title. His policies have gone far beyond simple dedication to removing noncitizens. By engaging in a policy roundly condemned for its heartlessness and human rights abuse, Trump deserves a new moniker: "Abuser-in-Chief."

In the midst of the family separation controversy, the Trump team struck another blow to asylum seekers. Sessions made asylum much more difficult for a large proportion of migrants fleeing for their lives from Honduras, Guatemala, and El Salvador. As reviewed in Chapter 4, most of the refugees from the Northern Triangle are escaping gang and/or domestic violence. In order to qualify for asylum, Chapter 5 described how these individuals often must establish that they are a member of a particular social group, such as boys or girls who have been beaten or raped after spurning gang recruitment, or women fleeing deadly abuse by partners whose conduct is ignored by local police. However, on June 11, 2018, Sessions issued an administrative precedent decision, *Matter of A-B-*,[31] that set a high bar for victims of domestic or gang violence to qualify for asylum.

The facts in *Matter of A-B-* involved a woman who suffered domestic abuse in El Salvador. Sessions criticized the Board of Immigration Appeals (BIA) for granting asylum without meaningfully considering whether the persecution was on account of membership in a particular social group and whether the Salvadoran government was unwilling or unable to control the assailant. Sessions wrote:

> Generally, claims by aliens pertaining to domestic violence or gang violence perpetrated by non-governmental actors will not qualify for asylum. While I do not decide that violence inflicted by non-governmental actors may never serve as the basis for an asylum ... based on membership in a particular social group, in practice such claims are unlikely to satisfy the statutory grounds for proving group persecution that the government is unable or unwilling to address. The mere fact that a

[28] Michelle Brané and Margo Schlanger, This is What's Really Happening to Kids at the Border, *Washington Post*, May 30, 2018.
[29] Adolfo Flores, The US Isn't Just Separating Children From Their Parents. It Also Has No Plan To Reunite Them, *BuzzFeed*, June 18, 2018, available at: www.buzzfeed.com/adolfoflores/dhs-border-patrol-ice-orr-no-reunification-children-parents?utm_term=.guaRv7roxd#.gkyOYX6oaB
[30] John Wagner, Trump Offers 'A Solution' for Separated Migrant Families: 'Don't Come to our Country Illegally', *Washington Post*, July 10, 2018.
[31] 27 I&N Dec. 316 (A.G. 2018).

country may have problems effectively policing certain crimes – such as domestic violence or gang violence – or that certain populations are more likely to be victims of crime, cannot itself establish an asylum claim.[32]

The BIA had recognized the applicant's particular social group of "El Salvadoran women who are unable to leave their domestic relationship where they have children in common" as at least one central reason that the ex-husband abused her. However, Sessions overruled the BIA and refused to grant asylum because there was no evidence that the husband mistreated the applicant "on account of" her membership in the social group; there was no evidence that her husband knew any such social group existed; he simply abused her because of their relationship.[33]

Sessions also overruled the BIA on the grounds that the applicant failed to demonstrate that the government of El Salvador was unable or unwilling to protect her from her ex-husband. Sessions admonished that "[n]o country provides its citizens with complete security from private criminal activity, and perfect protection is not required."[34] In fact, the applicant reached out to police, received various restraining orders, and had him arrested at least once. But dismissing ongoing violence against the applicant, Sessions declined to hold that the government was unable or unwilling to protect her: "The persistence of domestic violence in El Salvador, however, does not establish that El Salvador was unable or unwilling to protect A-B- from her husband, any more than the persistence of domestic violence in the United States means that our government is unwilling or unable to protect victims of domestic violence."[35]

Sessions made his intent clear: asylum should not be made available for those simply fleeing crime. "[V]ile abuse" may drive migrants from their home countries to "extricate themselves" for the "opportunity of a better life," but the "asylum statute is not a general hardship statute." Nothing in the text of the law supports the suggestion that Congress intended "membership in a particular social group" to be "some omnibus catch-all" for solving every "heart-rending situation."[36]

Sessions' decision in *Matter of A-B-* has impacted the border situation. Given its negative approach toward gang and domestic violence, on July 11, 2018 Border Patrol agents were given new instructions to follow at the border. Under new guidance, the officers who interview asylum seekers at the US borders and evaluate refugee applications initially through credible fear interviews, claims based on fear of gang and domestic violence will be immediately rejected. In addition, the guidance tells officers they should consider whether an immigrant crossed the border illegally

[32] Ibid., at 320.
[33] Ibid., at 343.
[34] Ibid.
[35] Ibid., at 344.
[36] Ibid., at 346.

and weigh that against their claim, potentially rejecting even legitimate fears of persecution if the immigrant crossed illegally.[37]

Sessions has become key to Trump's harsh immigration enforcement agenda. Acting on the instructions of the president, on September 5, 2017 Sessions announced that Deferred Action for Childhood Arrivals ("DACA") would end on March 5, 2018. This message was devastating for the hundreds of thousands of Dreamers who rely on DACA to remain in the United States. At the time of the announcement, almost 800,000 individuals had registered for the DACA program.[38] They registered for the program seeking assurance they would not be deported – that they could lead a semblance of a normal life in the United States. While neither President Barack Obama nor Congress guaranteed that the program would be permanent, DACA had provided hope to many.

Trump, as a presidential candidate, promised to rescind DACA immediately if he became president. After his 2016 election, however, Trump did not immediately move to rescind the program. He repeatedly spoke of having a soft spot for these young people who are leading productive lives and have few, if any, ties to the countries of their birth. Soon after taking office, Trump declared that DACA recipients "shouldn't be very worried ... I do have a big heart."[39] But on June 28, 2017, the Attorney General of Texas and several other states threatened to sue the Trump administration if DACA was not rescinded.[40] Thus, Sessions made the rescission announcement within six months of the Texas threat.

While the sense of safety from deportation is an obvious benefit of DACA, the opportunity to work is just as critical as DACA's protections against deportation. According to some estimates, approximately 700,000 Dreamers are employed and performing a wide variety of jobs in the United States. Consequently, they contribute mightily to the US economy. One report, published by the Center for American Progress, a progressive advocacy group and FWD.us (a bipartisan organization founded by tech leaders) found that repealing the program could cost the United States $460.3 billion in economic output over the next decade and that contributions to entitlement programs like Medicare and Social Security could drop by $24.6 billion.[41]

[37] *Asylum Seekers Claiming Fear of Gang, Domestic Violence to Be Immediately Rejected Under New Guidance*, CNN Wire, July 11, 2018, available at: ktla.com/2018/07/11/asylum-seekers-claiming-fear-of-gang-domestic-violence-to-be-immediately-rejected-at-border-under-new-guidance/

[38] Julia Glum, DACA by The Numbers: 15 Facts About the Youth Immigration Program Trump Could Soon Shut Down, *Newsweek* (Aug. 30, 2017).

[39] Alan Gomez and David Agren, First protected DREAMer is deported under Trump, *USA Today*, Apr. 18, 2017.

[40] Suzanne Gamboa, Texas AG, Others Demand Trump Stop New DACA Permits, End Renewals, *NBC News.com* (June 29, 2017), available at: www.nbcnews.com/news/latino/texas-ag-others-demand-trump-stop-new-daca-permits-end-n778371.

[41] Alana Abramson, Here's How Much Money Rescinding DACA Could Cost the U.S. Economy, *Fortune*, Sept. 6, 2017. All undocumented immigrants paid an estimated $11.7 billion in combined state and local taxes in 2014. Melissa Cruz, Yes, All Immigrants – Even Undocumented – Pay

The purchasing power of DACA recipients is significant. For example, in a survey of more than 3,000 DACA recipients, nearly two-thirds of respondents reported purchasing their first car in the United States for an average amount of $16,469. Large purchases such as these affect state revenue, as most states collect a percentage of the purchase price in sales tax, additional registration costs, and title fees. The data also show that 16 percent of all survey respondents purchased their first home after receiving DACA. Among respondents twenty-five years and older, this percentage rises to 24 percent. The broader positive economic effects of home purchases include the creation of jobs and the infusion of new spending in local economies.[42]

Driving out young workers who will pay into the system for many decades is, simply put, a very bad idea. Much of the anti-immigrant sentiment in the United States is based on the notion that undocumented immigrants are a drag on the economy.[43] However, the rescission of DACA actually would harm the economy and cost the US government a significant amount in lost tax revenue.[44] Dreamers are helping to offset America's aging population and declining fertility which results in fewer workers paying taxes to support federal programs like Medicare, Medicaid, and Social Security. This is especially poignant as these programs benefit US citizens. Research shows that the average wage for DACA workers is over seventeen dollars an hour. Their median age is twenty-two, meaning most are prime for careers, jobs, and incomes for the foreseeable future.

DACA recipients – and essentially all Dreamers – are part of the conscience of the country and a critical part of the economy. Dozens of CEOs from companies like Microsoft, Amazon, Netflix, AT&T, Wells Fargo, Google, and Facebook urged the president to preserve the program.[45] Mark Zuckerberg pledged that his immigration advocacy vehicle at FWD.us would be "doing even more in the weeks ahead to make sure Dreamers have the protections they deserve."[46] After the Sessions announcement, the Google CEO, Sundar Pichai, turned his attention to the need for legislation, stating, "Dreamers are our neighbors, our friends and our co-workers. This is their home. Congress needs to act now to #DefendDACA. #WithDreamers."[47]

Billions in Taxes Each Year, *Immigration Impact* (Apr. 16, 2018), available at: immigrationimpact .com/2018/04/16/undocumented-immigrants-pay-taxes/.

[42] Tom K. Wong, et al., DACA Recipients' Economic and Educational Gains Continue to Grow, *Center for American Progress* (Aug. 28, 2017), available at: www.americanprogress.org/issues/immigration/ news/2017/08/28/437956/daca-recipients-economic-educational-gains-continue-grow/.

[43] Pedro Nicolaci da Costa, Trump's Immigration Plans could Cripple the US Economy and Hurt the Workers He's Pledging to Protect, *Business Insider*, Feb. 24, 2017.

[44] Ibid.

[45] Aarti Shahani, Microsoft President to Trump: To Deport a DREAMer, You'll Have to Go Through Us, *NPR* (Sept. 5, 2017), available at: www.npr.org/sections/thetwo-way/2017/09/05/548686695/ 250-apple-employees-among-thousands-at-risk-from-daca-cancellation.

[46] Ibid.

[47] Ibid.

The plaudits continued. Over 800 American businesses including GM, Target, and Walmart signed onto a letter in support of the Dreamers.[48] The US Chamber of Commerce issued this statement: "DACA recipients are our friends, neighbors, and co-workers. The Chamber urges Congress to work quickly through the details of a legislative solution that treats these individuals with dignity and fairness. The Chamber stands ready to work with our leaders to ensure that the legislation is consistent with our nation's values and the best interests of our economy."[49] A group calling themselves the "Dream Coalition" that included Harvard President Catharine Faust, Apple CEO Tim Cook, New York Mayor Bill de Blasio, and former Secretary of State Madeleine Albright announced: "Collectively, we, the Dream Coalition, are committed to using our voices as business, civic, and government leaders to amplify the overwhelming American support for protecting Dreamers."[50] Dozens of human resource officers of large companies urged Congress and the Trump administration to consider the vital role foreign-born workers play in the US economy when making policy decisions. The letter, signed by chief human resource officers of 110 major companies such as Merck, GE, HP, IBM, and ManpowerGroup, notes the importance of foreign-born workers amid a workforce crisis characterized by six million unfilled job openings. As employers invest a cumulative $637 billion toward training and equipping the American workforce, foreign-born workers in the meantime help fill workforce gaps.[51]

As the DACA termination date of March 5, 2018, approached, however, Congress failed to enact legislation to provide relief for Dreamers or to otherwise extend DACA.[52] The failure was due, in part, to Trump's demand for border wall funding, the elimination of certain family immigration categories like siblings and married children and the diversity visa program in exchange for the Dream Act.[53] Ultimately,

---

[48] Stephen Nellis, Walmart, Target join call for "Dreamer" legislation, *Reuters*, Sept. 20, 2017, available at: www.reuters.com/article/us-usa-immigration/walmart-target-join-call-for-dreamer-legislation-idUSKCN1BV11E

[49] US Chamber of Commerce Letter: Thomas J. Donohue, *Clock is Ticking for DACA Solution*, Oct. 2, 2017.

[50] Madeleine R. Nakada, Faust Joins 'Dream Coalition' to Protect Undocumented Students, *The Harv. Crimson* (Oct. 19, 2017), available at: dev.thecrimson.com/article/2017/10/19/faust-joins-dream-coalition/.

[51] Steve Lee, Chief HR Officers Urge Rethinking on Immigration Policy and DACA, San Diego LGBT Weekly (Oct. 26, 2017), available at: lgbtweekly.com/2017/10/26/chief-hr-officers-urge-rethinking-on-immigration-policy-and-daca/.

[52] Mallary Shelbourne, Perez Pushes DREAM Act as Trump's DACA Deadline Passes, *The Hill* (Mar. 5, 2018).

[53] Gayle Putrich, California Republicans Close to Forcing Vote on DACA Bills in House, *S.F. Chron.*, May 17, 2018; Michael D. Shear and Sheryl Gay Stolberg, Trump Immigration Plan Demands Tough Concessions from Democrats, *New York Times* (Jan. 25, 2018). The DREAM Act (short for Development, Relief and Education for Alien Minors Act), is a bill in Congress that would have granted legal status to certain undocumented immigrants who were brought to the United States as children and went to school here. It was first introduced in 2001 and passed the House of Representatives in 2010, but never passed the Senate.

DACA did not end on March 5, 2018, because federal court challenges to the rescission announcement temporarily halted the termination.[54] However, Texas filed its own lawsuit on May 1, 2018, arguing that DACA is unconstitutional, and Sessions – a long-time opponent of DACA – announced that his Department of Justice would not defend DACA in the suit, referring to the program as "an open-ended circumvention of immigration laws."[55]

Trump likely will retain his title as Deportation King for years to come. Championed by the reign of ICE enforcement terror detailed in Chapter 6 and a cold-hearted family separation policy, his immigration exploits would be difficult to upstage. On June 26, 2018, the Supreme Court solidified Trump's legacy by upholding version three of his travel ban on a 5–4 vote.[56] Led by Chief Justice John Roberts, the court's conservatives said that the President's power to secure the country's borders was not undermined by Trump's history of incendiary statements about the dangers he said Muslims pose to the United States.[57] His place in history as the Commander-in-Chief, Deporter-in-Chief, and now Abuser-in-Chief, is officially sealed.

[54] Nicole Hong, Second Federal Judge Blocks Trump Plan to End DACA, *Wall St. J.* (Feb. 13, 2018), available at: https://www.wsj.com/articles/second-federal-judge-blocks-trump-plan-to-end-daca-1518567376

[55] Gabrielle Ware, DOJ Calls DACA Unlawful, Says It Won't Defend Program In Lawsuit, *Newsy*, June 10, 2018, available at: www.newsy.com/stories/doj-calls-daca-unlawful-won-t-defend-program-in-lawsuit/

[56] *See Trump v. Hawaii*, 138 S.Ct. 2392 (2018).

[57] Ariane de Vogue and Veronica Stracqualursi, Supreme Court Upholds Travel Ban, CNN, June 27, 2018.

Index